THE MAGILL BIBLIOGRAPHIES

The American Presidents, by Norman S. Cohen, 1989
Black American Women Novelists, by Craig Werner, 1989
Classical Greek and Roman Drama, by Robert J. Forman, 1989
Contemporary Latin American Fiction, by Keith H. Brower, 1989
Masters of Mystery and Detective Fiction, by J. Randolph Cox, 1989
Nineteenth Century American Poetry, by Philip K. Jason, 1989
Restoration Drama, by Thomas J. Taylor, 1989
Twentieth Century European Short Story, by Charles E. May, 1989
The Victorian Novel, by Laurence W. Mazzeno, 1989
Women's Issues, by Laura Stempel Mumford, 1989
America in Space, by Russell R. Tobias, 1991
The American Constitution, by Robert J. Janosik, 1991
The Classical Epic, by Thomas J. Sienkewicz, 1991
English Romantic Poetry, by Bryan Aubrey, 1991
Ethics, by John K. Roth, 1991
The Immigrant Experience, by Paul D. Mageli, 1991
The Modern American Novel, by Steven G. Kellman, 1991
Native Americans, by Frederick E. Hoxie and Harvey Markowitz, 1991
American Drama: 1918-1960, by R. Baird Shuman, 1992
American Ethnic Literatures, by David R. Peck, 1992
American Theatre History, by Thomas J. Taylor, 1992
The Atomic Bomb, by Hans G. Graetzer and Larry M. Browning, 1992
Biography, by Carl Rollyson, 1992
The History of Science, by Gordon L. Miller, 1992
The Origin and Evolution of Life on Earth, by David W. Hollar, 1992
Pan-Africanism, by Michael W. Williams, 1992
Resources for Writers, by R. Baird Shuman, 1992
Shakespeare, by Joseph Rosenblum, 1992
The Vietnam War in Literature, by Philip K. Jason, 1992
Contemporary Southern Women Fiction Writers, by Rosemary M.
    Canfield Reisman and Christopher J. Canfield, 1994
Cycles in Humans and Nature, by John T. Burns, 1994
Environmental Studies, by Diane M. Fortner, 1994
Poverty in America, by Steven Pressman, 1994

The Short Story in English: Britain and North America, by Dean Baldwin and Gregory L. Morris, 1994

Victorian Poetry, by Laurence W. Mazzeno, 1995

Human Rights in Theory and Practice, by Gregory J. Walters, 1995

Energy, by Joseph R. Rudolph, Jr., 1995

A Bibliographic History of the Book, by Joseph Rosenblum, 1995

The Search for Economics as a Science, by the Editors of Salem Press (Lynn Turgeon, Consulting Editor), 1995

Psychology, by the Editors of Salem Press (Susan E. Beers, Consulting Editor), 1995

World Mythology, by Thomas J. Sienkewicz, 1996

Art, Truth, and High Politics: A Bibliographic Study of the Official Lives of Queen Victoria's Ministers in Cabinet, 1843-1969, by John Powell, 1996

Popular Physics and Astronomy, by Roger Smith, 1996

Paradise Lost, by P. J. Klemp, 1996

Social Movement Theory and Research, by Roberta Garner and John Tenuto, 1996

Propaganda in Twentieth Century War and Politics, by Robert Cole, 1996

Propaganda in Twentieth Century War and Politics

An Annotated Bibliography

Robert Cole

Magill Bibliographies

The Scarecrow Press, Inc.
Lanham, Md., & London
and
Salem Press
Pasadena, Calif. / Englewood Cliffs, N.J.
1996

SCARECROW PRESS, INC.

Published in the United States of America
by Scarecrow Press, Inc.
4720 Boston Way
Lanham, Maryland 20706

4 Pleydell Gardens, Folkestone
Kent CT20 2DN, England

British Cataloguing-in-Publication Information Available

Library of Congress Cataloging-in-Publication Data

Cole, Robert, 1939–
Propaganda in twentieth century war and politics : an annotated
bibliography / Robert Cole.
p.   cm. — (Magill bibliographies)
Includes index.
1. Propaganda—Bibliography. I. Title. II. Series.
Z7204.S67C65   1996   016.3033'75—dc20   96–27825   CIP

ISBN 0-8108-3196-1 (cloth : alk.paper)

♾™ The paper used in this publication meets the minimum requirements of
American National Standard for Information Sciences—Permanence of
Paper for Printed Library Materials, ANSI Z39.48–1984.
Manufactured in the United States of America.

Books by the Same Author

The Dissenting Tradition (edited with Michael L. Moody), 1975
A Traveller's History of France, 1988
Britain and the War of Words in Neutral Europe, 1939-1945, 1990
A.J.P. Taylor: The Traitor Within the Gates, 1993
A Traveller's History of Paris, 1994

To Philip M. Taylor, friend and mentor in the study of propaganda.

CONTENTS

Acknowledgments xi

Introduction 1
  Bibliographies and Research Guides 9

Chapter 1 / Propaganda: The Concept 13
  General Studies 14
  Public Opinion, Public Relations, and Advertising 25
  Analysis and Measurement of Propaganda Effects 39
  Propaganda Channels and Techniques 56
  Mass Communications and Propaganda 71

Chapter 2 / Propaganda and World War I, 1914-1918 88
  History and Function 88
  Channels and Techniques 112
  Propaganda Material 122

Chapter 3 / Propaganda Before World War II: Variations on a
  Theme 134
  History and Function 134
  Channels and Techniques 159
  Propaganda Material 174

Chapter 4 / Propaganda and Authoritarian Ideologies 190
  History and Function 190
  Channels and Techniques 204
  Propaganda Material 219

Chapter 5 / Propaganda and World War II, 1939-1945 238
  History and Function 238
  Channels and Techniques 255
  Propaganda Material 266

Chapter 6 / Propaganda and the Cold War, 1945-1989 294
  History and Function 294
  Channels and Techniques 307
  Propaganda Material 321

Chapter 7 / Propaganda After World War II: More Variations
      on a Theme 336
   History and Function 336
   Channels and Techniques 345
   Propaganda Material 368

Author and Editor Index 381
Film Title Index 391
Subject Index 397

About the Author 403

Acknowledgments

An annotated bibliography is not accomplished without help. Therefore, I would like to express my gratitude for assistance, technical and other, to the following groups and individuals. At Utah State University: Lisa Olson, Regina Michaelson, and the Merrill Library Inter-Library Loan Services staff; John Elsweiler, and the Merrill Library reference staff; Ladell Hoth, Suzanne Scoresby, and Lorraine Kimber of Merrill Library Audio-Visual Services; Carolyn Fullmer, and Sally Okelberry (who proof-read the finished product), both secretaries in the Department of History; the History faculty generally for moral support; and my students Michael Grover, and C. Vance Doren. Elsewhere: Pat Davis at American Movie Classics, Charles Silver at the New York Museum of Modern Art, the programming staff at Turner Classic Movies, Ben Brewster at the Wisconsin Center for Film and Theater Research, Lou Ellen Kramer at the UCLA Film and Television Archive, Zoran Sinobad at the National Center for Film and Video Preservation, Rosemary C. Hanes at the Library of Congress, the National Archives, the National Audio-Visual Center, and the many writers and scholars whose work on propaganda and related subjects fills these pages, especially Philip M. Taylor, to whom this volume is gratefully dedicated. Finally, I thank my wife, Ilona Jappinen, whose patience and support never wavered, and whose language skills helped me over occasional rough spots with German sources. My gratitude to you all.

INTRODUCTION

Propaganda played a major role in war and politics in the twentieth century. There are various reasons for this. The twentieth is the century of total war and mass politics, democratic and otherwise. That being the case, governments, armies, political parties, ideological movements, and individuals with an ax to grind have recognized the value of persuading large numbers of people to see things their way. Note that only two of the five items in this list are extensions of the State, and therefore a source of "official" propaganda. Fully as much political and war propaganda has been conceived, created, and disseminated voluntarily, however much the effect may have been to benefit the State, as has been disseminated by the State. Finally, in the twentieth century, the technologies of mass communications made propaganda possible and potentially effective on an unprecedented scale.

A mass audience and mass communications are central to propaganda dissemination. Persuasive material may address the individual, as in the "Uncle Sam Wants *You*" posters from World War II, but the *You* is both one citizen and all citizens. Similarly, the 1935 German film *Triumph of the Will*, a propaganda documentary of the 1934 Nazi party rally at Nuremberg, was addressed to millions of individual Germans; however, it appealed to them collectively as the German nation. All of this suggests the simple fact that propaganda is a means to an end, not an end in itself. Political scientist Harold Lasswell defined propaganda as "the making of a deliberate one-sided statement to a mass audience"; Michael Balfour, who served in the British Ministry of Information in World War II, referred to the phenomenon (with tongue in cheek) as "the art of inducing people to leap to conclusions without first examining the evidence." Both descriptions indicate any systematic, widespread effort made by government, political party, ideological movement, or individual with access to channels of mass communications, to *propagate* (understood as to broadcast or spread with intent to persuade) a particular doctrine, practice, or cause.

Balfour's ironic sense may or may not have embraced a judgment on the morality of propaganda. Certainly the question of whether propaganda is a good thing or a bad thing is addressed by many of the authors listed in this volume, many of whom have used, in connection with "propaganda," phrases having negative connotations such as "psychological manipulation," "brainwashing," and "disinformation." Some have described propaganda use as destructive of democratic politics; others have averred that in certain circumstances propaganda is a necessary evil; still others, taking a positive high road, see propaganda as a means through which good things can be achieved—victory in war against fascism, or the spread of democracy, for example. In any case, by no means have writers on either the history or the theory of propaganda arrived at a consensus.

The term *propaganda* derives from the purpose endowed upon a committee of cardinals created in 1622 by Pope Gregory XV, which was to direct the foreign missions of the Roman Catholic Church. The Protestant Church of England created the Society for the Propagation of the Christian Gospel in Foreign Parts for a similar purpose. The object in both cases was to propagate religious doctrine. The means included preaching, publishing, and doing good deeds; these were the "channels" of propaganda, through which audiences were promised eternal salvation if they would but conform to the doctrines being propagated.

The principle remained the same in the propaganda of war and politics in the twentieth century. The doctrines in this case were political ideology, the party platform, the just cause in war, opposition to war, public policy and dissent from it, or social reform and control which always have been defined in part by political necessity. The Great War of 1914-1918 (World War I) was the first "total" war in history, and propaganda played a great role in it. Propaganda was disseminated to affirm the righteous cause, sustain morale, discomfit the enemy, placate allies, and pressure neutrals. The process continued in each war thereafter, down to and including the 1991 Gulf War, differentiating only to the extent that propagandists had access to ever more elaborate technologies of mass communications. Political propaganda followed a similar pattern, almost paralleling, on a party or movement level, the factors of cause, morale, discomfiting, placating, and pressuring that characterizes war propaganda. The "spin doctors" of today differ from their predecessors only in the multiplicity of methods and channels by which and through which they can disseminate their material.

With all of this in mind, certain questions arise: What does propaganda do, how does it differ from information, and how does it achieve its ends?

First, information is simply that: information. Propaganda, on the other hand, is information arranged in such a way as to appeal to the emotions of a given audience, for the purpose of persuading that audience in a particular direction. The propagandist must first identify that audience and then discover what emotions already exist within it and prepare the material accordingly. The British and German experiences in World War II are instructive. British propagandists learned that both home audiences and those in neutral European countries responded best to practical and information-grounded assessments of the progress of the war, couched in patriotic language in the first instance and in value-laden language in the second: appeals to democracy and warnings against the evils of fascism, respectively. The British also appealed to neutrals' concerns regarding postwar European economic and political relations, which was a practical consideration. For audiences in enemy-occupied countries, British propaganda promoted expectations of liberation and the defeat of fascism, and in enemy countries, doubt regarding the outcome of the war and the character and quality of fascist leadership. Nazi propaganda followed similar lines at home, save that the appeal to patriotism was more racially and ethnically biased. However, in neutral countries and those Germany had occupied, propaganda was predicated upon intimidation. The degree of success for any propaganda overseas remains a question. It is certain that Britain and its allies won the war while the Germans lost, but it is not certain that propaganda was the primary reason. On the other hand, it does seem likely that propaganda was a major factor in maintaining a "stiff upper lip" at home among all of the belligerent nations.

The question of how propaganda achieves its ends (or perhaps better, attempts to achieve its ends) involves what the propagandists do on a daily basis, and how they do it. Characteristically, they tell the truth selectively, suppress (censor) information that might be harmful to the cause, praise those values associated with the presumed social, political, and other assumptions of the audience, and also appeal to its inherent prejudices of class, race, or culture. If the propagandists have understood their audience and structured their material accordingly, if they have placed the appropriate "spin" on the factual information at their disposal, if they have disseminated what realistically promotes the cause and suppressed (without being found out) that which can retard it, then they may achieve their purpose. Of considerable interest here is the content of sources in this text which, on one hand, proclaim the great success of propaganda in particular cases and, on the other, proclaim with equal fervor how little was actually achieved. Some of the most skeptical comments come from those who have been practitioners of the propagandist's art, which is hardly surprising.

The point was made earlier that propaganda is a process of persuading groups rather than individuals. Therefore, propaganda is predicated upon the availability of such mass communications media as books, pamphlets, and flyers, mass-produced and distributed, the press (the oldest mass communications medium, in which manipulated news, censored news, and the political cartoon have become effective propaganda weapons), film, both documentary and feature, radio broadcasting, and most recently television broadcasting. Even the "mass meeting," the political rally with tens of thousands in the audience, has been most useful from a propaganda perspective when its content could be shared beyond the confines of parade ground, stadium, or arena with a larger audience via film, radio, or television.

A separate note about film as propaganda. While cinema existed for some time before 1914, it hit its stride as a communications medium during and after World War I. By the outbreak of World War II tens of millions of citizens in the United States, France, Great Britain, Germany, Italy, and the Soviet Union attended the cinema each week. Consequently, during that war film was among the most useful propaganda channels employed by each belligerent. Film came in three basic forms. One was documentaries, including newsreels, features, and cartoons. The documentary, for example *Desert Victory* (1943), brought information to the audience but presented it in such a way as to preclude a careful examination of the evidence supporting the information. Another was the feature film, such as the Hollywood production *Mrs. Miniver* (1942), which worked to influence the audience in favor of its message by showing soldiers as heroes, civilians as hardworking and determined in the face of adversity, and the enemy as always losing in the final scenes. American war-propaganda feature films always included a "speech" at some point, usually but not always delivered by the hero or heroine, in which all of the points the film sought to make were brought together in a single emotional appeal. British films followed similar patterns, as in *One of Our Aircraft Is Missing*, but usually were subtler. Nazi features showed Jews, the British, Russians, French, or some other group to be as evil as the Nazi party always had claimed they were. Finally, The propaganda cartoon had a particular role to play, for its purpose was to persuade through providing humorous entertainment at the expense of, for example, leaders or soldiers of enemy countries. Artists achieved amazing madcap results when they confronted the likes of Hermann Goering and Adolf Hitler with Bugs Bunny or Daffy Duck. In whatever form it was presented, film engaged its audiences for World War II propaganda purposes fully as effectively as television would do for political propaganda in later years.

Regrettably, many propaganda films are no longer available, and have been annotated here on the basis of printed descriptions and analyses found in secondary sources, themselves based upon film reviews and the memoirs and correspondence of filmmakers rather than upon the films themselves. This is particularly true of World War I feature films. The availability or lack of it of specific films is indicated in each film entry.

The nature of channels for reaching a propaganda audience naturally raises certain questions. What is that audience? How does it function? Does it have a reality beyond its individual members? Here is where propaganda theory draws heavily upon the behavioral methodologies found in both psychology and sociology. Simply put, the place of the individual within a group, the impact of group pressure upon an individual, and group conditioning of individual responses are the sort of issues which may be usefully addressed by behavioralists. Propagandists ignore these insights at their peril. Much of the theoretical material listed in the first chapter of this volume, "Propaganda: The Concept," is by psychologists and sociologists; moreover, much of the writing on propaganda produced by political scientists, opinion specialists, and communications experts is predicated upon paradigms suggested by behavioral theory.

The modification or, conversely, reinforcement of group behavior is central to propaganda technique. However, the process involved, offering material designed to encourage a particular response, has an "alter ego," so to speak: the process of *denying* certain kinds of information. This is censorship. Ultimately, it must form part of any discussion of propaganda. While the propagandist strives to provide particular interpretations of events, ideas, values, credos, heroes, myths, and realities in order to persuade, that process often faces the necessity of denying the validity of alternative interpretations. However, denial involves a form of debate, one possible outcome of which is that the audience may incline toward the wrong position. Therefore, the propagandist makes an ally of the censor, for a better way of denying alternative points of view may be simply to suppress them, thus leaving the audience with only one way of looking at the interpretations provided.

Censorship as an ally of propaganda has been around as long as propaganda itself. For example in the seventeenth century, the Inquisition censored writings by Galileo and others which challenged the Aristotelian precepts upon which rested Church teaching regarding the nature of the universe. Gabriel Nicholas de La Reynie, Paris prefect of police during the reign of Louis XIV, censored theater which parodied Louis' mistress, Madame de Maintenon. In the eighteenth century, Jonathan Swift's satire on British rule in Ireland, *A Modest Proposal* (1729), was censored in England, and both Voltaire and Rousseau suffered from the "blue pencil" in France. In the twentieth century, censorship became a feature of wartime and of political systems in which freedom of speech and information were considered neither necessary nor advantageous. Examples include political news in both Nazi Germany and Stalinist Russia, and war news distributed in all belligerent countries and in many neutral countries during both world wars. David Gray, United States ambassador to Ireland, remarked in 1945 that "censorship in Ireland is one of the scandals of Western civilization."

The reasons behind censorship were always the same: totalitarian states denied free speech and access to information on the grounds that the information sought was "false," and therefore dangerous to the state and to its citizens; nations at war censored war news on the grounds that publication of some kinds of information might be of aid to the enemy or else dangerous to domestic morale; and neutral countries used censorship as a weapon to protect themselves from the possibly un-neutral effects of propaganda disseminated among their citizens—and in the process, made a kind of propaganda in favor of neutrality. In each of these situations and many others, the function of propaganda was served by suppressing information and viewpoints that were at odds with its content. Without censorship, propaganda could be at least partially disarmed.

This volume collects and comments on materials that concern the theory and practice of propaganda in twentieth century war and politics, principally concerning the nations and states that took part in the two world wars and drove the dramatic political and social changes that occurred in part because of them. The opening chapter, "Propaganda: The Concept," annotates works about propaganda theory as well as theory pertaining to disciplines the content of which drives propaganda theory. Chapter 1 also lists materials relating to general histories of propaganda written by scholars and others seeking to evaluate the evolution of propaganda practice. The chapter focuses mainly on theory, however, and as theory has a history fully as much as does practice, the contents include early theoretical work produced in the explosion of interest in propaganda that followed World War I, through to that produced in the early 1990s. The writings of Sir Norman Angell, for example, are very instructive in helping students and scholars to grasp the concerns wartime propaganda produced among those whose primary interest was in seeing democracy take root and grow in the postwar world.

It must be pointed out that while books and articles continue to be written on propaganda theory, the bulk of the major theoretical work was actually done between the end of World War I and the end of the 1960s—that is, works on "propaganda," "propaganda and communications," "propaganda and persuasion," and "propaganda and public opinion." The explanation probably is threefold. First, a propaganda which embraced mass communications and the rapidly modernizing technologies associated with it came into its own only during the war of 1914-1918. Second, the methodologies of group psychology and sociology were forming and re-forming in the early years of the new century and were being associated with new research paradigms that seemed useful in addressing the reality of that mass propaganda, which was in fact the art of mass persuasion. Finally, the political movements that would draw heavily upon mass propaganda for their success began with Bolshevism, which came to power in Russia in 1917 and quickly expanded to embrace the political tactics of fascism and other radical right movements. Thereafter, interest in propaganda continued to be theoretical but more inclined to apply theory to practice, in historical terms with reference to what had been done in the world wars and the age of totalitarian dictatorship, and in contemporary political terms with regard to the role played by propaganda in the Cold War. Of course, there has always been criticism of propaganda, which in the Cold War era was increasingly associated not only with the "other side" but also with the presumption that Western governments were as capable of deception, disinformation, and outright lying as any other. Noam Chomsky, Edward S. Herman, and Anthony Pratkanis are a few of the names that stand out in this regard. As propaganda is a means to an end which employs mass communications and psychological and sociological manipulation, annotations in chapter 1 include material on the theories and uses of communications, on the evaluation of public opinion—how it is formed and what is expected of it—on the relationship of individual and group psychology to the techniques of manipulation associated with propaganda, and on the similar relationship between social organizations and group manipulation achieved through propaganda dissemination.

Chapter 1 is subdivided by subject matter. First is "General Studies," which includes works defining and describing propaganda and its history. The second, "Public Opinion, Public Relations, and Advertising" contains entries that explore the relationship between these subjects and propaganda. Third is "Analysis and Measurement of Propaganda Effects," in which entries concern psychological and sociological studies of mind manipulation on individual and group levels that is effected by propaganda. Next is "Propaganda Channels and Techniques," containing entries that examine how specific kinds of media are used in disseminating propaganda. Finally, "Mass Communications and Propaganda" includes sources pertaining to the relationship between communications theory and technology and propaganda dissemination.

Beginning with chapter 2, "Propaganda and World War I, 1914-1918," the chapters are organized chronologically, each addressing a particular epoch. Chapter 2 covers propaganda delivered in literature, press, pulpit, and film in the context of World War I. Chapter 3, "Propaganda Before World War II," lists materials pertaining to propaganda and revolution, reaction, social change, and international politics before 1939, much of which was a direct product of World War I and some of which helped condition the mentality of those who went to war in 1914. Chapter 4, "Propaganda and Authoritarian Ideologies," considers the propaganda of fascist and other totalitarian systems before and after World War II. Chapter 5, "Propaganda and World War II, 1939-1945" includes references to and examples of the variety of propaganda disseminated in World

War II, while chapter 6, "Propaganda and the Cold War, 1945-1989," lists materials on the propaganda of the Cold War and related subjects. The final chapter, "Propaganda After World War II," annotates postwar propaganda materials relating to subjects other than the Cold War, such as the Korean, Vietnam, and Gulf wars, international relations, and the remodeling of postwar Western societies.

Each chapter contains both primary and secondary sources. "Secondary sources" refers to books, portions of books, articles, and documentary films or audiotapes about the use of propaganda. Primary sources constitute such items as films, newspapers, cartoons, posters, radio transcripts, and pamphlets which were used as propaganda channels. As indicated above, chapters 2-7 refer to propaganda dissemination in particular historic periods. Consequently, each of these chapters is subdivided into three parts. First is "History and Function," in which sources deal with the motivation, planning, and purpose of propaganda that was disseminated in the particular historic context under consideration. Second is "Channels and Techniques," which includes sources relating to the media through which the propaganda was disseminated and the tactics propagandists employed in the hope of making their material effective. Third is "Propaganda Material," which includes samples of actual propaganda, ranging from feature films to published pamphlets. In each subdivision entries include information designed to aid the reader in finding the book or other source in question. Book and pamphlet entries include author, title, place of publication, publisher, and date. Journal articles include author, title, journal name, volume and issue number, date, and inclusive pages. Film information includes title, producer, director, studio, location of studio, date, length in minutes, and availability. Some of this information is abbreviated, using the following forms: min. (minutes), prod. (producer), dir. (director), and narr. (narrator). The video or archival source for a particular film is indicated by distributor and city wherever that information was available.

Finally, it should be noted that this is a select rather than a comprehensive bibliography. Far more books, articles, polemical pieces, and retrospectives have been written on twentieth century propaganda than could possibly be included in the space allotted to this volume, and that applies equally to films and other types of actual propaganda material. Therefore, the procedure followed in preparing this volume has been to select entries that provide the most useful sampling of the great variety of propaganda theory and practice that has developed in the twentieth century, with reference specifically to war, politics, and subjects that relate directly to war and politics. If, within that arena, any propaganda study—or propaganda sample—of truly seminal importance has been left out, the responsibility lies entirely with the author. Bibliographies on other areas of propaganda and related subject matter are entered below for the reader's convenience.

Bibliographies and Research Guides

Bishop, Robert L. *Public Relations: A Comprehensive Bibliography. Articles and Books on Public Relations, Communications Theory, Public Opinion, and Propaganda, 1964-1972*. Ann Arbor: University of Michigan Press, 1974.
Pages 139-143 are of use to the student of propaganda. They list or refer by number to 158 books or journal articles dealing with propaganda. All entries were published between 1964 and 1972 and cover a wide range of subject matter: propaganda theory, communist propaganda, World War II propaganda, and United States propaganda in Vietnam, to mention only a few. The remainder of the volume covers the wide variety of subjects indicated in the title, only some of which are directly applicable to the study of propaganda. Each entry contains a single line of annotation.

Campbell, Craig W. *Reel America and World War I: A Comprehensive Filmography and History of Motion Pictures in the United States, 1914-1920*. Jefferson, N.C.: McFarland, 1985.
One of the best resources on World War I United States propaganda films in existence. The first 145 pages are a history of United States filmmaking during the war years, operating from the premise that between 1914 and 1920 "movies developed into an important element of the mass American culture," and that as the United States became involved in the war, filmmakers attempted "both to shape and to follow public attitudes toward the ongoing struggle." The remainder of the volume is a series of "filmographies" subdivided into categories: features, shorts, and specific subject matter such as military preparedness, spies, the war, and bond drives. These lists are further subdivided by year, and each entry contains a one or two line annotation. Regrettably, they do not also indicate whether a print or videocassette of each film is available. Illustrations and select bibliography.

Hale, Hubert. *British Archives and the Sources for the History of the World War*. London: Oxford University Press, 1925.
A guide to public records in Britain relating to all aspects of World War I, with appropriate commentary. A select bibliography on record

guides is included. Of particular interest are the descriptions of Press Censorship records and the author's brief but negative description of sources from which propaganda was created.

Lasswell, H. D., Ralph D. Casey, and Bruce Lannes Smith. *Propaganda and Promotional Activities: An Annotated Bibliography.* Minneapolis: University of Minnesota Press, 1935.
This extensive bibliography lists a significant number of books and articles dealing with the theory and practice of political and war propaganda from the World War I period and the 1920s. It has a much greater number of entries concerning business management, public relations, public opinion, social psychology, the measurement of propaganda efficiency, and censorship. The volume includes German, French, and Italian materials as well as English. Unfortunately, the reference to "annotated" bibliography is somewhat overstated. Few of the annotations exceed one sentence, and perhaps two-thirds of the entries have no annotations at all.

Rose, Oscar. *Radio Broadcasting and Television: An Annotated Bibliography.* New York: H. W. Wilson Company, 1947.
Radio was a propaganda channel from early in its existence. It has been used extensively in war and peace time for promoting culture, political objectives, social change, morale, and victory over the enemy. This annotated bibliography, produced shortly after World War II, includes books and other sources on virtually every aspect of radio broadcasting: history, short wave, radio as a career, programming techniques, content, relationship to the listener, censorship, news, and radio in relation to other media. Many of the entries have little bearing upon the use of radio as a propaganda channel; many others do, such as a book edited by Margaret Mayorga, which contains four radio play scripts, each with a propaganda theme.

Singerman, Robert. *Anti-Semitic Propaganda: An Annotated Bibliography and Research Guide.* New York: Garland Publishing, 1982.
A foreword by Colin Holmes and an introduction by the compiler together describe in considerable detail the nature and widespread prevalence of anti-Semitism in modern times, noting in the process such classics of anti-Semitism as *The Protocols of the Elders of Zion.* Published early in the twentieth century, it was advertised as a master plan for a Jewish takeover of the world. It was actually a forgery put out by Russian authorities in order to justify the pre-1914 pogroms in western Russia. The remainder of the volume is a comprehensive

listing with annotations of more than 1900 examples of such propaganda. The listings are broken down by year, beginning with 1871, and by country. The annotations vary in length, and make clear that most of the entries are clearly anti-Semitic. A few entries are marginal, however. Each entry indicates where the item is held: for example, "ADL," which refers to Anti-Defamation League, New York. A key to holding institutions is included.

Smith, Bruce Lannes, and Chitra M. Smith. *International Communication and Political Opinion: A Guide to the Literature.* Westport, Conn.: Greenwood Press, 1956.
This annotated bibliography is somewhat different from others with which Bruce Lannes Smith was associated in the 1930s and 1940s. Here the emphasis is on electronic communications and there is a decided Cold-War flavor to the materials relating to political opinion. Propaganda and propaganda contexts are central to the organization of the bibliography, though many of the entries do not address propaganda directly. The annotations are much better in this volume than in Smith's other bibliographies.

Smith, Bruce Lannes, Harold D. Lasswell, and Ralph D. Casey, eds. *Propaganda, Communications, and Public Opinion: A Comprehensive Reference Guide.* Princeton, N.J.: Princeton University Press, 1946.
A continuation of the collection published by Lasswell, Smith, and Casey in 1935. The present volume includes a preface in which propaganda is defined as "the calculated selection and circulation of symbols, with a view to influencing mass behavior," and four essays by the editors commenting on the nature and content of political communication in the 1930s and 1940s. The annotations are much more complete than those in the earlier volume, and the contents include titles that appeared between 1934 and 1943. There are more than twenty-five hundred entries.

Thorpe, Frances, and Nicholas Pronay, eds. *British Official Films in the Second World War: A Descriptive Catalogue.* Oxford, England: Clio Press, 1980.
This catalogue of annotated film titles lists virtually every one of the nearly five thousand government-sponsored British films from World War II, and the archive where it was to be found at the time the listing was printed. Most are documentaries or newsreels; however, a few listings fit the term docudrama, such as *The Lion Has Wings*, which is described here as a "compilation film showing the events of the war to

date." The introduction describes the workings of government offices associated with wartime propaganda filmmaking. The volume is illustrated with war photos and includes several appendixes describing films that do not fit the general wartime category. There is also an index of titles and another of individuals associated with the making of particular films.

Young, Kimball, and Raymond D. Lawrence. *Bibliography on Censorship and Propaganda*. Eugene: University of Oregon Press, 1928.

Two-thirds of the materials in this bibliography concern censorship, and the rest propaganda. Inspired by the University of Oregon school of journalism, the entries are drawn almost entirely from the press and journals. Subject matter includes the nature and criticism of both censorship and propaganda, and some examples of print propaganda, such as pamphlets from World War I. Obviously, this reference source is limited to the early period of twentieth century concern with the use and abuse of both propaganda and censorship. It is among the first such compilations of propaganda materials ever made.

Chapter 1

PROPAGANDA: The Concept

Like all phenomena with practical applications, propaganda has a theoretical base. Practitioners of the art and science of propaganda must understand how it works. Otherwise, they risk failing in their ultimate goal of moving the attitude and outlook of a targeted audience in the desired direction. Consequently, linguists, political scientists, psychologists, historians, sociologists, communications theorists, and even literary and music critics have examined propaganda in terms of what it is, how it works, and in what areas it has been and may be applied as a process of mass persuasion.

This chapter on theory addresses a variety of research areas that contribute to understanding propaganda for both the practitioner and the critic. Questions raised in these areas include What is propaganda? How and why has it evolved? How does it work? How has research on the nature of propaganda, and those social and psychological realities which drive it, influenced our understanding of propaganda over time? and How does denying information (censorship) expand the parameters of propaganda? The books and articles annotated in this chapter range over six decades of the twentieth century. The aim is to provide as useful a list as possible in response to these questions.

The concept of propaganda covers many subjects both directly and peripherally connected with the practice of creating and disseminating propaganda. Those subjects are listed in this chapter in subdivisions that reflect their relationship to propaganda study and to one another. The first section, "General Studies," lists studies that define, theorize about, and provide history of propaganda. The second is "Public Opinion, Public Relations, and Advertising." These entries connect those sciences to propaganda. The third is "Analysis and Measurement of Propaganda Effects." Entries here concern the application of the psychological, sociological, and political sciences to propaganda study. The fourth is "Propaganda Channels and Techniques," in which the actual dissemination of propaganda is the subject. The fifth is "Mass Communications and Propaganda," in which entries concern mass communications theory and practice with application to propaganda dissemination.

General Studies

Angell, Norman. *The Public Mind: Its Disorders, Its Exploitation.* New York: E. P. Dutton, 1927.
Norman Angell was a major figure in British political life in the early years of the twentieth century and was a dissenter during World War I. This volume analyzes how propaganda affects what the author considered to be a confused and ill-prepared public. While it will interest historians of early theories about propaganda and opinion, and those interested in how intellectuals like Angell thought about democratic politics in the postwar years, it is limited by the fact that when it appeared, theorizing about propaganda and public opinion was the province of political writers, rather than of scholars trained in behavioral and other sciences.

Bartlett, F. C. *Political Propaganda.* Cambridge, England: Cambridge University Press, 1940.
This short volume was part of a series called Current Problems, edited by Ernest Barker and published by Cambridge University Press. F. C. Bartlett was a Cambridge professor specializing in experimental psychology. His contribution to the series has a contemporary flavor, as indicated by the opening line: "To-day propaganda is in the air and on it." Even so, the larger purpose is to "look at the activities of modern political propaganda mainly from the point of view of a psychologist." Bartlett's object is to define propaganda, explain its methods and why it became a fixture in the twentieth century, analyze its effects, and suggest whether propaganda could be put to the service of democracy. The book is a classic of its times, and Bartlett was among the theorists consulted—unofficially—by the planners of Britain's Ministry of Information for World War II. Limited bibliography.

Bem, Daryl J. *Beliefs, Attitudes, and Human Affairs.* Monterey, Calif.: Brooks/Cole, 1970.
A short, introductory volume on the role that beliefs and attitudes play in human affairs, particularly in relation to public policy-making. Useful for understanding how easily beliefs and attitudes can be manipulated by propaganda for political or other purposes. Select bibliography.

Bernays, Edward L. *Propaganda.* New York: Horace Liveright, 1928.
An early example of commentary on the nature of propaganda by a nephew of Sigmund Freud. Bernays accepts propaganda as a necessary, if perhaps not altogether welcome, feature of modern society. The

volume aims to explain the structure of "the mechanisms which control the public mind," and to find "the due place in the modern democratic scheme for this new propaganda and to suggest its gradually evolving code of ethics and practices." The author examines the psychology of propaganda and the link between public relations and political control in the United States as it was being discussed and viewed on the eve of the Great Depression. This work is proactive rather than reflective. No bibliography.

Brown, J. A. C. *Techniques of Persuasion: From Propaganda to Brainwashing*. Baltimore: Pelican Books, 1963.
Written by a trained psychiatrist, this volume begins by considering the extent to which persuasion usually, but not always, involves some form of propaganda. He then connects persuasion techniques to communications, the formation of attitudes, psychological warfare, politics, advertising, and religious indoctrination, with an eye always toward assessing their propaganda characteristics. This volume is a seminal work regarding the nature and evolution of propaganda as a means of persuasion. Select bibliography.

Chicken Little. Prod. Walt Disney, 9 min., 1943. Deerfield, Ill.: Coronet/MTI.
This nine-minute Disney cartoon, aimed at children, tells a cautionary tale about the negative side of propaganda. It features the old tale about foolish chickens and wily foxes, and the point is to show the children, through the chicken and fox metaphor, the pitfalls of following propaganda. Foxie Loxie uses psychology to fool the farmyard fowls into believing the sky is falling and convinces them that Chicken Little—portrayed here as a yo-yo champ and first-class chump—is a born leader. Naturally, persuaded by Foxie Loxie, they follow Chicken Little out of the barnyard and into Foxie Loxie's stomach. Cleverly done in the Disney style, this film is a period piece on propaganda theory.

Combs, James E., and Sara T. Combs. *Film Propaganda and American Politics: An Analysis and Filmography*. New York: Garland Publishing, 1994.
The authors describe the evolution over the twentieth century of American film as a propaganda channel. They note that its importance in this regard is connected directly with the development of mass communications as a "major new source of popular learning." An introduction describes film in relation to propaganda in general terms, ending with a definition of the relationship specifically in an American context. Subsequent chapters cover the history of American film

propaganda, and the development of film propaganda in specific contexts such as the two world wars, the interwar years, and American politics. Select bibliography and propaganda filmography.

Doob, Leonard W. "Propaganda." *International Encyclopedia of Communications*, vol. 3. Oxford, England: Oxford University Press, 1989, pp. 374-378.
A brief and very readable introduction to the phenomenon of propaganda. Doob begins by defining the concept as "communication, verbal or nonverbal, that attempts to influence the motives, beliefs, attitudes, or actions of one or more persons." The remaining pages survey the history of propaganda, noting in the process the evolving interaction of propaganda with advertising, public relations, lobbying, and political and ideological agendas generally. The article also includes commentary on channels and techniques, and counterpropaganda methodologies. A good starting place for understanding the basic concepts upon which propaganda rests.

Dovifat, Emil, ed. *Handbuch der Publizistik*. 3 vols. Berlin: Walter de Gruyter, 1968.
These three volumes constitute a virtual encyclopedia of the theory (volume 1) and practice (volumes 2 and 3) of European political communications in the twentieth century, through journals, films, poster art, and other media. It goes well beyond strictly propaganda materials, but the use of these channels of communication for political purposes involving propaganda is a constant theme. Aimed at a general but educated readership, it is immensely valuable for those who can read German. Select bibliography.

Ellul, Jacques. *Histoire de la propagande*. Paris: Presses Universitaires de France, 1967.
This volume follows the author's famous *Propaganda: The Formation of Men's Attitudes*, and to some extent is a demonstration of the earlier volume through examination of historical practice. Again Ellul asks What is propaganda? and cautions that contemporary definitions may not apply precisely to propaganda as deployed in past eras. The history opens with ancient Greece and ends with World War I; the underlying theme is the evolution of propaganda through various stages and uses into the propaganda that characterizes politics and war in the modern mass age. A very readable book for those who read French, in which the main points are clearly explicated. The reader will find that as Ellul presents his material, the difference between modern propaganda and

that employed by tyrants of ancient Greece is not so very great. Select bibliography.

_____. "Information and Propaganda." Translated by Elaine P. Halperin. *Diogenes* 18 (1957), pp. 61-77.
In this article, the author offers a criticism of existing writings which pronounce that information as distinct from propaganda is both a "good thing" and clearly definable. Not quite, he argues, and proceeds to set forth, in the context of his criticism, the nature of the complexities involved in trying to define propaganda as distinct from information. If it is true, he begins, that information is "by nature, completely honest, unadorned, and clear," then it is equally clear that propaganda is "falsehood, desire for power, Machiavellianism, crooked in intent." However, this is too easy, and the author devotes the remainder of the article to demonstrating how even the "purest information" is never free from a wish to influence. An excellent translation guarantees that the authors's well-structured arguments are clearly and readably presented.

_____. *Propaganda: The Formation of Men's Attitudes.* Translated by Konrad Kellen and Jean Lerner. New York: Vintage Books, 1965. Reprinted in 1973.
One of the classics of propaganda theory, this volume dissects the nature and purpose of propaganda, concluding among other things that by its nature, propaganda "is a direct attack against man," that it is destructive of democracy, and that it is the most dangerous phenomenon of twentieth century society. The author suggests quite clearly that propaganda also is inevitable in the present age, owing to the technology of mass communications and the continuing determination of political regimes to hang on to power. The bibliography lists the principal works of propaganda theory that appeared prior to the publication of this book. Argumentative and somewhat "preachy" in tone, this work nevertheless is an essential read for any student of propaganda theory, especially with reference to its history.

_____. "Propagande et personnalisation du pouvoir," in Léo Hamon and Albert Mabileau, eds., *La Personnalisation du pouvoir*. Paris: Presses Universitaires de France, 1964.
This collection of lectures is devoted to the idea of power coming to be associated with an individual in a virtually mythic sense: Winston Churchill, John F. Kennedy, Charles de Gaulle, and Nikita Khrushchev are a few of the examples. Not surprisingly, the lectures were published

when Charles de Gaulle was at the height of his powers as president of France, heading a regime very much identified with his personality. Jacques Ellul's lecture—fifteen pages in length—examines how the "personalization of power" can be effected through the use of propaganda: the use of symbols which mythologize the leader, for example. The entire process is naturally devoted to enhancing the power of the leader, perhaps at the expense of legal limitations on that power. Limited bibliography.

Ford, Nick Aaron, ed. *Language in Uniform: A Reader on Propaganda.* New York: Odyssey Press, Inc., 1967.
This anthology of essays and excerpts from books starts with the premise that "we are living in an age of propaganda" and therefore we must learn how to deal with it. The editor asserts that propaganda is sometimes used as a force for positive social and political change, as well as for less salubrious purposes. It can, therefore, be a useful tool in education. Examples of contents include extracts from John Milton, Adolf Hitler, Jonathan Swift, Sidney Hook, Walter Lippmann, and Senator Joseph McCarthy. The extracts are organized around such basic themes as "the nature of propaganda," "political and economic discussion," "racial and religious considerations," and "effective advertising." An introductory volume on propaganda history and theory which is weak on psychological analysis. Select bibliography.

Fraser, Lindley Macnaughton. *Propaganda.* London: Oxford University Press, 1957.
Written in the context of the Cold War, this concise volume surveys the nature and use of propaganda from World War I to its post-World War II application in commercial advertising, and operates on the premise that propaganda is an inevitable function of twentieth-century government and society. The purpose is to explain how propaganda has worked, worked at the time of writing, and will likely work in the future. Select bibliography.

Friedrich, Carl J. *The Pathology of Politics, Violence, Betrayal, Corruption, Secrecy, and Propaganda.* New York: Harper and Row, 1972.
Part 4, "Secrecy and Propaganda," is the portion of this volume of interest to the student of propaganda. These hundred-plus pages are addressed to the author's proposition that "the crucial function . . . of both propaganda and secrecy is to manipulate men in relation to the political order." The theme is the interaction of propaganda with political requirements. A readable and compelling study which sheds

much light on the use of propaganda in totalitarian societies as a control device, before, during, and after World War II. Significantly, with regard to the author's personal perspective, the volume is dedicated to the memory of the July 20, 1944, conspirators against Hitler. Select bibliography.

_____. "Propaganda and Education." *The Atlantic* 159 (June 1937), pp. 693-701.
The author was a prominent scholar before and after World War II on both propaganda and totalitarian politics and society. This article is a period piece in which the author argues that what "liberals" regard as "Truth" is largely based upon a set of naive assumptions about freedom of thought and expression. The author contends that Truth is relative and asks, as one example, What is the Truth about World War I? Because Truth is relative, it becomes increasingly difficult to separate education from propaganda. The effort to do so must be made however, and the author goes on to describe the importance to education of such concepts as scientific objectivity. At the same time, he argues that it may not be a bad thing for education to engage in a bit of propagandizing for "the maintenance of the human ideal."

Garnett, Maxwell. "Propaganda." *Contemporary Review* 147 (May 1935), pp. 574-582.
Once upon a time, the author begins, moral judgments were simple and straightforward. Words, despite their "elusive ways and their notorious inadequacy," were rarely highly charged with either vice or virtue. But World War I changed all that, he argues, because to a significant degree it was a propaganda war. Since then, words have been charged with all manner of "vice or virtue." This essay offers both a definition and an analysis of the function of propaganda that is directly related to the years between the world wars.

Hawthorne, Jeremy, ed. *Propaganda, Persuasion and Polemic.* London: Edward Arnold, 1987.
Ten articles by British literary critics and historians which inquire into approaches to research on the nature of propaganda and persuasion. The subject matter ranges from the political oratory of democratic Athens to the language of contemporary advertising, and the articles are uniformly well written and informative. Aimed at the educated reader rather than at the specialist. Bibliography is in endnotes.

Henderson, Edgar H. "Towards a Definition of Propaganda." *The Journal of Social Psychology* 18 (1943), pp. 71-87.

Despite being written in the middle of World War II, this article seems remarkably unaffected by the deluge of propaganda which characterized that conflict. Rather, it is a somewhat academic piece on propaganda theory, which takes issue with leading writers on the subject such as William Albig. The author's position is anti-propaganda, as evidenced by frequent references to the irrationality of propaganda and its purpose of circumventing critical thinking. Working from that perspective, the author addresses the issue of whether education is a form of propaganda and concludes that when teaching is done correctly, it is precisely the opposite of propaganda. The article is largely free of jargon and accessible to most readers.

Institute for Propaganda Analysis. *Propaganda: How to Recognize It and Deal with It. Unit of Study Materials in Propaganda Analysis for Use in Junior and Senior High Schools.* New York: Institute for Propaganda Analysis, 1938.

This typewritten eighty-page booklet provides basic information for young people who, the authors assume, know little or nothing about the subject. That they should is the primary reason for the booklet, which considers definitions of the term and arguments over whether propaganda is "good" or "bad," but does not actually take sides on that issue. The booklet is based upon the work of Leonard W. Doob and F. E. Lumley, two of the principal experts on propaganda of the 1930s. The authors attempt to cover everything, however briefly: the definition and role of propaganda, the "desirability of making young people critical of authority and able to recognize propaganda," how to study the subject, what interests it serves, and what are its principal instruments (channels), a list that includes both schools and churches. Limited bibliography.

Jowett, Garth S., and Victoria O'Donnell. *Propaganda and Persuasion.* Newbury Park, Calif.: Sage, 1992.

Two specialists in different aspects of communications collaborated on this volume. The object, in the authors' words, is "to clarify and distinguish propaganda as a form of communication." There is a brief "history" of propaganda, followed by consideration of such phenomena as the institutionalization of propaganda, the relationship of propaganda to persuasion in terms of a methodology of analysis, propaganda as psychological warfare, and propaganda technique. The volume offers little that is radically new in terms of conclusions or material covered; however, it does bring the subject up to date in a clear and readable manner. Designed for advanced undergraduates and post-graduates. Select bibliography.

Kamins, Bernard Francis. *Basic Propaganda*. Los Angeles: Houlgate House, 1951.
An attempt to walk a line between the "learned and scholarly" volume on propaganda theory and practice, and a superficial one written by the "wizened press agent" which "tells how smart the man is." The result is an enjoyable, highly readable volume of just 120 pages which approaches propaganda from the premise that the reader knows nothing about the phenomenon. The publishers' claim that the volume "has a bright future as a textbook in all schools of journalism" was optimistic. No bibliography.

Lambert, Richard S. *Propaganda*. London: Thomas Nelson and Sons, 1938.
A short but keen analysis of the history and nature of propaganda and propaganda channels, published in 1938 when Europe was again sliding toward a general war. It was written with the propaganda methods of totalitarian dictatorships clearly in mind. The purpose was to warn against the dangers of propaganda, which to the author's mind does far more harm than good. No bibliography.

Lasswell, Harold D. "Propaganda." *Encyclopedia of the Social Sciences*, vol. 12. New York: Macmillan, 1934, pp. 521-528.
Written by one of the leading authorities on propaganda theory, this essay offers a definition of propaganda, a brief history, and an analysis of how it works. There are also implied warnings that citizens of a democratic society should be on guard against propaganda, coupled with advice on how to combat it. It is useful to compare this essay with that by Bruce Lannes Smith written three decades later in the *International Encyclopedia of the Social Sciences* (see entry below) for a sense of changing perceptions regarding the nature and role of propaganda in society.

_____. "The Theory of Political Propaganda." *American Political Science Review* 21 (August 1927), pp. 627-631.
A brief overview of political propaganda: what it means, "the management of collective attitudes," and how it works, "the manipulation of significant symbols." Lasswell distinguishes propaganda from education as the basis of the manipulation factor, and warns that propaganda, which has it origins in classical times, continues to exist because of the "social disorganization which has been precipitated by the rapid advent

of technological change." An early, postwar writer on propaganda
theory, Lasswell takes a far more negative tone on propaganda than did
Edward L. Bernays writing on the subject at the same time (see entry
above).

Lee, Alfred McClung. *How to Understand Propaganda*. New York: Holt
Rinehart, 1952.
Designed as a recreation for the general reader of the author's writing
on propaganda over twenty years, this volume places a wide range of
propaganda-related subjects within reach of an uninitiated audience.
The author's object is to "inspire readers to go on to learn more and
more about how people can force propaganda and propagandists to
become instruments of a democratic mass society." Select bibliography.

Lipsky, Abram. *Man the Puppet: The Art of Controlling Minds*. New York:
Frank-Maurice, 1925.
This volume represents an early attempt at explaining mind control and
in the process makes a strong case for learning how to thwart it. The
relationship of mind control to propaganda is a major theme that runs
through the volume, either as the object of discussion or as an issue
related to other topics, but never far below the surface. The author notes
that in his day (the 1920s) interest in employing mind control—
whether by demagogues, salesmen, or politicians—was never higher,
and therefore it was important to expose the ways in which mind
control might be accomplished. Chapters cover such subjects as
"thwarting the common man," "public opinion," "spell-binding,"
"propaganda technique," "morale-making," "education," and "myth
and illusion." The experience of militarists and propagandists from
World War I provided some of the material, as did religious fanaticism
connected with such events as the Miracle of Lourdes (1876) and the
manipulation possibilities of such new inventions as radio. The book
is addressed mainly to historians of propaganda. Limited bibliography.

Lumley, Frederick E. *The Propaganda Menace*. New York: Century,
1933.
This volume examines propaganda from a theoretical and practical
perspective, and with a negative point of view. The author refers at one
point to a "slew of garbage" in such manner as to make clear that by
garbage he means propaganda. The object is to warn society that
propaganda endangers culture, politics, business, education, religion,
and virtually every other human activity. Propaganda methods are
explored, the "secrecy" of the propagandist is revealed, and the uses

and methods of propaganda in the classroom and in the promotion of religion are made clear. Published the year Adolf Hitler became chancellor of Germany, the volume clearly was shaped by the times through which the author lived. This argumentative exposé, so to speak, has a place among theoretical works on propaganda in the 1930s, and also among those which are pertinent to the history of the period itself. No bibliography.

Martin, L. John. *International Propaganda: Its Legal and Diplomatic Control.* Minneapolis: University of Minnesota Press, 1958.
A history of international propaganda in the twentieth century, and an analysis of efforts to control it through international law and by international agreement. The volume opens with a general history of propaganda, followed by a bibliographic essay on definitions of propaganda. The remaining chapters concentrate on the principal focus of the volume, which is legal aspects of international propaganda. This study is informative in a number of areas, and equally useful to students of propaganda and international relations. Well researched and written, the book is both readable and reliable. Bibliography other than the opening essay is contained in endnotes.

Robertson, James C. *The British Board of Film Censors: Film Censorship in Britain, 1896-1950.* London: Croom Helm, 1985.
The subject of this volume is how the BBFC came into existence and why, and its impact upon the developing film industry in Britain. The theme is the relationship of propaganda to censorship, which the author makes clear by discussing exactly why particular films were censored. Appendixes include an extensive list of censored films and a list of those that were banned altogether at one time or another by the censors. Select bibliography.

Short, K. R. M., ed. *Feature Films as History.* Knoxville: University of Tennessee Press, 1981.
Includes contributions from historians and others, such as Nicholas Pronay of Leeds University, one of the leading scholars on the history of propaganda. The editor's introduction makes the point that feature film has emerged as a major subject within historical research on the history of propaganda. Each essay deals with a particular film or aspect of film as propaganda: for example, D. J. Wenden on "*Battleship Potemkin*—Film and Reality," Elizabeth Grottle Strebel on "Jean Renoir and the Popular Front," and Thomas Cripps on "*Casablanca, Tennessee Johnson* and *The Negro Soldier*—Hollywood Liberals and

World War II." The conception, organization, research, and writing are of equally high quality. Bibliography is contained in endnotes.

Smith, Bruce Lannes. "Propaganda." *International Encyclopedia of the Social Sciences*, vol. 1. New York: Macmillan, 1968, pp. 579-589.
A comprehensive description of propaganda, this essay includes a definition, brief history, and summary of theoretical considerations applicable to propaganda. There also is a section titled "Factors in Propaganda," which summarizes such things as propaganda aims, ends, channels, symbols, psychological manipulation, and measurement of results. There is a bibliography of standard works on propaganda by such experts as Harold D. Lasswell, Bernard Berelson, and Leonard W. Doob. Compare this essay with that written in 1934 by Lasswell in the *Encyclopedia of the Social Sciences* (see entry above) for a sense of how perspectives on propaganda had changed on some levels, but remained the same on others.

Smith, Ted J., III, ed. *Propaganda: A Pluralistic Perspective*. New York: Praeger, 1989.
Eleven essays mostly by communications specialists on aspects of propaganda. Subjects include techniques, differences between democratic and totalitarian propaganda, propaganda definitions (one contributor confirms Jacques Ellul's "theory of information use in propaganda" for example), and whether the term "propaganda" continues to have validity. The editor stresses the element of controversiality in the essays, noting rightly that the study of propaganda deals with profoundly important issues, such as the "nature of truth, the morality of social influence, the role of the press in a democratic society, and the possibility of rational discourse." The essays are designed to inspire questions rather than to provide conclusive answers. Select bibliography.

Sproule, J. Michael. "Propaganda Studies in American Social Sciences: The Rise and Fall of the Critical Paradigm." *Quarterly Journal of Speech* 73, 1 (February 1987), pp. 60-78.
This article examines the reasons for propaganda study emerging as a major subject of social science after World War I. "A paradigm arises in response to social needs for knowledge," the author notes, and for this reason propaganda study emerged among social scientists in the 1920s. The "social need for knowledge" was predicated upon a complex interaction of reformist, scientific, economic, and government interests for which propaganda was a useful tool, once it was understood. A good

overview of the evolution of propaganda study, and the author notes many of the major contributors to the field along the way, including Leonard W. Doob, Ralph D. Casey, and Alfred McClung Lee.

Thum, Gladys, and Marcella Thum. *The Persuaders: Propaganda in War and Peace.* New York: Athenaeum, 1972.
Opening with the argument that everyone is a propagandist at least to the extent that we all use and respond to the language of propaganda, the authors proceed to survey how the "language" was used for propaganda purposes in American wars from the Revolutionary War onward, and in American politics beginning with the presidency of Martin Van Buren. The volume blends theory and practice as the authors demonstrate both how and why people may be easily misled, and how easily they may resort to misleading themselves. Illustrated, but no sources are cited, which raises questions about both theoretical and historical reliability.

Public Opinion, Public Relations, and Advertising

Abrams, Mark. "Opinion Polls and Party Propaganda." *Public Opinion Quarterly* 28 (1964), pp. 13-19.
This article examines how, for the first time in the 1950s, political parties in Britain structured party political propaganda upon assessments of public opinion. The conclusion drawn is that propaganda based upon such messages might be effective in winning voters, whether Labour or Tory. The author sketches both pros and cons of the use of polls and political propaganda.

Albig, William. *Modern Public Opinion.* New York: McGraw-Hill, 1956.
A contribution to explaining the evolving science of public opinion study, with particular reference to the effect of communications technology on both the measurement and shaping of public opinion. More than half of the book is devoted to propaganda, censorship, and the mass media. It serves as an introduction to public opinion theory and is accessible to the educated reader. No bibliography.

Allport, Floyd H. "Toward a Science of Public Opinion." *Public Opinion Quarterly* 1 (January 1937), pp. 7-23.
This article was the first substantive piece to appear in the *POQ*, a journal started specifically with the idea of making public opinion a subject for scientific inquiry. The author's point is to call for such inquiry in order to define and clarify the nature of public opinion and to remove

from it the "emotional bias" of writers who use the phrase "public opinion" for what amounts to propaganda purposes. An important early contribution to the definition of public opinion study as a science.

Annis, Albert D., and Norman C. Meier. "The Induction of Opinion through Suggestion by Means of 'Planted Content.'" *Journal of Social Psychology* 5 (February 1934), pp. 65-81.
Psychology early joined ranks with other disciplines interested in propaganda. This very science-based article makes the point that "power of suggestion" can be an effective means of opinion creation and by implication, a propaganda device. The channel in this instance is news reportage. The authors present the results of experiments using a number of participants, which produce the conclusion that "opinion can be induced by means of judiciously selected suggestion in as short a time as seven issues of a newspaper. . . ."

Berelson, Bernard. "Democratic Theory and Public Opinion." *Public Opinion Quarterly* 16, 2 (1952), pp. 313-330.
An article assessing the state of public opinion research in the post-World War II period and equating that research with theoretical evaluation of what a democratic electorate—those who hold "public opinion"—is all about. The author discusses the various components of democratic theory, such as the personality of the electorate, the decision-making process, and of what the outcome shall consist. His point is to encourage further research into opinion assessment. This article will help the reader to understand the opinion-assessment component in the propagandist's responsibilities.

Berelson, Bernard, and Morris Janowitz, eds. *Reader in Public Opinion and Communication*. New York: Free Press, 1966.
This collection of more than fifty essays on elements of the study of public opinion examines, among other things, the role of media in cultural and political contexts, persuasive strategies, and the nature and function of communication channels in connection with propaganda and opinion formation. These essays also consider communications tactics and opinion formation in a global setting, at least touching upon these questions in relation to Soviet Russia, communist China, and new nations of the Third World. They are a useful companion to Daniel Katz et al., *Public Opinion and Propaganda* (entry below). The underlying theme of both volumes is accurately stated by Berelson's observation regarding "concern over the pervasive effects of 'propaganda'" that began with World War I and grew thereafter. Select bibliography.

Bernays, Edward L. *Biography of an Idea: Memoirs of Public Relations Counsel Edward L. Bernays.* New York: Simon and Schuster, 1965.
This autobiography is an important document in the history of propaganda. Bernays was a pioneer in the development of the art or science of public relations in the United States. He learned the grounding for this work as a member of the United States Committee on Public Information during World War I, America's wartime propaganda department. This experience taught him that propaganda and public relations were inevitably interconnected, and he was among those in the 1920s to write at length on understanding the nature and uses of propaganda. This volume reflects the growing sophistication, in the years after 1920, of those factors that are characteristics of propaganda: advertising, public relations, public opinion assessment, mass communications, media technology, and political ideologies that embraced propaganda as a means to an end. This is the record of an "insider," so to speak, in the techniques of mass persuasion, which should be read by all historians of twentieth century propaganda. Illustrations but no bibliography.

_____. *Crystallizing Public Opinion.* New York: Liveright, 1923.
This was the first book written by the man who became the American doyen of public relations and the science of influencing public opinion. It explains, among other things, the function of the public relations expert, who "gives advice on the formulation of attitudes and actions which will win public favor and procedures by which they may be brought to public attention." In short, this volume is a description and analysis of public opinion and how it may be influenced through public relations. That Bernays understood public relations as a close relative of propaganda is clear from the fact that he wrote a book on propaganda (see entry above) just five years later, in which he—cautiously—gave his blessing to propaganda, so long as it was used in a good cause. He includes such topics as public relations as profession, what is public opinion, the powers that affect public opinion, the fundamentals of public motivation, the role of mass communications, and the ethics of the public relations counsellor. No bibliography.

_____. "Molding Public Opinion." *Annals of the American Academy of Political and Social Science* 179 (1935), pp. 82-87.
An argument for recognizing the importance of public opinion and the extent to which it can be molded by propaganda. Topics addressed in this short article include the use of symbols and the media in mounting a propaganda or public relations campaign (Bernays often uses the

terms interchangeably), what the public actually is, and what kinds of human motivations drive people in forming opinions. In each instance, he addresses his remarks to "the propagandist."

_____. *Public Relations*. Norman: University of Oklahoma Press, 1952.
With this volume, the author, who already had written on propaganda and public opinion, seeks to explain how public relations came into existence, how it works, and by implication, how it can be an adjunct of propaganda. He is in favor of public relations, so a major theme of the book is to justify the concept. Part 1 is a history of public relations. Part 2 describes how it works, the channels through which it works, and the objectives it strives to achieve. The author relates public relations to almost every aspect of American life from education to nursing and business. This volume is invaluable for understanding whether or not there really is a clear line dividing propaganda from public information. Extensive bibliography, much of which bears upon propaganda and mass communications.

Best, James J. *Public Opinion: Micro and Macro*. Homewood, Ill.: Dorsey Press, 1973.
The author's aim is to "define public opinion in a way which seems to make sense of the diverse kinds of research that deal with the subject." In short, he is striving for the articulation of a viable theory of public opinion: what it is, how it works, what drives it, and what is its impact on public policy. Along the way, he examines the interaction of public opinion and the elements of mass media, polling, public information campaigns and outright political propaganda which play into the process of forming or influencing opinion. The author draws his conclusions from scientific research but articulates them with a general though educated audience in mind. Select bibliography.

Buzzi, Giancarlo. *Advertising: Its Cultural and Political Effects*. Translated by B. David Garmize. Minneapolis: University of Minnesota Press, 1967.
Carefully avoiding almost all reference to propaganda, the author nonetheless analyzes advertising in terms of the characteristics of persuasion that it shares with propaganda. His theme, however, is that to the extent advertising is propaganda, it can be good propaganda with positive cultural and political effects, if properly used. However, he warns, when such propaganda is not used honestly and properly, the

result may have tragic consequences for culture and politics. Select bibliography.

Cantril, Hadley. *Gauging Public Opinion.* Port Washington, N.Y.: Kennikat Press, 1972. First published in 1944.
This is a reprint of a book the author first published in the midst of World War II. Some of the sample material incorporated in the analysis is drawn from that experience. Cantril, a major figure in the history of public opinion study, was concerned in this book to bring work on opinion polling up to date. (He dedicated the study to George Gallup, a leading figure in the development of opinion polling science.) He strove also to provide assessment of what research has demonstrated to be the "dos and don'ts" of polling. Chapters deal with such subjects as wording of questions, interviewer bias, the nature of "representative samples," how much opinion is determined by information, and measuring civilian morale. Data for the study were drawn from polls concerning such questions as public reaction to Pearl Harbor and whether Germany or Japan was considered to be the more important enemy, i.e. the greater threat, of the United States in World War II. Hadley Cantril made a seminal contribution over the years to the science of public opinion measurement, and in the process to the measurement of the effects of propaganda campaigns. Select bibliography.

_____, ed. *Public Opinion, 1935-1946.* Princeton, N.J.: Princeton University Press, 1951.
The word "editor" does not exactly fit Cantril's role in creating this unique compilation of public opinion surveys by various national polling services around the world; "organizer" is more to the point. The samples cover a twenty-one-year period, including everything from what Brazilians think of Americans to what anybody at all thinks of Charles de Gaulle. In the preface, Cantril reminds users of the volume what he was forever reminding readers of his books and articles on public opinion: opinion surveying is a scientific tool that is neutral in itself but that "can be used for good or evil according to one's own definition and purpose." The contents of this volume are valuable to propagandists, on whichever side of any issue they might stand.

_____. "The Public Opinion Polls: Dr. Jekyll or Mr. Hyde?" *Public Opinion Quarterly* 4, 2 (1940), pp. 212-217.
The author comments here on the controversy surrounding public opinion polls that raged throughout the 1930s. Are they a good or a bad thing? This short essay describes the questions which had been raised

and the issues which continued to be debated. In these pages, the author introduced an entire *POQ* issue devoted to discussing the pros and cons of opinion polling. Essays included some by those who thought that opinion polls actually impede social programs by misleading those questioned into thinking that they are "competent to judge complex social issues."

Childs, Harwood L. *An Introduction to Public Opinion.* New York: John Wiley and Sons, 1940.
The subject is public opinion; the theme is its relationship to propaganda; the purpose is to organize a theory of public opinion useful to all those who have an interest in its formation, and to clarify the meaning of such terms as "public relations," "public opinion," "public interest," and, of course, "propaganda." Written in 1940, the volume naturally is informed by opinion manipulation by Adolf Hitler and other dictators. Aimed at undergraduates. Select bibliography.

_____. *Public Opinion: Nature, Formation, and Role.* Princeton, N.J.: D. Van Nostrand, 1965.
This volume addresses the importance of public opinion in the shaping of public policy in the United States. It appeared at a time when the electronic mass media were exploding in importance within the framework of domestic and international politics. While only a small portion of the three-hundred-plus pages is addressed to propaganda by name, the role propaganda plays in the shaping of public opinion is clearly understood throughout. Select bibliography.

Christenson, Reo M., and Robert O. McWilliams, eds. *Voice of the People: Readings in Public Opinion and Propaganda.* New York: McGraw-Hill, 1962.
A collection of essays, articles, and speeches on virtually every subject related to propaganda theory and the application of the theory to practice: public opinion formation, group behavior, press bias, polling, censorship, and indoctrination. Scholarly and journalistic speculation about propaganda are included along with propaganda samples. For example, Richard Nixon's "Checkers" speech and a typical Harry Truman "Give 'em Hell" speech are interspersed with observations from such as Arthur Schlesinger, Jr., Harold Lasswell, and Edward Bernays. Novelist Aldous Huxley also appears, as does poet Carl Sandburg and such media specialists (or practitioners) as Newton Minnow. There are 107 contributions in all. The collection is designed specifically for undergraduates. No bibliography.

Clarke, I. F. *Voices Prophesying War, 1763-1984*. London: Oxford University Press, 1966.

This book looks at how predictions of the "shape of wars to come" in writing and in film have helped shape public opinion regarding the future. The author covers more than two centuries of such material, from predictions of the war between Britain and the American colonies to predictions of space invaders, as in H. G. Wells' *War of the Worlds*. In each instance, the book, essay, or film was directed at persuading its audience to be prepared. Select bibliography.

Davison, W. Phillips. "The Public Opinion Process." *Public Opinion Quarterly* 22 (1958), pp. 91-106.

This science-based article concerns the process of opinion formation, concluding that the behavior of "each member of a public in regard to an issue" is determined by that individual's expectation that others hold attitudes similar to his or her own. This article connects the nature of public opinion to the interaction of groups within a given society. The value of that understanding to the student of propaganda lies in the insights it provides into the audience toward which propaganda is aimed.

Does It Matter What You Think? Prod. British Information Services in New York, 16 min., 1945. Buffalo, N.Y.: SUNY Buffalo.

Set in the midst of an exhibition of wartime equipment, one piece of which is a propaganda leaflet bomb from World War II, this film examines the power and influence of public opinion. It enumerates the various kinds of mass media and their role in mass communications, and it shows how group opinion can be formed and made to operate for various purposes, such as within trade unions, charitable causes, and government. The ultimate point is how World War II raised public consciousness regarding the role propaganda could be expected to play in the future.

Doob, Leonard W. *Public Opinion and Propaganda*. 2d ed. Hamden, Conn.: Archon Books, 1966.

One of the most prolific writers on the theory of propaganda brings his 1935 volume on the subject up to date, in this systematic survey of the practical difficulties facing political and economic propagandists. Extensive bibliography.

Flynn, John T. "Edward L. Bernays: The Science of Ballyhoo." *Atlantic Monthly* 149 (May 1932), pp. 562-571.

Starting allegorically with a story about master showman Phineas T. Barnum, the author takes on the issue of influencing the "mass mind" as Edward L. Bernays approached it. Bernays was an early expert in public relations and had published a book on propaganda in 1928 (see entry above under "General Studies"). Flynn's assessment of Bernays' public relations style and interest in propaganda is full of astute observations regarding both Bernays and the nature and value of propaganda as it was understood in the 1920s. Skeptical in this regard though the author is, he nevertheless recognizes that propaganda is both important and inescapable in what, in 1932, was the new age of the "mass mind."

Ginsberg, Benjamin. *The Captive Public: How Mass Opinion Promotes State Power*. New York: Basic Books, 1986.
Propaganda as such is the subject here only in the sense that it is a device for the manipulation of public opinion. Public opinion is the subject, and this volume stands as an implicit warning against the abuse of propaganda. The author describes how democratic governments expand their power in direct proportion to their response to public opinion; that is, the State addresses the wants and needs of the citizens, and in so doing greatly increases its power. The next step, the author concludes, is "big brother" control and the propaganda and censorship used to maintain it. References to George Orwell and his 1949 dystopian novel *Nineteen Eighty-Four* occur frequently. A volume with a point of view, which helps explain what drives those who see propaganda as a negative factor in mass communications and opinion formation. Bibliography in endnotes.

Goodrum, Charles, and Helen Dalrymple. *Advertising in America: The First 200 Years*. New York: Harry N. Abrams, 1990.
Advertising is not a twentieth-century phenomenon, nor does it necessarily have political ramifications. However, as this volume makes clear, the techniques involved in advertising "cereals, soap, and sex" are precisely those that governments, politicians, and ideologists employ to sell war, political programs, and revolutions. Chapter 8, "Guilt, Shame, and Blame," makes this point very clearly. Chapters 1 and 2 provide an overview of the history of advertising in the United States over the nineteenth and twentieth centuries. Beginning with chapter 3, the authors concentrate on advertising techniques and channels, with reference to self-censorship—that is, when the advertiser decides that a given ad is, for example, too overtly sexual in its appeal and therefore might produce a negative response. The text is clear and informative, the illustrations are well done, and the bibliography is extensive.

Graves, W. Brooke, ed. *Readings in Public Opinion: Its Formation and Control.* New York: D. Appleton, 1928.
Consisting of more than twelve hundred pages and thirty-four chapters, this monumental collection of essays covers every aspect of public opinion. The essays connect public opinion to such issues as foreign policy, justice, censorship, war, freedom of speech, politics, legislation, reform, radio, art, and music—in short, nearly anything the editor could imagine. Published in 1928, the collection is dated; all the same, reference to such topics as the "tabloid press" strike a familiar chord. No bibliography.

Harrisson, Tom. "What Is Public Opinion?" *Public Opinion Quarterly* 11 (1940), pp. 368-383.
Written by the founder of Mass Observation in Great Britain, which was among the earliest efforts anywhere to apply scientific principles to opinion assessment, this article asserts the views that were standard as of 1940 regarding the importance of public opinion to democracy. The author writes about the assessment of opinion in relation to contemporary political issues such as whether or not Prime Minister Neville Chamberlain had lost the confidence of the British public and the way in which air raids were affecting public morale. The article is written in an informal, almost journalistic style but demonstrates a clear grasp of the techniques of opinion research.

Hennessy, Bernard C. *Public Opinion.* Belmont, Calif.: Wadsworth, 1965.
This study purports to explain the "true role of the *vox populi*," predicated on descriptions of the work of political campaigns, parties, pressure groups, and the institution and personnel of governments. Propaganda is an implicit element in the study, as the author describes the driving forces operating on opinion formation. These forces are simply those elements characteristic of propaganda, such as the psychology of persuasion and group dynamics. Aimed specifically at providing methodological direction for students of public opinion research, this volume is not for the general reader. Select bibliography.

Hiebert, Ray E. "Public Relations, Propaganda, and War: A Book Review and Essay on the Literature." *Public Relations Review* 19 (Fall 1993), pp. 293-302.
A short but thorough review essay which comments on books that describe the role of propaganda and public relations in major wars that have involved the United States, from the Revolutionary War through the Gulf War. The books discussed are listed in a select bibliography.

Hyman, Herbert H. "Problems in the Collection of Opinion Research Data." *American Journal of Sociology* 55, 4 (1950), pp. 362-370.
A major difficulty in collecting data for research in opinion formation is the effect of the interviewer on the quality of the result. The author describes the outcome of opinion research and concludes that the sometimes frustrating variations that are produced in the course of opinion research stem from interviewer fallibility, unreliability of respondents, and "interactional processes." This research indicates that better controls must be found for taking down opinion in order to make the results more reliable. This is supplemental reading on the relationship between propaganda campaign design and targeting audiences.

The Image Makers. Prod. Bill Moyers, 55 min., Prod. Public Broadcasting Service, 55 min., 1984. Alexandria, Va.: PBS Video.
Part of a Bill Moyers series for PBS television on how public opinion in the twentieth century is increasingly influenced through image manipulation, and how mass communications has made this possible. The film includes an interview with Edward L. Bernays, who coined the term "public relations" and was one of the pioneers of public relations as a science.

Irion, Frederick C. *Public Opinion and Propaganda.* New York: Thomas Y. Crowell, 1950.
The author claims complete objectivity in this work on the nature of the "forces that operate with respect to public opinion and propaganda" analyzed in the cultural context. He repudiates the idea that public opinion is inherently good or evil but suggests that it may become the latter when driven by propaganda. Little is left untouched as the author examines the influence of literature, the media, value-influencing institutions (such as family, church, and school), government, pressure groups, war, ideology, economic and social forces, and, finally, methodology. Writing in the early years of the Cold War, the author presses the point that propaganda study should be "divorced from missionary zeal of all sorts." No bibliography.

Jowett, Garth S. "Propaganda and Communication: The Re-emergence of a Research Tradition." *Journal of Communication* 37, 1 (Winter 1987), pp. 97-114.
This review essay covers fourteen books written between 1983 and 1986. The author contends that they reopen propaganda as a research interest in the communications field. His essay is an enthusiastic response to these volumes that pinpoint the wide variety of roles propaganda plays in contemporary society and make clear the extent

to which propaganda relies on the science of mass communications. This review also makes clear what was the latest round of writing on propaganda theory, practice, and history as of 1986.

Kapferer, J. N. "A Mass Poisoning Rumor in Europe." *Public Opinion Quarterly* 53 (Winter 1989), pp. 467-481.
This article draws upon the specific example of a rumor in the form of a leaflet that was spread across Europe over a ten-year period beginning in the late 1970s. The leaflet gave its readers to understand that ten well-known food products contained carcinogens. The article explores the effects of rumor upon opinion and the extent to which those who saw the leaflet reacted against the food producers without questioning the validity of the leaflet's contents. This pamphlet apparently succeeded in demonstrating Michael Balfour's dictum that propaganda seeks to induce people to leap to conclusions without first examining the evidence.

Karlins, Marvin, and Herbert I. Abelson. *Persuasion: How Opinions and Attitudes Are Changed.* New York: Springer, 1970.
The methodological base is psychology in this study of a book concerned with the *science* of persuasion. The book, in the authors' words, "seeks to identify, from evidence based on systematic procedure, the mechanism involved in successful persuasive appeals." From this description of intent, the authors respond to such questions as: How can you best use fear to influence people? Can a persuasive appeal be enhanced by distracting the person listening to it? How important are such groups as neighbors, family, fellow workers, and friends in molding opinion? Does a person have to believe in the persuader before believing in the message? and finally, What are the implications of persuasion research for society? The answers to such questions as these go to the heart of propaganda methodology and, indeed, the authors use the terms "propagandists" and "persuaders" interchangeably. The work is a revision of an earlier volume and purports to bring its predecessor up to date. Each section lists readings concerned with the topic of that section, and an extensive bibliography of works related to psychology and persuasion appears at the end of the volume. The work is aimed at "social scientists and their students."

Katz, Daniel, et al., eds. *Public Opinion and Propaganda: A Book of Readings.* New York: The Dryden Press, 1954.
More than ninety historians, psychologists, sociologists, anthropologists, and others contributed to this collection of essays on the relationship between public opinion and propaganda, and their impact upon

government and democracy. Topics include media, opinion research models, propaganda strategies and techniques, and cultural, social, and economic contexts involved in political opinion formation. Virtually every topic relevant to either public opinion or propaganda is considered and addressed in a manner accessible equally to professionals, students, and intelligent lay readers. Among the ninety-plus contributors are giants in the field of propaganda and opinion study: Bernard Berelson, Leonard W. Doob, Carl Hovland, Alfred McClung Lee, and Harold Lasswell, among many others. No bibliography.

Lasswell, Harold D. "The Impact of Public Opinion Research on Our Society." *Public Opinion Quarterly* 21 (1957), pp. 33-38.
Lasswell argues for the benefits democratic society derives from public opinion surveys, focusing on the importance to leaders of knowing what the public thinks and wants in order to lead more effectively. He also talks about research methodologies for assessing public opinion, and finally about how public opinion research actually strengthens "the institution of popular government." The article surveys the kinds of questions normally raised about opinion research, including some that imply uncertainty as to whether opinion research gives greater comfort to the public or to the propagandist. See John Riley and Leonard Cottrell's research on psychological warfare (entry below under "Analysis and Measurement of Propaganda Effects").

Lee, Ivy L. *Publicity: Some of the Things It Is and Is Not.* New York: Industries Publishing, 1925.
A series of published talks given by the author before the National Association of Teachers of Journalism, the Advertising Club of New York, and the American Electric Railway Association convention, this volume sets forth the principles and methods the author believes work best in creating publicity. The first section equates publicity with propaganda, and the author argues strongly that propaganda is an inevitable part of any appeal to opinion, whatever the subject. The remaining sections provide interesting but not wholly convincing arguments in favor of "publicity men." No bibliography.

McDowall, Duncan, ed. *Advocacy Advertising: Propaganda or Democratic Right?* Ottawa: The Conference Board of Canada, 1982.
A pamphlet examining the nature of "advocacy advertising," which is defined as the process of "getting the message across," be it from Mobil Oil or a political party. This volume argues that advocacy advertising is the exercise of the right of free speech, and describes it as "one of

the most powerful creative forces in our society." It argues as well that the purpose of advocacy advertising is information and enlightenment, rather than propaganda. However, the examples of advocacy advertising that are illustrated in the text very clearly employ propaganda techniques. No bibliography.

Noelle-Neumann, Elisabeth. *The Spiral of Silence: Public Opinion—Our Social Skin.* Chicago: University of Chicago Press, 1984.
This book argues that public opinion is often shaped by "trend-setters" with few ideas of their own, but who want to be leaders wherever they go. Their "trends" become the opinion of the crowd, which sooner or later falls in line with them, going so far even as to assume an air of moral superiority to complement the herd instinct. The author deals with such topics as social control, mass psychology, fashion as public opinion, challenging public opinion, mass media as an opinion influence, and stereotyping as a public opinion vehicle. Well written, the volume sheds light on many issues basic to links between public opinion formation and propaganda function. Select bibliography.

Odegard, Peter H. "Social Dynamics and Public Opinion." *Public Opinion Quarterly* 3, 2 (1939), pp. 239-250.
This article argues that public opinion experts must move beyond being describers and measurers of opinion, and become students of the "functional etiology of attitudes" as well. They should understand why people think what they think. An important article for historians of propaganda theory because it represents the movement—or at least the beginning of the movement—of public opinion theory beyond mere opinion sampling to opinion shaping, at which point it becomes a science of much expanded use to propagandists.

Ogle, Marbury Bladen, Jr. *Public Opinion and Political Dynamics.* Boston: Houghton Mifflin, 1950.
This volume addresses the role of public opinion in a democratic society: what it is and how it works. Topics include the conditioning of opinion by ideology, social myth as influenced by such social institutions as church, school, and family, psychological factors that work on opinion formation, measurement of public opinion, and the role of mass media in influencing opinion. Only one chapter is titled "Propaganda," but all chapters address aspects of the propaganda question relative to opinion formation. The book reflects political concerns that emerged with the advent of the Cold War. In more general terms, it is informative with reference to propaganda history and evolving

notions regarding opinion research. One-line annotations make the select bibliography containing works on propaganda, communications, and public opinion published prior to 1950 particularly useful.

Price, Vincent. "Social Identification and Public Opinion: Effects of Communicating Group Conflict." *Public Opinion Quarterly* 53 (Summer 1989), pp. 197-224.
Propaganda functions in some circumstances by playing off one social group against another. This article explains how public opinion tends to be influenced by an individual's identification with a particular social group, and how this opinion can be shaped in particular ways by the media reporting on conflicts between social groups.

Public Relations: A Founder's Perspective. Prod. C-SPAN, 89 min., 1989. West Lafayette, Ind.: Purdue University Public Affairs Video Archives. Edward L. Bernays was known as the "father of public relations." He was ninety-seven years old when he narrated this history of public relations in the United States and his contribution to it. He describes the history of public relations beginning with World War I, and concentrates from that start on public relations as politics. Bernays' point is that public relations concentrates on using "ideas as weapons" and that political leadership has an obligation to use public relations in leading society toward "righteous causes." Without saying as much, Bernays makes an excellent case for public relations as an aspect of propaganda. This film supplements Bernays' memoirs and writings on public relations over the years (see entries above).

Qualter, Terence H. *Opinion Control in the Democracies.* New York: St. Martin's Press, 1985.
A study of public opinion and democracy from the perspective of the role actually played by the former in sustaining—or conversely threatening—the latter. The author addresses the psychological and sociological characteristics of public attitudes and the role of propaganda and censorship in shaping them. This volume looks primarily at the future of democracy in Western society and suggests that this future will be determined by the mass media serving as a propaganda tool. Readable and well argued, if somewhat pessimistic. Limited bibliography.

Weiss, Janet A., and Mary Tschirhart. "Public Information Campaigns as Policy Instruments." *Journal of Policy Analysis and Management* 13 (Winter 1994), pp. 82-119.
Based upon a statistical study of one hundred public information campaigns, "or what might be called government propaganda," in

which effective outcomes, political benefits, and consequences for the democratic process were considered. The authors conclude that there are both disadvantages and advantages in the use of such campaigns. They further conclude that the disadvantages might be outweighed by the advantages, so long as the instruments of the campaigns (propaganda materials and channels) are used with care to emphasize the positive and mitigate the negative.

Analysis and Measurement of Propaganda Effects

Altheide, David L., and John M. Johnson. *Bureaucratic Propaganda.* Boston: Allyn and Bacon, 1980.
This volume concerns the kind of "public information" that results from bureaucratic communication. The study begins with a "reconceptualization" of propaganda against the background of its known history, in the process of which the authors create a theory of propaganda applicable specifically to its employment by bureaucrats. From that beginning, they go on to report on the results of their analysis of propaganda in relation to news, television ratings, welfare research, military preparedness and efficiency in combat, and even soul-counting by evangelists. The authors conclude that in all cases, the propagandists are bureaucrats, public or private, whose objective is to sell the public on the importance of their offices. Select bibliography.

Asher, R., and S. S. Sargent. "Shifts in Attitudes Caused by Cartoon Caricatures." *Journal of General Psychology* 24 (1941), pp. 451-455. A report on results of a study designed to discover "whether, and under what conditions, cartoon caricatures may cause significant changes in existing attitudes." Cartoons used in the research included "Uncle Sam," "Mussolini," and "John Bull," among others. It was discovered that caricatures could affect attitudes, but the researchers thought the parameters of their study too narrow to be conclusive. This raises the question of why they established the limits upon which the study was based in the first place.

Ball-Rokeach, S. J., and M. L. DeFleur. "A Dependency Model of Mass-Media Effects." *Communications Research* 3, 1 (January 1976), pp. 3-21.
"Do mass communications have widespread effects on individuals and society or do they have relatively little influence?" This is the question raised at the outset as the authors note that in spite of decades of research,

no one yet seems to have a clear answer. They suggest that researchers may be asking the wrong questions. "We propose that it is the nature of the tripartite audience-media-society relationship which most directly determines many of the effects that the media have on people and society." From this premise the authors build their "dependency model," looking in the process at the media's role in "attitude formation," "agenda setting," "expanding peoples' systems of belief," and "value clarification," concluding that the mass media certainly do have the capacity to influence, persuade, and otherwise affect their audience.

Bandura, Albert. *Principles of Behavior Modification.* New York: Holt, Rinehart and Winston, 1969.
A textbook for teaching psychological techniques that can be employed to modify behavior. The theme is modifying deviant behavior, but the underlying assumption is that there is a definably acceptable social or cultural "norm" for behavior, and that nonconformist behavior relative to these norms can be altered through psychological conditioning. Without intending it, the author has made clear that the techniques applicable to correcting deviant behavior among the mentally disturbed, for one example, are much the same as those which have been employed in mind-control, or "brainwashing." Written for the student of psychology, the bibliography is confined largely to reading in psychology and social psychology theory.

_____. *Social Foundations of Thought and Action: A Social Cognitive Theory.* Englewood Cliffs, N.J.: Prentice-Hall, 1986.
In this complex volume, the author presents a theoretical framework for analyzing human motivation and argues that central to motivation is social interaction. An optimistic work, the text asserts that people are quite capable of self-direction, once they understand the relationship between motivation and action. The author wants to direct understanding of social behavior onto this "higher plane," so to speak, of self-directed behavior. If his conclusions are correct, the individual may be less receptive to mass propaganda campaigns than most social psychologists have argued. The volume, filled with technical language, is intended for the specialist. Select bibliography.

Beyle, Herman C. "Determining the Effect of Propaganda Campaigns." *Annals of the American Academy of Political and Social Science* 179 (1935), pp. 106-113.
Since all of the social sciences "touch upon some phase of propaganda," it becomes necessary to develop techniques for understanding

how propaganda appeals and how the appeal can be measured. This article is, in part, a criticism of existing literature on the subject that the author finds both incomplete and somewhat superficial. It is important, he concludes, to adopt a scientific attitude for such study; otherwise, "assessment of propaganda may easily become only more propaganda."

Brown, Steven R. *Political Subjectivity: Applications of Q Methodology in Political Science*. New Haven, Conn.: Yale University Press, 1980. Most of this volume is theoretical beyond the capacity of all but the expert reader. However, chapter 3 brings the idea of political subjectivity to bear upon various factors in political science which relate directly to propaganda. These factors include political climate, political mood, public opinion and attitudes, political imagery, and personality. The conclusion of chapter 3 specifically targets political propaganda as a subject. A difficult book, but very instructive in relation to political propaganda for those who understand its technical language. An extensive bibliography of works mainly on politics, psychology, and related subjects.

Campbell, Donald T. "Stereotypes and the Perception of Group Difference." *American Psychologist* 22 (October 1967), pp. 817-829.
Stereotyping "the enemy" is standard in political and war propaganda. This article examines stereotyping as a psychological and anthropological phenomenon. The study upon which it is based concerns analysis of how specific behavioral as well as physical differences lead to stereotyping of individuals and groups. The author is opposed to stereotyping in principle, and conducted the study in order to demonstrate not only that it exists but also that it has negative social and other consequences. He provides clear evidence that propagandists have regularly employed stereotyping simply because the process works.

Canetti, Elias. *Crowds and Power*. Translated by Carol Stewart. New York: Continuum, 1973.
This volume is actually two books which have been described as one of the most monumentally important works on social psychology of the twentieth century. The first book is an analysis of "the crowd" as a factor in human history, which describes everything that relates to groups of people acting as crowds and to the individual's role within crowds. The second is a similar analysis of "power" as a factor in human history. It describes everything relating to power, using animal metaphors on occasion to make its points. The connection between the

two is that crowds are sources of power, or conversely are its victims. This eminently readable volume helps explain the social psychology that lies at the root of mass propaganda. Select bibliography.

Cantril, Hadley, and Gordon W. Allport. *The Psychology of Radio*. New York: Harper and Row, 1935.
A fascinating work published in 1935, this volume is among the first major, thorough studies of what at the time was a relatively new phenomenon of mass communications, the radio. The authors describe the book as "the first attempt by psychologists to map out from their own point of view the new mental world created by radio." Subjects scientifically examined include psychological and cultural factors that shape programming and determine audience response, the mental processes of listeners, and what are the practical applications of the results of experiments conducted with radio listeners. The authors also examine, in the context of these subjects, who owns radios in countries other than the United States, the voices and personalities of broadcasters, types of programming, and the differences in cognition between reading and listening. This volume was a virtual handbook for the radio propagandists who emerged before, during, and after World War II. No bibliography.

Chaiken, Shelly, and Charles Stangor. "Attitudes and Attitude Change." *Annual Review of Psychology* 38 (1987), pp. 575-630.
A long article in which the authors review what was, in 1986, recent literature on various aspects of how attitudes are formed and influenced. Their subjects include such items as "process models," "behavior and attitudes," "the influence of persuasive messages," and "minority and majority group influence" on attitudes. The language is technical and assumes a prior knowledge of the subject matter. The article is not intended for the general reader, but it can introduce the propaganda student to the many variants within the sociopsychological foundations upon which mass persuasion rests.

Child, Irvin L., and Leonard W. Doob. "Factors Determining National Stereotypes." *Journal of Social Psychology* 17 (1943), pp. 203-219.
This article describes a study carried out in 1939-1940 among college students regarding stereotypes based upon nationality. They were to consider specific traits—carefree, ambitious, religious, honest, cruel, gloomy, and materialistic, among others—in response to the questionnaire. The study demonstrated that positive traits were most often attributed to citizens of "preferred countries," while negative traits

were usually attributed to citizens of non-preferred countries. The authors conducted their study just before and after the outbreak of World War II. The implications for war propaganda are obvious and general, whether the context is World War II, Korea, Vietnam, or the Persian Gulf.

Cohen, Arthur R. *Attitude Change and Social Influence.* New York: Basic Books, 1964.
This relatively short volume is a study in social psychology in which the primary objective is to evaluate how people's minds are changed. The author phrases his purpose in this language: "Reformers, politicians, policemen, propagandists, educators, club members, and others have always been concerned with the conditions under which people can be influenced to accept new ideas and to cast off old ways of thought." To address these concerns, he examines the process of communication, the characteristics of the communicator, the effects, scientifically evaluated, of communication on groups, cognitive models of attitude change, and the influence of groups on their individual members. He concludes with a section on research still needing to be done on the subject of attitude change and social influence. The bibliography is limited to work by major mid-twentieth century American social psychologists.

Converse, Philip E. "The Nature of Belief Systems in Mass Publics," in David E. Apter, ed., *Ideology and Discontent.* New York: Free Press, 1964.
This essay focuses on differences in the nature of belief systems as held by "elite political actors" and the "masses." The point is that there are differences, and that these differences may be easily overlooked by behavioral theorists, who as a result may misrepresent the masses with which they are dealing. The author talks about psychological and social factors in the process of belief-system development, including the factor of "social groupings" as central objects in belief systems. Accurate mapping of belief systems within mass publics would greatly facilitate propaganda employment or, conversely, serve well to counter it.

Doob, Leonard W. *Propaganda: Its Psychology and Technique.* New York: Henry Holt, 1935.
Inspired by the realities of politics in the 1930s, at home and abroad, this volume is predicated upon the author's confessed belief that "the recognition and understanding of a phenomenon enables an individual to free himself to a certain extent from the forces which that phenome-

non represents." With that in mind, Doob proceeds to examine propaganda using what he terms the appropriate "weapons": sociology and psychology. The book is in five parts: the nature of psychology; the nature of propaganda; the scope of propaganda; the vehicles which carry propaganda (press, radio, film, etc.); and a summary of the arguments of the book and what they may mean. An accessible contribution to propaganda theory, which the author updated at the end of World War II. No bibliography.

Doob, Leonard W., and Edward S. Robinson. "Psychology and Propaganda." *Annals of the American Academy of Political and Social Science* 179 (1935), pp. 88-95.
An effort to correct certain "naive, yet widely current" views on the nature of propaganda which, the authors note, grew out of the negatives associated with the phenomenon in World War I. The article describes propaganda as "psychologically significant" because of its persuasive function, and therefore worthy of both more study and clearer understanding. The authors write generally but offer useful insights into the connection between propaganda and psychological influences in individuals and groups.

Faces of the Enemy. Prod. and dir. Bill Jersey, Public Broadcasting Service, 57 min., 1989. Alexandria, Va.: PBS Video.
Originally broadcast by the Public Broadcasting Service, this documentary is predicated upon the assumption that every society has an image of its enemies, and then asks how those images affect individual behavior within the society. Topics range from murder to war. The film looks at various kinds of propaganda messages, and then asks what takes place in the mind of an individual that allows him or her to kill the enemy whose image the propaganda exploits. The ideologically motivated murder of a family in Seattle is used as a case study.

Festinger, Leonard, and Nathan Maccoby. "On Resistance to Persuasive Communications." *Journal of Abnormal and Social Psychology* 68 (1964), pp. 359-366.
Research on resistance to opinion change carried out at three universities led to the conclusion that persuasion which argues strongly against an opinion to which an audience subscribes will be more effective if the audience is distracted in such a way as to be prevented from counter-arguing. Films were used in this manner to argue against fraternities. One was of a speaker making a speech. The other carried the same sound track, but with irrelevant and distracting visuals on the

screen. The researchers concluded that the second film was the most persuasive against fraternities. This article clarifies the importance in mind manipulation of sensory perception, which is a central feature of propaganda technique.

Freedman, Anne E., and P. E. Freedman. *The Psychology of Political Control: Comprising Dialogues Between a Modern Prince and His Tutor on the Application of Basic Psychological Principles to the Realm of Politics*. New York: St. Martin's Press, 1975.
This clever volume uses Niccolò Machiavelli's sixteenth century classic on political power *The Prince* as a metaphor in explaining how political power in the twentieth century can be understood in terms of psychological manipulation. The authors ask, "How do you get someone to do what you want him to do? How do the rulers control the ruled? What advice could a psychologist versed in the modern experimental literature of his field add to Machiavelli's shrewd dicta. . . ?" Each chapter is a "discourse" between a modern "prince" and his tutor, on such topics as control and human nature, control through positive reinforcement and through fear, the socialization of good citizens, and attitude change. Select bibliography and glossary of terms.

Freedman, Jonathan L., and D. O. Sears. "Warning, Distraction, and Resistance to Influence." *Journal of Personality and Social Psychology* 1 (1965), pp. 262-266.
The authors explore hypotheses concerning manipulation of the mind. Tell subjects they are about to receive a communication with which they will disagree, and those persons will resist its contents to a greater degree than otherwise. Distract subjects from the contents, and resistance to the message will be lessened. The authors report that experiments support the first hypothesis much more than the second.

George, Alexander L. *Propaganda Analysis: A Study of Inferences Made from Nazi Propaganda in World War II*. White Plains, N.Y.: Row, Peterson, 1959.
"Propaganda analysis," the author explains, "has two general purposes: (a) the summary, or selective description, of what is being said by the propagandist and (b) the interpretation of the intentions, strategy, and calculations behind propaganda communications." Nazi propaganda from World War II provides the perfect source material for applying this principle, for, as the author explains, "it would be difficult to reproduce in a research experiment the great variety of factors that affect propaganda analysis carried out under operational conditions."

This volume represents a step forward in developing a science of propaganda analysis having both theoretical and practical dimensions. The book is divided into four parts, each of which is subdivided into chapters. Subjects include propaganda analysis and the study of action, propaganda analysis and the study of communication, methodology and applications, and validation of inferences. The language is technical and will be of most value to readers with a working knowledge of communication and behavioral theory. Select bibliography.

Greenwald, Anthony G., Timothy C. Brock, and Thomas M. Ostrom, eds. *Psychological Foundations of Attitudes.* New York: Academic Press, 1968.
All of the contributors to this volume are academic psychologists, and their contributions here are highly technical studies of the psychology of attitude formation. The purpose is to offer alternative explanations to existing theories regarding the process. The language is scientific and is supplemented with charts, graphs, and equations which measure, in mathematical form, the effect of message sending upon attitude. The subject matter in this volume is the formation of individual rather than mass attitudes. Nevertheless, it points toward assessing how individual attitude formation is linked to the group attitudes that are the object of propaganda targeting. Bibliography in endnotes.

Herz, Martin F. "Some Psychological Lessons from Leaflet Propaganda in World War II." *Public Opinion Quarterly* 13, 3 (1949), pp. 471-486.
The author was chief leaflet writer for the United States Psychological Warfare Division in World War II. He discusses at some length how the effects of leaflets were measured. Examples of the lessons learned from this measurement include: do not export propaganda designed for domestic consumption, and be as truthful as possible. The author's comments here suggest ways in which psychological warfare experts can profit from the World War II experience, in terms of refining their analytical skills regarding the effects of propaganda.

Holt, Robert T., and Robert W. van de Velde. *Strategic Psychological Operations and American Foreign Policy.* Chicago: University of Chicago Press, 1960.
This volume falls somewhere between propaganda theory and propaganda practice at a particular point in history. It presents the reader with a theoretical analysis, developed within a historical and political context, of how psychological manipulation can be used as a means for achieving positive foreign policy results. The authors acknowledge that

what they are describing is propaganda, and note that to many people, propaganda carries negative connotations to such an extent that the real value of psychological strategies in foreign policy is overlooked. Their position is that it is time to put the negative aside and recognize that propaganda, understood as the use of mass communications to influence behavior, is simply psychological manipulation that can be used to advantage in the conduct of foreign policy. This volume is written for the informed student of propaganda history and theory and is likely to be somewhat beyond the general reader. Select bibliography.

Hovland, Carl I., Arthur A. Lumsdaine, and Fred D. Sheffield. *Experiments on Mass Communications*. Vol. 3, *Studies in Social Psychology in World War II*. Princeton, N.J.: Princeton University Press, 1949.
The authors describe the results of studies of mass communications through film that were conducted during World War II by the Research Branch of the United States War Department's Information and Education Division. The studies were based upon the "unprecedented utilization of films and similar mass communications media during World War II" as part of military training programs. They employed what were for the time standard social-psychological research techniques in evaluating the effectiveness of educational and indoctrinational films, and examined such questions as the advantage of presenting "one side" of an issue as opposed to "both sides." The results shed light on the effectiveness of film as a propaganda channel as it was used in World War II. No bibliography.

Hyman, Herbert H., and Paul B. Sheatsley. "Some Reasons Why Information Campaigns Fail." *Public Opinion Quarterly* 11 (Spring 1947), pp. 412-423.
The study here reported was based upon national sample polls, and it made the case that what the authors refer to as "psychological factors" are the principal reasons why information campaigns fail. Some examples: interested people require more information than uninterested or disinterested ones; people look for information that supports their existing attitudes; different groups of people interpret the same information differently. It makes clear that propagandists have much to take into account when they devise campaigns with the expectation that they will succeed.

Institute for Propaganda Analysis. *The Fine Art of Propaganda: A Study of Father Coughlin's Speeches*. New York: Harcourt Brace, 1939.
This study focuses on Father Charles E. Coughlin, one of the most notorious pro-fascist American radio rabblerousers of the 1920s and

1930s. The Institute for Propaganda Analysis, established in 1937 "to conduct objective, non-partisan studies in the field of propaganda and public opinion," found in the speeches of this Detroit priest a perfect set of materials upon which to practice its function. The result was this volume, which revealed "the present devices of undemocratic propagandists and the tests by which these techniques may be detected." There are twelve chapters, with such headings as "Name Calling," "Glittering Generality," "Testimonial," "Card Stacking," and "The Tricks in Operation." The contents of this study show clearly how propaganda analysis functioned in the 1930s. No bibliography.

Jahoda, Marie, and Eunice Cooper. "The Evasion of Propaganda: How Prejudiced People Respond to Anti-Prejudice Propaganda." *Journal of Psychology* 23 (1947), pp. 15-25.

This article examines the result of research on the question of how bigots responded to propaganda designed to "educate" them into being less prejudiced. The research was based upon an actual case study, in which the propaganda in question, a series of cartoons that made fun of prejudice in the form of a character named Mr. Biggott, failed to achieve its objective and, indeed, left its audience demonstrably more prejudiced than when it began. The authors' purpose was to explain how and why the propaganda had failed. They concluded that failure was owing to the audience's both misperceiving the object of the propaganda and evading its message, the latter being because the message ran counter to the values of the social group to which the audience belonged.

Lasswell, Harold D. "The Persons: Subject and Object of Propaganda." *Annals of the American Academy of Political and Social Science* 179 (1935), pp. 187-193.

This article challenges the assumption that propagandists are not influenced by their propaganda and that the propaganda audience is not capable of resisting propaganda. Topics touched upon in this short piece include the meaning of propaganda, the discrediting of traditional symbols of democracy because propaganda use has compromised them, the need for further study of propaganda, and questions of propaganda and ethics. Lasswell concludes by noting that propaganda is "a hazardous occupation," and that propagandists in their own lives give voice to "many of the major contradictions of our civilization": ambition, competition, frustration, and finally violence. Though the article was written in 1935, many of the author's contentions were still being raised years later.

Lindzey, Gardner, and Elliot Aronson, eds. *Handbook of Social Psychology.* 2 vols. New York: Random House, 1985.
Volume 1 concerns the theory and methods of social psychology, and volume 2 covers special fields and applications within the subject. While only volume 1 touches upon propaganda specifically as a technique for exercising social control, both volumes define, project analytical models for, and explain the interaction of the many aspects of social behavior and social manipulation that are part of propaganda technique. An understanding of social psychology is fundamental to understanding how propaganda works. These volumes are written in an encyclopedic manner but with a minimum of technical language. Select bibliography.

Marks, Melvin R., and Wilson L. Taylor. "A Methodological Study of the Effects of Propaganda." *Journal of Social Psychology* 65 (April 1965), pp. 269-277.
A report on research conducted to determine the most effective propaganda methodology. The test case was the idea of a powerful international police force. The subjects were students at Tulane University, and the propaganda materials included such items as prestigious-sounding but fictitious organizations that backed the police idea, and "blurbs" of varying degrees of literary quality. The breakdown of materials was: two kinds of sponsorship, scientific versus religious, and five degrees of intensity of the message, from "strongly for" to "strongly against." The conclusion drawn was that different approaches gained different results, and that it clearly is "no simple matter to conduct research on the effects of propaganda."

Martin, L. John. "Effectiveness of International Propaganda." *Annals of the American Academy of Political and Social Science* 398 (1971), pp. 61-70.
In this article on theoretical bases for international propaganda, the author argues that what is called international propaganda is actually "facilitative communication," as opposed to "persuasive communication," which, by definition, is propaganda. By facilitative communication the author means "an activity that is designed to keep lines open and to maintain contacts against the day when they will be needed for propaganda purposes." He argues that modern propaganda agencies rely only minutely upon persuasive communication, the reason being that in order for it to be effective, such communication must achieve an articulable objective. To accomplish that, the propagandist must control the propaganda vehicle and be able to predict the result of what is being done.

Merton, Robert K. *Mass Persuasion: The Social Psychology of a War Bond Drive.* Westport, Conn.: Greenwood Press, 1946.
Written on the morrow of World War II, this volume examines the concept of the war bond drive and how the kind of propaganda associated with such a wartime phenomenon works. The author is very aware of the impact the war had upon the prevalence of propaganda in American society and suggests at the outset that it needs more understanding as a concept. "A radio star succeeded in selling some $39,000,000 of war bonds in the course of one day's broadcasts," he notes, and then asks: "How did this come about?" What follows is a careful analysis of the propaganda of raising money for wartime, which considers such factors as ego, sociocultural context, repetition, sacrifice, guilt, and the absence of counterpropaganda. This volume has application equally to propaganda theory and the history of war propaganda. No bibliography.

Osterhouse, R. A., and T. C. Brock. "Distraction Increases Yielding to Propaganda by Inhibiting Counterarguing." *Journal of Personality and Social Psychology* 15 (1970), pp. 344-358.
In a research project similar to Jonathan Freedman's (see entry above), students were used in experiments in which communication that was propaganda espousing something they knew to be false was given to them while they were being distracted by having to call out a series of lights flashing at odd intervals. Their inability to concentrate clearly resulted in their reduced capacity to advance counterargument to the propaganda being received. Consequently, the propaganda, though known to be false, was at least somewhat effective, and far more than when there was no distraction. These tests seemed to invalidate Freedman's results from a similar experiment conducted a half decade earlier.

Petty, Richard E., Gary L. Wells, and Timothy C. Brock. "Distraction Can Enhance or Reduce Yielding to Propaganda: Thought Disruption Versus Effort Justification." *Journal of Personality and Social Psychology* 34 (1976), pp. 874-884.
More on distraction and propaganda. In this case, the discrepant messages differed in the degree of difficulty with which they could be countered. The research here concluded that "distraction works by inhibiting the dominant cognitive response to persuasive communication and, therefore, it can result in either enhanced *or* reduced acceptance." This conclusion would seem to put Freedman back on track and challenge Osterhouse and Brock (entry above). Interestingly, the Brock involved here was also an author of the Osterhouse study. All three

studies are of use in understanding propaganda theory, and if somewhat jargon-laden, they are nevertheless readable by the layperson as well as the expert.

Pratkanis, Anthony R., and Elliot Aronson. *Age of Propaganda: Everyday Use and Abuse of Propaganda.* Newark, N.J.: W. H. Freeman, 1992.
This volume addresses the question of how propaganda works—including subliminal messaging—and warns against it. The authors, both social psychologists, rightly see the techniques of advertising as central to propaganda and are critical of such techniques equally in terms of conspicuous consumption and their capacity to lead us down the garden path in politics and war. Their research appears extensive and scientific, in support of a clear desire to inform their readers in such a way as to make them propaganda-resistant. The volume is well written and informative, aimed at a mixed audience. That audience should pay attention to occasional use of terms or phrases that are of questionable definition. "Factoid," for example, is described here as information that is either misleading or simply false—which would come as a surprise to CNN-Headline News, which uses the term on a regular basis to introduce bits of generally unknown information. Even with this flaw, *Age of Propaganda* is a valuable addition to the literature on the subject. Select bibliography.

The Psychology of Mass Persuasion. Prod. Peter Cochran, 47 min., 1987. Pleasantville, N.Y.: Human Relations Media.
This film examines how attitudes are formed and changed within modern society, with the intent of showing the social psychology upon which much of the methods and ethics of propaganda rest. Propaganda is the point; mass psychology is the persuasion technique analyzed. The film is aimed at undergraduates.

Riley, John R., and Leonard S. Cottrell, Jr. "Research for Psychological Warfare." *Public Opinion Quarterly* 21 (1957), pp. 33-38.
This article was inspired by the fact of psychological warfare (military propaganda deployment) during World War II. Its point is that more precise research tools need to be devised if the "problem of psychological warfare" is to be understood and dealt with properly. Aspects of the problem treated in these pages include research on the target audience, the message content, and message effect; the latter connects this piece to problems on opinion research as discussed, also in 1957, by Harold Lasswell in his article "The Impact of Public Opinion

Research on Our Society" (see entry above under "Public Opinion, Public Relations, and Advertising").

Rokeach, Milton. "Attitudes: Nature." *International Encyclopedia of the Social Sciences*, vol. 1. New York: Macmillan, 1968, pp. 449-458.
The author defines attitudes as a "relatively enduring organization of interrelated beliefs that describe, evaluate, and advocate action with respect to an object or situation, with each belief having cognitive, affective, and behavioral components." He also describes the effects of interaction between two or more attitudes as defined above, and in so doing, describes what the propagandist addresses when designing a propaganda campaign. See M. Brewster Smith on attitude change (entry below), which follows the Rokeach entry in the *Encyclopedia*. Limited bibliography listing books on attitude theory.

_____. "The Nature and Meaning of Dogmatism." *Psychological Review* 61, 3 (1954), pp. 194-204.
The author sets forth a framework for empirical research into the phenomenon of dogmatism, the purpose of which is to determine the nature and significance of the concept. By dogmatism, he means a narrow set of beliefs, closed-mindedness, and intolerance of those with differing points of view. He points out that dogmatism cuts across ethnic, political, and economic lines, and applies equally to ethnocentrism, political-economic conservatism, and fascist authoritarianism. This article is not jargon-ridden, and supplements literature on propaganda as a means for sustaining dogmatic assumptions.

Rosnow, Ralph L., and Edward J. Robinson, eds. *Experiments in Persuasion*. New York: Academic Press, 1967.
A collection of journal articles by eminent psychologists and other behavioral scientists studying persuasion theory and methods, such as Carl Hovland, Kurt Lewin, Elliot Aronson, and Irving Janis. The articles are the outgrowth of experiments in persuasion technique and result, and are grouped in this volume around those themes that are central to persuasion: the credibility of the source of persuasion appeal, the message that is the appeal, the characteristics of the audience, individually and as a group, and finally, determinations of how far the persuader wants the audience to be moved in the course of the appeal. This is one of many such volumes produced in the 1960s in which behavioral scientists examined the hows and whys of persuasion and mind manipulation. Like many others from the period, this collection makes a valuable contribution to understanding the theoretical and

methodological issues that are germane to the study of propaganda. No bibliography.

Sargant, William. *Battle for the Mind: A Physiology of Conversion and Brain-Washing*. London: Pan Books, 1957.
At the outset the author, a medical doctor, points out that the purpose of this volume is "to examine some of the mechanics involved in the fixing or destroying of . . . beliefs in the human brain." The beliefs in question are political and religious, and the mechanisms are neurophysiological. He begins with the question whether or not beliefs can be forcibly implanted in the human brain; that is, how does "brain-washing" work, if it does. The result is a fascinating study in which nerve connections, psychoanalysis, drugs, and Pavlov's experiments with dogs play a part. A series of photographs illustrate the outward behavior of people supposedly in the throes of religious fervor. The conclusion is that while political or religious "conversion" may be induced by psychological manipulation, it should be remembered that the faculties thus affected are "physiologically entailed to the brain." A fascinating study of some bizarre forms of persuasion. Select bibliography.

Schoenewolf, Gerald. *The Art of Hating*. Northvale, N.J.: Jason Aronson, 1991.
The content of this unusual book is not quite what most readers might take the title to mean. It is not simply a guide to understanding and therefore resisting the emotion of hatred, an element central to many kinds of propaganda; rather, it is a psychological analysis of how hatred works as a human emotion, and how negative hatred can be turned into positive hatred, and thereby be made into a useful and constructive emotion. Virtually every application of hatred is examined, from individuals hating other individuals to hatred within cultures and political units. The link between hatred—positive or negative, by the author's definition—and the techniques of psychological manipulation employed by propaganda is made clear on every page, and in layperson's language. Select bibliography.

Smith, Bruce Lannes. "Propaganda Analysis and the Science of Democracy." *Public Opinion Quarterly* 5, 2 (1941), pp. 250-259.
This article concerns teaching the science of propaganda analysis, the methods for which, the author concludes, are sending students away filled with a "destructive cynicism." The remedy, he contends, is to create a "Science of Democracy" to define socially structured and individual motivation in a way both comprehensible and reassuring to

students. His point is that the propaganda students encounter, and which they are taught to analyze, leaves them distrustful even of their own democratically elected leaders. The author argues that this can only end in the destruction of democracy.

Smith, M. Brewster. "Attitudes: Change." *International Encyclopedia of the Social Sciences,* vol. 1. New York: Macmillan, 1968, pp. 458-467. This essay focuses on theories of attitude change and research on the subject. The author's purpose is to describe what the research is contributing to the theory. In the process, he defines and describes the factors that go into causing attitude change, all of which address the essential questions pertaining to how propaganda functions when it seeks to alter opinion as opposed to merely reinforcing it. See Milton Rokeach (entry above) on the nature of attitudes, immediately preceding Smith's essay in the *Encyclopedia.*

Stone, Vernon A. "Individual Differences and Inoculation Against Persuasion." *Journalism Quarterly* 46 (Summer 1969), pp. 267-273. A report on research into "strategies for building resistance to attitude change," or, to put it another way, how not to be affected by propaganda messages. In such research, persuasion sources, methods of persuasion, and gender were examined and found to hold no particular answers to the question of immunity. Self-esteem did, on the other hand; persuasion worked most effectively on those least certain of their ability to think for themselves. This conclusion is slightly at odds with Jacques Ellul's contention that intellectuals, by his definition those people who are always certain that they think for themselves, are among the most easily influenced by propaganda.

Swanson, G. E. "Agitation Through the Press: A Study of the Personalities of Publicists." *Public Opinion Quarterly* 20, 2 (1956), pp. 441-456. It would be wrong to treat propaganda as existing independent of the personality of the propagandist. This article makes that case with reference to press publicists. The author reports on a study of press publicists that was based upon the hypothesis that they "have strong needs to control their world and be protected from its unfavorable reactions." The study, based upon broad surveys of various kinds of press publicists and involving such factors as background and "need structures," proved the hypothesis. A considerable amount of technical language makes this article difficult for any reader not well versed in the science of personality study. For those who are, it is both interesting and informative.

Tanaka, Yasumasa. "Psychological Factors in International Persuasion."
Annals of the American Academy of Political and Social Science 398
(1971), pp. 50-60.
  The author argues that laws which operate in the formation of and
  changes in attitude are universal and not very susceptible to contami-
  nation by language or culture. Therefore, intercultural propaganda is
  possible so long as the nature of the target audience is examined,
  analyzed, and thereby understood by the propagandist; communication
  use is multifaceted; and communication is carried forward more by
  deeds than by words. However, the author continues, it is important to
  recognize that criteria used in making evaluations of the audience can
  be affected by cultural and individual differences.

Thompson, Wayne N., ed. *The Process of Persuasion: Principles and
Readings.* New York: Harper and Row, 1975.
  Propaganda is persuasion, or at least it is predicated upon being able to
  persuade, and this collection of readings seeks to integrate a wide variety
  of sources on how and why various techniques of persuasion work or do
  not work. In the process of presenting this material, the author covers
  virtually every aspect of how persuasive techniques can apply to propaganda, from the content of persuasive messages to crowd psychology.
  There is also a chapter on the ethics of persuasion, which mirrors decades
  of debate over whether or not propaganda is a "good thing." Designed
  mainly for undergraduate students. Bibliography contained in endnotes.

Turner, Ralph H. "The Public Perception of Protest." *American Sociological Review* 34, 6 (December 1969), pp. 815-831.
  This article examines "collective acts of disruption and violence" with
  regard to how the public may perceive and be influenced by them. Are
  they seen as legitimate, or as a crime or rebellion? What will be the
  effect upon the public in either case? The point is made that the
  protesters must persuade the public that what they are doing is legitimate and in the name of a valid cause or purpose. In the course of
  making this point, the author notes various types of action in response
  to protest, such as police confrontation, and explains how they too may
  influence public perception of the protest. This article compliments
  writings which relate propaganda to persuasion through group action.

Ursprung, Tobias. "The Use and Effect of Political Propaganda in Democracies." *Public Choice* 78 (March 4, 1994), pp. 259-282.
  The author examines the influence of political propaganda on voters
  and the behavior of interest groups resulting from that influence. Not

surprisingly, the analysis indicates that voters vote based upon their personal views, which are influenced by information received. That information, if it is in the form of propaganda, will be less than accurate or reliable, according to the research. The study is highly technical and will be of use mainly to the specialist reader.

Walster, Elaine, and Leon Festinger. "The Effectiveness of 'Overheard' Persuasive Communications." *Journal of Abnormal and Social Psychology* 65, 6 (1962), pp. 395-402.
    The authors conducted two experiments with "overheard" conversation in order to determine how such conversations affected the subjects. They found that the subjects were more influenced when they were told that the speakers knew they were listening, and that the degree to which the conversations concerned matters of interest to the subjects also influenced their response. This research is of particular relevance to understanding the impact of "whispering campaigns" used as propaganda.

Zajonc, Robert B. "Attitudinal Effects of Mere Exposure." *Journal of Personality and Social Psychology Monograph Supplement* 9, 2 (June 1968), pp. 1-27.
    This article reports on pure psychological research. The object of the research was to discover the impact upon an individual of the "mere exposure" to "stimulus effect." The procedure was to study word connotations and frequency of use, manipulated frequency of use of "nonsense words and symbols," and the effects of experimentally manipulated frequency of exposure to certain words on the attitude of an individual. The conclusion drawn from all of this is that "mere repeated exposure" to certain stimuli indeed enhances the individual's attitude toward those stimuli. The language is technical, and the conclusions are not surprising. The article does supplement the study of how propaganda materials work, all the same.

Propaganda Channels and Techniques

Ailes, Roger. *You Are the Message*. New York: Doubleday, 1988.
    Written by a television presentation expert and former producer of NBC-TV's *Tomorrow Coast to Coast*, this volume is partly autobiographical. Using the materials of practical experience as a broadcaster, the author examines how people may be influenced and persuaded by the way in which an individual presents himself or herself, fully as much as through what is said. The examples range from television news

presenters to political figures. This work sheds much light on how such historical figures as Adolf Hitler used public appearance and oratory for propaganda purposes. No bibliography.

American Institute for Research. *The Art and Science of Psychological Operations: Case Studies of Military Application*. 2 vols. Washington, D.C: American Institute for Research, 1976.
These two volumes are a United States government document, or collection of documents, prepared by experts on aspects of psychology, communications, propaganda, history, and ethnic studies. These experts come from the military, academia, journalism, and government. The purpose of the volumes is to analyze, assess, suggest, and reflect upon the issue of how propaganda can be used to enhance military operations. Much of the discussion is inspired by the reality of what was called "psywar" (psychological warfare) in World War II. The general topics are extensive: "The Nature and Scope of Psyop [Psychological Operations]," "National Policy and Psyop," "Organization," "Personnel," "Media, Methods, and Techniques," and "Foreign Ideology and Propaganda," to mention only a few. Each general topic is subdivided into a series of individual pieces written by such experts as Max Beloff, a British historian, and Zbigniew Brzezinski, President Jimmy Carter's national security advisor. Literally dozens of experts of this caliber contributed to this massive study. These volumes provide insight into psychological warfare as theory, Cold War propaganda techniques as theory and function, and assessment of the mass media as propaganda channels. No bibliography.

Annis, Albert D. "The Relative Effectiveness of Cartoons and Editorials as Propaganda Media." Paper presented at the Midwestern Psychological Association, May 6, 1939. Summarized in the *Journal of General Psychology* 22 (1939), p. 659.
A study was made of the response of college and high school students to editorials and accompanying cartoons on military and pacifist subjects. The students were asked to respond to the contents on the basis of subject matter, bias, and persuasion. The editorials were most effective with college students, and the cartoons with those in high school.

Art with a Message: Protest and Propaganda, parts 1 and 2. Slides. Prod. Center for Humanities, 1975. Dallas, Tex.: Dallas County Community College.
One hundred sixty slides with sound cassettes and instructor's guide that describe how art has been used as a vehicle for propaganda and

protest. Examples include such items as paintings of Benito Mussolini with clenched fist raised. The collection describes the power of art to persuade through distortion, and how war, government, politics, and political systems have been satirized through art. Designed as a teaching aid for secondary and undergraduate students.

Barnicoat, John. *A Concise History of Posters*. New York: Oxford University Press, 1972.
This volume is a history of poster art in the nineteenth and twentieth centuries. It crosses cultural and national boundaries, emphasizes the artistic aspect of poster design and production, but without exception recognizes that the poster was almost always used to sell an idea, a viewpoint, or a product, to make a protest, to recruit followers for a political party or movement, or to fight in war. This collection and attendant commentary provide an excellent resource on poster art and style with reference to the poster as propaganda. The illustrations cover a wider spectrum of examples in every regard than almost any comparable volume. Limited bibliography.

Barnouw, Erik. *Documentary: A History of the Non-Fiction Film*. Oxford, England: Oxford University Press, 1983.
First published in 1974, this volume aimed at providing a history of documentary film that would be of use in film writing, producing, research, and teaching, all of which the author had done at various times. The story begins with the work of Louis Lumière, who made the first documentaries in France in the 1890s, and proceeds through the decades, providing along the way an in-depth examination of the techniques of documentary filmmaking. Also along the way, the author looks at those who put documentary film to use for propaganda purposes, in chapters titled "Sound and Fury," "Clouded Lens," "Sharp Focus," and "Promoter." The author makes it clear, however, that few documentary filmmakers produced only propaganda films. The book is well written, illustrated with stills from many of the films discussed and complemented by an extensive film bibliography.

Bentley, Eric. *The Theater of Commitment and Other Essays on Drama in Our Society*. New York: Athenaeum, 1967.
First published in 1954, this volume is a collection of essays on theater by a critic who avers "I am a socialist and have been for thirty years." This relates to the present work in that he sees drama as a form of protest, argument, political propaganda, and social criticism. More than that, at least some of these essays suggest that this is the way it

should be. In the process, they explain how theater often uses psychological manipulation to sway the audience to embrace the agenda the playwright puts forth. In perhaps the most telling line, the author writes: "That propaganda falls far short of its objectives . . . is no reason why an artist should not be moral, or even didactic. It is not even a reason why he shouldn't write propaganda. . . ." Dramatists discussed include the likes of Bertolt Brecht, whose work was filled with propaganda messages and techniques of psychological manipulation. Not the best book on this subject, but a supplement of some value to the similar but better study by A. P. Foulkes, *Literature and Propaganda* (entry below). Bibliography in endnotes.

Berelson, Bernard, and S. de Grazia. "Detecting Collaboration in Propaganda." *Public Opinion Quarterly* 11, 2 (1947), pp. 244-253.
This article describes studies of radio propaganda carried out during World War II to determine whether Berlin and Rome were collaborating on their propaganda broadcasts into the United States. Surprisingly, the study shows that they were not. The point of the article, however, is to describe how the evidence in the study was collected and to comment on the analytical methodology used in the study with reference to its value for the future.

Brucker, Herbert. *Freedom of Information*. New York: Macmillan, 1949.
A study of how forces and institutions within society sometimes interfere with the free dissemination of communications, which is to say, a study of aspects of "unofficial" censorship. Topics analyzed include the theory and definition of mass communications and its relations to mass media, information gathering, news coverage and dissemination, institutional interference with news gathering and those who gather it, and the history of mass communications in the United States. The relationship between persuasion and censorship is the central theme. Limited bibliography.

Building Belief, Part 1. Prod. Dorothy Heathcote, 29 min., 1974. Evanston, Ill.: Northwestern University Film Library.
This film by Britain's Heathcote demonstrates how improvised drama can be used to create the concept of nationalism in her ten-year-old students' minds. The film was mildly controversial when first released, probably because it demonstrated putting theory into practice.

Caldwell, Jill. "Propaganda—Militant/Non-Militant." *Film Library Quarterly* 9, 1 (1976), pp. 52-53.
This short article examines propaganda technique and material in particular contexts. In just two pages, the author provides a brilliant

contrast between film propaganda styles, with observations on their effectiveness, by comparing Leni Riefenstahl's *Triumph of the Will* (see entry under "Propaganda Material" in chapter 4) and Ian Dalrymple's *Listen to Britain* (see entry under "Propaganda Material" in chapter 5) in terms of the stridency of the former and the quiet humanity of the latter. Both worked, she explains, because the mentality of Hitler's Germany required stridency, whereas democratic Britain wanted to stress its humanity.

Casey, Ralph D. "Party Campaign Propaganda." *Annals of the American Academy of Political and Social Science* 179 (1935), pp. 96-105.
"The central problem of political action today is propaganda," the author begins, and continues by describing how that problem manifests itself. He notes the various changes within society in modern times that have affected this political fact, such as growing literacy, popular education, and broadened suffrage, all of which render it impossible for political leaders to govern *without* resorting to propaganda techniques. The bulk of the essay describes propagandists, channels, propaganda organizations within political parties, and audiences to whom propaganda appeals.

Christensen, Terry. *Reel Politics: American Political Movies from "Birth of a Nation" to "Platoon."* London: Basil Blackwell, 1987.
This excellent and illuminating study of American film and politics has two objectives in its examination of the subject. The first is to explain what the films under consideration tell us about American attitudes toward politics at certain points in time, and the second is to explain how these films have influenced or even mobilized the American public. Among the films considered, in addition to those mentioned in the title, are *All Quiet on the Western Front*, *Mr. Smith Goes to Washington*, *The Grapes of Wrath*, *The Great Dictator*, *Mission to Moscow*, and *Dr. Strangelove*. Sixty films in all are discussed by the author, some of which, such as *Mission to Moscow* and *The Green Berets*, are blatant propaganda films and are explained here as such. There is also a chapter on the censorship of films under the umbrella of the House Committee on Un-American Activities during the worst years of the Cold War. Select bibliography and filmography.

Consuming Hunger. Prod. Freke Vuijst and Ilan Ziv, dir. Ilan Ziv. 187 min., 1983. Maryknoll, N.Y.: Maryknoll World Video Library.
"If the Vietnam conflict was a 'television war,' then the starvation in Ethiopia was a 'television famine.'" This set of three twenty-nine-

minute films focuses on how television imagery shapes popular perceptions of events. The films document how television images become public reality, specifically with reference to public thoughts and feelings about starvation in Ethiopia.

Culbert, David, ed. *Film and Propaganda in America: A Documentary History.* 4 vols. New York: Greenwood Press, 1990.
A collection of documents illustrating the role film has played in the development and dissemination of propaganda in twentieth century America. Volume 1 covers World War I; volumes 2 and 3 provide extensive materials for World War II; and volume 4 deals with the Cold War and after. The documents come mainly from government and film archives and cover a wide range of topics including censorship, propaganda organizations, film distribution, charges of "criminal wrongdoing in the army," and the making of army training films. Each volume includes illustrations, such as posters advertising propaganda films. The scope and number of documents are such that a propaganda film research seminar could be based upon the collection, at least to the level of first-year graduate students. This is an invaluable resource for the study of American film propaganda in its historic context. Select bibliography.

Cull, Nicholas. "Propaganda and the Art of Understatement: British Broadcasting and American Neutrality, 1939-1941." *Historical Journal of Film, Radio and Television* 13, 4 (1993), pp. 403-431.
An article examining radio as a propaganda channel using the specific example of British broadcasting to the United States prior to December 1941. The author describes the process, the role of censorship, and the politics involving both British and American government officials. He makes the point that in the delicate circumstances of the United States being neutral while Britain was at war, this radio propaganda worked best when it was subtle. In the author's words, it needed "neither ferocity nor falsehood," and above all likely would have been "held back by stridency." This article is the history of an event which also examines how a particular communications process works.

Daugherty, William E., and Morris Janowitz, eds. *A Psychological Warfare Casebook.* Baltimore: Johns Hopkins University Press, 1958.
This casebook on psychological warfare was the third in a series of such manuals. All were for the purpose of assisting anyone interested in psychological warfare planning or operations. Its contents were designed to support "both military and political operations," and, the editors note, it has application in both peace and wartime. Contributors

include many of the leading propaganda and psychology experts of the post-World War II period. All contributors, whatever their postwar occupations, had served in "psywar" operations during that conflict. Topics include such items as psywar history, psywar doctrine, organization and personnel, and the role of intelligence, research, and analysis. This volume should be used in conjunction with the two-volume *The Art and Science of Psychological Operations: Case Studies of Military Application,* published in 1976 by the American Institute for Research (entry above), and Daniel Lerner's *Sykewar* (see chapter 5). No bibliography.

Deacon, Richard. *The Truth Twisters.* London: MacDonald, 1986.
Disinformation is that approach to propaganda in which the truth is told, but in such a way as to encourage wrong conclusions to be drawn, and such "information spin" is the subject of this volume. The author explains that disinformation began with the Cold War following World War II and expanded to become a tool of a wide variety of causes, including world environmental organizations such as Greenpeace. He discusses techniques and channels for disinformation, describes the reasoning behind its use by the Soviet KGB, the American CIA, and even the U.S. Centers for Disease Control in seeking to allay public fears regarding the spread of AIDS. The volume explicates disinformation theory through example and demonstrates that the author has done his research well. Not wholly objective, as the author criticizes his subject matter even as he explains it. Photographs illustrate some of his examples. Bibliography is contained in endnotes.

Foulkes, A. P. *Literature and Propaganda.* London: Methuen, 1983.
A brief and excellent study of how literature—its forms and content—can be, and often is, adapted to propaganda usage, and how, on the other hand, literary forms and contents have been used to challenge or expose propaganda. Examples range from *Jud Süss,* a work of German literature upon which Veit Harlan based a propaganda film in 1940, to Arthur Miller's play *The Crucible* (1953), a work of exposition. This very readable volume is exceptionally insightful with regard to its subject. Select bibliography.

Furhammar, Leif, and Folke Isaksson. *Politics and Film.* Translated by Kersti French. New York: Praeger, 1971.
This volume provides an in-depth assessment of how film has been used as a means for conveying political messages throughout the twentieth century, which is to say how film has been used as a propaganda channel.

The authors open with a history of political film in such contexts as World Wars I and II, revolutions in Russia and Germany, the Spanish Civil War, and the development of democratic institutions in Britain and elsewhere. Part 2 examines, among other examples, *Hitlerjunge Quex*, a Nazi party propaganda film, and *The Green Berets*, a film made by and starring John Wayne, which idealized the Vietnam War. Part 3 looks at the principles involved in making political films under such headings as "The Aesthetics of Propaganda," "The Image of the Enemy," and "Myth, Magic and Politics." The authors conclude with a revealing chapter on the difficulty of their topic. The volume includes a select bibliography, filmography, and illustrations.

Gervereau, Laurent. *La Propagande par l'affiche*. Paris: Éditions Syros-Alternatives, 1991.
This volume presents an illuminating history of *l'affiche* (the propaganda poster) in France from the fifteenth through the late twentieth centuries. Examples range from royal placards made during the reign of Henri II to presidential campaign posters for François Mitterrand in the 1980s. Two-thirds of the volume concerns political and war posters from the twentieth century. The text provides clear and definitive explanations of the propaganda function of the posters in their historical context. The quality of the reproductions is uniformly high. The text is in French. Select bibliography.

Gordon, Robbie. *We Interrupt This Program . . . : A Citizen's Guide to Using the Media for Social Change*. Amherst: University of Massachusetts Press, 1978.
At the time of publication, the author was a member of the Citizens Involvement Training Project, which is an adjunct of the continuing education program at the University of Massachusetts. This volume is an illustrated training manual for, as the title indicates, those who want to use the media to effect social change. As presented, the guidelines describe the dissemination of "good" propaganda in the interest of promoting positive social effects. There are eight chapters, which range over topics from the theory of the media as a social force, through media exploitation strategies, to specifics on how to use the press, television, radio, and videotapes—and, most important, how to deal with those who own or control the media. Well organized and written, the volume straightforwardly shows how materials can be used to manipulate the audience; without apology, the volume is equally straightforward in recommending propaganda dissemination in the public interest. No bibliography.

Hummel, William, and Keith Huntress. *The Analysis of Propaganda*. New York: The Dryden Press, 1949.

Still another approach to understanding propaganda, inspired most likely by retrospection on the bewildering variety of propaganda messages disseminated during World War II. In this case, the authors begin by advising their readers to "use your head" when considering propaganda. The volume includes five chapters of analysis and a "reader" consisting of fourteen essays and extracts from books which either deal with subject matter that bears upon propaganda or are themselves expressions of what the authors regard as propaganda. These range from Robert M. Hutchins complaining against college sports to Jonathan Swift's satiric solution to Irish poverty in the early eighteenth century, *A Modest Proposal*. A clearly written and insightful early post- World War II volume that in no wise has lost its value as an approach to understanding propaganda. No bibliography.

Huse, H. R. *The Illiteracy of the Literate: A Guide to the Art of Intelligent Reading*. New York: D. Appleton-Century, 1933.

Not intended as a study of propaganda, this volume nevertheless addresses questions directly relevant to propaganda study. The theme is how words can be used for purposes of manipulation in discussion of political, social, and other issues. The author is unfortunately out of date in some of his assertions, such as that advertisers prefer to appeal to women because they "are more easily influenced" than are men.

Jacobson, David J. *The Affairs of Dame Rumor*. New York: Rinehart, 1948.

Rumor has long been an established channel of propaganda. Through rumor, or "whispering campaigns" as they were termed, the British in World War II sought to discredit the German war effort in neutral countries. Rumors often have been "blown out of proportion" by demagogues in an effort to sway a mass audience to their way of thinking. This volume takes up the question of rumor and analyzes the impact of rumor in hundreds of different examples. The author makes clear that rumor applied by politicians, demagogues, or simple con artists has been a most effective way to convey "disinformation" as well as outright lies, and as such has been a most effective channel of propaganda. Intended for the general reader. Extensive bibliography.

Keen, Sam. *Faces of the Enemy: Reflections of the Hostile Imagination*. San Francisco: Harper and Row, 1986.

This is a book about creating enemies, which is, as the author makes abundantly clear, one of the most important responsibilities of propa-

gandists, particularly in wartime. The author describes the many variations on the theme, from the example of the anti-Nazi propagandists'
view of Hitler, which seemed "almost realistic," to the Nazi propagandists' view of Jews, which was anything but realistic. The volume is
well illustrated with reproductions of posters, leaflets, and samples
from various wars and political campaigns. It covers such topics as
enemy archetypes, the psychology of enmity, and, at the end, a chapter
specifically on the interaction of propaganda with power, social
change, authority, conscience, and other elements within human society. The book adds much to understanding the uses of propaganda in
wartime, in particular. Written in an easy style, but without talking
down to the reader. Limited bibliography.

Lahav, Pnina, and Sue Curry Jansen. "Censorship." *International Encyclopedia of Communications,* vol. 1. Oxford, England: Oxford University Press, 1989, pp. 245-252.
Censorship is the other side of the propaganda coin. The issue is
introduced here in easily accessible language, and the authors, like
Leonard W. Doob on propaganda in a later volume of this encyclopedia, provide an excellent introduction to the subject. Divided between
"government" (Lahav) and "non-government" (Jansen) propaganda,
the article provides definitions, a brief history, and an overview of uses
to which censorship is put for social, cultural, or political control. There
is a section on "self-censorship," in which such bodies as film govern-
ing boards are explained.

Lane, Robert E. *Political Ideology: Why the American Common Man
Believes What He Does.* New York: Free Press of Glencoe, 1962.
This is not a book about propaganda and politics in the United States.
Rather it is about American political belief systems to which political
propaganda is addressed, their origins, and why they exist. The specifics of the volume concern the ideology. The underlying assumption is
that political parties and leaders appeal to the ideology through political propaganda at election time and when setting policy, in order to
solicit support for their particular agendas. The book is written in
philosophic rather than scientific language and, though complex, is
accessible to educated readers. See Robert Parry, *Fooling America:
How Washington Insiders Twist the Truth and Manufacture the Conventional Wisdom* (entry below). No bibliography.

MacLean, Eleanor. *Between the Lines: How to Detect Bias and Propaganda
in the News and Everyday Life.* Montreal: Black Rose Books, 1981.

An introductory study of the practical side of propaganda, that is, as it applies to everyday life. Emphasis is upon the use of propaganda in forming political and social opinion. Illustrations are drawn from the press (including popular cartoon strips), corporate advertising, and magazines. This volume is aimed at the lay reader but will also be of interest to the professional student of propaganda. No bibliography.

O'Connor, John E., and Martin A. Jackson. *American History/American Film: Interpreting the Hollywood Image.* New York: Continuum, 1988. Read between the lines in this volume. The authors have avoided discussion of film propaganda everywhere except in their introduction. Instead, they have discussed film as a way to assess American public attitudes at given times regarding given subjects. However, they have made clear that public opinion is affected by films, that messages regarding social, political, or other issues are sent *via* films, and that factual information is often twisted in films in order to make a particular point to the audience—all of which adds up to propaganda. Each chapter deals with a particular American feature film in the context of what that film said about a particular set of attitudes at a particular time. Some examples: *Drums Along the Mohawk*, 1939 (reaffirming American values); *Mission to Moscow*, 1943 (Stalin as wartime ally, a film recognized by all specialists as pure propaganda); *Dr. Strangelove: Or, How I Learned to Stop Worrying and Love the Bomb*, 1964 (distrusting the Pentagon); and *Platoon*, 1986 (A Vietnam War retrospective containing Oliver Stone's personal anti-United States government and antiwar agenda). A well-crafted book which provides a clear view of the role feature films can play in sending propaganda messages. Filmography and select bibliography.

O'Sullivan, Carol. *Television: Identifying Propaganda Techniques.* San Diego: Greenhaven Press, 1990. Aimed at young readers, this volume takes the issue of television watching—whether it is good or bad for children—and presents the opposing viewpoints of various educators and others. The author then explains the propaganda techniques that are employed by each presenter in an effort to persuade his or her audience. Limited bibliography.

Paret, Peter, Beth Irwin Lewis, and Paul Paret. *Persuasive Images: Posters of War and Revolution from the Hoover Institution Archives.* Princeton, N.J.: Princeton University Press, 1992. The propaganda poster collection at the Hoover Institution in Palo Alto, California, contains some 75,000 items. This volume is only a sampling of the collection. The early section deals with the nature of poster art and the poster as advertisement before 1914. Thereafter, the volume concentrates on the poster as a propaganda channel in war and politics. The posters come mostly from those nations involved in the two world wars, and from such interwar conflicts as the Spanish Civil War. Each chapter has an introduction, and a brief explanation accompanies each poster. The quality of reproduction is excellent, and the text is clear and informative. Select bibliography.

Parry, Robert. *Fooling America: How Washington Insiders Twist the Truth and Manufacture the Conventional Wisdom.* New York: William Morrow, 1992.

A sharp criticism of what the author terms the "conventional wisdom" ranking system conducted by Washington insiders; that is, the "what's hot and what's not" among issues of the day. The author contends that Americans are encouraged to base their decisions regarding what they will and will not think, and how they will and will not behave, on this ranking system. He questions the loyalty of such insiders to American interests and, above all, argues that devotion to "CW" trivializes important issues, reduces genuine critical thinking among constituents, and becomes, in this very negative way, a form of propaganda. The underlying theme is the relationship between political power brokers and persuasion through language, idea, and emphasis manipulation. Select bibliography.

Perris, Arnold. *Music as Propaganda: Art to Persuade, Art to Control.* Westport, Conn.: Greenwood Press, 1985.

This work lays out the theory that music appeals easily to the emotions, and as such can be made to function as a medium through which a cause, viewpoint, or loyalty (as to a nation) can be promoted effectively—in other words, as propaganda. The theory is demonstrated by example throughout the remaining book. The author cites Mozart's *Marriage of Figaro* (social issues), Dvořák's *Slavonic Dances* (nationalism), Prokofiev's *Alexander Nevsky* (patriotism in war), and Bob Dylan's *The Times They Are A-Changin'* (social protest), among dozens of others. "This book," the author sums up, "has attempted to demonstrate that [many] composers . . . have consciously used their craft to change the world outside their studios. . . . This is a record of . . . propaganda by means of the universal art of music." Although the author is interested in the tradition of music as a propaganda channel, his emphasis is upon the social and political role of musical propaganda as it has been manifested in the twentieth century. Well written, well argued, and well within the grasp of any literate reader with or without a broad knowledge of music. Select bibliography.

Phelan, John, ed. *Communications Control: Readings in the Motives and Structure of Censorship.* New York: Sheed and Ward, 1969.
Censorship is the other side of the propaganda coin; this collection of ten essays seeks to understand and explain censorship, rather than to criticize it. The editor introduces censorship in this manner: "As opposed to propaganda, which creates contents for communication to bring about a result in the target audience regardless of the truth or falsity of the content, censorship shapes and limits already existing contents for many purposes prescinding from the truth or falsity of the communication content." This approach can be helpful to the reader on propaganda, for it makes clear how the suppression of information—be it the contents of a novel, a newspaper report, or another source—creates an impression other than that intended by the author of the censored material. This, as the Irish censors well knew between 1939 and 1945, was fully as much a weapon of persuasion as was the propaganda-by-name that they were censoring. These essays are readable and interesting, accessible equally to the student and the professional. Select bibliography.

Propaganda Techniques. 11 min., 1950. Deerfield, Ill.: Coronet/MTI.
In this short film, a character named Chuck is having seven basic propaganda techniques explained to him by the campaign manager of a recently elected mayor. Examples include campaign posters, a campaign movie, and recorded broadcasts.

The Public Mind: 1—Consuming Images. Prod. Bill Moyers, Public Broadcasting Service, 58 min., 1989. Alexandria, Va.: PBS Video.
Part 1 of a four-part series which explores "image and reality in America" by looking at the impact on a "mass culture" of an information system based upon image making; that is, the film looks at the media, opinion polls, public relations, and overt forms of propaganda. It examines visual images which inundate society, such as billboards, rock video, and newsstands, all of which at some point have been used to disseminate political propaganda.

Rickards, Maurice. *Posters of Protest and Revolution.* New York: Walker, 1970.
As the title says, this collection of propaganda posters represents protest and revolution. Its purpose is to demonstrate how the poster has functioned as a propaganda channel, with examples drawn from

around the world and from a broad spectrum of causes ranging from animal rights to political uprisings. The lengthy and useful introduction describes the history of the propaganda poster as well as explains some of the symbolic nuances that have been embraced by poster makers in the course of sending their message. Campaign for Nuclear Disarmament posters, for example, sometimes superimposed the *N* and *D* in various ways on pictures of nuclear holocaust. All slogans on posters are translated into English. Regrettably, most of the examples are reproduced in black and white. See Peter Paret et al., *Persuasive Images: Posters of War and Revolution from the Hoover Institution Archives* (entry above). Limited bibliography.

Suleiman, Susan Rubin. *Authoritarian Fictions: The Ideological Novel as a Literary Genre.* New York: Columbia University Press, 1983.
This volume focuses on the French *roman à thèse*, defining it as a literary genre in which the novelist—for instance Charles Maurras or André Malraux—writes with a didactic purpose in order to demonstrate "the validity of a political, philosophical, or religious doctrine." An excellent study in which the author recognizes the link between the purpose of propaganda and that of the *roman à thèse*. See W. J. Reader, *'At Duty's Call'* (entry under "History and Function" in chapter 3), which explores the use of popular literature to propagate the mythos of the British Empire prior to 1914. Well written, but aimed at an audience with some literary background. Select bibliography.

Think Twice: The Persuasion Game. 19 min., 1978. Los Angeles: Churchill Films.
Part of the Think Twice series, this film presents vignettes from political speeches, governmental propaganda techniques (public information messages, for example), the media, advertisers, and personal appeals to dramatize the ways in which propagandists manipulate emotions in order to persuade people to act in predetermined ways. The film discusses the nature of appeals to fear, pride, vanity, a sense of justice (and injustice), and the normal human desire to belong to a group. Intended mainly as a university-level teaching tool.

Thomson, Oliver. *Mass Persuasion in History: An Historical Analysis of the Development of Propaganda Technique.* Edinburgh: Paul Harris, 1977.
This short volume opens with a descriptive analysis of the terminology and styles that have characterized the theory and practice of propaganda from early times onward. Historical examples then follow (from

as far back as Julius Caesar) to show how these characteristics applied to propaganda as a tool of politics and ideology in each era of its development. Twelve pages of photographic and other reproductions provide valuable illumination for the text. Virtually nothing is overlooked in this highly readable historical overview, whether it is the empire adventure novels of G. A. Henty or the character assassinations perpetrated by Senator Joseph McCarthy. Select bibliography.

Truth and the Dragon. 10 min., 1969. Evanston, Ill.: Perennial Education. A brief but instructive animated film guide to separating fact from fiction and propaganda from communication. It uses the symbolic figure of a dragon to represent propaganda, and deals with such examples of propaganda methods as name-calling, out-of-context statements, glittering generalities, the testimonial, the transfer guise, "plain folks," card-stacking, and the bandwagon. Designed for a youthful audience.

Wasburn, Philo C. *Broadcasting Propaganda: International Radio Broadcasting and the Construction of Political Reality.* New York: Praeger, 1992.
A well-researched and well-written study of the role of broadcasting in international propaganda. The first two chapters are a history of international broadcasting. Thereafter, Wasburn concentrates on the relationship between news and propaganda, control of media, broadcast counterpropaganda, the value of international broadcasting in evading censorship of news imposed on local broadcast sources, and some suggestions for future research on the nature of international broadcasting and its role in shaping political agendas around the world. Extensive bibliography.

White, Ralph K. "Propaganda: Morally Questionable and Morally Unquestionable Techniques." *Annals of the American Academy of Political and Social Science* 398 (1971), pp. 26-35.
Confusion over distinctions between morally defensible and morally indefensible propaganda inspired this piece. A comparison is made between *propaganda* and *persuasion*, in which it is concluded that the only difference is that the former has evil overtones. Persuasion which is "inherently legitimate" includes that which aims at getting and keeping attention, getting and building rapport, building credibility, appealing to "strong motives" including emotions, and "action involvement." What is not legitimate is lying, innuendo, misrepresentation, deliberate omission, and implying as obvious that which is

not—in other words, disinformation. There is a strong "good versus evil" element in this article, the validity of which contrast is a perennial question in the art of political persuasion.

Wooddy, Carroll H. "Education and Propaganda." *Annals of the American Academy of Political and Social Science* 179 (1935), pp. 227-239.
This article points out the differences between education and propaganda, and then suggests that those being educated are at the same time subject to propaganda influence through channels not employed in formal education, such as newspapers, radio, films, and advertisements. The purpose is to warn that schools must participate in preparing young minds to resist propaganda, which is described as irrational, containing false information, spreading belief in undesirable things, and so on. The description of propaganda here is somewhat single-minded.

Mass Communications and Propaganda

Altheide, David. *Creating Reality: How TV News Distorts Events*. Beverly Hills, Calif.: Sage, 1976.
"This is a study of television news," the author begins, the purpose of which is to clarify how television news works. His study is predicated on the central role played by TV news in the lives of most Americans. He argues that because news on TV is regarded as significant, the public tends to assume that whatever news is presented *is* significant; therefore TV news, by its process of selection and style of reporting, determines what is significant to the public mind. Topics discussed include the nature of news bias, differences between local and network news, the importance of camera operators in news coverage, and how notable public events such as Watergate were covered. The conclusion drawn is that TV news can be easily turned into a propaganda channel if the viewer is not aware of how easily news coverage can distort reality. Written in a popular style and remarkably free of jargon given that the author is a sociologist. The volume is accessible to any intelligent reader. Limited bibliography.

Bagdikian, Ben H. *The Information Machines: Their Impact on Men and the Media*. New York: Harper and Row, 1971.
This volume examines the impact of "information machines"—by which the author means the technology of mass communications (radio and television)—on broadcast news, the press, and the audience. On

the whole, he seems convinced that the result will be more people receiving more news, and that is a good thing—provided those who assemble the news act responsibly. "The information machines will do what they are instructed by their human masters," he points out, noting that "electrons have no morals. They serve free men and dictators with equal fervor." This volume sheds light on how technology is used to spread information over an ever-wider field and offers the *caveat* that this capability adds to the responsibility of those who run the machines. The author ends with the warning that "if the new communications are designed to serve people . . . it will require more than the new machines." By implication, if information can be enhanced by mass communications technology, so too can propaganda. Select bibliography.

Bettinghaus, Irwin P. *Persuasive Communications*. New York: Holt, Rinehart and Winston, 1968.

The author describes this book as being "about the ways in which people try to influence the behavior of others. It is specifically concerned with persuasion through communications." The methodology is behavioral, the source research drawn from psychology, sociology, communications, and psycholinguistics. The volume is aimed at students in a variety of fields. Among elements useful to understanding propaganda theory (though these may be somewhat dated in light of ever-advancing technologies and techniques associated with media advertising) are guidelines in chapters 1 and 2 for assessing the success of persuasive messages and for predicting how audiences, as individuals or groups, will receive particular persuasive messages, and a discussion in chapter 4 of how personality type may affect response to persuasion. This chapter also deals in an interesting way with the effectiveness, or lack thereof, of varying degrees of dogmatism, especially in official (government) persuasive efforts. Select bibliography.

Black, Edwin R. *Politics and the News: The Political Functions of the Mass Media*. Toronto: Butterworths, 1982.

The power of the press is enormous, the author begins, and goes on to explain how governments characteristically use this power for their own ends—that is, exploiting the mass media as a potent propaganda channel. This volume concentrates on the press as mass media, and the author, a former journalist, makes no bones about the propaganda aspect of his subject. His topics include communications theories, mass media "environments," manufactured news, reconstructed reality, elections and mass media, censorship, and the political functions of the press. Written for a general audience. Select bibliography.

Bloomfield, Leonard. *Language*. New York: Henry Holland, 1933.
From the perspective that this volume was inspired in part by the tensions of a period when politics were driven by propaganda, this may be considered an early work on the relationship of the characteristics, nature, and meaning of language to propaganda and opinion formation. Part of the focus of the volume is the meaning and function of language. The chapters that concentrate on these issues are the most important from the viewpoint of propaganda and opinion formation. Arguments are presented in a clear and informative manner. See S. I. Hayakawa, *Language in Thought and Action* (entry below). Extensive bibliography.

Chafee, Zechariah, Jr. Government and Mass Communications: A Report from the Commission on Freedom of the Press. 2 vols. Chicago: University of Chicago Press, 1947.
These volumes are an official report, so to speak, in which the central question is: "How can the communications industries realize their possibilities of meeting the needs of the kind of society we have and the kind of society we want? What obstacles—external and internal—hinder mass communications . . . ?" A major such obstacle, it is noted, might be governmental restriction, which, this report implies, means variations on censorship. These eight-hundred-plus pages undertake a thorough examination of where government may interfere in freedom of the press. Volume 1 deals with government restrictions, libel, legality and obscenity, customs control over imported materials, and the general question of what is government responsibility relative to freedom of the press in wartime. Volume 2 examines the positive side of the question in terms of how government can encourage mass communications as a channel for promoting progress and positive change.

Chaffee, Steven H., and Michael J. Petrick. *Using the Mass Media: Communication Problems in American Society*. New York: McGraw-Hill, 1975.
This volume is concerned with the role mass media play in modern society. The purpose is clear from the breakdown of subject matter. Part 1 introduces the problem of what constitutes the mass media, what the mass media do, and why the mass media can be a problem in American society. Part 2 looks at how the mass media are used for public information, which the authors argue is a good idea but one not always well addressed by the media. Part 3 examines how the media influence public behavior, which, along with social control (the subject of part 4), describes the role mass media play as a propaganda channel. The authors are academic communications specialists, and their work

here is directed at both students and communications specialists. Limited bibliography.

Chappell, Matthew N., and C. E. Hooper. *Radio Audience Measurement.* New York: Stephen Daye, 1944.
    Though written during World War II, this volume relates to the propaganda of that conflict only peripherally. The authors present a format and various models for advertising and media research with specific reference to measuring the impact of radio broadcasting on mass audiences. Topics include how to select an audience for measurement, sample selection, establishing statistical reliability, and how to combine measurement models in order to maximize reliability. The authors make clear that this book is designed for broadcasters competing for radio markets. Illustrations, charts, and a glossary of terms, but no bibliography.

Chase, Stuart. *The Tyranny of Words.* New York: Harcourt Brace, 1938.
    Human communication had bothered him for many years, the author admits, and in this book he hoped to come to terms with words: why their use seems to complicate rather than ease communication. "How often do minds meet; how often do they completely miss each other? How many of the world's misfortunes are due to such misses?" His chapters point to examples of the misuse of words that cause harm. The rhetoric of conflict between fascism and communism is a form of propaganda, he notes, and defines it as being propaganda because it uses "bad language"—that is, obfuscating language. Words which are used for political propaganda are not the only references in this volume, but they are a continuing theme of the book. This is not a scientific study of words and the semantics of language, but it contributes all the same to understanding of the word manipulation characteristic of propaganda. It supplements S. I. Hayakawa, *Language in Thought and Action* (entry below), and Leonard Bloomfield, *Language* (entry above). No bibliography.

Cherry, Colin. *World Communication: Threat or Promise? A Sociotechnical Approach.* London: John Wiley and Sons, 1971.
    Written when international television and telephone communications were just beginning to enter the "supertech" age, this volume raises the question: Is this new capacity to put communication on a world footing a danger more than an advantage? The author looks at language differences, differing ideas, sophisticated electronic advertising techniques, and, in one section, specifically at propaganda as carried

through international communications channels. While this is the only section that treats propaganda in so many words, the entire volume is directed at considering the advantages of instant communications offset by the dangers of using that technology for psychological manipulation and the dissemination of the kinds of information that have a specific propaganda purpose, whether political, social, or other. The volume is well and clearly written and cuts across disciplines whose work touches upon the techniques and methodologies of propaganda dissemination. Extensive bibliography.

Chester, Edward W. *Radio, Television and American Politics*. New York: Sheed and Ward, 1969.

This volume poses several questions regarding the role of radio and television broadcasting in American politics. They include, among others: How has the television role changed from campaign to campaign? How has radio and television been used in local campaigns? Why have American propaganda broadcasts overseas enjoyed a "checkered" career? What sort of ideas do censors most often bar from the airwaves? The book opens with a brief history of American broadcasting and thereafter discusses television in politics before and after 1960, commentary, editorials and propaganda—by which the author means Voice of America, primarily—and censorship, defamation, and "equal time." The volume is academic in nature but does not use jargon. It is accessible to a broad range of readers. The author does a fair job of answering the questions he set forth at the beginning. Extensive bibliography.

Clarke, Peter, and Eric Fredin. "Newspapers, Television and Political Reasoning." *Public Opinion Quarterly* 42 (1978), pp. 143-160.

People who read newspapers know more about political candidates then do people who only watch television, the authors conclude, based on data produced by a nationwide post-1974 election survey. They contend that the public actually relies on the press for its political information and that the more competitive a news market is the better the public will be informed. Therefore, the decline of the newspaper—which the authors argue was happening at the time this article was written—is a phenomenon to be feared. The result would be a voting public more susceptible to the propaganda put out over television by candidates for election. Since this article was written, television has expanded enormously as a medium of political information, and not necessarily to the benefit of voters; however, the decline of the newspaper has not materialized to the degree this article suggests.

Coggeshall, Reginald. "Diplomatic Implications in International News." *Journalism Quarterly* 11, 2 (June 1934), pp. 141-159.

This article combines theoretical speculation regarding the relationship of news reporting to the formation of public opinion with discussion of how that relationship may apply to international relations specifically. The author notes that foreign affairs are of less interest to the "man in the street" than are local or national concerns, which may render the citizen more susceptible to press influence regarding international relations. He cites various scholars in warning against the press's allowing bias or sensationalism to distort coverage of foreign affairs, for while newspapers can start "war talk," for example, "once momentum is gained, they cannot . . . easily check it."

Corcoran, Paul E. *Political Language and Rhetoric*. Austin: University of Texas Press, 1979.

This volume is a communications study in which the author undertakes a careful analysis of political language and rhetoric, the latter defined as a method of discourse. The author operates on the assumption that "language is a technology . . . or a technique of human performance." The object of the book is to identify the "great variety" of techniques which that assumption covers and to examine their "political and social implications," in a historical as well as contemporary context. That is, how has political language and its expression evolved over time? This study has profound implications for the use of language for persuasion. The author makes several large points, among the most important being that political rhetoric has evolved beyond persuasion and into language meant to prevent thought, rather than to stimulate it, and to control rather than to persuade. This, in simple language, is the dark side of propaganda. There is some technical language in the volume, but it remains accessible to the educated reader and supplements reading on propaganda analysis. Bibliography is contained in the endnotes.

Curran, James, Michael Gurevitch, and Janet Woollacott, eds. *Mass Communication and Society*. Beverly Hills, Calif.: Sage, 1979.

A collection of eighteen essays on aspects of mass communications. The unifying theme is the control by capitalist organizations over mass media, in the context of which much is written about the need to free media from such controls. The essayists examine a variety of aspects of mass broadcasting, including how the personality of the "professional broadcaster" can influence the nature of broadcasts and how politics and the mass media interact. The ultimate point of this collection is that mass communications are a natural means through which propaganda is to be transmitted, because of the ways in which the media can be manipulated and their access to a mass audience. Each essay includes a bibliography.

Curran, James, Anthony Smith, and Pauline Wingate, eds. *Impacts and Influences: Essays on Media Power in the Twentieth Century.* London: Methuen, 1987.

There are fourteen articles in this collection by leading historians and other scholars on the relationship between mass media and public influence, such as Tony Aldgate, Deian Hopkin, and Nicholas Pronay. Subjects include the "Independent Labour Party Press and the Boer War," "Rearmament and the British Public," "The Press and the Battle for London, 1981-6," "Broadcasting and National Unity," and "Broadcasting Culture." It is an outstanding collection for students interested in mass media as a propaganda channel, despite the fact that propaganda as such is only an implicit topic. The essays concentrate on the technical side of media and influence and on public opinion as a political force needing to be either shaped or responded to by government and media policy makers. Bibliography in endnotes.

Davitz, Joel R., ed. *The Communication of Emotional Meaning.* New York: McGraw-Hill, 1964.

At first glance, this collection of articles describing research on emotional communication does not appear to have much connection to propaganda theory. In reality, the research addresses exactly the avenues through which propaganda appeals to emotions rather than to reason. It deals with such questions as how messages containing love, hate, anger, sadness, or joy may be transmitted through facial expression, tone of voice, volume of sound, and metaphor, among other devices. Such emotional content is central to propaganda, whether it is being used by a political leader inspiring the led, a nation gearing its population for war, or an auto manufacturer trying to create a market for cars. Bibliography in endnotes.

DeFleur, Melvin L., and Sandra J. Ball-Rokeach. "The Effects of Mass Communication," in *Theories of Mass Communications.* 5th ed. New York: Longmans, 1989.

The volume as a whole provides an in-depth analysis of the media in all of their forms, and their uses in the process of mass communications. Part 2, titled "The Effects of Mass Communications," deals specifically with media and communications in the context of propaganda and its uses. The content is complex and intensely theoretical, drawing heavily upon concepts and terminology associated with psychology, sociology, and communications. The text has been updated so that, though a fifth edition, the volume is in line with the most contemporary theoretical language, such as "media system dependency" theory. Though well written, part 2, like the rest of the text, will be most accessible to readers already familiar with both propaganda and communications terminology and concepts.

Friedson, Eliot. "Communications Research and the Concept of the Mass." *American Sociological Review* 18, 3 (June 1953), pp. 313-317. This brief article describes rising interest in communications research among sociologists. The author argues that a theory of mass communications ought to be developed in order to bring together the "practical orientation" of this research up to 1953, when the article was written. He argues further that such a theory should begin with a "concept of the mass" and the nature of its behavior. From there it would be possible to develop a concept regarding how mass audiences receive communication and respond to it.

Fyfe, Hamilton. *Sixty Years of Fleet Street*. London: W. H. Allen, 1949. A memoir by a London newspaper man, whose career covered the evolution of London journalism from the Victorian Age to immediately after World War II. Fyfe leaves little untouched, ranging in his recollections from the political influence of the press through to occasional government censorship efforts. This volume reveals the role of the British press in propaganda only peripherally, but it provides excellent insight into how governments as well as individual politicians have used the press and how journalists and news publishers have used governments and politicians for what amount to propaganda purposes. No bibliography.

Godefroy, Christian H., and Stephanie Barrat. *The Power Talk System: How to Communicate Effectively*. London: Piatkus, 1991. This is a home-study workbook. It teaches students how to "have the edge" when studying, speaking before an audience, or being interviewed. It promises to turn the reader into an effective communicator, the result of which will be to gain all of that power and success that the reader hitherto has been denied owing to shyness. The book "synthesizes all researches," in the authors' words, in the power communication field. The language of the volume (periodically including quotations from such famous persons as Albert Einstein) is such that it becomes a piece of propaganda itself, as well as a guide to how to use what might be termed the "propaganda of personal presence." Interestingly, politicians are the example of success referred to in the introduction. No bibliography.

Halloran, J. D. *The Effects of Mass Communication with Special Reference to Television. Leicester, England: Leicester University Press, 1965.*
A survey of research on the issue of how television influences viewers, particularly young ones. The issue of how viewers are persuaded to accept or reject certain behaviors is central to the research. The implications for propaganda study are obvious. Accessible to educated readers, who need not possess specialist knowledge of communications theory. No bibliography.

Hayakawa, S. I. *Language in Thought and Action.* 4th ed. New York: Harcourt Brace Jovanovich, 1978.
This book, whose first edition appeared in 1939, concentrates on the uses and abuses of semantics, which are the "spins" we put on words and phrases to give them value-laden meaning well beyond their literal and objective definition. The volume is a classic contribution to the field of semantic language study in English, originally published, ironically, by a Japanese American on the eve of World War II. Hayakawa draws upon a variety of sources to make his points, including the language of *Uncle Tom's Cabin*, the political speeches of Malcolm X (in Hayakawa's 1978 edition only), and poets and songwriters such as Francis Scott Key, author of "The Star-Spangled Banner." On page after page the relationship between semantics and propaganda is made perfectly clear, though Hayakawa never actually uses the word "propaganda." An instructive and entertaining volume, it is accessible equally to professional and lay readers; however, it would be well to read it in connection with a work specifically on propaganda theory, such as Jacques Ellul's *Propaganda* (entry under "General Studies").

Howitt, Dennis. *Mass Media and Social Problems.* Oxford, England: Pergamon Press, 1982.
This volume asks the in-depth questions about the persuasive influence of television that J. D. Halloran's *The Effects of Mass Communication with Special Reference to Television* (entry above) only surveys. Indeed, Halloran is cited by the author. Written for a specialist audience, but still accessible to the general reader. Extensive bibliography.

Irwin, Will. *Propaganda and the News; or, What Makes You Think So?* New York: Whittlesey House, 1936.
Aimed to some extent at the emergence of propaganda associated with European fascism, this volume nevertheless provides an overview of

the history and contemporary practice of journalists who, as often as not, practiced propaganda rather than straight reportage. Subjects include propaganda and propaganda agencies, and such related topics as "yellow" journalism, press agents, public relations, and "gutter" journalism, which is simply an extreme version of yellow journalism. Aimed at a popular audience. No bibliography, save that the author adds a page at the end which reads: "Bibliography. The Book of Experience."

Jowett, Garth S., and James M. Linton. *Movies as Mass Communications.* 2d ed. Newbury Park, Calif.: Sage, 1989.
This short but insightful study examines the degree to which film has penetrated to the very core of modern culture, becoming in the process a medium for communication of ideas, values, and beliefs. The authors do not make an argument for film as a propaganda medium; they do, however, explore many of the elements of film and film audiences upon which film as a propaganda medium has rested from the first moment. Select bibliography.

Katz, Elihu, and Tamás Szecskö, eds. *Mass Media and Social Change.* Beverly Hills, Calif.: Sage, 1981.
Fourteen essays dealing with aspects of the influence of mass media— principally the press and television—on attitudes regarding social issues. Topics include such items as the mass media and: systemic, historical, and comparative perspectives; processing social development; managing social change; managing social change in developed societies; revolution, communication, and the sense of history; and the image of women. The essays are linked by their consideration of the various ways in which mass media plays a role in persuading opinion in particular directions through both informing and manipulating a mass audience. No bibliography.

Knightly, Phillip. *The First Casualty. From the Crimea to Vietnam: The War Correspondent as Hero, Propagandist, and Myth Maker.* New York: Harcourt Brace Jovanovich, 1975.
Written by an English investigative reporter, this volume traces the history of the war reporter from the Crimean War (1854-1856) to the Vietnam struggle of the 1960s and 1970s. The author makes the point—reflecting his subtitle—that war reporters have played the role of hero certainly, but more often that of propagandist and myth maker. A title page illustration shows a journalist taking notes while standing with one foot on the body of a woman wearing a sash labeled "Truth." Each chapter reads like an op-ed piece but is well documented and informative. Some of the themes stressed include the selling of British

heroism in 1940, reporters creating a heroic image for Russia in World War II, reporters who did propaganda for and against Algeria in the struggle with France in the 1950s, and the battle journalists have had historically with generals and governments in the search for what was really happening in a given war. While the volume is critical of subjective war reporting, it does not take the line that this is the primary contribution of journalists in wartime. Select bibliography.

Kraus, Sidney, and Richard M. Perloff, eds. *Mass Media and Political Thought*. Beverly Hills, Calif.: Sage, 1985.
There are twenty-four contributors to this volume drawn almost exclusively from the fields of psychology and political science. Their combined purpose is to identify how the political communication process works, "from input of the message to cognitive processing of its content to output in terms of effects on the individual and the larger political system." The volume brings together a variety of scientific research projects into the political communication process. The individual essays tend to be technical in language and based upon scientific paradigms of investigation and analysis. Topics covered include, among other things, emotional and cognitive response to television images, the psychology of agenda setting, relating the relevance of political campaigns to personal interest, and cognition and the public mind. Each essay includes its own bibliography.

Lakoff, Robin Tolmach. *Talking Power: The Politics of Language in Our Lives*. New York: Basic Books, 1990.
This volume is about the manipulation of language by people who use it, in turn, to manipulate those to whom they address it. The author, a linguist, begins: "We feel ourselves at the mercy of language and its manipulators the slick professionals—advertisers, politicians, televangelists—who use it with cynical skill to entice us, innocent amateurs, into their webs of words." However, the point this volume makes is that everyone uses language to persuade, "to achieve something at the expense of someone else." In sum, "language is politics, politics assigns power, power governs how people talk and how they are understood." To analyze language therefore has become a survival skill. The book is divided into sections dealing with everyday language, language and institutions, cross-cultural language, and the language of power. The propaganda element in political and social language is a continuous theme in each. The volume is competently and interestingly written, and includes an extensive specialist bibliography on language and communication.

Lasswell, Harold D., Daniel Lerner, and Hans Speier, eds. *Emergence of Public Opinion in the West.* Vol. 2, *Propaganda and Communication in World History.* Honolulu: University Press of Hawaii, 1980.
   This collection of nineteen articles opens with a historical assessment of such developments as the Reformation era, the emergence of "political fanaticism," and, of course, the invention of the printing press, all of which contributed to the development of modern forms of propaganda communication. The overall theme is the use of propaganda as an instrument in managing "crisis politics." The bulk of the volume contains essays on twentieth century uses and abuses of propaganda and communication, and concludes with a plea for another kind of communication, that is, cooperation between peoples and nations in the interest of peace and harmony. This plea discusses how uses of the term "peace" can be deceptive and can be made to take on a propaganda value. On the whole, the articles are well written by scholars and others with impressive credentials. Bibliography in endnotes.

_____. *A Pluralizing World in Formation.* Vol. 3, *Propaganda and Communication in World History.* Honolulu: University Press of Hawaii, 1980.
   These fourteen essays take on the contemporary world with reference to communication and propaganda. Arranged in three sections, they examine communication first in a "multivalue context," in which such issues as the relationships between science and technology, on the one hand, and the media and transforming social values, on the other, are examined. This is followed by the "multivariate process" section, wherein essays explore political language, audience composition in relation to the mass media, and the impact of the mass media upon both. Everything is brought together (in very theoretical language) in the final section, which discusses, among other things, changing social structures and the future of propaganda as part of world communication. The essays provide context for theoretical thinking about future linkages among propaganda, society, politics, technology, and power. Bibliography in endnotes.

Lemert, James B. *Does Mass Communication Change Public Opinion After All? A New Approach to Effects Analysis.* Chicago: Nelson-Hall, 1981.
   "This book is meant for audiences in several social sciences, including political science, mass communication research, and sociology," the author begins. Such clearly is the case. The volume is an analysis of the relationship between opinion formation and mass communications

on various levels, and the impact of that influence on politics and society. Themes include the need to develop a new model for media in relation to public opinion, linkage between opinion, decision makers, and journalists, "mobilizing information," and the nature of attitude change and formation. It is written in a sufficiently popular style to be accessible to readers at various levels, and the author clearly has a sense of humor, the "run-on-horsemeat" example being a case in point. Select bibliography.

McCombs, Maxwell E. "Mass Communication in Political Campaigns: Information, Gratification, and Persuasion," in F. Gerald Kline and Phillip J. Tichenor, eds., *Current Perspectives in Mass Communications Research.* Beverly Hills, Calif.: Sage, 1972.
This essay essentially describes current research on political communications and the use of mass media. It is critical of that research and urges movement in a new direction, as indicated in this line: "What has passed for mass communication theory has been, in reality, a loose collection of orientations toward data and a few empirical generalizations. While our knowledge has high empirical import, it has little of theoretical import to contribute to an explanation of mass communication and its role in political behavior."

McCombs, Maxwell E., and Donald L. Shaw. "The Agenda-Setting Function of Mass Media." *Public Opinion Quarterly* 36, 2 (Summer 1972), pp. 176-187.
The authors analyze how media editors, newsroom staff, and broadcasters help shape political reality through their choice and manner of displaying news. Readers, viewers, and listeners learn both what happened and how much importance attaches to it, not from their personal assessment of the information but from the emphasis the presentation gives to the information. This becomes a propaganda technique, if perhaps an unintentional one, simply because the hierarchy of significance established by the news personnel predetermines the conclusions the audience may draw about events.

McCrosky, James C. "A Summary of Experimental Research on the Effects of Evidence in Persuasive Communication." *Quarterly Journal of Speech* 55, 2 (April 1969), pp. 169-176.
A very technical report on twenty-two studies relating to evidence and persuasion. The question asked was whether or not documented evidence is vital to producing attitude change. The answer, these studies suggest, is that sometimes evidence helps, but it is not always a

necessary part of the process. This leads the author to conclude that more research is needed. The language is sufficiently technical to make the article difficult for the general reader.

Molotch, Harvey, and Marilyn Lester. "News as Purposive Behavior: On the Strategic Use of Routine Events, Accidents, and Scandals." *American Sociological Review* 39, 1 (February 1974), pp. 101-112.
This article describes, in the language of the authors, how "by suspending belief that an objective world exists to be reported, we develop a conception of news as a constructed reality." In other words, news is news because it is "created" as news by the reporter, rather than because of its inherent importance. In the process of "created" news reporting, journalists may shape, or contribute to shaping, opinion on politics, war, and other events, and become a type of propagandist. This is a very technical piece written for professional sociologists, but still accessible to nonspecialists. See also Phillip Knightly, *The First Casualty. From the Crimea to Vietnam: The War Correspondent as Hero, Propagandist, and Myth Maker* (entry above).

Pool, Ithiel de Sola, et al., eds. *Handbook of Communication.* Chicago: Rand McNally, 1973.
Thirty-four experts on communications theory contributed to this 900-plus-page volume. Part 1 covers "The Communication Process," part 2 concerns "Communication Settings," and part 3 examines "Communications Research." Each part contains numerous essays on such specific topics as sociolinguistics; channels and audiences; persuasion, resistance, and attitude change; political persuasion; film as communication; the press as communication; communication in totalitarian societies; public opinion; and propaganda. Each essay sets forth a definition and brief discussion of its topic. Paul Kecskemeti on propaganda, for example, defines the concept, examines its conceptual aspects, presents its sociological and psychological aspects, discusses propaganda theory, and concludes with an overview of the language of propaganda. Each essay includes a short bibliography relative to its specific topic.

Reardon, Kathleen Kelley. *Persuasion: Theory and Context.* Beverly Hills, Calif.: Sage, 1981.
This volume repudiates a decade of argument that persuasion should not be the primary process for communication study, and places an expanded concept of persuasion "squarely in the center of peoples' daily communication transactions." Much of the book is focused on interper-

sonal communications and on a challenge to certain "methodological traditions" for the study of persuasion. Only one section deals specifically with mass persuasion and mass communications; however, all of the volume is concerned with those persuasion techniques, and psychological and sociological responses to them, that inform mass persuasion and therefore propaganda. Too technical to be of interest to a general audience, but valuable to the informed student of persuasive communication and its application to propaganda. Extensive bibliography.

Robinson, Michael J., and Andrew Kohut. "Believability and the Press." *Public Opinion Quarterly* 52 (Summer 1988), pp. 174-188.
The press has long been used for propaganda dissemination, particularly in wartime. This article presents the results of a study of how people perceive the press in terms of information reliability. The conclusion is that most people do believe what they see, hear, and read in the press, thus demonstrating how effective the press can be as a propaganda channel.

Schramm, Wilber, and Donald F. Roberts, eds. *The Process and Effects of Mass Communications.* Rev. ed. Urbana: University of Illinois Press, 1971.
This excellent collection of articles cover a wide range of what the editors term "old classics, new classics, and reports on 'state of the art' in important areas of communication studies." Of course, the latter do not include advancements along the "information superhighway," which came into existence well after these articles were published. The subject is mass communications; the theme is the way mass communications techniques operate. The implication of mass communications for propaganda lies barely beneath the surface, as much of the material presented deals with persuasion, the effectiveness of mass communications in forming beliefs, attitudes, or values, the way in which mass communications are adapted for political purposes, and so forth. Bibliography with each article.

Speier, Hans. *The Truth in Hell and Other Essays on Politics and Culture, 1935-1987.* New York: Oxford University Press, 1989.
Part 2 in this volume, "Communications and Propaganda," is the section of principal interest to the student of propaganda. Speier, who was twenty-eight when he emigrated to the United States from Germany in 1933, understood very well the relationship between propaganda and the totalitarian society. He also soon came to understand the relationship between propaganda and psychological warfare. No bibliography.

Sproule, J. Michael. "Progressive Propaganda Critics and the Magic Bullet Myth." *Critical Studies in Mass Communication* 6, 3 (September 1989), pp. 225-246.
This article challenges the standard account of the beginnings of American mass communications research, which claims that propaganda critics between the world wars accepted the European version of the mass audience and treated messages as "magic bullets" directed at a passive audience. Not so, the author contends. He argues that such a claim overlooks the "progressive reformists' mission of propaganda analysis to help an essentially competent public against the new co option of communications channels by powerful institutions." The magic bullet myth, the author claims, was the product of social scientists after 1940 who hoped to use propaganda as a weapon against fascism and communism. This article is a well-argued contribution to the history of propaganda theory.

Stevens, John D. "Press and Community Toleration: Wisconsin in World War I." *Journalism Quarterly* 46 (Summer 1969), pp. 255-259.
During World War I, anti-German sentiment ran high in Wisconsin, which had a large ethnic German population. This brief article reports a study which noted that wherever the press was tolerant of German ethnicity, so too were the citizens. Such was the case also with regard to socialists, radicals, pacifists, and religious minorities. The author notes that the newspapers which preached toleration were few in number, and that by disseminating a "yellow journalism" style of propaganda, the press on the whole contributed to a "mob spirit" in World War I Wisconsin.

Storey, Graham. *Reuters' Century.* London: Max Parrish, 1951.
This volume tells the history of the Reuters news service from its inception through 1951. Written by a Reuters journalist, it is hardly an objective work. The author argues throughout for freedom of the press and against the dissemination of false information, and claims that throughout its history, Reuters was a bulwark for the former in defiance of the latter. This readable, if somewhat panegyrical, volume provides valuable insight into the relationship between information, censorship, and propaganda. Limited bibliography.

Waples, Douglas, ed. *Print, Radio, and Film in a Democracy.* Chicago: University of Chicago Press, 1941.
This collection of ten papers was presented at the Sixth Annual Institute of the Graduate Library School at the University of Chicago. They are devoted to "the problem of administering mass communication in the

public interest, that is, for the common good and without exceeding the democratic limits of popular consent." Presenters included such propaganda theory luminaries as Harold D. Lasswell and Ernst Kris. Subject matter of the papers includes communication in totalitarian states and in democracies, radio and public opinion, film and public opinion, public opinion analysis, and public education and communications. Each essay includes a short bibliography.

War Reporters. 55 min., 1985. Princeton, N.J.: Films for the Humanities. War reporting can be a tricky business, and not just because it is dangerous. The needs of governments in wartime and the priorities of journalists sometimes conflict, and when they do, journalists are often pressured to send back what amounts to government propaganda. This documentary discusses, against a background of actual filmed war sequences, how reporters must work objectively and must recognize and reject propaganda. See Phillip Knightly, *The First Casualty* (entry above).

Willey, Malcolm M. "Communication Agencies and the Volume of Propaganda." *Annals of the American Academy of Political and Social Science* 179 (1935), pp. 194-200.
This article proposes that the advent of mass communications is the key to understanding the role of propaganda in modern politics, war, and society in scientific yet jargon-free language. The author describes how modern mass communications distinguish modern propaganda from its historical predecessors. He also argues that mass communications have forced schools to take responsibility for education in areas once confined to home, family, and church, and have brought confusion to people by disrupting the traditional "folkways" that define social values. This piece ultimately is a warning that mass communications— press, radio and film—constitute a communication system "fraught with greater possibilities for evil or for good" than has ever existed.

Wirth, Louis. "Consensus and Mass Communications." *American Sociological Review* 13, 1 (1948), pp. 1-15.
The presidential address at the 1948 meeting of the American Sociological Society (subsequently renamed the American Sociological Association). It focuses on the effect mass communications may have upon "building consensus" within society and what the science of sociology will need to do in order to study that phenomenon. The author speaks from the premise that persuasion will play a central role in building consensus.

Chapter 2

PROPAGANDA AND WORLD WAR I, 1914-1918

The Great War of 1914-1918, recalled later as World War I, was a mechanized total war, which produced millions of casualties and engaged civilian populations as much as armies. In consequence, propaganda, disseminated at home, to allies, and to enemy soldiers and civilians, played an ever-expanding role in sustaining morale—or, conversely, undermining it—and the will to fight. This propaganda was organized and controlled by government offices, and its content drew upon channels and employed psychological manipulation in a manner that presaged the propaganda work that would become commonplace after the war.

The citations in this chapter represent the gamut of propaganda, including censorship and antiwar protest. Propaganda channels in the Great War included print media (press and magazine), posters, books, sermons, leaflets and flyers, and, for the first time on a large scale, film (silent, to be sure), including features. How large may be inferred from an assertion by George Creel, director of the United States Committee on Public Information, that one of the "three great agencies of appeal in the fight for public opinion" was the motion picture. Sadly, most propaganda films from this period are available only in archives, if at all. Nevertheless, representative samples of such films are annotated here, based upon descriptions found in printed sources, along with more accessible propaganda materials. Specific entries indicate whether or not it was possible to locate, in positive print, videotape, or archive, the film being described.

History and Function

Abrams, Ray H. *Preachers Present Arms: The Role of the American Churches and Clergy in World Wars I and II, with Some Observations on the War in Vietnam.* Scottdale, Pa.: Herald Press, 1969.
This volume, a study of "pulpit propaganda" with specific reference to World War I, originally appeared in 1933. The present edition includes thirty pages of commentary on the clergy in more recent conflicts. The original purpose was to "provide insight into the mechanisms of social control" employed during World War I, specifically the role of American churches and clergy. Much attention is given to how churches were used as "agents of propaganda." Billy Sunday, the famous evangelist, is quoted on one occasion as "laying down the gauntlet to the Ger-

mans," when he "shrieks in a cracked voice: 'I today . . . declare war against Hell and all its commissaries and all its cohorts. You can't shoot your cursed Kulture and your damnable Hohenzollernism down our throats.'" The volume is written in narrative style, well documented, and with an extensive bibliography.

Barkhausen, Hans. *Filmpropaganda für Deutschland im ersten und zweiten Weltkrieg*. Hildesheim, Germany: Olms Presse, 1982.
Both world wars are covered in this volume, but more attention is paid to World War I than to World War II. The text provides an overview of organizations which made propaganda films, early and later film technologies, internal debates regarding how filmmaking should be approached, and the propaganda innovations of Joseph Goebbels. The volume includes a lengthy list of newsreel-type documentaries from World War I and immediately after, with an extensive bibliography on propaganda film and filmmakers. The text is illustrated with photographs and charts showing the organization of Bild-und-Film-Amt (BUFA) which oversaw German propaganda films in World War I.

Becker, Jean-Jacques. *The Great War and the French People*. Leamington Spa, England: Berg Publishers, 1985. Translation of *Les Français dans la grande-guerre*. Paris: Robert Laffont, 1983.
This volume seeks with only moderate success to explain why the French people endured more than fifty months of war between 1914 and 1918, and arrives at the conclusion that it was mainly the strength of national feeling that sustained them. Along the way, the author argues that propaganda played only a minor role in maintaining public morale and commitment to the struggle. On the other hand, he claims that censorship played a considerable role by denying to the public the true story of what was happening at the front. All the same, he admits that teachers, writers, the press, and trade union leaders all exhorted their students, readers, and members to stay the course—which is, of course, an exercise in propaganda. Well written and translated, but flawed somewhat by its subjectivity, with the consequence that the study is of uncertain value to gaining a proper understanding of French propaganda in the Great War. Extensive bibliography.

Blakey, George T. *Historians on the Home Front: American Propagandists for the Great War*. Lexington: University Press of Kentucky, 1970.
This short study analyzes how "America's young historical profession" was mobilized in 1917 to conduct a moral crusade against "teutonic

militarism" and in support of the United States war effort. While there were questions of ethics—how far should professional historians go in patriotic appeal—for the most part the profession dug in. The author describes how the historians were "organized" for the propaganda war, and what kinds of propaganda pamphlets with historical themes that they produced. The volume is well written and appears to be competently researched. Bibliographical essay.

Bruntz, George H. *Allied Propaganda and the Collapse of the German Empire in 1918*. Stanford, Calif.: Stanford University Press, 1938.
In an introduction to this volume, Harold D. Lasswell asserts that World War I "led to the discovery of propaganda by both the man in the street and the man in the study." There is an element of truth in this. Propaganda was a key element in the defeat of Germany at the front, just as it was in stirring up popular antipathy to Germany at home. Bruntz describes how the Western allies worked to disseminate propaganda into Germany that was designed to destroy public morale. He also credits Western propaganda—perhaps with slightly less credibility—with "revolutionizing" Germany in 1918. To do so certainly was the aim of allied propaganda, and there was a German revolution at war's end. That allied propaganda made it happen is not quite so clear. A very readable and scholarly work, with an extensive bibliography.

Buitenhuis, Peter. *The Great War of Words: British, American, and Canadian Propaganda and Fiction, 1914-1933*. Vancouver: University of British Columbia Press, 1987.
The reference to fiction in the title may have a double meaning. Certainly the author means the likes of Edith Wharton, Ford Madox Ford, and other writers of novels and poetry; perhaps he also means the content of the propaganda as being fiction. This excellent and readable survey of "literary" propaganda produced during and after World War I is accurate on both levels, for it details the work of literary people who became propagandists and has some equally enlightening observations to make about the subjectivity of the contents of their propaganda product. The book analyzes the major sources upon which this propaganda was based, from stories of atrocities to the execution of Nurse Edith Cavell. Those who wrote war propaganda felt disillusioned afterward, and the author makes a point of discussing the apparent effect of writing war propaganda on the writers' work in the postwar period. The volume is illustrated with photographs, reproductions of posters, and other propaganda materials. Limited bibliography.

Carsten, F. L. *War Against War: British and German Radical Movements in the First World War.* Berkeley: University of California Press, 1982.
In this volume, F. L. Carsten, Thomas Garrigue Masaryk Professor of East European Studies at the University of London, examines the antiwar campaigns of radical groups in Germany and Britain during World War I. These include, among others, the Sparticists in Germany, which was a Bolshevik-style political movement, and the Union of Democratic Control in Britain, which was dominated by socialist pacifists. Both used public demonstration and the printed word to oppose the war and press their own political agendas. Professor Carsten's excellent study is not principally about propaganda, but it describes political movements which used propaganda to achieve—or attempt to achieve—their goals, regarding both opposition to war and preference for political change along socialist lines. Extensive bibliography.

Chambers, Frank P. *The War Behind the War, 1914-1918: A History of the Political and Civilian Fronts.* New York: Harcourt, Brace, 1939.
In this early "social history" of World War I, the author touches on propaganda as being profoundly important, but not yet a subject to which historians ought to pay great attention. He puts it in this language: "[Propaganda] is a subject which should fill an important place in any history of the War, but it is also a subject on which our judgements are still apt to be unsafe. We now live in the classic age of propaganda, and, as is the case of every art in its classic age, we have not yet developed a recognized critique of it." With that in mind, he presents economic and political materials upon which propaganda regularly played, and otherwise describes propaganda briefly in terms of the kinds of materials it used, how it was organized and disseminated, and whether it worked. German propaganda in the United States did not, he concludes, while French propaganda against Germany late in the war, did. The volume provides a valuable context for evaluating World War I propaganda. Extensive bibliography, but the entries do not relate directly to propaganda.

Cockerill, George. "The Lure of Bloodless Warfare," in George Cockerill, *What Fools We Were.* London: Hutchinson and Company, 1944.
In this section of his retrospective on war and politics, the author reflects on how Britain employed intelligence, censorship, and propaganda in World War I. An officer in army intelligence with the rank of brigadier general, he knew of what he spoke, and, moreover, in later years had second thoughts about the war and all it involved. Each

chapter of this section opens with a quote from the likes of Cicero indicating that war is a fool's occupation—hence the title of the book. The volume as a whole combines the brigadier's memoir of his professional life with a statement against war and tyranny. No bibliography.

Collins, Ross F. "The Development of Censorship in World War I France." *Journalism Monographs* 131 (February 1992), pp. 1-25.
This monograph, as the series is titled, looks at censorship and propaganda in France in World War I, specifically at the methods which the French government employed to control public opinion through the press more efficiently than it had ever been done before. The author examines a "vast bureaucracy" devoted to the task, the law which established press censorship on August 3, 1914 (the day war was declared), the rigor with which censorship was maintained, and finally, the manner in which negative control of the press—straight censorship—evolved into positive control—censorship which faded into disinformation. An easy read for students, and well documented from both archival records and published sources.

Cornebise, Alfred E. *War as Advertised: The Four Minute Men and America's Crusade, 1917-1918*. Philadelphia: American Philosophical Society, 1984.
This is a study of the government spokesmen (women did not participate in this program) who appeared during the period of United States involvement in World War I in movie houses, among other venues, to make a precisely four-minute pitch aimed at enhancing support for the war effort. This propaganda channel took the place of radio and television, neither of which were yet available for propaganda purposes. These "four-minute men," in the authors words, renounced "subtlety and ideological refinement . . . [and] unabashedly went for the jugular." Accessible to a general audience, which likely will find it entertaining as well as informative. Illustrations and a short bibliography.

Dahlin, Ebba. *French and German Public Opinion on Declared War Aims, 1914-1918*. New York: AMS Press, 1971. Reissue of earlier publication.
The focus is on public opinion; the subject is the formation of public opinion in France and Britain relative to national aims in World War I. The author concludes that censorship of news played as great a role as did outright propaganda in the formation of that opinion. This short

study surveys government considerations of possible war aims, argument among segments of the population—the press, political parties, etc—and the role played in the formation of war aims by strikes among workers and, after 1917, by a growing public desire for peace. The bibliography draws upon mainly French and German sources.

Dodge, Raymond. "The Psychology of Propaganda." *Religious Education* 15 (October 1920), pp. 241-252.
Written soon after World War I, this article examines propaganda as used in the war and concludes that its long-term impact would be horrific. "Paper bullets, according to Mr. Creel, won the war," the author notes, and adds, "but they have forever disturbed our peace of mind." He briefly traces the history of propaganda, and then examines ways in which it affects emotions and distorts rational thought. His principal concern is that given the experience of the war, propaganda might emerge as a persuasive tool that would be dangerous to the social and moral order. This article is part of the for-and-against argument regarding the future of propaganda that began even before the war was over, and the author's examples are all drawn from poster and other propaganda channels from World War I.

Ernst, Wilhelm. *Die Antideutsche Propaganda durch das Schweizer Gebiet im Weltkrieg, speziell die Propaganda in Bayern.* Munich: C. H. Beck'che Verlagsbuchhandlung, 1933.
This pamphlet is part of a historical series published in Munich between the world wars. It contains two quite unconnected items, the second being a selection of correspondence involving Eugen von Frauenholz and Feldmarshalleutnant Alfred Freiherr von Henikstein, in anticipation of the Austro-Prussian war of 1866. The first item is of interest here, a brief assessment of anti-German propaganda introduced into Bavaria during World War I through neutral Switzerland. It includes the example of an anti-German propaganda pamphlet. Needless to say, the author is not sympathetic to allied efforts in this regard, which fact makes this work a useful resource for post-World War I German resentment of allied war propaganda. Select bibliography.

Felstead, Sidney Theodore. *Horatio Bottomley: A Biography of an Outstanding Personality.* London: John Murray, 1936.
"Never did mortal man have such wonderful possibilities thrust upon him," the author writes with reference to Horatio Bottomley and World War I, and ends the sentence with "never was a nation's trust so grossly abused." This is the earliest biography of one of England's shadiest

twentieth-century characters, who ended his life trying to survive as a London West End stage performer. Broken, weak-voiced: "Did it seem possible," the author asks, "that this poor shambling figure . . . could be the mighty magician whose pen had stirred the emotions and actions of millions of his countrymen, whose platform oratory had swayed the applause of the multitude?" This biography has much in common with those by Alan Hyman and Julian Symons (entries below), in that all three trace the course of Bottomley's life and career chronologically, and all agree that he was a charlatan. These studies are of value to this bibliography because they place Bottomley firmly in the context of being a war and peacetime propagandist as well as a charlatan.

Ferguson, John. *The Arts in Britain in World War I*. London: Stainer and Bell, 1980.
Designed as a textbook for Britain's Open University, a television university which operates over the BBC (the British Broadcasting Corporation), this volume places British creative arts produced between 1914-1918 in the context of World War I. Artists, composers, poets, and novelists responded to the hard realities of the war. Not all of them produced work with propaganda content, but many did. The text provides an overview of the war under the headings of "outbreak," "heart of," and "finale and aftermath." In this context the author evaluates the effect of the war on Wyndham Lewis, Ford Madox Ford, D. H. Lawrence, Edward Elgar, Edward Wadsworth, and many other creative artists. Some of the painters did propaganda posters; some of the writers wrote patriotic fiction; some painters and writers created antiwar material, which was propagandistic in its own right. Select bibliography.

Gilmour, T. L. "The Government and Propaganda." *The Nineteenth Century* 85 (January 1919), pp. 148-158.
Propaganda played a major role in Britain's effort in World War I, and this article was inspired by that fact. It appeared the month that the Paris Peace Conference opened, and even before the Ministry of Information had been disbanded. The author is not wholly convinced that government propaganda was worth the expenditure, noting that "it must never be forgotten that the propaganda value of any particular happening will vary according to the view-point of the person to whom it appeals. . . ." However, he goes on to argue that propaganda would appear to be something that will be around in future wars, and therefore it must be properly understood. The bulk of the essay is an overview of propaganda which attempts to define it, assess its channels, and call

attention to how it may be abused. This essay is a primary source on the debate over propaganda which began even before World War I ended.

Grahame, Jeanne. "The Four-Minute Men: Volunteers for Propaganda." *Southern Speech Journal* 32, 1 (1966), pp. 49-57.
One of the more successful World War I United States propaganda operations was the Four-Minute Men program. These volunteers—some 75,000 of them—presented four-minute pitches for bond sales, food conservation, and similar wartime needs. Usually they spoke in cinemas before the presentation of the feature. This brief article provides a descriptive overview of the subject. The author concludes by observing that "the Four-Minute Men had proved the power of men armed with words." The article should be read as an introduction to Alfred E. Cornebise, *War as Advertised: The Four Minute Men and America's Crusade, 1917-1918* (entry above).

Hachey, Thomas E. "British War Propaganda and American Catholics in 1918." *Catholic Historical Review* 61 (1975), pp. 48-66.
This article concerns British war propaganda aimed at Catholics in the United States after the United States entered into World War I, a propaganda inspired by concern in the Foreign Office over anti-British propaganda in the United States, particularly that generated by Irish-American Catholics. The article is mainly a consideration of certain Foreign Office documents relating to the subject, such as a memorandum by Geoffrey Butler (January 28, 1918) which discusses the "Catholic Question" in the United States. This document is reproduced in its entirety, and there are detailed extracts from other Foreign Office minutes as well. The article lies somewhere between a primary and a secondary source for the history of World War I propaganda.

Hanak, Harry. *Great Britain and Austria-Hungary During the First World War: A Study in the Formation of Public Opinion.* London: Oxford University Press, 1962.
When this book was published, it joined a growing list of works on aspects of the history of propaganda in World War I. In this case, the subject was how various kinds of propaganda were used by Hungarians, Czechs, and other peoples of the lands of the Dual Monarchy (Austria-Hungary) to shape public opinion in Britain before and during the war. This propaganda was very effective, the author argues. On the other hand, British propaganda going in the opposite direction, aimed at the peoples of the monarchy for purposes of undercutting the

Austro-Hungarian war effort, was not so useful. An interesting and well-researched study written for historians, but still accessible to the general reader. Extensive bibliography.

Haste, Cate. *Keep the Home Fires Burning: Propaganda in the First World War.* London: Allen Lane, 1977.

This volume concentrates on British propaganda in World War I, though it draws its theoretical definition and description of propaganda from American sources. The object is to describe why propaganda was a necessary part of the Great War and how it came of age in that war. In the author's words, "it became increasingly necessary to professionalize propaganda. . . ." The research comes mainly from the Public Records Office and the Imperial War Museum in London, and there are a number of illustrations of propaganda materials. The bibliography is limited and could be more usefully organized. However, the volume is well written and aimed at a general audience.

Hiley, Nicholas. "Sir Hedley Le Bas and the Origins of Domestic Propaganda in Britain, 1914-1917." *Journal of Advertising History* 10, 2 (1987), pp. 30-46.

This article looks at the origins of British home propaganda in the early years of World War I and asserts that a 1960s revision of what was once consensus about the importance of domestic propaganda in those years may have been only a "changing fashion in historical analysis." He argues that the problem may lie in the fact that historians have looked for evidence principally in government documents. Rather, "it is to advertisers and not government officials that British historians must look for the roots of domestic propaganda." Operating on this premise, the author examines the role of Hedley Le Bas, a publisher, who represented an advanced attitude toward the value of advertising and who became involved in developing British domestic propaganda upon the outbreak of war. The article draws heavily upon the Le Bas papers as well as on other sources to make a coherent and compelling argument.

Home Front, 1917-1919: War Transforms America. Prod. Columbia Broadcasting System, 17 min., 1967. Minneapolis: University of Minnesota.

Narrated by actor Robert Ryan, this short documentary looks at posters, newspaper pages, newsreels, and contemporary feature films in order to show how pacifists in the United States were changed into militants during World War I. The agency was the Committee on Public Information, which the film depicts as stirring the nation with volunteer drives, bond rallies featuring the likes of Douglas Fairbanks, and other forms of "win-the-war" propaganda. An excellent film for use in secondary schools or university classrooms.

Hoover, A. J. *God, Germany, and Britain in the Great War*. New York: Praeger, 1989.
A short but well-crafted study of how British and German clergy preached nationalism from the pulpit during the Great War. In the process, they became propagandists for the war and at the same time inspired a kind of religious revival. The bibliography contains a representative list of pamphlets and published sermons relating to the central theme, as well as a short listing of secondary works on nationalism, war propaganda, and churches in Germany and Britain.

Hopkin, Deian. "Domestic Censorship in the First World War." *Journal of Contemporary History* 5 (1970), pp. 151-169.
This article examines how and why the British government practiced press censorship during World War I. Initially, censorship was to be voluntary; when that proved inadequate, an official Press Bureau was established, which issued a "D (Defense) Notice" whenever a press item overstepped the bounds. Occasionally, the police would actually raid the premises of a newspaper and seize offending copies. Virtually no one was exempt. Few liked the censorship, but the government was reluctant to give it up after the war owing to the advent of a new "threat," Bolshevism. All the same, the author concludes, censorship did disappear, "imperceptibly," in 1919. It reappeared, however, in 1939. Well written, readable, and thoroughly researched from materials in the Public Records Office in London.

Huber, Georg. *Die französische Propaganda im Weltkrieg gegen Deutschland, 1914 bis 1918*. Munich: Dr. Franz A. Pfeiffer-Verlag, 1928.
The French anti-German propaganda effort in World War I is seen here through the eyes of its victim, which should stand as a warning that this volume, though written by a reputable historian at the university in Munich, is not entirely objective. This assessment of French propaganda is divided between a section on the channels and tactics of French propaganda and another which analyzes its content. The first covers such things as the press, books, pamphlets, and the use of caricature, while the second describes French criticism of German imperialism and accusations that Germany committed atrocities. There are a few examples of cartoon propaganda, much of it crudely done, and a select bibliography.

Hyman, Alan. *The Rise and Fall of Horatio Bottomley: The Biography of a Swindler.* London: Cassell, 1972.

Horatio Bottomley was many things, including a propagandist, though never one in the employ of the British government. That he also ended up in prison convicted of stealing money entrusted to him by investors is beside the point. A probably apocryphal story is associated with his time in prison, where, as was the custom, he sewed mail bags. A visitor came, saw him at work, and said, "Ah, Bottomley. Sewing?" The prisoner sighed, and replied, "Reaping, I'm afraid." In any event, a significant portion of the volume explains Bottomley's efforts as an unofficial propagandist in World War I and after, using his newspaper *John Bull* to promote wartime enlistment, among other things. There are a number of photographs of Bottomley and others who figured prominently in his life. Select bibliography.

Isenberg, Michael T. "The Mirror of Democracy: Reflections of the War Films of World War I, 1917-1919." *Journal of Popular Culture* 9, 4 (Spring 1976), pp. 878-885.

A short but thoroughly documented article which examines United States World War I films that called upon the nation to go to war for the defense of democracy. The further purpose of these films was to teach democracy abroad. The author describes how the National Association of Motion Picture Producers worked with the government from the start to plan films for overseas that would "teach the lessons of democracy to Europe." Films with this specific agenda included, among others, *The Pride of New York* (Fox, 1917), *For the Freedom of the World* (Lowry-Goldwyn, 1918), and *The Unbeliever* (Edison, 1918). A few of the films referred to in this article are available on videocassette. The rest, if they survive at all, are to be found only in such archives as the American Film Institute. Isenberg's materials are drawn from contemporary print sources such as reviews of the films and correspondence between filmmakers and others. See Timothy J. Lyons, "Hollywood and World War I" (entry below).

_____. *War on Film: The American Cinema and World War I, 1914-1941.* London and Toronto: Associated University Presses, 1981.

Not all of the film discussed here is propaganda, and in any case, the author's purpose is to look at how film can be used as historical evidence. However, in the process, he discusses a number of films which decidedly were made for propaganda purposes, and therein lies a major part of the value of this volume. Propaganda films are sources for the history of propaganda, and much of the material analyzed in this book contributes on that level. There is an extensive list of films by title that were made in the United States during World War I and after in which the war, or aspects of it, was the subject matter. See Larry Wayne Ward, *The Motion Picture Goes to War: The U.S. Government Film Effort during World War I* (entry below). Extensive bibliography and film lists.

_____. "World War I Film Comedies and American Society: The Concern with Authoritarianism." *Film and History* 5 (September 1975), pp. 7-15, 21.
This article argues that World War I comedies provide evidence of such films being used for at least a quasi-social propaganda purpose. The heroes were "raffishly proletarian," and the purpose was, as the author quotes Mack Sennett, "the discombobulation of authority." Films cited include *Yankee Doodle in Berlin* (entry below under "Propaganda Material"), *Kicking the Germ out of Germany*, and *Too Fat to Fight*, among others. The author, a specialist in World War I film as historical evidence, argues that all of this comedy carried an anti-authoritarian message. He also argues that it was not very effective. See the author's other writing on World War I film (entries above).

Johnston, Winifred. *Memo on the Movies: War Propaganda 1914-1939*. Norman, Okla.: Cooperative Books, 1939.
The author's expertise came from having been "one of the victims of World War propaganda," by which she meant that she worked for the Signal Corps of the War Department of the United States. Just how this victimized her is not explained. Her book is brief, critical of propaganda and censorship, and roughly two-thirds of it concerns the use of film and film stars for propaganda purposes in World War I. The remaining third summarizes the kinds of themes that appear after 1919 mainly in British, American, German, and French films. Social, political, and war retrospective subjects are her principal interests here. Too summary to be of great value to the historian of film propaganda. Limited bibliography.

Jones, Barbara, and Bill Howell. "Propaganda and Morale," in Barbara Jones and Bill Howell, *Popular Arts of the First World War*. New York: McGraw-Hill Book Company, 1972.
The book covers a wide variety of "popular arts" from the World War I period, that is, art for popular consumption. This chapter deals with items having specific propaganda value: statuettes of Joan of Arc made in Britain with "Vive la France!" painted on the base, posters, draw-

ings, and other art forms. It includes 11 pages, with illustrations and text, and is prepared for the general reader.

Jusserand, Jean Jules. *Le Sentiment américain pendant la guerre*. Paris: Payot et Cie, 1931.
In this highly readable and not overly subjective work, the author, a former ambassador to the United States, recalls how opinion in the United States was formed relative to France's part in World War I. This memoir gives credence to the popular postwar notion that Americans remembered French support after 1776 when the American colonies rebelled against England, and that this sentiment encouraged enthusiasm in the United States for the French cause. The volume includes two interesting and useful chapters specifically on German and French propaganda and opinion in the United States. No bibliography.

Knoles, George H. "American Intellectuals and World War I." *Pacific Northwest Quarterly* 59 (October 1968), pp. 203-215.
This article examines the response of various American intellectuals, principally writers, to World War I, with reference to how they regarded the purpose and function of the war in relation to the society of the United States. Some of them wrote for or against the war in propagandistic language. John Dewey, for example, urged his readers that the war had a "compelling moral import," namely to achieve a new social order. Such is the author's ultimate point: that these writers used the war as a springboard to launch their advocacy of the Progressive Era "that emerged triumphant after Versailles." The author does not contend that these intellectuals' advocacy was in any way official; rather, these were individuals with an ax to grind and with access to a mass readership, who seized the opportunity to use it in support of their agenda.

Larson, Cedric, and James R. Mock. "The Lost Files of the Creel Committee of 1917-19." *Public Opinion Quarterly* 3, 1 (1939), pp. 5-29.
This article describes the contents of lost archival materials relating to United States propaganda in World War I, which was found two years before this article appeared. These files contained material needed to write a thorough and scholarly history of World War I propaganda that would go well beyond what had been done before, at least so far as the bureaucratic background of the effort was concerned. This article is, in a sense, a summary of that history. The principal point is that what had been written before on the work of the Committee on Public Information (Creel Committee) was revealed by virtue of these lost

files to have been more legend than fact. The authors published this article as an introduction to their book, which appeared the same year and which was based upon the lost files. See James Robert Mock and Cedric Larson, *Words That Won the War* (entry below).

Lowell, Abbott Lawrence. *Public Opinion in War and Peace*. Cambridge, Mass.: Harvard University Press, 1923.

Written not long after World War I ended, this volume clearly was inspired by the use made of propaganda to influence public opinion in that war, and by the author's observation of the "political attitude of thoughtful people" in Britain in the year following war's end. In his view, postwar political opinion in Britain lacked aggressiveness, but was both confident and antagonistic on matters of national policy in a manner that was "unusual in English-speaking countries." He concluded that this was at least in part a response to the strain placed upon public opinion during the war. Much of this strain was the result of vigorous propaganda campaigns. The volume offers an analysis of public opinion and an assessment of the effects of the war on postwar public opinion in former belligerent countries. This is a long essay rather than a work of theoretical analysis, and provides insight into early rounds of reflection upon where public opinion was headed as a result of World War I. No bibliography.

Lutz, Ralph Haswell. "Studies of World War Propaganda, 1914-33." *Journal of Modern History* 5 (1933), pp. 496-516.

This bibliographic essay describes writings on World War I propaganda by historians, political scientists, and other specialists from both sides of the battle lines; that is, books by writers in the United States, Germany, Britain, and France are included. The reader is brought up to date (1933) on war propaganda scholarship and on arguments and discussion over just what that scholarship was proving. The author, himself a knowledgeable student of the subject, offers his own views on definitions, uses, and abuses of war propaganda, and concludes that even with all that had been written, "it is too early to estimate the part played by world war propaganda in victory and defeat." The essay makes reference to more than one hundred sources.

Lyons, Timothy J. "Hollywood and World War I, 1914-1918." *Journal of Popular Film* 1, 1 (Winter 1972), pp. 15-30.

Film, the author argues, was a major contributing factor in preparing the populace of the United States to enter World War I. He stresses the rising popularity of films in the years of United States neutrality, and notes that "much had been discovered about the American popular mind, its common beliefs and prejudices, and its way of accepting war as a necessary evil." The remaining pages describe the major Hollywood films of the war period, noting both their propaganda content and their often brutal manner of presenting it. See Michael T. Isenberg's writings on World War I film (entries above).

Marquis, Alice Goldfarb. "Words as Weapons: Propaganda in Britain and Germany During the First World War." *Journal of Contemporary History* 13, 3 (July 1978), pp. 467-498.
The author argues that while many people saw World War I propaganda as a momentarily exciting event of no lasting significance, others recognized that it was a profound revelation of the value of "words as weapons" in a total war. This article provides an overview of how British and German propagandists approached their work, and notes how government, the press, censorship, and propaganda came together. The author carries her story into the postwar period when words became weapons in the rise of fascism. The point is made that Nazi propagandists used British war propaganda as a model. Well written but not altogether convincing.

Marrin, Albert. *The Last Crusade: The Church of England in the First World War*. Durham, N.C.: Duke University Press, 1974.
This volume focuses on the Church of England during World War I as a religious body rather than as a propaganda channel. All the same, the author makes it clear that the clergy played an important role in promoting support at home for "England's Holy War," and for those who were fighting it. The volume includes an extensive bibliography of sermons, speeches, and pamphlets produced by the English clergy during the war, many of which, judging from their titles, clearly served a propaganda function.

Messenger, Gary S. *British Propaganda and the State in the First World War*. Manchester, England: Manchester University Press, 1992.
Two opening chapters define and characterize official British propaganda in World War I, followed by chapters that profile the contributions to wartime propaganda of some fifteen of its principal organizers, disseminaters, and controllers. Some of these were Charles Masterman, Douglas Brownrigg, Lord Beaverbrook, and Horatio Bottomley. The author takes a positive line on the value of propaganda in wartime and concludes that it was naive for the British government to turn against propaganda after the war. This attitude merely impeded progress when

it became necessary to organize official propaganda for World War II. Well researched and written with an extensive bibliography.

Metzl, Irvine. "The Poster Goes to War," in Irvine Metzl, *The Poster: Its History and Its Art*. New York: Watson-Guptill, 1963.
The poster has a long history, going as far back as the late Middle Ages. The chapter noted here specifically concerns posters used as war propaganda between 1914 and 1945. The author claims that in wartime, posters "became more effective than all the patriotic oratory of their day." Plentiful illustrations, mainly from World War I, and an easily readable text. Limited bibliography.

Mock, James Robert, and Cedric Larson. *Words That Won the War: The Story of the Committee on Public Information, 1917-1919*. Princeton, N.J.: Princeton University Press, 1939.
The records of the Committee on Public Information (CPI) were deposited in the Washington National Archives in 1937. They told "the story of America's first 'propaganda ministry,' and its dynamic leader, George Creel." Using these documents, the authors set down that story in the 350-plus pages of this volume. They describe in the first part, "The American Mind in Wartime," the imposition of wartime censorship, and the particular stamp George Creel placed on the organization. The second part deals with the press, broadcasting, film, historians, business, and trade unions as domestic propaganda channels. The last section covers United States propaganda efforts overseas, ending with a chapter describing a CPI "blue print" for future wars. The book includes examples of propaganda, and a limited bibliography of other writings about World War I propaganda. The book is eminently readable and clearly reflects the rising danger of that "future war" in 1939, when the volume appeared.

Mould, David H. *American Newsfilm, 1914-1919: The Underexposed War*. New York: Garland, 1983.
A study of wartime newsfilm, specifically that from World War I, this volume discusses newsreels and war documentaries shown in the United States during two distinct periods: before the United States entered the war in 1917, and in the two years after entry. The author also describes film censorship and, more important, the degree to which film producers and exhibitors were inclined to fake and restage supposed newsfilm scenes in order to present "attention-grabbing, heart-warming, tear-jerking" subjects. In short, he argues, "newsfilm was erratic, censorship capricious and exhibition unashamedly propa-

gandistic." An excellent study by a young historian of World War I propaganda, who had access to advice from some of the best film scholars available, such as Kevin Brownlow, Garth Jowett, and Nicholas Pronay. The study concludes with a bibliographical essay.

The Moving Picture Boys in the Great War. Prod. Post-Newsweek Stations, 52 min., 1975. Los Angeles: Republic Pictures Home Video.
This documentary narrated by Lowell Thomas points out how attitudes in the United States toward isolationism in World War I were affected by film. Special attention is paid to how newsreels were adapted for propaganda use. There are also extracts from commercial films with explanation of how they served a propaganda purpose. The point is clear that film was well established as a propaganda channel in the United States as elsewhere during World War I.

Nicholson, Ivor. "An Aspect of British Official Wartime Propaganda." *Cornhill Magazine* 70 (1931), pp. 593-606.
This article notes that the British government recognized the importance of propaganda "for the first time" during World War I, and that a thorough history of propaganda in that war had not been written and "perhaps it never will be written now." An odd statement, since it is based upon the fact that the three men most involved in developing wartime propaganda in Britain had died. It does not take into account that even with the "fifty-year rule" for keeping government archives under wraps, eventually those years would pass and Ministry of Information files in the Public Records Office would be opened to historians. In any event, the author, who worked at Wellington House, one of the propaganda headquarters during World War I, offers here a general survey of the kinds of things that were done in propaganda work, including references to the role played by the British Board of Film Censors, the press, British artists, and others. This piece is primary material for the propaganda historian, but in the manner of a memoir, and therefore not without limitations over and above its brevity.

Nielsen, Keith. "'Joy Rides'?: British Intelligence and Propaganda in Russia, 1914-1917." *Historical Journal* 24, 4 (1981), pp. 885-906.
At the time, some referred to British propaganda and intelligence work in wartime Russia as "joy rides," because they were such exercises in futility. The object was to promote greater coordination between the two allies in war, and that did not happen. The author acknowledges that in this regard the charge of uselessness is well founded, but notes that it is useful to survey the activities of British intelligence and propaganda

agents who were in Russia, and to assess whether or not they had any influence on British wartime policy. This article opened the door to a previously neglected area of World War I propaganda history.

Noble, George Bernard. *Policies and Opinions at Paris, 1919: Wilsonian Diplomacy, the Versailles Peace, and French Public Opinion.* New York: Macmillan, 1935.
This is in part an apology for the statesmen who met in Paris in 1919 to make the Versailles and other treaties, suggesting that they should not be blamed for the ills of the present (the 1930s), though these ills are the direct result of the Versailles Treaty. Rather, the author argues, the fault lay with "the turbulence of popular feelings, inflamed by falsifying wartime propaganda and distorted by a stupid censorship." For the most part, the author treats with the Paris peace conference in the context of opinion as it was crafted by propaganda. Select bibliography.

Over There: 1914-1918. Prod. CRM Films, writ. Cécil Saint-Laurent, 90 min., 1963. Tucson: University of Arizona.
This documentary combines German and French newsreels, official army films, censored films, propaganda productions, and film taken by "amateur soldier-cameramen" from World War I. Only the latter tend to have no particular propaganda function. The film shows the horrors, betrayals, victories, and defeats of the war from a European point of view. An excellent teaching aid for secondary and university students.

Peterson, H. C. *Propaganda for War: The Campaign Against American Neutrality, 1914-1917.* Norman: University of Oklahoma Press, 1939.
Writing on the eve of World War II, the author asserts that the "enduring effects" of propaganda disseminated in the United States during the early years of World War I are measurable by the fact that "concepts which grew out of the wartime propaganda are still being accepted even though they are fundamentally inaccurate. As a result, the United States seems to have become a partisan to all the world's troubles." Despite having a clear pro-neutrality agenda, the author has written a remarkably objective and well-documented history of the role allied, in particular British, propaganda played in persuading America into the war in 1917. Extensive bibliography, and graphs showing United States trade with belligerent nations in Europe on the eve of World War I.

Peterson, H. C., and Gilbert C. Fite. *Opponents of War, 1917-1918.* Madison: University of Wisconsin Press, 1957.
This book examines the conflict in the United States between prowar and antiwar individuals and groups, the methods they used to promote

or oppose World War I, and who and what they were. It is a story, in Gilbert Fite's words, "which abounds with violent words, violent deeds, violent laws, and violent individuals." The authors cover the activities of the radical left—Industrial Workers of the World (IWW) and various socialist groups—and conservative Americans "who displayed an intemperance that would do credit to the wildest of radicals." In short, this is the history of a propaganda war waged equally by crackpots and government agencies against and for the involvement of the United States in World War I. It is illustrated with examples of the propaganda and photographs of some of the propagandists, such as Bill Haywood, head of the IWW. Extensive bibliography.

Rappaport, Armin. *The British Press and Wilsonian Neutrality*. Stanford, Calif.: Stanford University Press, 1951.
A study of how the 37 leading newspapers and periodicals in Scotland and England responded to the United States neutrality policy prior to 1917. The volume assesses British public opinion and how the British press both reflected and shaped it. The propaganda element in this press coverage was both obvious and ran counter to British government policy. As the author notes, "the use of intemperate and reckless language by certain sections of the press increased the government's difficulties."

Read, James Morgan. *Atrocity Propaganda, 1914-1919*. New Haven, Conn.: Yale University Press, 1941.
Inspired by the realities of World War II, in progress when the author began writing, this volume examines how belligerents on both sides in World War I used stories about atrocities for propaganda purposes. Well and clearly written by a professional historian, the volume is accessible to any informed reader. Curiously, there are no illustrations even though posters were used extensively in the atrocities propaganda war. Extensive bibliography.

Reeves, Nicholas. "Film Propaganda and Its Audiences: The Example of Britain's Official Films During the First World War." *Journal of Contemporary History* 18 (1983), pp. 463-494.
A scholarly article that examines how the British government disseminated "official," which is to say newsreel, film propaganda during World War I in an effort to win public support for its policies. The author explains official views on the value of film propaganda as opposed to other channels, notes that from the start the government formed a partnership with commercial enterprise for distribution of

these newsreels, and comments on the lack of quality which often defeated the propaganda purpose. He also points out that early on, the propaganda and foreign ministries were in conflict with one another over who would control the propaganda. This argument never went away, and was again a problem during World War II.

Sanders, M. L. "Wellington House and British Propaganda During the First World War." *Historical Journal* 18, 1 (1975), pp. 119-146.
The author begins by noting that upon the outbreak of World War I, Germany "poured out propaganda"—a fact that upset the British government no end. Officials were particularly concerned over the virulence of the German material, much of which was aimed at influencing the United States. Consequently, the British government established a war propaganda bureau at Wellington house for purposes of designing a counter to this onslaught. This article describes their efforts, noting the contributions of such people as the novelist John Buchan, noting also the great secrecy in which they labored, and describing the policy of telling the truth "as often as possible" that characterized British propaganda. There is an appendix showing the bureaucratic structure at Wellington house.

Sanders, Michael, and Philip M. Taylor. *British Propaganda During the First World War, 1914-18.* London: Macmillan, 1982.
The volume attempts, in the authors' words, "the first modern study of this controversial subject based upon unpublished primary source material," taking into account that some of the primary documentation relevant to the subject was destroyed in 1920, or else "lost" in the years since. This is a pioneering work by two outstanding British historians of propaganda, and should be of great value to students of the subject. The research is thorough, including work done in archives as far afield as the Hoover Institution in Palo Alto, California, and the Public Records Office in London. The writing is clear and cogent, and the select bibliography includes nearly five pages of titles of wartime propaganda pamphlets.

Schwertfeger, Bernhard. "Propaganda," in Gerhard Anschütz et al., eds., *Handbuch der Politik.* Vol. 5, *Der Weg in die Zukunft.* Berlin-Grune-wald: Dr. Walther Rothschild, 1922.
Volume 5 in this five-volume encyclopedia of politics includes an entry on propaganda which was derived from the experience of World War I. The author, a Reichswehr colonel, appears to have been involved in Germany's propaganda activity. This short essay talks about German

war propaganda and also the propaganda efforts of Germany's enemies. The point is to suggest a role for propaganda in Germany's efforts
at recovering its position in postwar Europe.

Shover, Michele J. "Roles and Images of Women in World War I Propaganda." *Politics and Society* 5 (1975), pp. 469-486.
An excellent study of various propaganda channels employed to publicize the roles played by women during World War I. The author notes
that it was traditionally thought that women were assigned passive
wartime roles on the strength of their "innately passive natures."
However, she argues, the evidence of World War I propaganda suggests
that policy was dictated by role management (manipulation) rather
than role recognition (passive nature). The author concentrates on
poster art for her evidence, the purpose of which was to generate
anti-German feeling at many levels. She evaluates the female image
that was used in, respectively, troop recruitment, factory work recruitment (of both men and women), as national symbol, and as victim of
German atrocities. The author also notes that this propaganda "effectively encouraged a controlled expansion of women's established
social roles." However, at war's end, the push was toward a restoration
of traditional social roles for women.

Squires, James Duane. *British Propaganda at Home and in the United
States from 1914 to 1917*. Cambridge, Mass.: Harvard University
Press, 1935.
This 82-page volume is a long essay rather than a book, a point
acknowledged by the author. His purpose was to write the history of
British propaganda during the period of American neutrality, an area
which in 1935 had not yet been explored. The theme is propaganda
against United States neutrality and for sustaining British morale
against the horrors of the Western Front. The conclusion is that "British
propaganda was a real force in winning the World War." This study is
a very readable if somewhat skimpy historical treatment of the propaganda issue. There is a thirteen-page bibliography of wartime pamphlets, most of which were written for propaganda purposes, and a very
brief list of major early works about propaganda.

Swartz, Marvin. *The Union of Democratic Control in British Politics
During the First World War*. Oxford, England: Clarendon Press, 1971.
Not all propaganda in 1914-1918 supported war. The Union of Democratic Control (UDC) was a British organization that opposed the war,
and agitated against it through leaflets, pamphlets, and public oration.

Its numbers counted both men and women, including such luminaries of the English left as Sir Arthur Ponsonby, C. P. Trevelyan, and Lady Margaret Sackville. This scholarly volume includes a select bibliography and appendixes related to UDC leaders and branch organizations.

Symons, Julian. *Horatio Bottomley: A Biography.* London: Cresset Press, 1955.

This biography of one of the more shady as well as colorful figures in Britain during the first third of the twentieth century provides a useful compendium for the study of propaganda in World War I. First, it deals with Horatio Bottomley, publisher of *John Bull*, a tabloid-style journal that was by its nature propagandistic, and which Bottomley used, along with a compelling style of public oratory, to disseminate unofficial propaganda during the war. Second, the volume examines, through Bottomley's life and exploits, a period of British history when propaganda was becoming an ever more important part of the way governments, as well as individuals with an ax to grind, communicated with the public. The volume includes several photographs but no bibliography. See Sidney Felstead and Alan Hyman on Bottomley (entries above).

Taylor, Philip M. "The Foreign Office and British Propaganda During the First World War." *Historical Journal* 23, 4 (1980), pp. 875-898.

Even though the British Foreign Office embraced propaganda deployment during World War I, it was the opinion of Lord Northcliffe, the press lord responsible for Britain's overseas propaganda in wartime, that "propaganda and diplomacy were incompatible." Much of his reasoning was the result of disillusionment after a number of clashes between his organization and the Foreign Office. This article is a brief history of the propaganda-foreign policy relationship in World War I placed in the context of Britain's need to disseminate propaganda abroad as an aspect of the conduct of the war. Thoroughly researched, cogently written, and compellingly argued.

Thimme, Hans. *Weltkrieg ohne Waffen: Die Propaganda der Westmächte gegen Deutschland, ihre Wirtung und ihre Abwehr.* Stuttgart and Berlin: J. G. Cotta'sche Buchhandlung Nachsolger, 1932.

This volume critically surveys allied propaganda disseminated against Germany during World War I, including leaflets fired by rockets behind enemy lines. Examples of leaflet propaganda are included, along with an appendix of German military correspondence related to propaganda and the intelligence work connected with it. The volume takes on a special significance since it was written during that period of political

crisis in Germany out of which emerged the dictatorship of Adolf
Hitler. Much of Hitler's own propaganda was an attack upon how the
Western democracies treated Germany at the end of the war. Difficult
to read, as the print is old German script. Limited bibliography.

Vaughn, Stephen. *Holding Fast the Line: Democracy, Nationalism, and
the Committee on Public Information.* Chapel Hill: University of North
Carolina Press, 1980.
A scholarly monograph which details the domestic propaganda efforts
in World War I of the United States Committee on Public Information.
This was the so-called Creel Committee, after its director, George
Creel, the function of which was to sell to United States citizens the
idea of being nationalistic and of participating in the war. In the
author's argument, the Creel Committee was "a nationalizing agent,
encouraging American nationalism." Illustrations include photographs
of Creel and other CPI members, and reproductions of propaganda
material disseminated by the organization. This volume does for the CPI
what Allan M. Winkler's *The Politics of Propaganda* (entry under
"History and Function" in chapter 5) does for the Office of War
Information in World War II.

Viereck, George Sylvester (George F. Lorners). *Spreading Germs of Hate.*
New York: Horace Liveright, 1930.
A very personalized retrospective examination of World War I propaganda in the United States by one who was deeply involved in creating it.
What Viereck created, however, was pro-German propaganda, an activity
in which he engaged again during World War II. The author's description of propaganda is revealing: "Propaganda is the primary weapon
of the world's invisible government. The microbes it scatters infect
humanity like a plague. My book is an attempt to administer an antidote
or a serum against this scourge by inculcating Propaganda Resistance."
Written sometimes in narrative, sometimes in novel form. The volume
includes examples of cartoon and other propaganda. No bibliography.

Wallace, Stuart. *War and the Image of Germany: British Academics,
1914-1918.* Edinburgh: John Donald, 1988.
This volume clarifies the role prominent British historians and other
academics played as propagandists in World War I. They helped create
the negative image of Germany that was essential to the domestic
propaganda campaigns orchestrated to gain support for the war effort.
An interesting question raised in this volume is whether these academics were supporting propaganda purely for Britain's sake in all in-

stances, or partly for the sake of their own conscience, once they were convinced that the Germans were committing atrocities on a broad scale. Extensive bibliography and several appendixes, including such items as how many British academics worked in Whitehall, how many attended German universities, and so forth.

Williams, John. *The Other Battleground. The Home Fronts: Britain, France, and Germany, 1914-18.* Chicago: Henry Regnery, 1972.
This is a history of life on the home front in three of the principal belligerent nations in World War I. Propaganda and censorship are among several themes that run through the book. Others include regulation, regimentation, morale, and daily discomfiture owing to shortages. In a very real sense, the propaganda-censorship issue is central to these themes, for as the author makes clear, it was through manipulation of opinion that the governments of these nations dealt with morale, patriotism, regulation, and the rest. The format of the book is chronological, the style narrative, and the conclusion is that in the end, propaganda and censorship slipped in effectiveness when it became clear that what civilians were told about victories in the field and the need for an ever more bloated bureaucracy did not quite mesh with reality. The book is illustrated with photographs and includes a select bibliography of secondary works.

Willis, Irene Cooper. *England's Holy War: A Study of English Liberal Idealism During the Great War.* Reissue of earlier publication. New York: Garland, 1972.
A three-part study of wartime press propaganda concentrating on the way Liberal Idealism in England was "harnessed to the war chariot," written during the decade after the event. Somewhat short on objectivity, the volume nevertheless provides considerable insight into how David Lloyd George's Liberal party used the English press to sell its war aims, once they had been determined. The foreword by J. A. Hobson, one of the leading English radicals of the pre- and postwar period, is an added attraction. Well written with a sense of humor. The only bibliography is contained in the author's preface, in which she refers to having drawn her material from the leading English newspapers, which she names.

Wilson, Trevor. "Lord Bryce's Investigation into Alleged German Atrocities in Belgium, 1914-15." *Journal of Contemporary History* 14, 3 (July 1979), pp. 369-383.
Accusations of atrocities were central features of allied anti-German propaganda in World War I. This article by a leading historian of early

twentieth-century British history examines the work of the Lord Bryce Committee, which was set up to investigate the truth or falsity of alleged German atrocities committed in Belgium. The committee found them to be much exaggerated. Needless to say, since Britain was in the middle of the war, these findings were not made public.

Wright, D. G. "The Great War, Government Propaganda and English 'Men of Letters' 1914-16." *Literature and History* 7 (1978), pp. 70-100.
This article examines the role of men and women of letters in developing British propaganda in World War I. Their influence, the author argues, was the result of the great respect Edwardian England had for literary figures. The writers discussed include Arnold Bennett, Arthur Benson, H. G. Wells, Arthur Conan Doyle, Gilbert Murray, John Galsworthy, and G. M. Trevelyan, among others. The author also examines the propaganda office, Wellington House, which was created to employ them. A major theme of this article is that these writers brought a certain idealism to their work; that is, many of them would only write in favor of the war when convinced that the English side was fighting for ideals. Not everyone fell in with C. F. G. Masterman, the organizer of this literary propaganda corps. He was never able to engage Thomas Hardy, for example.

Channels and Techniques

Blankenhorn, Heber. *Adventures in Propaganda: Letters from an Intelligence Officer in France.* Boston: Houghton Mifflin, 1919.
A collection of letters written by Blankenhorn to his wife—who wrote the preface to this volume—while he was a United States intelligence officer in France toward the end of World War I. His job was to liaise with other allied propaganda offices and gather information that was then used for propaganda against the enemy. These letters offer an intriguing firsthand account of how propaganda materials were gathered and deployed, providing insights into how propaganda seemed to affect the opinions of people the officer met. Not all of the contents bear upon propaganda, but this in no way detracts from the value of the book to the student of propaganda. No bibliography.

Bornecque, Henri, and J. Germain Drouilly. *La France et la guerre: Formation de l'opinion publique pendant la guerre.* Paris: Payot et Cie, 1921.
This volume, published within three years of the end of World War I, is both an explanation and an apology for propaganda disseminated in

France during that conflict. Once it became clear that neither the German "blitzkrieg" of August 1914 nor the French all-out counterattack in response to it would end the conflict, France resorted to propaganda to maintain public morale for the duration. The authors take no responsibility for commenting on the accuracy of propaganda content, but only indicate what it contained and how it was designed to vindicate France, praise French allies, and excoriate the enemy, the last in part through the dissemination of atrocity stories. The volume is readable and, though not a scholarly work, appears to be based upon a clear reading of the propaganda materials under discussion. Limited bibliography.

"British Propaganda in Enemy Countries." *The Times History of the War*, 21. London: The Times, 1920.

This volume is part of a multivolume set which, taken together, is an excellent resource on World War I. The entry for propaganda in enemy countries is invaluable. It explains the nature of propaganda as understood in both general theory and specific practice, describes how Britain's enemies used propaganda in neutral and belligerent countries, and shows how Britain itself organized the dissemination of propaganda to enemy countries. The bulk of the piece details the techniques, channels, and contents of British propaganda as deployed against Germany and the Austro-Hungarian Empire. There are numerous photographs of principals in the propaganda war, and of their wares. Among these items: a manifesto written by Thomas Masaryk in Czech for leaflets dropped by balloon into areas where Czech soldiers fought for Austria-Hungary; a leaflet showing the growing strength of the American field army; and another leaflet showing the breaking of the Hindenburg Line. Well and clearly written within a year of war's end, this article is virtually a primary source on World War I propaganda.

Brownrigg, Sir Douglas. *Indiscretions of the Naval Censor*. London: Cassell and Company, 1920.

Another wartime memoir, this by a British Admiralty censor. His aim is to describe how the censorship was established, how it worked, and what was its ultimate purpose. The author is detailed on the nature of the job, its degree of difficulty, and, of course, its importance to winning the war. Chapter headings indicate the scope of the censors' concerns. They include "Publicity and Propaganda," "Educating the People," and "Pressmen of Allied Countries," among many others. The illustrations are mainly military photographs. No bibliography.

Cadogan, Mary, and Patricia Craig. *Women and Children First: The Fiction of Two World Wars*. London: Victor Gollancz, 1978.
Not every piece of writing considered in this volume was propaganda. However, much of it was, and, as the authors note in their introduction, "the fiction of the second world war largely reflected the pattern of 1914-1918. Official propagandists and popular novelists joined forces to urge housewives out of their homes into war work. . . ." With wit, skill, and clarity, the authors have made an important contribution to a major propaganda subject, written fiction as a propaganda channel, specifically in Great Britain. This genre played a propaganda role much like that of the feature film, both in wartime and between the wars. There is a select bibliography of books about women in wartime; curiously, the titles of novels discussed are indicated only in the text.

Cook, Sir Edward. *The Press in War-Time: With Some Account of the Official Press Bureau*. London: Macmillan, 1920.
Written by an official of the British Press Bureau, which had responsibility in World War I for press censorship, this volume has three themes: first, to explain why press censorship was necessary in wartime; second, to note that a free press is essential to a democracy at peace; and third, to commend the British press for its wartime cooperation with the censor, in the process of which it "contributed largely to the success of the Allies." Something of an *apologia*, the book nevertheless is well written and presents compelling arguments for press censorship in wartime. No bibliography.

Creel, George. *How We Advertised America: The First Telling of the Amazing Story of the Committee on Public Information That Carried the Gospel of Americanism to Every Corner of the Globe*. New York: Harper and Brothers, 1920.
George Creel was director of the Committee on Public Information (CPI) in World War I. This is a personal history of what that office did to propagandize the United States, not only or even mainly with an eye toward the war, but for influence in the world after the war. The volume explains the organization, the philosophy, the work, and the successes and failures of the CPI. This is a primary document on United States propaganda in World War I, much in the manner of Sir Campbell Stuart's memoir on Crewe House, the British equivalent of the CPI. It is equally subjective. Creel's volume contains an appendix of correspondence and a bibliography of CPI publications, which includes the number of copies printed.

Crozier, Emmet. *American Reporters on the Western Front, 1914-1918.*
New York: Oxford University Press, 1959.
Strictly speaking, this is not a book about propaganda. It is rather about
war reporters who, as the author points out, "risked their lives and
fought the censors in France." It is, therefore, a book about one of the
channels, the press, through which propaganda in World War I was
funnelled to people at home, in this case, to the United States. The
author looks at the lives of American journalists working in Paris and
London as well as at the front, considers the difficulties they faced in
getting access to certain kinds of military information, and notes that
sometimes the stories they filed emphasized those parts of events
which made good propaganda. Written in a journalistic style by a
former newsman, the volume is a somewhat subjective commentary
on the press in action in wartime. The extensive bibliography includes
a number of books by former war correspondents.

De Chambure, A. *Quelques Guides de l'opinion en France pendant la
grande guerre, 1914-1918.* Paris: Celin, Mary, Elen et Cie, 1918.
Dedicated to the French press, this volume addresses the issue of how
Paris newspapers and journalists guided French public opinion during
World War I. The author makes clear that there were good and bad
journalists influencing opinion, some *vrai journalistes* (true journalists) and some who were "sans conscience, comme sans talent" (without conscience as without ability). Papers discussed include *La Liberté,
Le Gaulois, Le Matin,* and *L'Echo de Paris,* among many others, and
journalists and other writers discussed include Maurice Barrés of
L'Echo, and Léon Daudet and Charles Maurras of *L'Action Française.*
Written literally as the war was ending and filled with the author's
patriotic fervor, this book is not only a critique of the press as an
opinion-forming or propaganda channel, but is itself a piece of pro-
press propaganda. Limited bibliography.

Demartial, Georges. *La Guerre de 1914: Comment on mobilisa les con-
sciences.* Paris: F. Rieder et Cie, 1922.
This volume denounces anti-German commentary during and immediately after World War I for being based upon lies and misrepresentation.
The author claims that a nation (France) if truly pacific, would have
opposed the false patriotism that was brought to play in anti-German
propaganda. Almost an academic writing but with highly argumentative
overtones, it is a most unusual book to come out of France at that point
in time. An interesting volume which sheds light on how intellectuals
sometimes lent themselves to making propaganda. Limited bibliography.

Demm, Eberhard. "Propaganda and Caricature in the First World War." *Journal of Contemporary History* 28, 1 (January 1993), pp. 163-192.
The theme of this article is that total war is possible only with the full consent of the people. The conclusion is that this is possible only through the effective use of propaganda and censorship. The author describes, in general terms, the propaganda organization and activities on both sides in World War I, focusing his detail only on the propaganda role played by caricature. He points out that German caricature was as effective as any other, at least in Germany.

The First Casualty. Prod. Thames Television, 55 min., 1974. Santa Monica, Calif.: BFA Educational Media.
John Terraine narrates this film examination of World War I British propaganda through which morale was boosted, soldiers were recruited, war bonds were sold, and the "Huns" were assailed. Samples include posters, magazines, animated cartoons, and newspapers. The film has a point of view, as the theme is propaganda used to "dominate" the masses, and argues from the premise that "the first casualty when war comes is truth."

Ford, Guy Stanton. "The Committee on Public Information." *Historical Outlook* 11, 3 (March 1920), pp. 97-100.
A short essay which provides an overview of the purpose, nature, and function of the World War I Committee on Public Information (CPI). It is somewhat subjective, probably because the author worked for CPI. Written on the morrow of the war, the essay suggests a positive view of America's propaganda work. The author urges that the American effort brought war propaganda "up to the level of truth telling."

Gallo, Max. "1914-1924: Images of War and Revolution," in *The Poster in History*, translated by Alfred and Bruni Mayor. Secaucus, N.J.: Wellfleet Press, 1989.
An analysis with samples of how posters were used as propaganda during and after World War I. The text is easily readable, the poster samples are well reproduced, and there is virtually no aspect of this propaganda channel left untouched. The samples are drawn from every nation which participated in the war and the events which followed it. Limited bibliography.

Ingersoll, William. "The Future of the Four Minute Men." *Quarterly Journal of Speech Education* 5 (March 1919), 175-178.
The Four-Minute Men became famous as fund raisers in the United States in World War I by giving precisely four-minute pitches to cinema

audiences prior to the start of a feature film. The author suggests that these men might now organize local forums on a weekly or monthly basis so that they could use the skills they developed as war propagandists to address and clarify public questions in peacetime.

Landau, Captain Henry. *The Enemy Within: The Inside Story of German Sabotage in America.* New York: G. P. Putnam's Sons, 1937.
One function of propaganda is to undercut enemy morale and reduce fighting efficiency. With that in mind, sabotage, whether of enemy shipping, factories, or communications, becomes a propaganda channel. This volume, written by a British army officer from World War I, purports to explain how German agents carried out certain acts of sabotage in the United States during World War I. There are numerous illustrations, but no bibliography or documentation, save for the author's assertion that "I have endeavored to present the true facts, as far as they are known."

Lasswell, Harold D. *Propaganda Technique in the World War.* New York: Garland, 1972. Reissue of earlier publication.
One of the leading theorists of propaganda between the world wars, Lasswell here describes World War I propaganda in terms of techniques and channels with an eye toward commenting on the continuing role of propaganda in international and national politics. His study is based to some extent upon behavioral theory; however, he insists that his principal analytical methodology is common sense. Subjects in this volume include organizations that run war propaganda, long-term propaganda goals such as elaborating war aims and assessing war guilt, reassuring allies and demoralizing the enemy, and assessment of results. The volume is somewhat dated with regard to the last subject. Otherwise, it is a useful if rather pontifical survey of World War I propaganda work. Select bibliography.

McEwen, John M. "The National Press During the First World War: Ownership and Circulation." *Journal of Contemporary History* 17, 3 (July 1982), pp. 459-486.
This article surveys the British press in World War I in terms of whether circulation figures and the relationship between press proprietors and politicians determined how the press sought to influence public opinion. The author refutes long-held assumptions regarding the British press as an arbiter of public affairs and the direction of the war. However, he remains convinced that the press was a potent force for molding opinion to accept government policy during the war, simply because they were "practically the sole medium of communication" between events and the public.

McLaughlan, Andrew Cunningham. "Historians and the War." *The Dial* 62 (May 17, 1917), pp. 427-428.

A letter to the editor, actually, this short piece calls upon American historians (Frederick Jackson Turner and James T. Shotwell being the most famous of those named) to lend their talents to helping win the war. The author mentions as one possibility how they can write about history in such a manner as to stir up patriotism. This was gilding the lily somewhat, since most historians of that era already wrote history from a patriotic perspective.

Millard, Oscar E. *Uncensored: The True Story of the Clandestine Newspaper "La Libre Belgique" Published in Brussels During the German Occupation.* London: Robert Hale, 1937.

This volume is a narrative history of *La Libre Belgique*, a clandestine Belgian resistance newspaper published during World War I. The book is based largely upon the version of events told to the author by Eugène van Doren, one of its editors. It describes the events leading to the invasion and occupation of Belgium, the founding of the resistance paper, much about its principal editor, Victor Jourdain, and the role the paper played (which is somewhat romanticized) in sustaining Belgian morale while giving the occupiers a hard time. The volume is written in the style and form of an adventure novel. There is no bibliography, but the book contains a few illustrations and an outline map of Brussels.

Mock, James R. *Censorship 1917.* New York: Da Capo Press, 1971. First published in 1941.

Two themes run through this highly critical study of censorship in the United States during World War I. The first is the extent to which censorship was practiced as one technique for achieving popular support for the war; the second is to reveal the dangerous evil that censorship represents to civil liberties. With this in mind, the author describes how censorship was applied in the immediate postwar period to "anyone with ideas of which the [censorship] officials as individuals disapproved." That included anarchists, communists, and radicals of various kinds. This volume is a useful study of censorship in World War I and an example in its own right of free-speech propaganda. There is an extensive description of sources connected with the subject.

Ponsonby, Sir Arthur. *Falsehood in War-Time: Containing an Assortment of Lies Circulated Throughout the Nations During the Great War.* London: George Allen and Unwin, 1928.

Ponsonby was a leading figure in the antiwar Union of Democratic Control in Britain. This book is a continuation of the pacifist program which the UDC advanced. Its premise is that governments cannot tell the truth in wartime, else no one would fight. Therefore, they tell lies. This volume is a collection of wartime falsehoods perpetrated, the author claims, by the British government: Russian troops passing through Britain; Germany's sole responsibility for the war; the mutilated nurse (an atrocity story); the corpse factory; and many more. In simplest terms, it is the author's point that propaganda is central to modern war, and that lying is one of its techniques. No bibliography.

Rawls, Walton. *Wake Up, America! World War I and the American Poster.* New York: Abbeville Press, 1988.
Another contribution to the study of posters as channels of propaganda. These samples come from all belligerent countries, but mostly from the United States. This collection can be used with Max Gallo's *The Poster in History* (entry above). Indeed, the two volumes are very similar, save that Rawls limits himself to the war period. High-quality color reproductions of samples are accompanied by an easily readable explanatory text that puts the posters in context. Limited bibliography.

Reeves, Nicholas. *Official British Film Propaganda During the First World War.* London: Croom Helm, 1986.
This volume analyzes British film propaganda in World War I, and describes the relationship between those who made the films and the propaganda offices that contracted for them: Wellington House, the Ministry of Information, and the War Office Cinematograph Committee. The volume is divided into sections which provide a general description of official British war propaganda, the administration of official film propaganda, film production, the films themselves, and film audiences. The author considers newsreels, documentaries, and commercial features made with the cooperation of the government. There are a few illustrations, a select bibliography of primary and secondary sources, and an extensive list of films by title, producer, and location of extant prints.

Roetter, Charles. *The Art of Psychological Warfare, 1914-1945.* New York: Stein and Day, 1974.
This volume concerns psychological warfare in both world wars. However, the first third of the book defines the concept and explains how it was developed during the Great War as a propaganda weapon to both unsettle the enemy and manipulate the feelings of neutrals. The author describes psychological warfare in general terms as a process

whereby illusions are created that present an audience with a false perception of reality: guards regiments marching past a visiting dignitary's reviewing stand, quickly changing uniforms once out of sight, and marching past again in order to create the illusion that they are far more numerous than is the fact. The author provides examples from both sides in both wars, with illustrations. No bibliography.

Silver, Kenneth E. *Esprit de Corps: The Art of the Parisian Avant-Garde and the First World War, 1914-1925*. Princeton, N.J.: Princeton University Press, 1989.
This volume describes both how French artists contributed to wartime propaganda in World War I and how their postwar art was influenced by the experience of the war. The forms of visual art most commonly employed in this context included photography, painting, poster art, and sculpture. There is an extensive bibliography, and the volume is illustrated by 243 examples of the art being considered. Gris, Picasso, and Ozenfant are but three of the many artists represented.

Street, C. J. C. "Propaganda Behind the Lines," *Cornhill Magazine* 48 (1919), pp. 490-495.
The author worked as a military propagandist for Great Britain in World War I, and this essay describes how military propaganda worked. In the process, the author argues that the Allies did it much better than did the Germans. The reason, he claims, was that "the Allies, keener students of psychology, substituted persuasion for brutality and developed a system of military propaganda that has never before been equalled." The propagandists' principal task, which drew upon this keen understanding of psychology, was "to produce depression and unrest in the enemy camp." The purpose of that was to render the enemy less resistant to attack. This propagandist goes so far as to argue that if the propaganda was properly done, it produced the desired effect better than the most intense artillery bombardment.

Stuart, Sir Campbell. *Secrets of Crewe House: The Story of a Famous Campaign*. London: Hodder and Stoughton, 1920.
Campbell Stuart was a mainstay of British "enemies" propaganda, as it was termed, during World War I, which operated from headquarters in Crewe House, London. This is his personal history of that "famous campaign." Stuart begins with a general definition and description of the good and bad sides of propaganda, and progresses to explain how Crewe house was organized, who ran it, its close relations with military intelligence, and how various propaganda campaigns proceeded. He

also discusses allied cooperation on propaganda. This volume is a primary source on World War I propaganda, in the sense of being a memoir. It also includes the limitation of subjectivity from which memoirs normally suffer. Even so, it is well written and is illuminated with maps, samples of propaganda materials, and photographs of principals within the propaganda organization. No bibliography.

United States Committee on Public Information. *The Creel Report: Complete Report of the Chairman of the Committee on Public Information, 1917, 1918, 1919.* New York: Da Capo Press, 1972. First published by the USCPI in 1920.

This is the complete and detailed report by its director, George Creel, of how the Committee on Public Information (CPI) conducted its "advertising of America" campaign during World War I. Through that campaign, in his words: "We fought indifference and disaffection in the United States and we fought falsehood abroad," which is at least partially true. This volume contains a breakdown of the CPI organization, the work of every division (including the Cartoon Bureau), how enemy propaganda was studied, and much else besides. Creel based his memoir of wartime propaganda work, *How We Advertised America* (entry above), on this report. No bibliography.

Ward, Larry Wayne. *The Motion Picture Goes to War: The U.S. Government Film Effort During World War I.* Ann Arbor, Mich.: UMI Research Press, 1985.

This volume explains United States government use of film in World War I as a medium of both information and persuasion. It also surveys the history of the development of film in the United States prior to the war. Many stills are included as examples of both information and propaganda films. The latter category includes, for example, *Heart of Humanity* (entry below) in which a German officer (Erich von Stroheim) throws a baby out of a window. The former includes public relations shorts such as film of Charlie Chaplin selling war bonds. Select bibliography and film lists.

Warner, Arthur H. "'Sainte-Anastasie': The Censorship in France." *The Outlook*, June 13, 1917, pp. 258-262.

This is a short but useful piece of primary material for the history of World War I propaganda as it relates to censorship. The author describes how the French government was practicing censorship of such French journals as the satiric *Le Rire*. The author lists a number of other censored journals as well, noting the kinds of items that they could not

print, and describes ways in which journalists sought—with only
limited success—to get around the censors.

Welch, David. "A Medium for the Masses: UFA and Imperial German
Film Propaganda During the First World War." *Historical Journal of
Film, Radio and Television* 6, 1 (1986), pp. 85-91.
This short article comments on a set of documents from German
archives which shed further light on the founding of Universum-Film-
Aktiengesellschaft (UFA) in 1917. The documents indicate clearly that
UFA's purpose was to direct both domestic and foreign film propa-
ganda for the German government, and coordinate the activities of
commercial filmmakers to this end. This volume is also an introduction
to the wide range of materials on German film propaganda held in the
Bundesarchiv-Militararchiv in Freiburg-im-Breisgau, Germany.

Propaganda Material

The Adventures of Dick Dolan. Prod. Broadwest Film Company for the
National War Savings Committee, length unknown, 1918. London:
Imperial War Museum Film Archive.
This film encourages British citizens to save rather than squander their
money. Those who save are shown to be admirable, as contrasted with
those who do not and are shown to be self-indulgent and extravagant.

America's Answer. Prod. Committee on Public Information Film Division,
approx. 60 min., 1918. Washington, D.C.: National Archives.
A typical propaganda product put out by the films division of the
official Committee on Public Information, known as the Creel Committee after its director. The films division went into operation on a
wide scale at the end of 1917. This film is full of patriotic title cards.
It opens with a tableau of flag-draped doughboys and a leering "Hun."
It concludes with the title, *America's Answer*, spelled out by hundreds
of sailors who are throwing their hats in the air.

The Battle Cry of Peace. Prod. Vitagraph Company, approx. 80 min.,
1915. Rochester, N.Y.: Eastman House, fragments only.
In this film aimed at convincing a neutral population to be prepared in
the event of war, a young American, Harrison, is converted to the cause
of preparedness. He tries but fails to convert his fiancée's father,
Vandergriff, who is the leader of a peace movement which has been
infiltrated by enemy agents. The climax comes when Vandergriff
releases a flock of doves at a peace rally, and an artillery shell crashes

through the building, killing him and Harrison. The enemy have invaded. Harrison's fiancée is also killed, but by her mother so that she will not be ravaged by the invaders, who look vaguely Germanic.

Be Neutral. Prod. Universal-Powers, approx. 20 min., 1914. Unable to locate copy.

According to some sources, this short film was produced in forty-eight hours by the Universal Film Manufacturing company to plump for President Woodrow Wilson's neutrality proclamation. The work was undertaken without the president's prior knowledge, and certainly was not an official propaganda film. All the same, propaganda it was. A group of factory workers become engaged in a heated argument about the war, and in the process let their factory burn down. If anyone in the audience missed the point, they could hardly misunderstand the supplementary title cards which said: "Don't Take Sides," "Be American First," and "Forget the Horrors of War." Opinion in the United States was given plenty of support in this period for neutrality. See Larry Wayne Ward, *The Motion Picture Goes to War* (entry above under "Channels and Techniques").

Bevan, Edwin. "The Truth About Lies." *The Nineteenth Century* 80 (September 1916), pp. 612-622.

This article attacks official propaganda being disseminated on all sides in World War I. The author points out that no belligerent government can make a comment without having a specific audience in mind, and that leads to lying. He notes various examples from Germany in particular; in fact, Germany is the point of the article. The author goes so far as to argue that allied propaganda lies were actually necessitated by German attitudes toward the Allies from before the war. Being that it is propaganda in its own right, this article is primary source material for the history of World War I propaganda. See Wilson Crewdson, "French Heroes and German Barbarians" (entry below).

The Bond (also known as *Some Bonds I Have Known*). Prod. Charlie Chaplin, approx. 10 min., 1917. Washington, D.C.: Library of Congress/American Film Institute Collection.

This short Charlie Chaplin contribution to the United States war effort features Chaplin's famous little tramp character. Charlie looks at the various kinds of bonds: friendship, love, marriage, and duty. At the end, he points out that the most important bond of all is the Liberty Bond. To show the audience in graphic manner what can be expected from the purchase of war bonds, the tramp pounds the German Kaiser senseless with a huge mallet bearing the inscription "Liberty Bonds."

This film was typical of the involvement of Hollywood stars in selling war bonds. Effective, though said not to be up to Chaplin's usual art.

Britain Prepared. Prod. Charles Urban Trading Company, approx. 20 min., 1916. London: Imperial War Museum.
Charles Urban organized this documentary. He was a naturalized British citizen and campaigner for British propaganda film since the beginning of the war. The film describes how Britain had prepared for war prior to 1914. When it was released in the United States, the point was obvious. Though neutral, the United States also should be "prepared." The film title in the United States was *How Britain Prepared.* It was distributed by the Patriot Film Company, a group with strong British ties. See Larry Wayne Ward, *The Motion Picture Goes to War* (entry above under "Channels and Techniques").

Buchan, John. *Mr. Standfast.* New York: George H. Doran, 1919.
A novel of heroism in defense of the just cause by one of the great adventure writers of World War I. The narrator tells the story of Mr. Standfast, his exploits and heroics, from the Boer War until his death as a British pilot when shot down on the Western Front. Through novels such as this, the British public were given an idealized view of the Great War and what British soldiers were fighting for.

_____. *The 39 Steps.* London: Longman, 1938. First published in 1915.
An adventure novel set in World War I, this story warns the British to be alert for enemy agents in their midst. The hero, Hannay, discovers a German spy ring operating in England. Its agents have killed one man who found them out, and Hannay must expose them without himself being killed. Needless to say he succeeds, and in the process reinforces the danger German espionage represents to Britain and the values for which the British were fighting. Alfred Hitchcock's film version of this novel was set in the 1930s, and the German agents were obviously working for the Nazis, though the British Board of Film Censors would not allow Hitchcock to actually say so.

Chenault, Libby. *Battlelines: World War I Posters from the Bowman Gray Collection.* Chapel Hill: University of North Carolina Press, 1988.
This 200-page volume of World War I posters is from the Bowman Gray III collection at the University of North Carolina. There is a foreword by historian Arthur S. Link, who makes the point that in World War I, "posters were the belligerents' prime means of propaganda and recruitment," and that as they covered virtually every aspect

of war—fund raising, rationing, help for the wounded, support for men in the trenches, and maintaining morale among women and children at home—they reveal "in graphic form much of the military and social history of the wartime period." Libby Chenault opens with a one-page introduction which only indicates the number of examples contained in the Bowman collection. Otherwise, there is no text, only reproductions, mostly in black and white, with translations when needed. The posters cover every conceivable wartime subject from all belligerent countries. No bibliography.

Civilization. Prod. and dir. Thomas Ince, Ince-Triangle, 86 min., 1916. Chicago: Facets Video; New York: Museum of Modern Art; Washington, D.C.: Library of Congress.

A Thomas Ince production which was a classic of pacifist films made in the United States before that country entered World War I. This film features Christ reincarnating himself as a dead submariner in order to rise up and preach the gospel of peace to the world. President Wilson is seen in the epilogue offering his best wishes to Ince for having made the film. It was thought at the time that this film helped Wilson win reelection in 1916, in a United States that was determined to stay out of war. Be that as it may, the film sent another message also, by presenting the Germans as brutes, warmongers, and generally not very nice. In fact, there was so much of this kind of material that the film was censored in Sweden as unsuitable for showing in a neutral country.

Crawford, Anthony R., ed. *Posters of World War I and World War II in the George C. Marshall Research Foundation*. Charlottesville: University Press of Virginia, 1979.

This is an inventory of the 697 posters from both world wars in the George C. Marshall collection. Each one is reproduced in this volume, with a short description of the contents, all in a listing which comprises the second half of the short volume. There is also an introduction by O. W. Riegel, a propaganda analyst for the United States Office of War Information in World War II. Approximately one third of the list pertains to World War I, and the rest to World War II. In both cases all of the principal belligerents are represented.

Crewdson, Wilson. "French Heroes and German Barbarians: Some Impressions of an Englishman Amongst the French Wounded." *The Nineteenth Century* 80 (September 1916), pp. 623-635.

Written by an English visitor to French military hospitals in 1916, this essay is a piece of anti-German propaganda which also makes an appeal for Anglo-French friendship. The language appears detached at first, but subtle phrases give the author away. The Germans "swarmed" over northern France, is one example. The author also contends that barbarous German behavior not only was commonplace but also was carried on under direct orders from German commanders. He offers no proof of this beyond a sort of logic derived from his idea that the close discipline maintained within German army units would have prevented soldiers acting barbarously on their own. Primary material for the history of World War I propaganda. See the essay by Edwin Bevan in this volume of *Nineteenth Century* (entry above).

Darracott, Joseph, ed. *The First World War in Posters.* New York: Dover Publications, 1974.
Assembled by the assistant director and keeper of the department of art at the Imperial War Museum in London, this volume complements that prepared by Darracott and Belinda Loftus on World War II poster art (entry in chapter 5). The contents are reproduced from Imperial War Museum holdings and represent all belligerent nations in the Great War, including French posters extolling the role played in the war by troops from French colonies in Africa. The reproductions are of the highest quality, and the artist is indicated with each poster. Limited bibliography.

Doin' His Bit. Prod. Universal-Powers, approx. 5 min., 1918. Washington, D.C.: Library of Congress/American Film Institute, partial print.
Happy Hooligan, the principal cartoon character, is behind enemy lines. He steals German war plans and, when trying to escape, is forced to hide inside a large German artillery piece. The Germans fire the gun and unwittingly send Happy, clinging to the shell, flying across no-man's-land with the plans tucked in his pocket. Cartoons of this sort were a propaganda forerunner of such World War II classics as "Commando Daffy," which featured Daffy Duck as a British Commando.

The Fall of a Nation. Prod. and dir. Thomas Dixon, National Drama, approx. 90 min., 1916. Unable to locate copy.
This Thomas Dixon feature described a vaguely German military force (though unnamed as such) invading Long Island. There is only token resistance to this invasion that was prepared by enemy agents and misled pacifists. One of the latter, a caricature of William Jennings Bryan, is depicted peeling potatoes in the enemy mess hall. Finally, the enemy are distracted by a large force of American women, whose husbands and sons then lead a successful counterattack. The point

obviously was to rally public opinion to be prepared in the event the United States was forced into World War I. President Woodrow Wilson opposed the project, which he thought would stir up public sentiment needlessly. The film bore a close resemblance to *The Battle Cry of Peace* (entry above) released in 1915. See Larry Wayne Ward, *The Motion Picture Goes to War* (entry above under "Channels and Techniques").

The Great Liberty Bond Hold-Up. Prod. Lasky Studios, approx. 10 min., 1916? Unable to locate copy; however, portions of this film may be in the Library of Congress, Washington, D.C.
Lasky Studios donated this film to the United States government for raising money. The set is a teller's window where war bonds are being sold. Each of a number of Hollywood stars appears and purchases bonds. In each case they appear as a familiar screen character. Mary Pickford is the girl next door, William Hart is a cowboy, and Douglas Fairbanks is a swashbuckler as he leaps over the top of the teller's cage for his bonds. See Larry Wayne Ward, *The Motion Picture Goes to War* (entry above under "Channels and Techniques").

Hapgood, Norman. "Atrocities." *Harper's Weekly* 61 (July 10, 1915), pp. 28-30.
The author, who was editor of this journal, describes his journey to the Western Front and the horrors committed there by the Germans. He asks his readers to consider whether the extent to which atrocities are attributed to the Germans is justified by evidence and responds that from what he has seen, readers can conclude that it is. The ultimate point is a call for punishing Germany when the war is over. The author assures his readers that he does not advocate hate, but rather is only seeking justice. Another example of the German atrocities theory used as a basis for anti-German propaganda.

Heart of Humanity. Prod. Universal-Jewel, 110 min., 1919. Chicago: Facets Video, Washington, D.C.: Library of Congress.
One of many films featuring German atrocities. Erich von Stroheim plays a German officer who enjoys raping Red Cross nurses and throwing babies out of windows. He is finally shot for his troubles by the soldier husband of a nurse. In other examples of this genre, Stroheim played German officers who, variously, burned civilian houses, murdered women and children, and lusted after Belgian maids. In *The Unbeliever* (Edison Company, 1918) Stroheim's character is so vicious he frightens his own men.

Hearts of the World. Prod. and dir. D. W. Griffith, 123 min., 1918. Chicago: Facets Video; London: National Film Archive; Los Angeles: Republic Pictures Home Video; Washington, D.C.: Library of Congress.
A film made in the United States that was also released in Great Britain, this is the story of a young couple's romance interrupted by war. The boy is conscripted and is soon defending his own village against German attack. Many of the couple's relatives are killed in the war, and boy and girl both have narrow escapes. A heartrending moment comes when the girl thinks the boy has been killed. The Germans are portrayed as brutal and unfeeling, the young couple as totally sympathetic, courageous, and long-suffering. The London print is truncated, as extensive cuts were taken from it after the war to remove the extreme anti-German material. This does not appear to apply to the videocassette version.

The Kaiser, the Beast of Berlin. Dir. Rupert Julian, Universal-Jewell, approx. 70 min., 1918. Unable to locate copy.
A major work of the atrocity propaganda genre. This film catalogued every atrocity the Germans were believed to have committed from the first day of the war, including sinking the *Lusitania* and "raping" Belgium. Posters advertising the film drew upon the "melodrama" tradition in music halls in the United States and advised the audience to "hiss the Kaiser" whenever he appeared on screen. (See Larry Wayne Ward, *The Motion Picture Goes to War*, entry above under "Channels and Techniques.")

The Little American. Dir. Cecil B. DeMille, Paramount-Artcraft, approx. 90 min., 1917. Chicago: Facets Video; Rochester, N.Y.: George Eastman House; Washington, D.C.: Library of Congress.
Still another film which features atrocity propaganda. In this instance a young American girl on her way to visit an aunt in France is on a ship, the *Veritania*, which is torpedoed by a German submarine. She survives and finds her way to Europe, where after observing a number of German atrocities, she becomes a spy for the French. She is arrested, is sentenced to face a firing squad, but is saved at the last moment by French soldiers. One of many propaganda films produced in the United States during World War I featuring heroic women.

The Man Who Was Afraid. Dir. Fred E. Wright, Essanay, American Motion Pix, approx. 100 min., 1917. Washington, D.C.: Library of Congress.
Benton Clune is the son of an overprotective mother who has taught him to fear life; however, at heart, he is not a coward. His National

Guard unit is called up when the United States enters World War I, and his terrified mother persuades him to resign from his unit. He is branded a coward as a result, and his girlfriend spurns him. Clune is hurt by the taunting he confronts on all sides, and he leaves his mother to rejoin his unit at the front. He finds them confronted with a much larger enemy force and being threatened with annihilation. The colonel calls for a volunteer to go for reinforcements, and Clune responds. He undergoes many harrowing experiences as he slips through enemy lines, but survives and emerges a hero. His girl comes back to him, his honor is restored, and the audience watching this potboiler may take comfort in the idea that American soldiers will always come through in the end.

Marshall, Logan. *Horrors and Atrocities of the Great War including the Tragic Destruction of the Lusitania.* Branford, Ontario: L. T. Myers, 1915.
Anti-German in large part, the main thrust here is propaganda against war using the commission of atrocities as a major theme. Much of that material cites the Germans, of course: references to the Kaiser as murderer, German barbarism, and the massacre of innocent Belgians, for example. However, the destruction of cathedrals and the horrible weapons of war take over and are applied to all sides. A concluding essay points toward the war as leading, hopefully, to a world where war will never again be permitted. No bibliography.

Ministère des Affaires Étrangères (France). *The Deportation of Women and Girls from Lille.* Translation of a French note to allied governments, 1917, with untranslated documents. New York: George H. Doran, 1917.
These documents, published during the war, contributed to what was known as "atrocity propaganda," in which the other side was accused of committing atrocities against innocent civilians. Posters that sought to spread hate for the enemy among the populations of the belligerent nations were derived from sources such as this. Both sides did it, and it was not without effect, in part because at least some of the allegations—on both sides—were true.

Mothers of France. Prod. Pathé, approx. 100 min., 1917. Unable to locate copy.
This is a Franco-American production starring the aging Sarah Bernhardt, which presents heroic French mothers sending their brave sons off to fight the *boche*. Its propaganda message is, simply, sacrifice for

the cause. It appears to have succeeded. A reviewer noted that the film was "propaganda so subtle and powerful that it must move even the most calloused and neutral observer." (See Larry Wayne Ward, *The Motion Picture Goes to War*, entry above under "Channels and Techniques.")

My Four Years in Germany. Prod. Warner Brothers, approx. 70 min., 1918. Madison: Wisconsin Center for Theater Research; Washington, D.C.: Library of Congress.

Based on the memoirs of the same name written by former United States ambassador to Germany James W. Gerard, the film is presented as "fact not fiction." It is pure propaganda. The German high command is presented through superimpositions comparing each of them to an animal, and the kaiser is displayed as a man with mental problems. He rides a hobbyhorse while making plans to start World War I. Atrocity in Belgium follows, prisoners of war are tormented, and near the end a German officer promises that "America won't fight." This title dissolves into newsreel footage of President Wilson and United States soldiers on the march. The Americans storm across the battlefield, bayonetting Germans left and right. Boasts one soldier, "I promised Dad I'd get six."

Our American Boys in the European War. Prod. American Triangle Company, approx. 60 min., 1916. Washington, D.C.: Library of Congress.

This was an "official," meaning not staged, film shot in Europe by a United States film company with additional footage supplied by the French government. It highlighted activities of volunteers from the United States in such organizations as the American Ambulance Corps in France, and the Franco-American Flying Corps. Made and released while the United States was neutral, the film nevertheless was enormously successful as a fund-raiser in support of these volunteers—not exactly neutral behavior.

"Over There." George M. Cohan, 1917.

The classic patriotic song from World War I, composed and performed on Broadway by one of the most patriotic show-business personalities in the United States. This song became the symbol of United States participation in the war. The lyrics are filled with references to American idealism and not-too-subtle hints that the "Yanks" were coming to save the Europeans from themselves. The song is a major feature of a World War II film about Cohan called *Yankee Doodle Dandy* (entry in chapter 5 under "Propaganda Material") starring James Cagney.

Passelecq, Fernand. *Les Déportations belges à la lumière des documents allemands*. Paris: Berger-Levrault, Libraries-Éditeurs, 1917.

More sources for "atrocity propaganda." This volume presents documentary evidence with commentary regarding the deportation of Belgian citizens, principally male, for forced labor in Germany. The introduction deplores the horror of such an act. The author was an appeals court lawyer in Brussels who was in Paris during the war as a refugee. No bibliography.

The Prussian Cur. Dir. Raoul Walsh, Fox, approx. 65 min., 1918. Unable to locate copy.

One of a number of genuine potboilers which advocated violence against enemy spies. When a German agent tries to induce an aircraft worker to engage in sabotage, the worker reports the agent, who is arrested. A group of pro-Germans seek to rescue him, but they are thwarted at the last minute by the Ku Klux Klan, whose members arrive on horseback, throw the agent back in jail, and force the sympathizers to kiss the American flag. With that particular group emerging the heroes, it is not surprising to learn that Raoul Walsh of D. W. Griffith's *The Birth of a Nation* fame, directed this film. See Larry Wayne Ward, *The Motion Picture Goes to War* (entry above under "Channels and Techniques").

Rickards, Maurice. *Posters of the First World War*. London: Evelyn, Adams and Mackay, 1968.

A collection of wartime posters from all belligerent countries. One theme is to show how different countries used similar representational images to convey certain themes. For example, Austrian and British posters sometimes used nearly identical images of a dragon-slaying knight as a metaphor calling for public support of their respective war efforts. The introduction discusses the aims of the nations in producing posters, and describes a few of the major names associated with poster art. There is an index of all of the artists included in the collection. The variety is wide, and the reproductions excellent. Limited bibliography.

Rudolph, G. A. *War Posters from 1914 through 1918 in the Archives of the University of Nebraska-Lincoln*. Lincoln: University of Nebraska Press, 1990.

A descriptive listing of war posters from the Great War contained in the University of Nebraska archives; 453 entries describe posters from Canada, France, Italy, Great Britain, and the United States, with an index of artists at the end. One of the most complete collections available for posters as a propaganda channel in the Great War. No bibliography.

Stanley, Peter. *What Did* You *Do in the War Daddy? A Visual History of Propaganda Posters*. Melbourne, Australia: Oxford University Press, 1983.
The title of this volume of propaganda posters refers to a particular poster issued in Britain between 1914 and 1918. A little girl sits at the feet of her father and asks what he did in the Great War. On his face is a look of chagrin, indicating that he did very little and is ashamed of the fact. The volume contains materials mainly, but not exclusively, concerned with World Wars I and II. Selections come from all belligerent nations and theaters of war. The volume departs from most collections of war posters, however, in that it includes samples from Australia. This is not surprising as the contents are drawn from the Australian War Memorial and include Australian anti-Vietnam War protest posters from the 1960s. There is an excellent introduction, which explains both the purpose and artistic quality of war posters as the genre evolved over some four decades. Limited bibliography.

Strang, Herbert. *Great Britain and the War: A Book for Boys and Girls*. London: Henry Frowde, 1918.
This pamphlet sets out to explain why Great Britain entered the Great War. Its audience is British children; its purpose to justify the war to them. That justification is the German attack on Belgium and the Austrian attack on Serbia, and that in any case, the war was thrust upon Britain, which the author describes as a nation not normally inclined toward war. The pamphlet is anti-Germany, naturally, which nation is described as a cruel tyrant that preys at sea upon innocent ship travelers. Britain and the United States, the "English-speaking races," are those who will save the day. Of course, the members of the British Empire are included in this linguistic-racial designation. Students of propaganda history may draw useful comparisons between the approach to justifying war taken in this pamphlet addressed to children, and that which argued for imperialism in Robert Baden-Powell's writings on scouting. No bibliography.

Swat the Spy. Prod. Fox, approx. 70 min., 1918. Washington, D.C.: Library of Congress.
In this film, the issue of German spies is treated as comedy, probably because by the time the film was made in 1918, the issue was no longer of great concern. The story concerns a maid and butler who are actually

German agents. The maid even keeps a picture of the kaiser in her quarters. Two small girls throw a pie at it and treat the whole servant spy ring to a series of hilarious indignities. An inept spy catcher also figures in the film. After tracking down a German agent named Schwartz, he throws a sack over the man's head and hauls him off to the police. However, Schwartz turns out to be a "respectable colored gentleman," and the spycatcher is run out of the police station.

Yankee Doodle in Berlin. Prod. Mack Sennett, dir. Richard Jones, Universal, 60 min., 1919. Chicago: Facets Video.

World War I used comedy for propaganda, just as did World War II, and in some cases probably with more effect. In this film, comedian Ben Turpin plays a German squad leader who is so inept as to be a danger to all around him. It is the Keystone Kops in German uniforms at the front. There is also some slapstick in Kaiser Wilhelm's garden, involving an American spy masquerading as a woman.

Chapter 3

PROPAGANDA BEFORE WORLD WAR II:
Variations on a Theme

The first half of the twentieth century was a period of unprecedented change in the industrialized world. Cracks appeared in the facade of empire, social hierarchies were challenged from below, economies were strained by war and depression, revolutions introduced ideologically radical regimes, relations between nations became even more complicated, and democracy often seemed at once the last best hope of humanity and an ideal whose time was past. It was a time also when mass communications raised the impact of advertising to new levels, which had a telling impact upon the cultural, economic, and political behavior of industrial societies.

Propaganda activity reflected all of this. The age of mass communication was a reality after World War I, and organizations, governments, and individuals could now have access to mass communications channels as never before. Therefore, demands for change, whether the change was revolutionary or merely reformist, as well as defense of the status quo, were frequently expressed in propaganda form. Appeals to the emotions of a targeted audience were made through broadcasting, film, press, posters, books, public demonstrations, and oratory. With the growth of mass communications the possibilities of spreading misleading information, or "disinformation," also increased. Resources listed in this chapter address as wide a variety as is possible of propaganda with political ramifications other than waging war, prior to 1939.

History and Function

Akzin, Benjamin. *Propaganda by Diplomats*. Washington, D.C.: Digest Press, 1936.
This essay by the associate editor of *Annuaire Interparlementaire* describes how, in the nineteenth century, foreign diplomats established contact with the small but powerful elites—aristocrats, officials, clerical hierarchy, and social and intellectual circles—in the countries to which they were posted, in order "to establish cordial relations which might be used for discreet propaganda." This is no new discovery, but the author makes the point that this process continued down to and beyond World War I. He describes *agents provocateur* working with diplomatic propagandists, national laws aimed at preventing such opera-

tions, and the role of the press as a channel through which diplomats could operate for propaganda purposes. Appendixes are attached which contain documents relating to the subject matter. No bibliography.

August, Thomas G. *The Selling of the Empire: British and French Imperialist Propaganda, 1890-1940.* Westport, Conn.: Greenwood Press, 1985. This volume is a history of British and French imperialist propaganda during a period when the respective empires of Britain and France reached their zenith and began to decline. The latter fact resulted in ever more zealous efforts on the part of the governments in London and Paris to promote the ideal of empire. The author's main emphasis is on efforts to shape opinion among colonial peoples in favor of imperial ties. The propaganda disseminated in this regard included hints at closer economic ties with the mother country, and more equality between the mother country and certain colonies (those with dominion status in the case of Britain). Themes include imperialism as ideology, propaganda in the classroom, and empire at war. This study complements studies of empire and propaganda by W. J. Reader and John M. MacKenzie (entries below). Select bibliography.

Bagley, William C. "The Army Tests and the Pro-Nordic Propaganda." *Educational Review* 67 (April 1924), pp. 179-187. An intriguing article which criticizes claims made by a "determinist psychologist" named Carl C. Brigham, based upon the results of intelligence tests carried out by the United States Army. Brigham's claim, the author explains, was that these tests demonstrated the innately superior intelligence of whites over non-whites (chiefly blacks), and that the government should pursue immigration and eugenics policies accordingly. The author protests that such a claim would simply "fan the fires of race prejudice with alleged scientific findings." The bulk of the article is devoted to systematically destroying Brigham's argument by explaining how he misused the army research data. The author ends with a plea for racial understanding and against racist propaganda.

Berchtold, William E. "The World Propaganda War." *North American Review* 138, 5 (November 1934), pp. 421-430. "There is hardly a nation in the world whose government is not busier tampering with public opinion than seeking solutions to grave and universal problems," the author writes. His essay surveys the censorship and propaganda "wars" going on at the moment of writing, across Europe, Asia, Latin America, and the United States, and the channels being exploited by them. He describes Nazi and fascist, communist and New Deal propaganda, warns of the danger to democracy in the United States of "the flood of foreign propaganda which has washed our shores," and concludes that if the propaganda wars continue—and he believes that they will—then the result will be that the public no longer trusts any aspect of the media. The author also has an essay criticizing efforts by religious groups to censor Hollywood, beginning on page 503 of this volume.

Borchard, Edwin M. "Dragging America into War." *Current History* 40 (July 1934), pp. 392-401.
The author, a Yale law professor, makes a case for United States isolationism and for the League of Nations doing the job for which it was intended: pressing the peace of Europe through negotiation. He warns against allowing propaganda on behalf of any nation or cause to disrupt American commitment to, and regard for, international law. This article clearly was inspired by the breakdown of international disarmament talks in 1934 and by the danger that fact posed to creating an environment conducive to war. The tone indicates that the author was very conscious of the role propaganda was playing between the world wars in international relations generally.

Buchsbaum, Jonathan. "Vote for the Front Populaire! Vote Communiste! *La Vie est à nous.*" *Quarterly Review of Film* 10 (Summer 1985), pp. 183-212.
In 1936, the French Communist party commissioned Ciné-Liberté, a fledgling film company dedicated to the use of film for political purposes, to make a propaganda film supporting the *Front Populaire* in the upcoming national assembly elections. The film was called *La Vie est à nous* (entry below under "Propaganda Material"), and it purported to be a documentary. This article analyzes the film and how it was made in the context of French politics in that tumultuous decade, pointing out the various ways in which the filmmakers used trick photography to make fascists look foolish in some cases, and menacing and dangerous in others. The author tends toward hyperbole in praise of the film, but the article makes a useful contribution to French political filmography all the same.

Casey, Ralph D. "The National Publicity Bureau and British Party Propaganda." *Public Opinion Quarterly* 3, 4 (October 1939), pp. 623-634.
This article describes what was at the time of writing the recent history and function of political party propaganda in Great Britain, as associ-

ated with general (parliamentary) elections. The specific reference is to propaganda created and disseminated by the National Publicity Bureau (NPB). This organization was created by the National Government which had formed across party lines after the great financial crisis of 1931, and which caused the Labour party to break with its leader and then prime minister, Ramsay MacDonald. The author's point is that the NPB's contribution to improving the quality and sophistication of electoral propaganda through film and broadcasting had been overlooked, and that this contribution changed forever the "traditions of British electoral propaganda." See also Mariel Grant, *Propaganda and the Role of the State in Inter-War Britain* (entry below).

Clements, Frank. "The British Council in Europe." *Quarterly Review* 273 (1939), pp. 33-45.
This article, published on the eve of World War II, describes the work of the British Council in Europe, the function of which, then as later, was to acquaint people with English language and culture. The author begins by pointing out that the Council's "aims are strictly limited," and that it in no way resembles an official propaganda ministry. Be that as it may, what follows is a description of an agency operating under the auspices of the British Foreign Office to promote British interests abroad. Perhaps it was a slip of the pen when the author referred to a future when Britain had "ten times" existing funds "to spend in Europe on propaganda." The main objective of the article appears to be to convince the British government that an increase in British Council funding would be money well spent. See Philip M. Taylor, *The Projection of Britain* (entry below).

Cockett, Richard. *Twilight of Truth: Chamberlain, Appeasement and the Manipulation of the Press.* New York: St. Martin's Press, 1989.
The outgrowth of a Ph.D. thesis at the University of London, this volume offers an explanation for why the mainstream British press supported Neville Chamberlain and appeasement from 1937 to 1939, engaging in what the author terms an "incestuous relationship between Whitehall and the press." His argument is that the press had no choice, for the various major newspapers had evolved in the 1930s into party political weapons. The next step, by implication, was for the press generally and certain papers in particular to become political propaganda channels for the government as well as for political parties. The author concludes that this was what had transpired by the time appeasement policy took the negative turn in 1937 with which it has since been associated. Extensive bibliography.

Cole, Robert. "The Conflict Within: Sir Stephen Tallents and Planning for Propaganda Overseas Before the Second World War." *Albion* 14 (1982), pp. 50-71.

Planning for what became the wartime British Ministry of Information began in the mid-1930s under the direction of British Broadcasting Corporation Controller of Public Relations Sir Stephen Tallents. This article describes the slow and painful progress of that experience with reference to overseas propaganda, with opposition coming mainly from Foreign Office turf protectors and treasury traditionalists who considered the process wasteful. It ends with Tallents being dismissed from his responsibilities for challenging the views of those who wished to proceed cautiously with propaganda planning. His successor, Ernest Fass, knew little about propaganda, but he "would do what he was told." The result was a propaganda bureau that was ill-prepared when war came in 1939.

Cornebise, Alfred E. "The Refinement of Allied Propaganda: The Case of *Nachrichtendienst.*" *German Studies Review* 2, 1 (February 1979), pp. 30-48.

This article examines allied press propaganda during the occupation of the Ruhr which followed Germany's default on reparations payments in 1923. First the Allies cracked down on German newspapers in the Ruhr which called for resistance to occupation. Then the French launched their own propaganda effort, which included distributing broadsides, posters, and pamphlets, and, above all, establishing a propaganda newspaper called *Nachrichtendienst.* It was published in Düsseldorf on confiscated presses and circulated in French occupied territory. The paper pursued a "divide and conquer" policy; that is, it called for separation of the Ruhr from Germany. The author concludes that the lesson of this press propaganda campaign by France was remembered above all by Adolf Hitler, who employed *Nachrichtendienst* propaganda techniques as the National Socialist leader.

Davey, Arthur. *The British Pro-Boers, 1877-1902*. Cape Town, South Africa: Tafelberg Publishers, 1978.

The author tells the history of a British political movement that was anti-imperialist and Little England in its orientation. His book also is the history of how that political movement used the mass media in an effort to place the British public on its side in opposition to that of the Unionists and other imperialist political groups. The study carries through to the end of the Boer War in 1902, by which time press propaganda on the issue of pro- and anti-Boer as party politics had become virulent. The author draws upon the contents of dozens of newspapers as well as pulpit polemics and pamphlets written by prominent men, all of which aimed to influence public opinion. The volume provides insights into both turn-of-the-century British politics and the manipulation of the media by politicians pushing a not always straightforward agenda. Select bibliography.

Eberle, Matthias. "George Grosz: The Irate Dandy: Art as a Weapon in the Class Struggle," in Matthias Eberle, *World War I and the Weimar Artists*. New Haven, Conn.: Yale University Press, 1985.
This chapter looks at the work of a German artist who devoted his work after World War I to an attack on the Weimar establishment. He was inspired by the war, and by the bitterness which it engendered in Germany, to turn his art into a political and social weapon. In consequence, this art fits comfortably within the "individuals with an ax to grind" classification of propagandists. His art attacked all of the pillars of Weimar society, from bureaucrats and authority figures to clergy. Ironically, when the Nazis, who also regularly propagandized against Weimar, came to power, his was among the art that they proscribed. This chapter sheds much light on the relationship between satire and propaganda in the particular setting of pre-Hitler Germany.

Fielding, Raymond. *The American Newsreel, 1911-1967*. Norman: University of Oklahoma Press, 1972.
Like *The March of Time* by the same author (next entry), this book provides the history of one particular example of film as a news communication channel that often played a propaganda role. This was particularly true in wartime when newsreels portrayed "us" in valiant or even heroic terms, and "them" as the ugly enemy. The author suggests that in at least one respect the newsreel was made for propaganda: the newsreel was a "potpourri of motion picture news footage" which offered only a very superficial look at the news. It was easy to misrepresent reality, and that, the author concludes, was precisely the reason newsreels lost credibility after World War II when television began providing news coverage in much greater depth. This volume describes all aspects of newsreel filmmaking and showing, including the politics sometimes associated with it. Illustrations and an extensive bibliography.

_____. *The March of Time, 1935-1951*. New York: Oxford University Press, 1978.
This volume tells the history of *The March of Time*, a film documentary series associated with *Time* magazine founder Henry Luce. Its purpose

was to explore vital social and political issues in the United States and elsewhere. The films were released monthly and were shown in movie houses preceding the feature of the evening. Intended as educational documentaries, *March of Time* films played a propaganda role as well. Many episodes in the later 1930s, for example, sought to raise sympathy for victims of Depression-induced unemployment and hunger, while others took a stand against such Depression-era demagogues as Huey Long, Gerald L. K. Smith, Father Charles Coughlin, and, in Europe, Adolf Hitler and Benito Mussolini. The author describes the series carefully and notes that sometimes the filmmakers "created" scenes that did not exist in fact—such as when James Conant and Vannevar Bush shook hands, ostensibly while lying on the sands of the New Mexico desert, following the successful 1945 atom bomb test. They were actually filmed lying on the floor of a garage in Boston. Illustrations and extensive bibliography.

Fraser, Lindley. *Germany Between Two Wars: A Study of Propaganda and Guilt.* London: Oxford University Press, 1945.
As World War II was winding down, historians understandably began to examine that horrendous event, seeking explanations for what had happened. Why had Germany gone so terribly wrong? Such is the point of this volume, started not long before the allied landing in Normandy in June 1944. In this instance, the author argues that the Germans had been misled by their own propagandists both before and during the National Socialist period. Therein lay the explanation for "what went wrong." He writes about German response to the Versailles treaty of 1919 (the "stab-in-the-back" theory), and about propaganda disseminated before and during the Nazi period to persuade the Germans that they were not responsible for World War I and that they had a right to "living space" even if it came at the expense of others. He ends with speculation about whether or not future propaganda might produce World War III. No bibliography, but Woodrow Wilson's Fourteen Points document is reproduced in the appendix.

Grant, Mariel. *Propaganda and the Role of the State in Inter-War Britain.* Oxford, England: Clarendon Press, 1994.
The author explores British domestic propaganda prior to World War II. Her point is to demonstrate that thinking about, and understanding of, propaganda in Britain when the wartime Ministry of Information was being planned in the late 1930s was more sophisticated than historians and others have generally thought. The book opens with an overview of a half century of writing about British

propaganda in the prewar period. It then explores the role played in interwar propaganda by such organizations as the Stationary Office and the General Post Office. The author concludes with a discussion of the debate which went on in that period concerning whether or not control over official propaganda should be centralized. Extensive bibliography of primary and secondary sources.

Grierson, John. "Propaganda: A Problem for Educational Theory and for Cinema." *Sight and Sound* 2 (1933), pp. 119-121.
This article was written in the early days of talking pictures by the architect of Britain's Documentary Film Movement. The author examines the potential use of propaganda film in education. "Propaganda is the art of public persuasion," he explains, and goes on to argue that while the word "savours of the bamboozling and bludgeoning of public opinion with which it was associated during the war," this need not be its only function. He then makes a case for producing and disseminating propaganda that would serve the public good, by which he means propaganda to educate the British public in the practice of democracy.

Gross, John, ed. *The Age of Kipling.* New York: Simon and Schuster, 1972.
Twenty writers contributed to this anthology of essays about English writer Rudyard Kipling, many of which concern the question of Kipling as propagandist. Few writers were more committed to the British Empire than was Kipling, who filled his novels and poetry with the idea that it served a great purpose and must be preserved. Among the essays which indicate Kipling's propaganda bent are George Shepperson, "Kipling and the Boer War," Eric Stokes, "Kipling's Imperialism," and Bernard Bergonzi, "Kipling and the First World War." The volume is thoroughly illustrated with photographs and reproductions of propaganda posters and cartoons that illuminate elements of Kipling's life and work. An informative and entertaining collection which not only explains Kipling, but explains how literature can be used as a propaganda channel. Bibliography in endnotes.

Hale, Oron James. *Publicity and Diplomacy: With Special Reference to England and Germany, 1890-1914.* Gloucester, Mass.: Peter Smith, 1964.
A history of war-origins, in one respect, but specifically a history of war-origins with reference to how publicity that "sprang from private sources" influenced British and German foreign policy prior to 1914. The author argues that "newspaper editors, party leaders, private persons, and pressure groups employed all the techniques of propa-

ganda, agitation and advertising to bend the foreign policy of the government to their will." Chapter headings include "The Press and the Kruger Telegram," "Publicity and the Birth of *Weltpolitik*," and "Interviews and Indiscretions," among others. Bibliography only in footnotes.

Hall, Alex. "The War of Words: Anti-Socialist Offensives and Counter-propaganda in Wilhelmine Germany, 1890-1914." *Journal of Contemporary History* 11, 2 and 3 (July 1976), pp. 11-42.
The German Socialist Party (SPD) was a growing concern during the reign of Wilhelm II, which worried the government and its upper- and middle-class allies. This article examines how newspapers and such patriotic groups as war veterans' organizations were used to propagandize against the socialists. It also assesses the nature of SPD propaganda put out in order to further its own development. The conclusion drawn is that as the SPD held 110 seats in the 1912 Reichstag, their propaganda was apparently the more effective.

Harding, T. Swann. "Genesis of One 'Government Propaganda Mill.'" *Public Opinion Quarterly* 11 (1947-1948), pp. 227-235.
The author, a longtime official of the United States Department of Agriculture (USDA), provides here a brief history of USDA information services, public relations, "or 'propaganda mill' as you wish." He traces that history since the 1860s, and his point appears to be that this form of "propaganda" provides an indispensable service to American agricultural interests. An implicit additional point may be to challenge the idea that propaganda should be regarded primarily in negative terms.

Hays, Will H. *The Memoirs of Will H. Hays.* New York: Doubleday, 1955.
This is the autobiography of the man best remembered as head of the Motion Picture Producers and Distributors of America (MPPDA) from 1922 to 1945. During those years, Hollywood "came of age," so to speak, and undertook, with Hays at the helm, to regulate itself in order that such people in Congress as Senator Gerald P. Nye of North Dakota would have no excuse for instituting the kind of film censorship that existed in Great Britain under the British Board of Film Censors. The last third of this autobiography is of primary interest for the study of censorship. In those pages, Hays tells the story of his years with the MPPDA, recounting in detail his defense of certain Hollywood films, particularly those in the 1930s which were thought to be urging the United States away from its isolationism and toward taking a stand

against fascist dictatorships in Europe. A single illustration—a photograph of Hays—and no bibliography.

Higham, Charles Frederick. *Looking Forward: Mass Education Through Publicity*. New York: Alfred A. Knopf, 1920.
Written shortly after World War I by a member of Britain's parliament, this volume tries to make a case for linking the functions of propaganda to the business of education in the modern world. In Higham's words, "this small book is an attempt to show the educational value of organized publicity in educating people in the mass." He argues that "uninformed democracies are the greatest danger confronting modern states." In order to fulfill their proper role of making appropriate responses to issues that may confront the state of which they are a part, citizens of democracies must be well informed. The author warns against "haphazard publicity," calls for a proper science of public opinion and a state publicity bureau, and draws attention to the potential importance to his schemes of such new mass communications media as the cinema. This is primary source material for propaganda history. No bibliography.

Himelstein, Morgan Y. *Drama Was a Weapon: The Left-Wing Theatre in New York, 1929-1941*. New Brunswick, N.J.: Rutgers University Press, 1963.
"Armed with the slogan, 'Drama is a weapon,' the Communist party attempted to infiltrate and control the American stage during the Great Depression of the nineteen-thirties." From this opening, the author proceeds to examine how that effort was the central feature of the New Theatre movement in New York. Advocates of the movement encouraged new dramatic forms and techniques in order to "propagandize the radical ideas of the thirties." The author refers to "agitprop" being much in evidence within the movement. The volume follows a topical history approach, dealing in turn with "workers theatres," theater union, labor stage, and specific theatres such as the Mercury. It ends with a chapter on the failure of the Communist party to carry out its long-term purpose. The volume is illustrated with photographs of theatrical performances, while the bibliography lists both titles of plays that figured in the movement and secondary sources dealing with such issues as fascism, racism, the Ku Klux Klan, and trade unions.

Hobson, J. A. *The Psychology of Jingoism*. London: Grant Richards, 1901.
This volume is (a) a criticism of "jingoism" functioning as a propaganda channel, and (b) a piece of propaganda in its own right. J. A. Hobson was an activist in Britain against the Boer War in South Africa

(1899-1902), which fact inspired him to write this book, and against the Great War in 1914-1918. Hobson defines jingoism as "that inverted patriotism whereby the love of one's own nation is transformed into the hatred of another nation, and the fierce craving to destroy the individual members of that other nation." He proceeds to examine how jingoism appeals to those emotions engendered by hate, citing such examples as a line from the *Indian Planters' Gazette*, to the effect that Boers should be "slain with the same ruthlessness that they slay a plague-infected rat." This is an easily read volume, because Hobson hoped to make his point clear to anyone willing to pick up the book.

Johnson, Niel M. *George Sylvester Viereck: German-American Propagandist*. Urbana: University of Illinois Press, 1972.

"The biography of an enigma" might be an accurate description of this study of the life of George Sylvester Viereck, who was an apologist for Germany before and during both world wars. The author, along with a great many others who knew of Viereck, reckoned him to be a failed propagandist for Germany who, not surprisingly, eventually was tried for sedition. However, this writer differs from many others in that he claims Viereck's complex mentality makes it impossible to judge him so simply, and that even though he was pro-German and even pro-fascist, Viereck was primarily committed to the United States. This biography places Viereck in the context of the world wars, but its emphasis is on the evolution of the subject's views and how he was led into being a sometimes anti-Semitic propagandist for German interests. Extensive bibliography.

Juergens, George. *News from the White House: The Presidential-Press Relationship in the Progressive Era*. Chicago: University of Chicago Press, 1981.

A history of how the presidency first used the press as an instrument of policy, beginning during the administration of Theodore Roosevelt. The author explains that it was possible to appropriate the press in this way because during this period, the "Progressive Era," the press evolved into big business. Newspapers were under enormous pressure to increase circulation, and as they did, they opened up contact with a mass readership. Roosevelt appealed as a Progressive to that mass audience through the press, and, the author argues, he did so consciously. Roosevelt's strategy was: "If he could seize the headlines and influence the way reporters wrote about him, it would not matter a great deal what the press might have to say about him on its inside pages." Illustrations and an extensive bibliography.

Knowles, Dorothy. *The Censor, the Drama and the Film, 1900-1934.* London: George Allen and Unwin, 1934.

Censorship grew increasingly strict in Britain between the world wars. This volume argues that the effect upon society was strictly negative, doing damage to both democracy and human rights. Every institution practices censorship, the author argues, noting that when one asks "Who are the censors?" the answer is that the censors are "Society, the Church, Educational Authorities, the local Fire Brigade, the Police, the Board of Trade, the Admiralty, the War Office, the Home Office, the Foreign Office, the Lords, and the Commons." That half of the book concerned with film pays a great deal of attention to film censorship, whose purpose was thought to be propaganda. Extensive bibliography.

Leeper, R. A. "British Culture Abroad." *Contemporary Review* 148 (August 1935), pp. 201-207.

R. A. Leeper was an Australian who served for years in the British Foreign Office as a cultural propagandist. He was a major figure in organizing the British Council, the main function of which was, and continues to be, to disseminate cultural propaganda abroad. This essay describes what useful and good things cultural propaganda achieves, and indicates some of the ways in which it may be disseminated. See Philip M. Taylor, *The Projection of Britain* (entry below).

MacCann, Richard Dyer. *The People's Films: A Political History of U.S. Government Motion Pictures.* New York: Hastings House, 1973.

This book was first written in the early 1950s as a Ph.D. thesis at Harvard University. Here is the published—and updated—version that appeared twenty years later. For this reason, the bulk of the volume deals with government official films and their propaganda function from before and during World War II. Only three chapters, added for purposes of this volume, concern official films from the postwar period. The author's purpose remains unchanged from the original version: to examine the extent to which "official" films can be called documentaries rather than propaganda. In his words, "Government tasks are diverse and sometimes delicate. When the persuasive purpose is agreed upon and dramatic weapons acceptable, there may occur what can be called a 'documentary movement'": in other words, the type of film made in Britain in the 1930s to "educate" the public about the post office, empire free trade, British industry, and so forth. The author applies the same principle to official United States government films. His topics in this volume include consideration of these official films in relation to both domestic and foreign policy, such organizations as the Creel Committee (World War I) and the Office of War Information (World War II) which made, or commissioned, films for propaganda purposes. Illustrations; bibliography is limited to footnote entries.

MacDonald, Callum A. "Radio Bari: Italian Wireless Propaganda in the Middle East and British Countermeasures, 1934-38." *Middle Eastern Studies* 13 (1977), pp. 195-207.
The Middle East was an area of considerable stress for Britain between the world wars, owing to the British having "inherited" a significant portion of that area following the collapse of the Ottoman Empire at the end of World War I. However, fascist Italy had designs on the Middle East as part of Mussolini's policy of making the Mediterranean into an "Italian lake." During the 1930s, Italy began broadcasting anti-British propaganda into the Middle East, particularly into Palestine and Egypt, with a view to rousing Arab resistance to British control. This article describes the motivation, analyzes the nature and content of the broadcasts, and examines the debate in Britain within and without parliament, regarding how to respond. Sir John Reith, British Broadcasting Corporation (BBC) director general, insisted that British broadcasts be "straight news" and not propaganda. Many members of the House of Commons insisted that only propaganda would provide an effective counter to the Italian broadcasts. In the end, a compromise was reached. When the BBC began broadcasting in Arabic in 1938, the content was propaganda, but of a sort much milder than what the Italians were disseminating.

MacKenzie, John M., ed. *Imperialism and Popular Culture*. Manchester, England: Manchester University Press, 1986.
This collection of ten articles, including an introduction by John MacKenzie, examines aspects of how the British Empire was popularized from the late nineteenth through the mid-twentieth centuries, in literature, art, music hall, feature film, and radio. In some instances, the popularizing was conducted through direct propaganda campaigns, such as the Empire Marketing Board scheme to sell the idea of empire free trade. These articles are well researched and well written by professional historians. A few illustrations and bibliography contained in footnotes. See W. J. Reader, *'At Duty's Call'* (entry below).

Marchand, Roland. *Advertising the American Dream: Making Way for Modernity, 1920-1940*. Berkeley: University of California Press, 1985.
In essence, this book is a study of how a social revolution was created in the post-World War I United States, through the art of advertising.

The social revolution in question was the "American dream": conspicuous consumption of a wide variety of products, without which, the consumers were told, their lives would be incomplete and their place in society lessened. It is the author's contention that advertising created the dream and in the process persuaded the American people to embrace it. "I marvelled," the author writes in his introduction, "that historians could have written so much about social values and popular attitudes without examining the ads—a profusion of documents aimed precisely at reflecting those values and shaping those ideas!" Advertising as social propaganda is the point here, and it is made extremely well. The volume is illustrated with examples of advertisements which contain variations of classic propaganda techniques including heroic imagery and the appeal to such emotions as love, joy, fear, and even hate. Bibliographic essay.

Martin, Kingsley. "Public Opinion: Censorship During the Crisis." *Political Quarterly* 10 (1939), pp. 128-134.
The author, a noted twentieth century English journalist, comments on how "the present British government have been insidiously destroying the traditional liberties of Britain out of a desire to appease the dictators." The context is the Sudeten crisis of September 1938, which led to the Munich Agreement, and the subject is censorship of press and public meeting, which sought to suppress opposition to the governments' handling of the crisis. The author describes accusations against the government delivered in parliament and argues that they are well founded.

Morris, A. J. A. *The Scaremongers: The Advocacy of War and Rearmament, 1896-1914*. London: Routledge and Kegan Paul, 1984.
This is not a study of war origins, the author points out, but rather of British journals and journalists which, for all practical purposes, worked to convince the British public that war with Germany was to be expected and that increasing Britain's armaments was an inescapable requisite for survival. There is some speculation in an "epilogue" as to what is required for a newspaper to be a persuasive influence upon public opinion, using as context the British public mind before 1914. Select bibliography.

Nelson, Joyce. "*Mr. Smith Goes to Washington:* Capra, Populism and Comic-Strip Art." *Journal of Popular Film* 3, 3 (Summer 1974), pp. 245-254.
Many United States senators were outraged by Frank Capra's 1939 film, *Mr. Smith Goes to Washington*. Was this because Capra made the film as propaganda for the New Deal? At least partially true, the author

argues, but suggests that the propaganda was populist "wish fulfill-
ment" rather than serious New Deal ideology. The article describes
scenes from the film which support this thesis and discusses Capra's
personal commitment to the New Deal.

Odegard, Peter H. *Pressure Politics: The Story of the Anti-Saloon League*.
New York: Columbia University Press, 1928.
A study of the Anti-Saloon League, which was one of the organizations
that helped effect the 1919 Volstead Act prohibiting the sale of alcoholic
beverages in the United States. The author is interested mainly in the
League's tactics. That these tactics and the messages they disseminated
were propaganda is clear from the author's description, and from the
fact that the index entries under "Propaganda" run to more than one
entire column. The book also contains reproductions of Anti-Saloon
League leaflets and cartoons which are very obviously propaganda. The
author's purpose, in part, is to recognize that the League's campaigns
were political and that it had the right to engage in politics (a right many
people disputed), even though it was a religious organization. There are
extensive appendixes with documents showing voting patterns for and
against Prohibition. This study is only marginally biased despite being
written during the Prohibition Era. Bibliography in footnotes.

Pronay, Nicholas, and Philip M. Taylor. "'An Improper Use of Broadcasting . . . ': The British Government and Clandestine Radio Propaganda
Operations Against Germany During the Munich Crisis and After."
Journal of Contemporary History 19, 3 (July 1984), pp. 357-384.
This article is based upon a document called the Wellesley Memorandum, discovered ca. 1982 in British government archives. The memorandum told the story of secret British radio broadcasts into Germany
made during the period of the 1938 Sudeten crisis from broadcast
stations in Luxembourg and elsewhere on the continent, by order of
Prime Minister Neville Chamberlain. The object was to present Britain's position concerning the crisis to German listeners, which, of
course, was not in the interests of the Nazis. The authors describe the
contents of the memorandum and comment on their significance for
rethinking the use made of propaganda in international affairs by the
British government before World War II.

Reader, W. J. *'At Duty's Call': A Study in Obsolete Patriotism*. Manchester, England: Manchester University Press, 1988.
Why did millions of British men and women volunteer for service to
the nation at the time of the Great War? This volume examines a gener-

ation of cultural propaganda which inculcated a positive view of the empire and an attitude of cultural, national, and even racial superiority. This propaganda was disseminated through popular entertainment, education, juvenile literature, the arts, the press, and even from the pulpit. The author argues that the result was a set of attitudes favorable to war and a willingness to make the ultimate sacrifice. Select bibliography.

Reid, Franklyn. *The British Press and Germany, 1936-1939*. Oxford, England: Clarendon Press, 1971.
The subject here is appeasement, Britain's German policy in the last years before World War II. It is treated in the context of the role played by the British press generally and British foreign correspondents specifically, in the shaping of public opinion regarding foreign policy. The author notes leftist correspondents who railed against fascist movements, and rightist correspondents who "glorified the civilizing mission of the British Empire ... and saw the greatest threat Western Civilization had ever faced ... in Soviet Russia." The latter also put the case, directly and indirectly, for Germany's position in European affairs. The ultimate point in this volume is that British newspapers of the later 1930s provided the "funnel" through which appeasement policy was sold to the British nation. The bibliography is mainly of secondary sources.

Renshaw, Patrick. "The IWW and the Red Scare of 1917-1924." *Journal of Contemporary History* 3, 4 (October 1968), pp. 63-72.
A brief but pithy examination of how the Industrial Workers of the World (IWW) movement touched off the "Red Scare" paranoia that informed populist politics in the United States during and after World War I. The author shows that xenophobia played a role in this paranoia, since many of the "Wobblies," as IWW members were called, were immigrants. Otherwise, the paranoia was produced by the IWW itself, which was "little more than a free-wheeling propaganda organization." Indeed, the author argues, the whole experience was a form of a propaganda war waged between the IWW and its supporters on one side, and the Red-baiting, anti-Bolshevik press, supported by Ku Klux Klan hate campaigns against foreigners and for racial purity, on the other.

Reynolds, Mary T. "The General Staff as a Propaganda Agency, 1908-1914." *Public Opinion Quarterly* 3, 3 (July 1939), pp. 391-408.
The author looks at the organization of the general staff of the United States Army prior to World War I for the purpose of explaining how it was used as a propaganda agency in support of preparedness. A brief explanation of how the General Staff was conceived and created is

followed by analysis of its propaganda work through reports to the public on the state of the army, efforts to influence legislation (a practice continued by the Joint Chiefs of Staff after World War II), and dramatization through press manipulation of the "glamour of war." The author discusses differences between "official" and "un-official" propaganda disseminated by the General Staff and concludes by taking notice of what General Staff propaganda says about power, government, and government service.

Rice, Arnold. *The Ku Klux Klan in American Politics*. Washington, D.C.: Public Affairs Press, 1962.
This history of the Ku Klux Klan aims at assessing how it attempted to influence politics in the United States, and to secure its particular racist, anti-Semitic, and anti-Catholic agenda. It traces Klan activities from its origins in 1915 through and after World War II. The author describes Klan efforts at political influence as being both largely ineffective and largely carried out as crude propaganda, which mostly was the propaganda of terror and intimidation. However, the Klan Propagation Department set up in 1920 also put out print propaganda that "strove to show how the Klan was the country's only bulwark against the evil forces of the Negro, Catholic, Jew, and immigrant." The Klan was most successful in selling this viewpoint in the South, from which region it recruited most of its members. Bibliography is in endnotes.

Richards, Jeffrey. "The British Board of Film Censors and Content Control in the 1930s: Images of Britain." *Historical Journal of Film, Radio and Television* 1, 2 (1981), pp. 95-116.
British cinema came into its own between the world wars, and so did the British Board of Film Censors. BBFC control, the author notes, was much tighter over film than over live stage performance, simply because "film was *the* mass medium, regularly patronized by the working class." He draws upon examples of several films to demonstrate his points when he analyzes the attitude, which he describes as elitist, the purpose, and nature of the BBFC, an organization created originally by the film industry itself. See James C. Robertson, *The British Board of Film Censors* (entry in chapter 1 under "General Studies").

Riegel, O. W. *Mobilizing for Chaos: The Story of the New Propaganda*. New Haven, Conn.: Yale University Press, 1934.
Written and published during the years of political crisis in Germany that produced the regime of Adolf Hitler, this book warns that propaganda dissemination can be abused in order to further the interests of

anti-democratic politics. The volume opens by quoting Joseph Goebbels, the Nazi minister of propaganda, who claimed that "it is the absolute right of the State to supervise the formation of public opinion." The author sees nationalism as the driving force in anti-democratic propaganda and describes how communications may be manipulated for negative propaganda purposes. The cynicism behind this volume is evident in the final chapter, which is titled "Toward a New Dark Age?" Endnotes include bibliographical references.

Rosenthal, Michael. *The Character Factory: Baden-Powell and the Origins of the Boy Scout Movement.* New York: Pantheon Books, 1984.
This volume is a study of Robert Baden-Powell in the context of his greatest achievement, founding the Boy Scout movement and, subsequently, the Girl Guides auxiliary, in Great Britain. The author argues that from the beginning the purpose of Scouting was to save Britain from what Tory politicians, social imperialists and military leaders perceived as moral, physical, and military weakness. The object of moral, physical and military strength was to maintain the empire. As Baden-Powell liked to say (the phrase originated with David Lloyd George), "You cannot maintain an A-1 Empire on C-3 men." Scouting was used to indoctrinate young male Britons with those values which would maintain the empire, and which, in due course, encouraged them to volunteer in their hundreds of thousands for the Western Front in World War I, while Guiding served to indoctrinate young females with those values considered appropriate to the role of women within British society. Scouting and Guiding proved to be one of the most successful ventures into social propaganda with long-term political goals in the twentieth century. Select bibliography.

_____. "Knights and Retainers: The Earliest Version of Baden-Powell's Boy Scout Scheme." *Journal of Contemporary History* 15, 4 (October 1980), pp. 603-617.
This article contributes further evidence that Boy Scout founder Robert Baden-Powell was a propagandist of British patriotism, whose vision of service contributed much to preparing British youth for the trials of World War I. The author argues that a letter written by Baden-Powell to the Eton College *Chronicle* in 1904 makes clear that he meant scouting to instill patriotic idealism in boys who participated. He further points out that Baden-Powell joined others in the National Service League to warn repeatedly of the threat of foreign invasion (see Erskine Childers, *Riddle of the Sands*, entry below under "Propaganda Material"), using this propaganda to "sell schemes for the proper indoctrination of youth."

The title of this article reflects Baden-Powell's equation of public school prefects and scout patrol leaders as "knights," while public school boys and boy scouts were equated as "retainers."

Rotha, Paul. *Documentary Diary: An Informal History of the British Documentary Film, 1928-1939.* New York: Hill and Wang, 1973.
The author's primary theme in this volume is the history of documentary filmmaking in Britain. That history includes the deployment of documentary film for propaganda purposes. Such chapters as "The EMB (Empire Marketing Board) Film Unit," "The GPO (Government Post Office) Film Unit," and "The Peace Film," make clear how important such films were thought to be in disseminating propaganda relative to the issues of working conditions in mines and factories, the use of telephones, sustaining peace through international negotiation, and bolstering resistance to fascism. The author touches all bases, including points of criticism against many of the films produced by GPO and others. Select bibliography more useful to film students than to those interested mainly in film as propaganda. See Paul Swann, *The British Documentary Film Movement* (entry below).

Rühlmann, Paul M. *Kulturpropaganda: Grundsätzliche Darlegungen und Auslandsbeobachtungen.* Charlottenburg, Germany: Deutsche Verlagsgesellschaft für Politik und Geschichte, 1919.
Published the year after World War I ended, which may have been at least part of the inspiration (that is, defeated Germany needing to reconstruct its image abroad), this volume offers a study of cultural propaganda disseminated in foreign countries. The first chapter lays down definitions of what cultural propaganda involves, and extrapolates principles upon which it should rest. This chapter also includes discussion of, among other things, institutions that may be used for propaganda purposes such as language schools in foreign countries, theater, the arts generally, and tourism. Remaining chapters cite examples of the above, beginning with France and going on to include Spain, the United States, Great Britain, and Japan. France occupied most of the author's attention, however, which suggests once more that the recently ended world war may have had much to do with inspiring this volume. Limited bibliography.

Russell, Bertrand. *Free Thought and Official Propaganda.* London: George Allen and Unwin, 1922.
Bertrand Russell, British philosopher and political activist for much of the twentieth century, gave the talk of which this volume is the printed

text, in March 1922, less than three years after World War I had ended. The propaganda operations which had been a prominent feature of that conflict, were much on his mind in this talk, as was official censorship. His ultimate object was to promote the importance of free thinking in opposition to the employment of propaganda, particularly as a function of education and economic development. With regard to education, for example, Russell argued that "the power is in the hands of the State, which can prevent the young from hearing of any doctrine which it dislikes." As to economics, he reckoned that no university in the United States would hire a professor who had criticized Standard Oil, because "all college presidents have received or hope to receive benefactions from Mr. Rockefeller." This is vintage Russell, whose observations help illustrate what was a fairly common attitude toward propaganda among postwar intellectuals in Britain and elsewhere. No bibliography.

Silverman, Joan L. *"The Birth of a Nation*: Prohibition Propaganda." *Southern Quarterly* 19, 3 and 4 (Spring-Summer 1981), pp. 23-30.
This article puts D. W. Griffith's film *Birth of a Nation* in the context of the prohibition movement that gained ground during the years of World War I, and resulted in the Eighteenth Amendment. Griffith, the author argues, had already made a number of pro-temperance films. In *Birth*, the message is made crystal clear that drinking is an evil thing. It is conflated with southern racism. Certain scenes show "Negros" carrying whisky jugs as they come to vote in the elections of the immediate post-Civil War period, through which process, it is made clear, they threaten to usurp the place of whites.

Simcovitch, Maxim. "The Impact of Griffith's Birth of a Nation on the Modern Ku Klux Klan." *Journal of Popular Film* 1, 1 (Winter 1972), pp. 45-54.
The author notes that while it had long been thought that *Birth of a Nation* was linked to Klan revival in 1915, the evidence had not been presented in clear detail. This article does that, describing among other things how it was by design that Klan organizer William Joseph Simmons went public with the revival of the Order just ten days before the film premiered. Putting this with other evidence connecting the film to Klan recruitment, the author concludes that the film "seems to have played a major role in finally bringing the Klan to reality."

Southworth, Herbert Rutledge. *Guernica! Guernica! A Study of Journalism, Diplomacy, Propaganda, and History.* Berkeley: University of California Press, 1977.

The bombing of the Basque town of Guernica by German flyers during the Spanish Civil War became one of the most significant symbolic events in twentieth century history. It was made to represent the willingness of fascists to visit wanton destruction upon innocent people. Picasso recorded the event in one of the most famous paintings of modern times. Guernica seemed to epitomize the fateful struggle between democracy and tyranny. This volume asks: How was Guernica destroyed? By whom? And why? These questions naturally raise further questions: To what extent was the picture painted of the event reality, and to what extent was it propaganda based upon misrepresentation of what really happened? To what extent did journalists, knowingly or unknowingly, lend their support in this? The inspiration for the book was a controversy at the time over whether the Basques actually destroyed their own town and blamed it on the Spanish nationalists and their German supporters. The author's exhaustive research leads him to conclude that those who accused the Basques lied as part of a propaganda campaign in support of the Spanish Catholic Church. Extensive bibliography.

Stead, Peter. "Hollywood's Message for the World: The British Response in the Nineteen Thirties." *Historical Journal of Film, Radio and Television* 1, 1 (1981), pp. 19-32.
A fascinating article which examines the impact of Hollywood films on Britain after World War I, and resistance to that impact from the British government. Several parliamentary acts were passed that limited the number of films imported from the United States. Hollywood films were seen by some as having a negative impact upon the shaping of postwar British society. The author discusses the role of the British Board of Film Censors as well as that of the government in opposing what they apparently regarded as a propaganda film campaign from the United States to induce British people to chew gum and speak in nasal accents. The debate was a class issue in part, for working-class British audiences liked American films, compared to the upper classes, who preferred British films. This article sheds light on the extent to which film played a role in shaping British attitudes toward the United States between the world wars.

Steele, Richard W. *Propaganda in an Open Society: The Roosevelt Administration and the Media, 1933-1941*. Westport, Conn.: Greenwood Press, 1985.
This book rests upon an interesting premise: that Franklin D. Roosevelt wanted to solve domestic economic and social problems and challenge Axis expansionism but was not certain that his experiments would work or that the public would have the patience to see his efforts

through. The author argues that the "we have nothing to fear but fear itself" speech was the first expression of the central theme of his entire administration. From this initial assertion, the author goes on to develop the argument that Roosevelt's sometimes radical social, economic, and political policies were, from the first moment, put over to the American people through press, radio, film, and poster propaganda. From start to finish, the book is a history of New Deal social, political, and foreign policy propaganda. Extensive bibliography. See R. Fielding, *March of Time* (entry above) and *Mr. Smith Goes to Washington* (entry below under "Propaganda Material").

Steinson, Barbara J. *American Women's Activism in World War I*. New York: Garland Publishing, 1982.
A study of various women's groups in the United States that took a stand either for or against the fighting of World War I, this volume also shows how the foundations were laid for the struggle for women's rights after the war. The author's purpose, as she explains it, is to increase understanding of the role of women in the war, the pacifist controversy surrounding the entry of the United States into the war, and "the role and operation of organized advocacy groups in American society." This last is a major element of the book. While the author concentrates on the structure, perspectives, and activities of several women's groups in the context of the war, she examines those issues in the context also of how the groups conducted propaganda and what the propaganda contained. Select bibliography.

Stenton, Michael. "British Propaganda and Raison d'Etat 1935-40." *European Studies Review* 10 (1980), pp. 47-74.
This article analyzes how the British government pursued its foreign policy during the period of appeasement using censorship and at least considering seriously the use of propaganda. Much of the author's discussion includes the planning and early deployment of the wartime Ministry of Information, why Neville Chamberlain became an enthusiast for propaganda as a foreign-policy weapon, and how he failed to make effective use of it. The materials upon which this article is based were drawn mainly from the Public Records Office in London. See Robert Cole, "The Conflict Within" (entry above), and Philip M. Taylor, "If War Should Come" (entry below).

Swann, Paul. *The British Documentary Film Movement, 1926-1946*. Cambridge, England: Cambridge University Press, 1989.
The author calls this book "a political and social history of the British documentary film movement," including a biographical sketch of its

founder, John Grierson. A central theme links the various parts of the volume: that there was a close administrative, ideological, and intellectual relationship between the British state and the making of documentary films. That relationship, the text makes clear, encouraged the use of documentary films for domestic propaganda by the General Post Office and the Empire Marketing Board. One chapter is devoted to the use of propaganda documentaries for projecting trade and a national image abroad. Stills from various of the films illustrate the volume. This is among the best studies of documentary film extant. Extensive bibliography.

Taylor, Philip M. "If War Should Come: Preparing the Fifth Arm for Total War, 1935-39." *Journal of Contemporary History* 16 (1981), pp. 27-51. This article describes the first three years of planning for the British Ministry of Information in World War II, with particular emphasis upon the organizational structure. It points out the conflicts, uncertainties, and resistance to the planning that came from many sources within government, but also the determination showed by many in overcoming such obstacles. See Robert Cole, "The Conflict Within" (entry above).

_____. *The Projection of Britain: British Overseas Publicity and Propaganda, 1919-1939*. Cambridge, England: Cambridge University Press, 1981.
This work grew out of the author's Ph.D. research. It is among the first major archival studies of how the British government undertook to further its foreign policies through the use of both political and cultural propaganda. The theme is the development of a propaganda awareness in the Foreign Office, and subjects related to this theme include relations between the Foreign Office and the press, the British Council and the British Broadcasting Corporation as propaganda channels, and preparation to engage in overseas propaganda in wartime. That preparation began when it became clear in the mid-1930s that a repetition of 1914-1918 was not out of the question. Extensive bibliography.

_____. "Publicity and Diplomacy: The Impact of the First World War upon Foreign Office Attitudes Towards the Press," in David Dilks, ed., *Retreat from Power: Studies in Britain's Foreign Policy of the Twentieth Century*. Vol. 1, *1906-1939*. London: Macmillan, 1981.
This essay is one of the author's early contributions to the study of foreign policy in relation to propaganda. It provides an excellent overview of how the exegeses of a militant and outspoken British press in World War I compelled the British Foreign Office, always among the most hidebound and conservative of Britain's government minis-

tries, to adopt a policy of harnessing both the propaganda and censorship potential of newspapers to the interests of furthering Britain's
foreign policies after the war. See Philip M. Taylor, *The Projection of
Britain* (entry above).

Taylor, Richard, and Nigel Young, eds. *Campaigns for Peace: British
Peace Movements in the Twentieth Century.* Manchester, England:
Manchester University Press, 1987.
Public demonstration is a form of propaganda because the assembled
demonstrators hope to persuade those watching them and those against
whom they are demonstrating, to move their thinking or their feelings
in a particular direction. Each essay explores an example of propaganda for peace, from antiwar protest before and after World War I,
through the Campaign for Nuclear Disarmament (CND) in the 1950s
and 1960s, and to the Greenpeace movement in the 1980s. This is not
a detached collection, for most of the authors are members of various
peace groups including the CND. Even so, their descriptions and
analyses of what war protesters in Britain were doing throughout the
twentieth century is fair and balanced. Limited bibliography.

Waddington, Geoffrey. "Fifth Arm or Fifth Column? Nazi Propaganda
Activities in Britain." *Historical Journal of Film, Radio and Television* 6, 1 (1986), pp. 93-99.
This short piece analyzes a Foreign Office communication which
details the existence of German propagandists resident in the United
Kingdom beginning May 1933. The author argues that the document
clearly indicates the importance Hitler placed upon propaganda as an
element in foreign policy, and suggests that there is still much to
understand about the extent to which British rearmament in 1934-1935,
and the formulation of Britain's appeasement policy which aided
Germany in expanding its control in eastern Europe prior to 1939, were
a response to German propaganda.

Waley, Daniel. *British Public Opinion and the Abyssinian War, 1935-6.*
London: Maurice Temple Smith, 1975.
This is the author's first book that does not deal with some aspect of
the Middle Ages. Rather, it examines a twentieth-century topic, Italy's
war against Abyssinia, in the context of British public opinion. The
author addresses such questions as: How did the British public respond
to events in Abyssinia and Britain's position on the concept of Collective Security, which underscored Western Europe's approach to such
"revisionist" nations as fascist Italy? What influence did public opinion

have on the pronouncements of the National Government in Britain and on its policy? To what extent did the National Government shape opinion on the Abyssinian question? That is, what kinds of propaganda was disseminated to direct opinion in directions the government wanted it to take? Bibliography only in endnotes, except for a listing of primary source collections. There are two illustrations, which are reproductions of cartoons dealing with the Abyssinian question.

Walker, Graham. "The Irish Dr. Goebbels: Frank Gallagher and Irish Republic Propaganda." *Journal of Contemporary History* 27, 1 (January 1992), pp. 149-165.
From the Civil War in Ireland (1920-1921) to well after World War II, the Irish Republican Army was a thorn in Britain's side. Terrorism and propaganda against the British Empire had been standard parts of the conflict between Britain and Ireland. This article analyzes the contribution to the struggle made by Frank Gallagher as a creator of propaganda tracts and articles. *The Irish Bulletin* was his main channel, and the author acknowledges that what he wrote was effective. The "Dr. Goebbels" metaphor in the title may be revealing of sympathies, for the author is a lecturer at Queens University, Belfast. He displays respect for Gallagher's skills but describes the creed for which the Irish propagandist labored as "self-righteously narrow," denying an alternative vision for Ireland and the Irish.

Warren, Allen. "Sir Robert Baden-Powell: The Scout Movement and Citizen Training in Great Britain, 1900-1920." *English Historical Review* 101 (April 1986), pp. 376-398.
This article on the origins of the Boy Scout and Girl Guides movement in Britain, is concerned with the propaganda element inherent within the movement's values and ethic. Baden-Powell is described as a proselytizer whose idea for Scouting grew out of his efforts as an army officer to reform cavalry training. At the core was the aim of instilling in Britain's youth values worth fighting for. These came in handy in World War I. The author argues that Scouting also prepared them to withstand the eroding of those values in times of social and political dislocation, such as occurred in Britain in the 1920s. This article was part of a 1980s debate among historians in Britain over the true purpose of the origination of the Boy Scout movement.

Willcox, Temple. "Projection or Publicity? Rival Concepts in the Pre-war Planning of the British Ministry of Information." *Journal of Contemporary History* 18, 1 (January 1983), pp. 97-116.

This article is one of the early efforts at historical analysis of the preliminary debates over planning the British Ministry of Information for World War II. It evaluates the impact on planning had by the debate and conflict within Whitehall over what exactly the planners were trying to construct. The author describes the conflict as being principally between the Foreign Office-run British Council concept of "projection" and the more forceful element from within British Broadcasting Corporation (BBC) ranks which wanted "publicity"—by which Sir Stephen Tallents, the director of planning and a BBC executive, was understood to mean propaganda. Subsequent research on this issue supports the conclusions offered here. See Robert Cole, "The Conflict Within," and Philip M. Taylor, "If War Should Come" (entries above).

Youngblood, Denise J. *Soviet Cinema in the Silent Era, 1918-1935.* Austin: University of Texas Press, 1991.
   This volume is not strictly about propaganda but rather is about the evolution of Soviet filmmaking in an era when many, if not most, film productions in the Soviet Union had a propaganda purpose. As the author notes in her introduction, "political radicals . . . were drawn to cinema because they considered it, unlike theater, an art of the *people*, a mass medium." Subject matter in this volume includes the connection between Soviet politics and filmmaking, with special attention in the later chapters to the impact of Stalinism on Soviet cinema. Thoroughly researched and well written, with a text accessible to most readers; not so the bibliography, which consists of mostly Russian-language sources.

Channels and Techniques

Ainsworth, Gardner. "The New York Fair: Adventure in Promotion." *Public Opinion Quarterly* 3, 4 (October 1939), pp. 694-704.
   The New York World Fair of 1939 was in progress when this article was written. The author describes the fair as an "adventure in promotion," by which he means a propaganda show with the object of promoting "world peace," "the humanitarian aims of the Roosevelt administration," and "free enterprise." He argues that the effort is not always successful in its propaganda aims, owing to some less-than-effective promotion techniques. However, he concludes that on the whole, the fair is a propaganda success which "deserves first mention in the annals of great promotional projects." See Bernard Lichtenberg, "Business Backs New York World Fair" (entry below).

Albert, Ernst. "The Press in Nazi Germany." *Contemporary Review* 154 (November 1938), pp. 693-699.

The author, an anti-Nazi Austrian, describes how little there is of "truth" in Nazi-controlled German newspapers, and how much of propaganda. "If repetition is the secret of successful propaganda, as Adolf Hitler points out in *Mein Kampf*," he writes, "the Nazi Press ought to have achieved unrivalled results after five years of power." The remainder of the article describes German press propaganda in the context of comparisons with other channels. The author ends by offering a warning to the Germans that their press propaganda, most of it containing anti-foreign themes, has driven an ever widening gulf between Germany and the rest of the world.

Aldgate, Anthony. *Cinema and History: British Newsreels and the Spanish Civil War*. London: Scolar Press, 1979.

This volume examines how British newsreels covered the Spanish Civil War (1936-1939). The author looks at the motives of those who filmed the war and edited the result, and the messages about Spain which they transmitted to Britain as a result. The purpose here is twofold: one, to examine how film can be used as historical source material—newsreels of an event such as the Spanish Civil War, for example—and two, how film in this particular instance came to serve a propaganda function. The author fulfills both ends by describing the contents of newsreel film of particular events in very specific detail, noting that as often as not, the newsreel makers used their films to send either pacifist messages or messages which encouraged taking one side or the other in the war. Illustrations and select bibliography.

Bent, Silas, Edgar Dale, and Lester Ziffren. "Channels of Communication." *Public Opinion Quarterly* 1, 3 (July 1937), pp. 112-125.

Each of the authors contributed a subsection of this essay: Silas Bent wrote "International Broadcasting" as his part; Edgar Dale, "Need for the Study of Newsreels"; and Lester Ziffren, "The Correspondent in Spain." Taken together they describe events, news trends, and development, and problems having special significance for public opinion, propaganda, and censorship relating to the press, radio, and film. Ziffren's contribution is of particular significance owing to his "hands on" experience in Spain as a correspondent during the early days of the Spanish Civil War.

Bigelow, Burton. "Should Business Decentralize Its Counter-Propaganda?" *Public Opinion Quarterly* 2, 2 (April 1938), pp. 321-324.

A brief commentary by a contemporary on the interaction of New Deal and big-business propaganda. The author raises the question whether New Deal propaganda that challenges big business represents social reform or simply political demagoguery, and suggests that either way, business has no clear idea how to counter it. He contends that "the place for the businessman to begin effective counterpropaganda is right in his own community" and suggests various channels through which this might be effected, such as bypassing the "discredited" United States Chamber of Commerce in favor of organizing the support of local public opinion leaders. The author's pro-business bias is evident throughout.

Brown, Harold Chapman. "Advertising and Propaganda: A Study in the Ethics of Social Control." *International Journal of Ethics* 40 (1929), pp. 39-55.

During the 1920s and 1930s, observers of spreading mass publicity began to see the specific connections that existed between propaganda and advertising as a concept which employed propaganda techniques. This author is no exception. He sees advertisers and propagandists as increasingly the same, both of which embrace methods and techniques for the sale of their "product" that employ social control. He argues that people are capable of making their own decisions and should be left to do so without the intervention of propagandists and advertisers.

Calder, Robert Lorin. *W. Somerset Maugham and the Quest for Freedom.* London: Heinemann, 1972.

Literature has long been a channel of persuasion on various levels. The subject here is novelist W. Somerset Maugham, who was a British propagandist and espionage agent in Russia at the time of the Bolshevik Revolution. In this critical study, the author does not make an outright case that Maugham wrote propaganda novels, but does describe the novelist's early work as belonging to the "pot-boiler" school, which expressed forceful criticism of various social ills. The author describes such later Maugham novels as *The Moon and Sixpence* as being similar social criticism, though expressed in a different way: the artist as hero struggling against convention and for freedom, on behalf of himself and the larger society. An appendix includes documents concerning Maugham's activities in Russia. The limited bibliography is of use to literary historians far more than to those concerned with propaganda.

Callcott, W. R. "The Last War Aim: British Opinion and the Decision for Czechoslovak Independence, 1914-1919." *Historical Journal* 27, 4 (1984), pp. 979-989.

According to this author, Thomas Masaryk, founder of Czechoslovakia in 1919, was an effective propagandist. He was supported by a number of patriotic Czech groups who were organized principally to make propaganda, which they disseminated through pamphlets and other printed media. Masaryk and his Czech followers, aided by an often sympathetic British press, persuaded the British public to believe in the principle of an independent Czechoslovakia. More important, Masaryk persuaded the British Foreign Office to agree, and the result was Britain leading the Allies in backing the creation of the Czechoslovak Republic.

Carr, E. H. *Propaganda in International Politics.* Oxford, England: Clarendon Press, 1939.
Edward Hallett Carr was in the British Foreign Office between the world wars and ran British external propaganda (except for that aimed at enemy and enemy-occupied countries) in the first two years of World War II. This pamphlet brings those areas of his expertise together, as he talks about the uses and abuses of propaganda in international affairs, and about how modern mass media are made to order as channels for propaganda dissemination. Carr was not opposed to propaganda, but he did have high standards for it, noting among other things that "the more nearly propaganda approximates the truth, the better it will be." This piece is part of the Oxford Pamphlets on World Affairs series, actually written before the outbreak of war in 1939, but published only after war began. No bibliography.

Childs, Harwood Lawrence, and John B. Whitton, eds. *Propaganda by Short Wave.* Princeton, N.J.: Princeton University Press, 1942.
Though published during World War II, this collection of essays is not about war propaganda as such, but about shortwave radio broadcasting as an international propaganda channel. It was inspired by the Princeton Listening Center, established in 1939, which is described here as "America's eavesdropper on the radio propaganda of the world." There are eight essays. The first introduces the concept of international broadcasting, and those which follow cover wartime broadcasting from Germany, Britain, Italy, Paris, and the United States. One essay concerns atrocity propaganda used in German broadcasts of 1939-1940, while another analyzes the techniques of persuasion by radio. The contents reflect primarily on what was heard at the Listening Center, so there is no bibliography or footnoting. The authors were all experts on aspects of broadcasting and propaganda, and the essays are informative as well as readable.

Clark, David C. "Radio in Presidential Campaigns: The Early Years (1924-1932)." *Journal of Broadcasting* 6, 3 (Summer 1962), pp. 229-238.

The author examines the role of radio in presidential campaigns when radio was still in its infancy. At first, radio broadcasts in support of candidates (Herbert Hoover in 1924 was the start of it) were considered a "stunt." After all, the number of people with access to receivers was still low. However, that changed quickly. By 1932 there were 12 million radios in the United States, which meant that perhaps twice that number, who were potential voters, were radio listeners. With this development, the "stunt" became a serious election propaganda channel. However, the author notes, it was not overly successful in this period, owing to a lack of sophistication regarding propaganda technique. To hear the scratchy voice of a southern politician in place of regularly scheduled music programming did not always impress listeners.

Crew, T. *Health Propaganda (Ways and Means)*. Leicester, England: Leicestershire Health Insurance Committee, 1935.

This volume is equally a description of propaganda techniques and channels, and propaganda material in its own right. Put out by the Leicester Health Insurance Committee, it first explains the importance of good health and then describes, in detail and with illustrations, the many kinds of propaganda being used to promote it. The object is to encourage such agencies as the National Baby Week Council to use propaganda to promote practices resulting in healthy babies. Publications (leaflets, pamphlets, and books), films, posters, cartoons, and even poetry are extolled as propaganda channels that can have positive effects. There is even a crossword competition sponsored by the National Baby Week Council. To say that the volume is illustrated is an understatement. No bibliography.

Dobyns, Fletcher. *The Amazing Story of Repeal: An Exposé of the Power of Propaganda*. Chicago: Willett, Clark, 1940.

This is a study of anti-Prohibition propaganda—that is, propaganda aimed at overthrowing the Eighteenth Amendment—written in the language of a pro-Prohibition propagandist. The point is to warn against propaganda opposing Prohibition. The author begins by charging that the instruments of publicity—he names the press, radio, telegraph and telephone—are used for propaganda put out by pressure groups "motivated by selfishness and greed to deceive, mislead, inflame and regiment the people to pursue courses of action inimical to their economic and spiritual interests." As the book was published in 1940, naturally there is a reference to the "totalitarian states'" use of propaganda in the interests of their dictators. The author claims to have seen a government document to the effect that some of the principal industrial, financial, and social leaders of the United States organized a propaganda war to set prohibition aside. The author obviously was offended by this and makes it clear that he favors prohibition. No bibliography.

FDR and Hitler. Prod. Public Broadcasting Corporation, 51 min., 1989. Alexandria, Va.: PBS Video.

This PBS film traces in a comparative manner the coming to power in the midst of Depression of Franklin D. Roosevelt and Adolf Hitler, who would later face each other as war leaders. The film concentrates on the role played by mass communications in their respective administrations, citing FDR's "fireside chats" and Hitler's effective use of radio and film propaganda. This film is recommended for use as an undergraduate teaching tool in history, political science, and communications.

Foster, H. Schuyler, Jr. "The Official Propaganda of Great Britain." *Public Opinion Quarterly* 3, 2 (April 1939), pp. 263-271.

The author begins by noting that Britain disseminates far less propaganda than do the totalitarian states, and goes on to argue that what Britain does disseminate is aimed at constructive rather than negative purposes: improving British society and assuring Britons that the menace of foreign dictators is not being ignored by the government. The author examines five examples of British official propaganda, including "the milk campaign," "physical fitness," "air raid precautions," "the British Council" (external cultural propaganda), and "foreign broadcasts." He contends that none of this has anything substantial in common with the propaganda bombast produced in Italy and Germany. See Mariel Grant, *Propaganda and the Role of the State in Inter-war Britain* (entry above under "History and Function").

Freeman, Judith. "The Publicity of the Empire Marketing Board, 1926-1933." *Journal of Advertising History* 1 (1977), pp. 12-14.

This brief article surveys the particular advertising style used by the British Empire Marketing Board to promote its objectives. Several EMB posters are reproduced in the text as examples. Some of the EMB officials discussed here were involved later in the planning stages of the World War II Ministry of Information, notably Sir Stephen Tallents and Frank Pick. See Mariel Grant, *Propaganda and the Role of the State in Inter-War Britain* (entry above under "History and Function").

Got, Ambroise. "La Littérature pangermaniste d'après-guerre." *Mercure de France* 167 (October 1923), pp. 403-421.
This article describes and analyzes the pan-German literature produced in Germany following World War I. The author cites numerous examples which he claims uniformly promote the idea of German cultural superiority, attack the Versailles Treaty and those who imposed it upon Germany, and call for a restoration of prewar German boundaries. It is probably not a coincidence that the article appeared several months after French troops had occupied the Ruhr in response to Germany defaulting on reparations payments. The occupation provoked outrage in Germany, which resulted in an increased output of pan-German writing. This author clearly was offended by what he was reading, and he warns the Germans that if they continue with this propaganda, they will bring down upon themselves the "odieuse au monde entier" (contempt of the entire world).

Gruening, Ernest. *The Public Pays: A Study of Power Propaganda.* New York: Vanguard Press, 1931.
The "Power" in the title is electric power. This volume examines the propaganda put out by public utilities which at the time of writing was being investigated by the United States Federal Trade Commission. That propaganda, the author contends, was disseminated to "shape public opinion to serve private ends." The author asserts very firmly that his own comments are "not propaganda on either side of the controversial issue involved." The study is based on FTC documents, which, so far as that is possible, are allowed to "speak adequately for themselves." The author describes how the propaganda was "uncovered" by a Senate enquiry. He discusses the originators of the propaganda campaigns—the leaders of utility companies—and how universities and colleges, the press, women's clubs, political parties, radio, film, and even music were pulled into the process of propaganda dissemination in favor of the power companies. The study ends with the less than objective conclusion that "the public pays" and that private enterprise may be a negative in the electric power field. No bibliography.

Hamlin, Charles Hunter. *Propaganda and Myth in Time of War: The War Myth in United States History* and *Educators Present Arms.* New York: Garland, 1973. *War Myth* was first published in 1927, and *Educators* in 1939.
In these two long essays, the author seeks to expose the manipulation of the public mind through the perpetration, in the guise of being

history, of certain "myths" about the moral justification for war. In the first essay he examines what he terms the "false representation historically" of every war in United States history, such as the Revolutionary War, presented as a patriotic uprising, but actually forced upon the colonists by a small minority. He also exposes the representation of every such war in history as having a morally justified basis. This was the "myth in time of war" of the title. In the second essay, the author describes how during World War I the teaching of history in schools and colleges was exploited for propaganda purposes. These essays were first published by the Association to Abolish War and were dedicated to the memory of the author's brother, a victim of World War I. They express a point of view that is both opposed to propaganda and an example of it. In the latter manifestation, it seeks to further a pacifist agenda. Limited bibliography.

Hanson, Elisha. "Official Propaganda Under the New Deal." *Annals of the American Academy of Political and Social Science* 179 (May 1935), pp. 176-186.
Written when the Roosevelt administration was well on the way to making the New Deal a reality, this article surveys the propaganda techniques and channels through which a "depression-weary public" was sold on the philosophy of the New Deal and its programs. The author claims that New Deal propaganda was spread mainly through two instruments, the press and radio, and that while the Roosevelt administration did not actually control the press, they were good at manipulating it. The article includes a list of press and public relations persons in each of the main departments of the government, ranging from the State Department to the National Labor Relations Board. It ends with a warning that propaganda works only when its audience does not recognize it, and now that the audience is aware, "what will come next?"

Hollins, T. J. "The Conservative Party and Film Propaganda Between the Wars." *English Historical Review* 96, 379 (April 1981), pp. 359-369.
In the 1920s, the British left blamed its electoral failures on the "deeply rooted propaganda of the right." Meanwhile, the right feared the propaganda of the left. Both believed film would become a major propaganda channel through which the "untested" and "uneducated" mass electorate created by the Representation of the People Act in 1918 could be manipulated. The author shows that to some extent this was true, and that the right profited from it the most, through both commercial films and newsreels which traveled around the country in National

Publicity Bureau (NPB) vans. Political film propaganda had become a British reality by 1939, and the Conservative party led the way. See Ralph D. Casey, "The National Publicity Bureau and British Party Propaganda" (entry above under "History and Function").

Huxley, Aldous. "Notes on Propaganda." *Harper's Magazine* 174 (December 1936), pp. 32-41.
The author, writer of futuristic novels (*Ape and Essence*, for one) with their purpose planted firmly in the present, describes in this essay the state of propaganda technique and deployment in the mid-1930s as he sees it. He crosses the spectrum from commercial to political propaganda, looks at literary propaganda (Erich Maria Remarque's *All Quiet on the Western Front* is cited specifically), and concludes by observing that over time, people are more likely to respond to negative than to positive propaganda, simply because the latter tends to become boring. This is not an optimistic essay, which makes it perfectly consistent with the author's other writings.

Lacey, Kate. "From *Plauderei* to Propaganda: On Women's Radio in Germany, 1924-1935." *Media, Culture and Society* 16 (1994), pp. 589-607.
This article argues that radio developed a form of talk that was at once intimate and public, and which was crucially important at a time when "definition of the gendered boundaries" between public and private was in a volatile state. In Germany, the author continues, radio talk evolved the idea of the "fireside chat," the essence of which was *plauderei* (chitchat), specifically in the realm of women's programming. *Plauderei* was pioneered in the 1920s, and the author contends that it proved to be of strategic value later in the domestic propaganda of the Third Reich. She explains that unlike other kinds of Nazi propaganda, radio propaganda aimed at women was very much in the "chitchat" mode.

Lawrence, Raymond D. "Haldeman-Julius Has Made Propaganda Profitable." *Public Opinion Quarterly* 3, 1 (January 1939), pp. 79-91.
When this article appeared, the subject, E. Haldeman-Julius, was a publisher and paperback book seller in Girard, Kansas. The author claims that he had "produced and sold more than 200,000,000 books," largely literary classics, many of which contained sexual themes that Bible Belt moralists considered scandalous. The author claims also that Haldeman-Julius was "one of the most prolific of the radical American symbol-manipulators," which is to say propagandists. This essay analyzes the quantity, methods, and techniques of the propaganda Haldeman-Julius disseminated, and looks for an explanation of

why he was a propagandist. The conclusion drawn is that Haldeman-Julius' contempt for the "cultural bankruptcy" of his small Kansas community provides that explanation. The author praises Haldeman-Julius for his propaganda skill, adding tongue-in-cheek that his propaganda had also make him a fortune.

LeMahieu, D. L. *A Culture for Democracy: Mass Communication and the Cultivated Mind in Britain Between the Wars.* Oxford, England: Clarendon Press, 1988.
In this volume, the author makes clear the connections between propaganda techniques and mass communications as a force in social-political change. He analyzes how mass communications—radio, press, and film—helped transform British culture in the 1920s and 1930s from a traditional class-based culture to one with a more democratic content. The main thrust is not toward defining this phenomenon as being the result of propaganda; however the author makes it clear that the persuasive purposes and techniques associated with mass propaganda were a fundamental part of this democratic development. The volume deals with advertising, press coverage of major events, advancing communication technologies, and film. All contributed to at least challenging, if not breaking down entirely, the traditional social divisions that characterized Britain between the wars. The bibliography runs to fifty pages.

Levin, Jack. *Power Ethics.* New York: Alfred A. Knopf, 1931.
This volume is an analysis of propaganda used by private power companies to retain monopoly over the production of electricity in the 1920s, and as he argues against that monopoly and against power company publicity tactics, the author indulges in a kind of propaganda of his own. Coming on the eve of the great controversy over the Tennessee Valley Authority (TVA) power project, the volume is immensely valuable to understanding the propaganda battles between public control and private ownership which characterized the TVA debate. Limited bibliography. See Ernest Gruening, *The Public Pays* (entry above).

Lichtenberg, Bernard. "Business Backs New York World Fair to Meet the New Deal Propaganda." *Public Opinion Quarterly* 2, 2 (April 1938), pp. 314-320.
The author describes how businessmen recognized, from the first moment of planning it, that the New York World Fair, projected for 1939, could be exploited to promote business by showing "what an indispensable contribution industry is making to social and economic

existence." He then describes the channels that would be exploited for the purpose, presenting them as explicitly propagandistic in nature, and predicts that they would make the fair "the greatest single public relations program in all history." See Gardner Ainsworth, "The New York Fair" (entry above).

MacKenzie, John M. *Propaganda and Empire: The Manipulation of British Public Opinion, 1880-1960*. Manchester, England: Manchester University Press, 1984.
Each chapter of this study of imperial propaganda covers a specific aspect of propaganda dissemination designed to sell the British Empire to the British public. They cover such subjects as "The Vehicles of Imperial Propaganda," which is about the earliest propaganda materials containing imperial references, and "Imperial Propaganda Societies and Imperial Studies" and "Imperialism and the School Textbook," both of which describe themselves. Each of these and the six other chapters open with an illustration; the chapter "Cinema, Radio and the Empire," for example, is introduced with a still from a 1940 film, *The Sun Never Sets*. Select bibliography. See John M. MacKenzie, ed., *Imperialism and Popular Culture* (entry above under "History and Function").

Marshall, Herbert, ed. *The "Battleship Potemkin": The Greatest Film Ever Made*. New York: Avon Books, 1978.
This volume is an anthology of writings about the Soviet film classic *Battleship Potemkin*, which is set in the time of the 1905 Revolution in Russia and is one of the best pro-Revolution propaganda films ever made. The book opens with the editor's description of the film, its context, its purpose, and its place within the world of Socialist Realism art criticism. The remainder of the volume consists of director Sergei Eisenstein's own comments on the film, correspondence and news reports concerned with the film and the events it describes, items on censorship connected with the film, and reviews of and articles about the film that were published in the USSR, the United States, Germany, Great Britain, France, Holland, Spain, Czechoslovakia, and Poland. Limited illustrations but no bibliography.

Montague, Ivor. *The Political Censorship of Films*. London: Victor Gollancz, 1929.
Ivor Montague wrote this short tract as a protest against censorship of films in Britain being a practice, but not at the same time being legal: no parliamentary Act establishing censorship had ever been passed. In practice, he argues, the Cinematograph Act of 1909, which was passed

for other purposes, was being interpreted as legitimizing what amounted to film censorship. The author is certain that the practice has political motives, and refers to such films as *Battleship Potemkin* having been effectively censored by government regulators in conformity with an anti-Bolshevik agenda. The pamphlet includes appendixes that list legal decisions affecting censorship, film distribution costs, correspondence, and a "model organization" for distributing vetoed films. No bibliography.

Mott, Frank Luther. "Newspapers in Presidential Campaigns." *Public Opinion Quarterly* 8, 2 (Fall 1944), pp. 348-367.
Franklin D. Roosevelt won his presidential elections seemingly in spite of opposition from the press. This article notes that the effect was to lead some people to fear that the press was failing to play the public opinion role that was thought necessary for it in a democracy. After extensive analysis of the press on this issue, the author concludes that such fears were unfounded, that Americans still read their newspapers without thinking that the press had sold them out by representing only a minority opinion. There is an extensive appendix listing where major newspapers stood on presidential candidates all the way back to George Washington.

Pohle, Heinz. *Der Rundfunk als Instrument der Politik: Zur Geschichte des deutschen Rundfunks von 1923/38.* Hamburg: Hans Bredow Institut, 1955.
It is a given that mass propaganda depends for its success as much upon mass communications as upon any other thing. Radio broadcasting was the specific form of mass communications which made propaganda such a potent force in twentieth century ideology and politics. This volume puts that reality into the context of German political life between 1923 and 1938, which period encompassed the storm and stress of the Weimar collapse and the victory of the Nazi revolution. It describes the German radio system, its expansion, its popularity, its uses in German foreign policy, and above all, for more than half of the book, its employment in disseminating Nazi propaganda. Extensive bibliography.

Potter, Pitman B. "League Publicity: Cause or Effect of League Failures?" *Public Opinion Quarterly* 2, 3 (July 1938), pp. 399-412.
The author measures the reality of League of Nations publicity work against his own theory of how it should work, and how the League seemed to think it should work—the latter not being the same as how League publicity *did* work. The essay is somewhat abstract and theo-

retical in nature, though the materials to which the theories are applied are drawn from actual experience. The author concludes that the issue is very complex and indicates that if the League had a clearer sense of what was needed to promote its work, some of its failures might have been prevented, such as those connected to League efforts to impose sanctions against Italy over the Italian invasion of Abyssinia in 1935.

Pronay, Nicholas. "British Newsreels in the 1930s: Audiences and Producers." *History* 56, 188 (October 1971), pp. 411-418.
This is the first of a two-part essay (see next entry) on British newsreels before World War II. Here the author describes the limitations of newsreels as a record of historical events, but notes that their value is considerable to historians as a record of what people were being told was happening by filmmakers, and by government and other organizations who sponsored newsreels. Against this record, historians could assess what *was* happening from other sources and determine whether given newsreels encompassed a specific propaganda purpose. This essay clearly sets forth a context in which newsreels can be viewed as a propaganda channel.

_____. "British Newsreels in the 1930s: Their Policies and Impact." *History* 57, 189 (February 1972), pp. 63-72.
In this second part (see entry above) of the author's essay on British newsreels, he looks at editorial policy concerning the films and its impact on the audience. He describes censorship, the sometimes stormy relations between newsreel makers and the "radical and usually well-born, hence guilt-ridden" Documentary Film Movement members, and the influence of press style on newsreels. His conclusion is that on the whole, much public perception of world and national political and social developments in the 1930s was influenced, if not actually shaped, by what the newsreel makers selected to show their audience. Again, a context is described in which newsreels can be studied as a propaganda channel.

Pronay, Nicholas, and D. W. Spring, eds. *Propaganda, Politics and Film.*
London: Macmillan, 1982.
These essays focus on the role of film in political, cultural, and social propaganda. They are written by some of Britain's leading historical and analytical specialists in this area. The essays concern Britain mostly though not exclusively, and cover such topics as external cultural and diplomatic propaganda, the working class and film, poli-
tics, and film censorship, news and propaganda film in wartime, film

and public opinion, and the "projection of the Soviet Union" on film. This collection aims in part at encouraging further research on film, politics, and propaganda, especially with reference to the impact of improved film technology on the propaganda product. Bibliography in endnotes.

The Radio Priest: The American Experience. Prod. WGBH-TV, Boston, 60 min., 1988. Rutgers, N.J.: Rutgers University.
This documentary tells the story of Father Charles Coughlin, the "radio priest" who became an anti-Semitic propagandist during the Depression era. Coughlin also took on the government and democracy, allying himself with the programs of fascist dictators in Europe. This program interweaves his personality with the issues of his times, in the context of the value of radio as a mass propaganda channel. His weekly radio broadcasts touched off a heated debate in the United States over whether or not there should be censorship of the airwaves.

Radio, Racism and Foreign Policy. Prod. Anthony Potter, 30 min., 1978. Ames: Iowa State University.
The United States tried to isolate itself from the rest of the world during the decades between the world wars. This documentary explores that phenomenon with particular emphasis on the fact that racism and xenophobia were never more intense or intensely expressed in the United States than in that period. Radio served as a propaganda channel in terms of projecting a uniform image of the "good American," an image that excluded foreigners and persons of color. News of rising difficulties in Europe and Asia only reinforced isolationism and xenophobia.

Riegel, O. W. "Press, Radio, and the Spanish Civil War." *Public Opinion Quarterly* 1, 1 (January 1937), pp. 131-136.
This brief commentary looks at the Spanish Civil War in the context of manipulation of the mass media by both sides. At issue is concern that propaganda has replaced reporting, with the effect that both disinformation and manipulated information are misleading public opinion on the issues involved in the struggle.

Rogerson, Sidney. *Propaganda in the Next War.* London: Geoffrey Bles, 1938.
This book was part of a series called *The Next War* edited by Basil Liddell-Hart. Between the world wars, particularly in Great Britain, educated opinion was both fascinated by propaganda and convinced that its role in war was permanently established. "Large as [was] the

part played by propaganda in the war of 1914-1918," Liddell-Hart wrote in the preface, "there is every indication that it will fill a still bigger rôle in any future 'great war.'" The author knew of what he spoke, Liddell-Hart continued, and brought to this book the expertise he had acquired by working for British propaganda dissemination during World War I. The author's theme is how propaganda would expand in quantity and quality in the next war. He first describes it, then examines the distrust persisting in postwar Europe among people who were propaganda's "victims" in the Great War. Finally, he speculates about channels and techniques, and potential audiences at home and abroad, the latter including enemy, neutral, and allied countries. No bibliography.

Seldes, George. *You Can't Print That! The Truth Behind the News, 1918-1928*. Garden City, N.Y.: Garden City Publishing Company, 1929.
That the volume is dedicated to the author's father, a "libertarian," is an indication of its direction: the right to know, a critique of censorship, and an exposé of propaganda. In one instance, the author describes European "presidents, kings and dictators" having their "friendly or purchased press in Great Britain," through which they spread false ideas. No subject of interest in the 1920s about which propaganda was disseminated or to which censorship was applied, is overlooked. The author, a foreign correspondent for a press he does not identify, addresses himself to, for example, "The Truth about Fascist Terrorism and Censorship," "the Pope and Fascism," "Censorship in Red Russia," "Catholic Trials in Moscow," "German Censorship," and last but not least, "D'Annunzio, or the Bow-Legged Napoleon." A chapter on Lenin describes the founder of the Soviet Union in great and almost entirely negative detail, in order to show how easily the Russian people were duped by Bolshevik propaganda. No bibliography.

Smith, A. C. H. *Paper Voices: The Popular Press and Social Change, 1935-1965*. London: Chatto and Windus, 1975.
The purpose of this book is to analyze how the popular press "interprets social change to its readers," and to suggest an analytical methodology for this kind of study "as a contribution to the general field of cultural studies." The author headed a research "team" for this purpose, which included Elizabeth Immirzi and Trevor Blackwell. They specifically examined the *Express* and the *Mirror*, starting from the assumption that popular press performs, especially in times of rapid social change, "a significant role as a social educator," or to put it another way, social propagandist. Select bibliography.

Wright, Quincy, ed. *Public Opinion and World Politics*. Chicago: University of Chicago Press, 1933.

Five lectures delivered in 1933 at the Tenth Institute under the Norman Wait Harris Memorial Foundation at the University of Chicago. The theme is the rising influence of propaganda on the formation of public opinion with regard to international politics beginning with World War I. The authors of these lectures were a mix of journalists and academics who obviously were both alert to and concerned by the development of fascism and totalitarianism then beginning to take shape in Europe. No bibliography.

Propaganda Material

À nous la liberté. Dir. René Clair, Société des Films Sonores Tobis, 104 min., 1931. Chicago: Facets Video.

Two prison inmates escape. One becomes a tycoon and the other is hired at his factory, where he becomes an assembly line automaton. This film is a satire on the dehumanization of industrial workers. It precedes Charlie Chaplin's indictment of the industrial revolution in *Modern Times* (entry below) by five years.

Aerograd. Dir. Alexander Dovshenko, Mosfilm-Ukrainfilm, 81 min., 1935. Berkeley: University of California.

In this film, a new Siberian city is nearly destroyed by Japanese saboteurs who smuggle dynamite across the border from Manchuria and try to blow it up. Superpatriotic to a fault, the film stereotypes the saboteurs, uses rhetorical language, and presents the audience with a clear dichotomy between the villainous "them" and the heroic "us"— all classic techniques of propagandistic feature films. This film reflects the rising tensions in the 1930s between the Soviet Union and the Japanese empire.

Alexander Nevsky. Dir. Sergei Eisenstein and D. I. Vassiliev, Mosfilm, 107 min., 1938, Chicago: Facets Video.

As Soviet concern increased with regard to perceived threats to the Soviet Union from Nazi Germany in the 1930s, Russian nationalism became a part of official Soviet ideology. Stalin ordered this film by Sergei Eisenstein, music by Sergei Prokofiev, which glorified Alexander Nevsky's resistance to a Teutonic invasion of medieval Russia, just as he ordered films glorifying the eighteenth-century Czar Peter the Great. *Alexander Nevsky* has come to be regarded as one of the great classics of Soviet cinema. It is also a film that, though based upon actual events which occurred in the thirteenth century, uses its subject for propaganda purposes. The hero is Prince Alexander Nevsky, who arouses the Russian people to defend themselves. Images of the Orthodox Church indicate that the Russians are on the side of justice, while the Germans, their helmets decorated with all manner of satanic symbols, are depraved criminals who burn children alive and are on the side of evil. The film was effective both as cinema and as propaganda.

And So They Live. Dir. John Derno and Julian Roffman, New York University and the University of Kentucky, 25 min., 1940. New York: New York University Film Library.

This film indicts an outdated school in a poor Kentucky community. The curriculum has no bearing on reality for the daily struggle these mountain people wage against poverty. This was one of a number of films produced in connection with the Educational Film Institute of New York University. They were intended to comment on whether functional education as opposed to traditional education would raise the level of living in these backward communities. They did not, however, examine questions concerning social structure. As propaganda, this film made the point clearly that these backward Kentuckians deserved better; it did not also give a clear indication of how that was to be achieved.

Baden-Powell, Sir Robert. *Scoutmastership: A Handbook for Scoutmasters on the Theory of Scout Training.* New York: G. P. Putnam's Sons, 1920.

This volume carries forward Baden-Powell's original purpose in starting the Boy Scout movement in Britain: to instill in boys and young men the values and commitments necessary to defend and maintain the British Empire. These values include hard work, service, healthy habits, and, as one chapter puts it, "Be Ye Prepared!" This scoutmaster's guide fits nicely with the propaganda campaigns organized by Baden-Powell and others in the 1920s, in which the nation's youth were encouraged to rededicate themselves to these same values in order to rebuild Britain in the aftermath of World War I.

Body and Soul. Prod. and dir. Oscar Micheaux, 80 min., 1924. New York: Museum of Modern Art.

This silent, all-black production seeks to reverse the negative stereotype of African American men prevalent in films of the 1920s, by showing a strong, masculine black man in a heroic role. Paul Robeson plays a black preacher who appears to live two lives. On the one hand he is a preacher; on the other, he is apparently a wicked man who associates with criminals and cardsharps in a speakeasy, and is shown trying to dupe a pious mother into marrying off her daughter. By the end of the film, however, the latter role is shown to have been a sham, and Robeson emerges as a righteous man who had ingratiated himself with the speakeasy patrons only in order to close the place down.

Carroll, Gordon. "Dr. Roosevelt's Propaganda Trust." *American Mercury* 42, 165 (September 1937), pp. 1-31.
This essay is a propaganda piece against the New Deal. It uses as its technique accusations that the Roosevelt administration disseminates propaganda even while deploring it. The author opens by complaining at the amount of "propaganda *about* propaganda" that comes out of the White House, while the White House itself uses propaganda to impose the New Deal on the United States. He claims also that White House propaganda is aimed more at enhancing Roosevelt's power than at resolving issues created by the Depression. His main target is the Works Progress Administration and other New Deal agencies, all of which, he claims, are being sold to the American people using fascist propaganda tactics. This was the first in a series of three articles targeting the Roosevelt administration that appeared in this volume of *American Mercury*. The others include "How the WPA Buys Votes" (pp. 194-231) and "Propaganda from the White House" (pp. 319-336). The latter ends by describing White House propagandists as offering a "shabbier spectacle" than even their European fascist counterparts.

Century of Progress. Prod. New York and San Francisco Film and Photo League, approx. 20 min., 1932. New York: Motion Picture Center.
The irony of the title is the focus of this film about Depression era suffering in the United States. It contrasts the reality of life for unemployed citizens for whom progress is a meaningless expression, with the boasting about progress that characterized the Chicago World Fair.

Childers, R. Erskine. *The Riddle of the Sands: A Record of Secret Service*. London: Smith, Elder, 1903.
In this novel, the theme is a German plot to launch a secret attack on Britain from the sea. The novel appeared at the height of the pre-1914 Anglo-German naval race, and spoke to British fear that under their sometimes bellicose emperor, the Germans indeed were up to no good. The author was a veteran of the Boer War and a committed British Imperialist—which is ironic, since he later embraced Irish nationalism and became an enemy of the empire. *The Riddle of the Sands* is sometimes described as the prototype of the modern spy novel genre.

China Strikes Back. Prod. Frontier Films, 24 min., 1937. New York: Museum of Modern Art.

This documentary provides one of the first film treatments of the Chinese Communist Eighth Route Army in their Shensi province fortress after the Long March. A variety of activities are covered: the march itself, guerrilla tactics, army training, political programs, relations between the army and the peasants of the province, the leadership focusing on Mao Zedong, and the Communist movement's efforts at indoctrinating the people. The propaganda elements lie in the film's positive and hopeful view of Mao's revolutionary movement.

Coal Face. Prod. and dir. John Grierson, Empire Marketing Board/General Post Office, 24 min., 1935, on *Benjamin Brittain.* New York: Kino International.

A John Grierson documentary which honors both the contributions and sacrifices of Britain's coal miners. It also stresses the importance of mining to the British economy. The object of the film is to promote good public relations at a time when miners and the industry generally were suffering from the effects of the Depression. Some of the footage used in this film appears also in *Industrial Britain* (entry below).

Constantine, Stephen. *Buy and Build: The Advertising Posters of the Empire Marketing Board.* London: Her Majesty's Stationery Office, 1986.

The Empire Marketing Board (EMB) was established in May 1926 and survived for seven years despite being very controversial. Among its essential functions was to encourage commitment to empire and to develop innovative ways of selling Britons on that commitment. This volume contains reproductions of EMB advertising posters which were part of the propaganda disseminated in connection with economic and other kinds of empire development. Posters display Australian wheat, South African oranges, Sudanese cotton, travel to India, and many other elements central to advertising the empire. The originals of these posters are in the Public Records Office in London. Limited bibliography. See Judith Freeman, "The Publicity of the Empire Marketing Board" (entry above under "Channels and Techniques").

Le Crime de M. Lange. Prod. André Halley des Fontaines, dir. Jean Renoir, Oberon, 90 min., 1936. Chicago: Facets Video.

This is anticapitalist propaganda as only a French filmmaker could organize it in the era of the leftist *Front Populaire* government of Léon Blum. It extols the idea that a collective can overthrow a capitalist tyrant and run things better as a result. In this case, the collective is the employees of a publishing house who take control and make the publishing house profitable after their employer is reported killed. However, their employer is not dead. He returns and demands a share of the profits created by the collective. They hold the line and even consider whether or not they would be justified in killing him—a scene which clearly considers whether a workers' revolution is justified.

Dangerous Hours. Prod. Thomas Ince, dir. Fred Niblo, 84 min., 1919. Chicago: Facets Video.
A college student in the United States is duped by evil Marxists into embracing their communist ideology. In due course, he sees the error of his ways, realizes the truth of his upbringing and point of view, and repudiates the Marxists. Among the first Hollywood anti-communist propaganda films which perfectly reflects the anti-Bolshevik paranoia that existed in the United States following the 1917 Revolution in Russia.

DeNoon, Christopher. *Posters of the WPA.* Los Angeles: Wheatley Press, 1987.
The Works Progress Administration was an integral part of the New Deal program of the Franklin D. Roosevelt administration. This volume is a collection of murals and posters created by the WPA Federal Art Project. Their purpose was to advertise programs through which the administration hoped to improve the economic, social, cultural, and physical well-being of United States citizens in the Depression era. The Federal Art Project also provided employment for artists, who responded with an output as varied as could be imagined in both content and style.

Drums. Prod. Alexander Korda, dir. Zoltan Korda, Korda/London Films, 96 min., 1938. London: Polygram Video.
In this unabashed glorification of British imperialism, a wicked native prince faces off against a British captain and garrison which are more than a match for him. The wicked prince has murdered the rightful native ruler and threatens the life of the heir apparent. The heir is just a boy, and he finds refuge with the British. They teach him proper British military discipline and, in the process, to love the empire as well. The British soldiers are friendly, fun-loving, and caring; apparently they have not a single "white man's burden" bone in their collective body.

Eric Severeid's "Not So Wild a Dream." Prod. WGBH-TV Boston, 60 min., 1988. Columbia: University of Missouri.
This documentary is based on journalist Eric Severeid's memoirs. It traces his evolution from a student pacifist and isolationist into a champion of the United States playing a role in the world. He became

a CBS correspondent in Europe during the era when fascism was taking over, and it was this experience that changed him. Once he had decided that the United States must act against fascism, Severeid became an anti-isolationist propagandist, his object being to persuade his fellow citizens to take up the fight against the rising tide of European fascism and dictatorship.

Friedl, Bettina, ed. *On to Victory: Propaganda Plays of the Woman Suffrage Movement*. Boston: Northeastern University Press, 1987.
This volume is an anthology of twenty plays written by American playwrights between the 1850s and 1919, when the Nineteenth Amendment, which gave the vote to women, was passed. The object of these plays was to dramatize the desire and right of women to vote, and they are unabashedly propagandistic in tone. The collection includes such titles as "Lords of Creation" by Ella Cheever Thayer (1883), "The New Woman" by George Rugg (1896), "A Suffragette Baby" by Alice C. Thompson (1912), and "On to Victory" by Hester N. Johnson (1915). This is some of the earliest women's suffrage propaganda, which the editor has introduced and described with great skill.

G-Men. Prod. Louis F. Edelman, dir. William Keighley, 85 min., Warner Brothers, 1935. Chicago: Facets Video.
A rough-and-ready character played by James Cagney becomes an equally rough-and-ready FBI agent when his friend is killed by gangsters. His motive is revenge, and as this film makes clear, revenge is a perfectly justified motive for pursuing gangsters. The film was fully supported by FBI director J. Edgar Hoover, who provided some real FBI agents to take part in it. His motive was to ensure that the FBI would be presented as he wished. It was, and *G-Men* emerged as an effective piece of FBI propaganda.

La Grande Illusion. Dir. Jean Renoir, 112 min., 1937. Washington, D.C.: Library of Congress; Westlake Village, Calif.: Western Film and Video.
This film includes Erich von Stroheim in the cast and describes the fate of French flyers shot down and taken prisoner by the Germans in World War I. It is shown that differences of class are harder to overcome than differences in nationality; in other words, the aristocratic French officers get on better with the aristocratic German officers than they do with their own men. This film is antiwar propaganda in the tradition of Erich Maria Remarque's novel *All Quiet on the Western Front* (entry below), with the additional element of propaganda against class consciousness.

The Grapes of Wrath. Prod. Darryl F. Zanuck, dir. John Ford, Twentieth
Century-Fox, 128 min., 1940. Chicago: Facets Video.
Henry Fonda and Jane Darwell star in this Depression-era film based
on a novel by John Steinbeck. It tells the story of the migration of the
Joad family from Oklahoma to California, and the persecution they
experience at the hands of police and others, who are prejudiced against
"Okies." The story makes a case for the poor and dispossessed, and
against the representatives of the social and political establishment.
Steinbeck's writings on the Depression-era United States are among
the outstanding examples of literature as propaganda; this film version
of his best known novel makes his message crystal clear.

Hunger: The National Hunger March to Washington. Prod. Workers' Film
and Photo League, 24 min., 1932. New York: Motion Picture Center.
Made by some of the same Workers' Film and Photo League filmmakers who produced *The National Hunger March* (entry below), this
documentary explains the purpose, program, and organizing of the
December 1932 hunger march, which was in response to an appeal
from the National Unemployed Councils. It focuses on the plight of
the workers and the sometimes violent opposition to their march by
police in Boston and Washington, D.C.

I Am a Fugitive from a Chain Gang. Prod. Hal B. Wallis, dir. Mervyn Le
Roy, Warner Brothers, 93 min., 1932. Chicago: Facets Video.
Based on the writings of Robert Elliot Burns, who escaped from a
Georgia chain gang. Burns became a successful magazine editor even
though he lived in constant fear of being recaptured and returned to
Georgia. The story is of a man who is framed for robbery and sentenced
to ten years' hard labor on a chain gang. He is degraded, abused, and
nearly worked to death. The film is an indictment of the horrors of the
post-World War I Georgia penal system, in which the chain gang
figured prominently. This is hard and uncompromising propaganda in
support of reform of an inhuman system.

Industrial Britain. Prod. and dir. John Grierson, Gaumont British Films
for the Empire Marketing Board, 21 min., 1933, on *E.M.B. Classics*.
New York: Kino International.
A product of the British Documentary Film movement started by John
Grierson in the 1920s, this is a public relations film for British industry
released at the worst point in the 1930s depression. It covers mining,
steel, and glass production, transportation including air, and concludes
with the ringing assertion: "These are the products of Industrial Britain!"

The Informer. Prod. Cliff Reid, dir. John Ford, Radio Pictures, 91 min., 1935. Chicago: Facets Video.
Victor McLaglen, Heather Angel, and Preston Foster star in this film version of Liam O'Flaherty's novel of betrayal in the Irish Republican Army's ongoing war against the British Empire. Jocko sells out an IRA officer for twenty English pounds. (It requires an effort to miss the symbolism of this transaction.) The film appealed to the sympathies of an American audience which, in the 1930s, was more likely to favor Ireland than Great Britain. It contains almost every characteristic of Hollywood propaganda features that appeared during World War II, only on a more sophisticated level.

J'accuse. Prod. and dir. Abel Gance, Pathé, 127 min., 1938. Chicago: Facets Video; Washington, D.C.: Library of Congress.
This is Abel Gance's remake of his 1919 classic of the same title, which was released in the United States under the title *That They Might Live*. It features stark scenes of slaughtered soldiers rising from their graves to march upon the cities of the world. In particular, they march on Paris, where they contrast vividly with victory parades along the Champs Élysées. The death, destruction, and mindlessness of trench warfare are made starkly real in a film which is pacifist from start to finish. Gance included some actual war film footage and this version employs much of the same imagery, but within a slightly different story line than appeared in the 1919 original. In the view of most critics, that film remains the superior version.

Kameradschaft. Dir. G. W. Pabst, Nerofilm, 92 min., 1931. Chicago: International Historic Films.
This film argues for cooperation between France and Germany after a decade of revenge-seeking (France) and resentment (Germany), and in the context of a rising tide of authoritarian nationalism in Germany. Based upon a real event, the story is that French coal miners trapped by a cave-in are rescued by German miners in an outstanding example of Franco-German cooperation. However, the film ends with French and German bureaucrats and policemen reestablishing the border between the two nations and peoples, complete with gates and barriers. Presumably Pabst was not overly optimistic that his point would have much effect on the reality of Franco-German relations.

Kirkpatrick, George R. *War—What For?* New York: Garland, 1971.
This is a reprint of an antiwar diatribe published in 1910. The author was a radical socialist in the United States who dedicated the volume

to "the victims of the civil war in industry; that is . . . the working class, the class who furnish the blood and tears and cripples and corpses in all wars—yet win no victories for their own class." He was a member of the Industrial Workers of the World, and, along with Eugene V. Debs and others, was inspired to join in an international protest against what the protesters defined as a capitalist system bent on drawing the industrial nations of the world into a world war. In that eventuality, the author argues, those who would pay the price are the workers. The book is filled with facts and figures, but presented in language that is inflammatory and emotional. See H. C. Peterson, and Gilbert C. Fite, *Opponents of War, 1917-1918* (entry above in chapter 2 under "History and Function").

The Lady Vanishes. Prod. Edward Black, dir. Alfred Hitchcock, Gaumont-British, 97 min., 1938. Chicago: Facets Video.
The most political of a series of espionage and terrorist thrillers Hitchcock made prior to World War II, which began with The Man Who Knew Too Much (1934). The vanishing lady is Miss Froy, a British agent conveying an important political secret home to the Foreign Office. She disappears from a train passing through the fictitious Central European country of Bandrieka. Her young English friend, Iris, persuades another Englishman, Gilbert, that Miss Froy has been made to vanish somehow. Eventually they find her, there is a shoot out with foreign agents who are thinly disguised representations of the Nazi secret police, and the secret is brought safely home to London. The film boasts a number of very specific jibes at the appeasement foreign policy of the pre-1939 British government, including the line: "Never climb a fence when you can sit on it. Old Foreign Office proverb."

The Lives of a Bengal Lancer. Prod. Louis D. Lighton, dir. Henry Hathaway, Paramount Pictures, 110 min., 1935. Chicago: Facets Video.
Though made in Hollywood, this adventure film is based on a novel by Francis Yeats-Brown set in British India in the 1930s. The theme is how imperial troops deal with uprisings among the Afghans and others along the Northwest Frontier. British rule is shown as just and strict, but also benevolent, and that when treated with such benevolence, the Indians are keen to remain under British rule. The rebels are shown to be cruel and ineffective. This is not serious propaganda, but it serves the purpose of sustaining assumptions characteristic of the 1930s that Asians, Africans, and other nations of color were barbarians best looked after by enlightened Europeans. Such films also served to defend imperialism at a time when it was coming increasingly under attack.

Low, David. *A Cartoon History of Our Times*. New York: Simon and Schuster, 1939.

New Zealander David Low was the celebrated political cartoonist of the London Evening Standard, who gave the world Colonel Blimp and some of the most potent illustrated political and social commentary the English-speaking world saw during the 1930s. Low addressed every major issue of the day, from fascism to social distress, and in the process caricatured every major European and American political figure. This included the likes of Winston Churchill, Neville Chamberlain, Franklin D. Roosevelt, Adolf Hitler, Benito Mussolini, and Francisco Franco. This volume is a select collection of those cartoons, which represent Low's personal political perspective and which attempt, as do all political cartoons, to urge a particular point of view upon a mass audience. A typical example is the last cartoon, which depicts a tiger wearing swastikas in place of stripes devouring Neville Chamberlain, the apostle of appeasement policy. That Low was exceptionally talented and exceptionally witty merely makes his personal propaganda more effective. Every student of the interwar period, whether of propaganda, politics, or foreign policy, will appreciate this collection. There is a brief text with each cartoon.

La Marseillaise. Dir. Jean Renoir, World Pictures Corporation, 135 min., 1938. Chicago: Facets Video.

Set in the early days of the French Revolution, this film tells the story of volunteers who march to Paris from Marseilles to take part in the uprising. They inspired Roget de Lisle's famous song, *Les Marseilles*, which became the French National Anthem. The film was sponsored by the French trades unions with the intention of linking their struggle with the Revolution of 1789. They described the film as "the film of the union of the French nation against a minority of exploiters, the film of the rights of man and the citizen."

Meet John Doe. Prod. and dir. Frank Capra, Warner Brothers, 135 min., 1941. Chicago: Facets Video.

A female newspaper reporter, fired from her job, tries to regain her place through sensationalism. She creates in print the myth of an idealistic American named "John Doe," who, tyrannized and mistreated by tycoons, moguls, magnates, and captains of industry, will file his protest by leaping to his death from the top of City Hall on Christmas Eve. The public pours out its heart in response to her reporting on the fictional character, so she must find a real John Doe. She does, and though he does not leap at the appointed time, he indicates that he would be willing to do so in order to make what had begun as the reporter's fictitious point. The film is pointedly anti-fascist and targets among others the pro-Nazi, German-American Bund movement. With this film, Capra warned his compatriots against the fascist elements then very much in evidence in the United States.

Metropolis. Dir. Fritz Lang, Universum-Film-Aktiengesellschaft (UFA), 153 min., 1926. Chicago: Facets Video.
An underground workers' city is contrasted with an above ground bourgeois playground for the rich owners of the factories in which the subterranean workers labor. These workers are portrayed as over-worked and abused automatons. There is an abortive rebellion, but in the end the son of the factory owner sees the errors of his father's ways, and the ideal solution emerges: capital and labor are reconciled through the love of the capitalist's son for a worker's daughter. This film is not necessarily clever propaganda, but it was effective in the sense of using revolutionary cinema techniques to make its case. Later, when the Nazis achieved power in Germany, they were so impressed with Lang that they wanted him to make propaganda films for the regime. He responded by emigrating to the United States.

Millions Like Us. Prod. American Labor Films, 17 min., 1934-1935. New York: Motion Picture Center.
This film examines the plight of millions of Depression-era unemployed in the United States surviving through soup kitchens and bread lines. They are contrasted with the millions who are still working. There is a work stoppage, and a young man is shown being driven by hunger to become a scab. However, his experience in that capacity demonstrates to him that his interests are the same as those of the strikers, and he is converted to trade unionism. This act sums up the propaganda message of the film.

Mr. Smith Goes to Washington. Dir. Frank Capra, Columbia Picture Corporation, 125 min., 1939. Chicago: Facets Video.
Jeff Smith is an innocent bumpkin pitted against corrupt politicians in a United States Senate that leaves much to be desired in terms of integrity and concern for the people of the nation. Smith is appointed a United States senator on the assumption that he will do what he is told. Instead, he heads for Washington full of ideals and purpose, and defies the party machine, the leadership of which is in the hands of the governor of Smith's state and a newspaper publisher. While he discovers that his ideals will not win the senators to his side, he is able to

expose their corruption to the public. Capra's message is clear: "every-man" is the true guardian of democracy, whereas those with power and position tend to be its enemies.

Modern Times. Prod. and dir. Charlie Chaplin, 85 min., 1936. Chicago: Facets Video.
This is a Chaplin Little Tramp film, which sees the tramp traverse from a day working at a factory (which features work-induced twitches) through an accidental arrest because he has been labeled a communist, to a stint as a waiter, and finally to his disappearance as he walks down the road with Paulette Goddard toward, one hopes, a brighter horizon. This was Chaplin's attack on industrial dehumanization in which he expresses a basically Luddite disaffection with mechanized society. See *À nous la liberté* (entry above).

A Mormon Maid. Dir. Robert Z. Leonard, 60 min., 1917. Chicago: Facets Video.
Anti-Mormon hate propaganda, this film depicts a woman driven to suicide as the result of being forced into a polygamous marriage. Her daughter is faced with the same marriage prospects, but reacts by fleeing from the Church of Jesus Christ of Latter-day Saints figuratively, and into the arms of her true love literally. See *Trapped by the Mormons* (entry below).

The National Hunger March. Prod. Workers' Film and Photo League, approx. 15 min., 1931. New York: Motion Picture Center.
A film record of the first massive protests raised against the failure of government and industry to even try to alleviate the miserable condi-tions of some 12,000 unemployed men, women, and youths in major industrial cities during the early period of the Great Depression. This is a condensation of the original film, with scenes of protesters march-ing through various towns en route to Washington, D.C., and of their protest marches in Detroit, Cleveland, St. Louis, Indianapolis, New York City, and other industrial centers.

Native Land. Prod. Frontier Films, 84 min., 1939-1941. New York: Museum of Modern Art.
This docudrama is based on the hearings held by the Senate Civil Liberties Committee chaired by Senator Robert La Follette in the 1930s. At issue were violations of civil liberties by industry. Six dramatized sections are linked with documentary material to show the continuing struggle to gain their rights by male and female workers and farmers of various racial and ethnic origins. This is a documentary

with a clear propaganda purpose; there is not even a pretense of objectivity.

Night Mail. Prod. Basil Wright and Harry Watt, Government Post Office, 24 min., 1936, on *Benjamin Brittain*. New York: Kino International.
The purpose of this film is both to explain and to praise the work of those who collect, carry, and sort the mail. This production takes place almost entirely aboard a train taking mail from one part of the country to another for delivery the following day. This is a public relations film for the Government Post Office, in the docudrama form, using GPO employees acting out what they do in the normal course of their work.

The Old Way and the New. 8 min., 1912. Los Angeles: Film Classic Exchange.
Among the earliest propaganda films ever, this satire with an edge depicts greedy and exploiting businessmen robbing honest workers. It was used in Woodrow Wilson's first campaign for the presidency.

Our Daily Bread. Prod. and dir. King Vidor, Viking Productions, 71 min., 1934. Chicago: Facets Video.
The debasing effects of the Great Depression on the rural United States is the focus of this King Vidor film. The story depicts a group of otherwise unemployed and homeless people, who, inspired by a young city couple, join together on a subsistence farm. They work together almost like members of a commune, including a climactic and heroic effort to dig an irrigation canal. When finished, the canal irrigates the barren soil and makes it bountiful. This is a classic of "social consciousness" propaganda as well as of cinematographic excellence.

People of the Cumberland. Dirs. Sidney Meyers and Jay Leyda, Frontier Films, 18 min., 1938. New York: Motion Picture Center.
Documentary footage and dramatic reenactment were combined in this docudrama to publicize the struggle of poor whites living in the badlands of the Cumberland mountains in Appalachia to organize unions and fight for their rights.

Pett and Pott: A Fairy Story of the Suburbs. Prod. John Grierson, Government Post Office, 33 min., 1934, on *England in the Thirties*. New York: Kino International.
This John Grierson film was made for the Government Post Office, which ran the British telephone system. It depicts two families, the "good" Petts and the "evil" Pottses. After a burglary in the neighborhood, the Petts install a telephone; the Pottses, urged on by Mrs. Potts

(who smokes cigarettes, a certain indication of her wickedness), hire a maid instead. Things go well for the Petts, who are a loving and ideal family, while things go badly for Mrs. Potts, including that the maid is useless, save for her availability to Mr. Potts when he makes a pass at her. The climax comes when the burglar reappears, does Mrs. Potts an injury, but is caught when Little Polly Pett uses the telephone to summon the police. A delightful example of Documentary Film Movement work. The style is a foretaste of instructive documentaries with a humorous twist that appeared in the United States during the 1940s and 1950s.

Professor Mamlock. Dir. Adolph Minkin and Herbert Rappaport, Lenfilm, 100 min., 1938. New York: Museum of Modern Art.
In 1933, a surgeon in a Berlin hospital was degraded because he was a Jew. An impassioned speech against the Nazi regime led to his assassination. This event provided Soviet filmmakers with a subject for an anti-Nazi propaganda film five years later. Indeed, it was initially banned in Britain, then in the throes of appeasement policy, because of its anti-German agenda. It is well made and far subtler than the usual Soviet anti-German films of the 1930s, which perhaps makes it all the more effective as propaganda.

Reefer Madness. Dir. Louis Gasnier, Festival Films, 70 min., 1936. Chicago: Facets Video.
"The motion picture you are about to see may startle you," the film begins. It proceeds from there to describe the horrors of marijuana, the "real public enemy number one!" The film was made in cooperation with the United States government as anti-drug propaganda. The story is that a group of drug dealers are involving young people with marijuana, with the result that one goes mad, another is murdered, a third leaps to her death from a window—all because of the drug. In style and quality, the film is typical of "public service" cinema propaganda that existed from the 1930s through the 1950s. That is, the acting, cinematography, and writing are of uniformly poor quality, and the audience is beaten over the head with the message. This particular film became a "cult" film during the 1960s flower child era, as an example of the adult establishment's paranoia about the dangers of what much of the younger generation perceived to be a relatively benign drug.

Remarque, Erich Maria. *All Quiet on the Western Front.* Boston: Little, Brown, 1929.
Probably the most powerful pacifist novel ever written with particular reference to World War I. Remarque was a veteran of the German army

who spent several years engaged in the trench warfare of the Western Front. This novel chronicles the experience of a group of schoolmates who, in a fit of wartime patriotism, volunteer for the army. They are soon disillusioned, both with the futility of the struggle and with the lack of understanding of those at home. One after another they are killed as the film reaches its conclusion. The message is crystal clear, and the evocative style makes it difficult to resist. The novel was made into a film in 1930, for which Remarque wrote the screenplay. Many critics have argued that the film is not as powerful as the novel, however.

Return to Life. Prod. Medical Bureau and the North American Committee to Aid Spanish Democracy, dir. Henri Cartier Bresson, Frontier Films, 10 min., 1939. New York: Museum of Fine Art.
This French film, edited in Paris and New York, shows the behind-the-scenes work of American and Canadian doctors and nurses who volunteered medical aid to the Loyalists in the Spanish Civil War. The propaganda point is made by showing the heroism of those who oppose the Nationalist (fascist) rebels.

Sanders of the River. Dir. Zoltan Korda, London Films, 85 min., 1935. Rutgers, N.J.: Rutgers University.
Paul Robeson plays the role of West African Chief Bosambo in this British film that extols the British Empire. It has much in common with *The Lives of a Bengal Lancer* (entry above), save that it is superior in quality. The story: rebel natives are confronted by Commissioner Sanders, and under his direction, British imperial forces thwart the warlike plans of the West Africans. In this film, the British are humane rulers in Africa confronted by ungrateful natives who do not understand what is best for them.

Stop Japan. Prod. Tom Brandon, dir. Leo Selzer, Garrison Films, 20 min., 1935-1936. New York: Motion Picture Center.
This film depicts the invasion of China by Japan and lauds the Chinese struggle to resist the Japanese. It is among the first Western films to treat this subject, and it helped lay the foundation for the anti-Japanese sentiment in the United States that characterized response to the bombing of Pearl Harbor in December 1941.

Trapped by the Mormons. Dir. H. B. Parkinson, 97 min., 1922. Chicago: Facets Video.
Also known by the title *The Mormon Peril*, this film accuses "evil Mormons" of seducing innocent young girls into joining their polyga-mous society. Latter-day Saints men are depicted here as keeping

harems. The film is characteristic of what may be termed "paranoid propaganda." Ku Klux Klan supporters used the technique against African Americans during this period, and Nazi filmmakers used it against Jews a decade later. The idea is to depict the object of the propaganda as thoroughly evil, degenerate, or monstrous. See *A Mormon Maid* (entry above).

La Vie est à nous. Dir. Jean Renoir et al., Partie Communiste Français, 66 min., 1936. Paris: Arlequin Video; Reims, France: Bibliothèque de l'Université de Reims.
Newsreels, political speeches, and sketches are used to put forward the policies of the French Communist party. Staged scenes include a bailiff being driven off a farm by peasants, an unemployed intellectual joining the party, and fascist thugs beating up a newspaper vendor who is selling the Communist newspaper, *L'Humanité*. It was made specifically with the upcoming 1936 national elections in mind, elections which took place in one of the most critical moments in interwar French history. The film was later banned, and resurfaced only in 1968. It is not clear whether the reappearance was inspired by *les événements*, the student uprising in Paris in 1968, or was merely a fortuitous coincidence.

Westfront, 1918. Dir. G. W. Pabst, Nero-Film, 96 min., 1930. Chicago: Facets Video.
An antiwar film which appeals to the pacifism that was widespread in Germany and throughout Europe in the 1920s. It was released the same year as the film *All Quiet on the Western Front* and to some extent is similar to it, though not as well done. The horror as well as monotony of life in the trenches is captured through the experience of four soldiers. When they go home, they face ignorance regarding the reality of war from their families. In 1930 both films had a ready audience; within five years, in Germany at least, pacifism was being replaced by militant nationalism. Or so Nazi propagandists were proclaiming, though the reality may have been something less than Joseph Goebbels would have had the world believe.

What Eighty Million Women Want. 50 min., 1913. Los Angeles: Film Classic Exchange.
A film promoting women's suffrage, this documentary argues that society is fraught with ills: political bosses who control the courts, elections won by fraud, packed ballet boxes, and multiple voting. The message is that all of this will end once women get the vote. See Bettina Friedl, ed., *On to Victory* (entry above).

Chapter 4

PROPAGANDA AND AUTHORITARIAN IDEOLOGIES

World War I left Europe in a state of uncertainty regarding the future. This was so in part because the war had wrecked such havoc upon the European peoples, but also because the war shattered the sense of confidence regarding the future that characterized the several decades prior to 1914, known then and since as *la belle époque*. The postwar period began with revolution and civil war, economic collapse and hunger, and as is often the case in such circumstances, the appearance of a wide range of ideological and political revolutionaries and extremists. Among these were Adolf Hitler, leader of the National Socialist party in Germany and Reich chancellor after 1933, and Benito Mussolini, the Italian fascist leader who became premier of Italy in 1922. These were right-wing extremists; on the left were the Bolsheviks in Russia who, after 1929, were led by Joseph Stalin, a dictator every bit as bad as Hitler. The object of all of these leaders was to impose their authoritarian will upon the states they ruled—to establish, in short, what has frequently been termed totalitarianism. Propaganda was one of the means used to achieve this end.

This chapter lists books, articles, films (including distributors, where known), and other materials that relate directly to the propaganda of authoritarian ideologies and systems that came into existence after World War I, and some of which continued to exist after World War II. The Soviet Union, Nazi Germany, and fascist Italy were the principal sources of such material, though not the only ones. Radical movements of right and left with totalitarian solutions to social and other problems also figured from time to time in the political life of Great Britain, France, Spain, and the United States.

History and Function

Adam, Peter. *Art of the Third Reich*. New York: Harry N. Abrams, 1992. This collection of examples with text is drawn from a wide range of art produced in Germany between 1933 and 1945. Two points are made clear: one, that for the most part it was not very good art, and two, that it was mostly produced with propaganda in mind. Arno Breker's sculpture portrayed ideal Nordic types, which was propaganda for Nazi racial ideology. Jürgen Wegener created murals which linked the Hitler Youth movement to the same racial ideology. Werner Peiner's series of tapestries included scenes of Frederick the Great in battle, which idealized the German military tradition. Even architecture reflected the ideological perspectives of the Reich, whether it was the grand buildings on a heroic scale designed by Albert Speer or the *Hitlerdorf* (Hitler village) opened in Bavaria in 1934. The text is clear, the analysis of the work is carefully drawn, and the examples reproduced are fully representative. They include, for instance, Herman Goering's country estate, Karinhall, which was designed to reflect the Gothic character that Nazi ideology claimed to reflect. The bibliography cites mostly German-language sources.

Architektur des Untergangs. Prod. Peter Cohen, Filminstitute Sveriges Television Kanal 1, 119 min., 1989. New York: Icarus Films.
This black-and-white documentary looks at the arts and architecture of the Third Reich in the context of the rise to power of the Nazi party. The object is to demonstrate how Hitler used the arts for propaganda purposes, and to reflect certain elements of Nazi policy, such as exposition of the ideal of absolute power and racial purity. In German with English subtitles.

Baird, Jay W. "From Berlin to Neubabelsberg: Nazi Film Propaganda and *Hitler Youth Quex.*" *Journal of Contemporary History* 18 (1983), pp. 495-515.
This article analyzes how "film, myth, and history" were integrated into the making of the Nazi propaganda film, *Hitlerjunge Quex*. The author is concerned equally with the nature of film propaganda and the "use of poetic license in the mythical interpretation of history." He provides a historical background for Herbert Norkus, the subject of the film, showing how the facts differed from the idealized version of his life portrayed in the film. The author also analyzes the propaganda techniques employed in demonizing the communists. By killing Norkus, they turned him into a Hitler Youth martyr.

_____. "Hitler's Muse: The Political Aesthetics of the Poet and Playwright Eberhard Wolfgang Möller." *German Studies Review* 17, 2 (May 1994), pp. 269-285.
A thoroughly researched and well written commentary on the contributions of German poet Eberhard Wolfgang Möller to what the author terms the "distorted concept of the beautiful" espoused by the Nazis. As he makes clear, that concept was an idealization of racial type and of German cultural superiority, and was an integral part of Nazi propaganda. Möller wrote both anti-Semitic poetry and poetry that called upon the German people to embrace Adolf Hitler as their savior.

The Birth of Soviet Cinema. Prod. Mosfilm Studies, 49 min., 1972, English-language version prod. Harold Mantell, 1989. Princeton, N.J.: Films for the Humanities.

Through the efforts of such film pioneers as Sergei Eisenstein and Vsevolod Pudovkin, the Soviet Union was able to use film as an effective propaganda channel virtually from the moment the 1917 revolution was over. This documentary, produced originally in Moscow, explains how the Soviet government attracted the best writers, directors, and producers to make films that promoted the party line. This point is made clearly here through the use of scenes from some of the most famous examples of their early films, such as *Strike*, *Battleship Potemkin*, and *October*.

Bramstead, Ernest K. *Goebbels and National Socialist Propaganda.* East Lansing: Michigan State University Press, 1965.

The purpose of this volume, in the author's words, "is to place the development of National Socialist propaganda and the role of Joseph Goebbels as its chief protagonist in a clearer and better proportioned perspective than has hitherto been possible." It is among the first complete histories of Nazi propaganda, and as such endeavors to be all-inclusive. The author analyzes the propaganda of the early Nazi party in opposition, the creation of the propaganda ministry, the particular kinds of propaganda used to build up Nazi ideology such as anti-Semitic and Führerprinzip propaganda, war propaganda, and propaganda battles specifically between Deutsche Rundfunk (German radio) and the British Broadcasting Corporation. There is an appendix called "What Goebbels Left Out," a reference to his published diaries. Select bibliography. See Erich Ebermayer and Hans-Otto Meissner, *Evil Genius* (entry below).

Burden, Hamilton T. *The Nuremberg Party Rallies: 1923-39.* New York: Frederick A. Praeger, 1967.

This volume traces the evolution of Nazi party rallies as a propaganda channel from the very beginning to the outbreak of World War II. Such events were "among the most significant activities of the National Socialist German Workers' Party." For that reason, the author argues, it is important to understand these rallies and the role they played throughout the history of Nazi Germany. Each chapter looks at a particular rally, beginning with "Party Day, 1923." Among others are "Party Day of Victory, 1933," "Party Day of Freedom, 1935," and "Party Day of Labour, 1937." The author explains that it was through these rallies that Hitler and other Nazi leaders reaffirmed the mythic values upon which

Propaganda and Authoritarian Ideologies
193
Nazi ideology rested. There are numerous illustrations, a select bibliography, and appendixes containing examples of party rally programs.

Bytwerk, Randall L. *Julius Streicher: The Man Who Persuaded a Nation to Hate Jews*. New York: Stein and Day, 1983.
"Why did the Germans kill six million Jews?" the author asks. He answers that it was owing to the propaganda of Julius Streicher, publisher of the violent anti-Semitic propaganda newspaper *Der Stürmer*. Streicher's message was Jewish depravity of both spirit and blood as compared to Aryan purity. He sent this message through some of the most vicious hate propaganda material ever published. Much of it was sexual in nature: for example, a cartoon of Jewish doctors preparing to violate an Aryan female patient, and photographs touched up to accent stereotypical images of Jewish Hollywood film producers ogling scantily clad blond, blue-eyed females. The volume is thoroughly researched, clearly written, and illustrated with reproductions from *Der Stürmer*. Select bibliography.

Catlin, George E. G. "The Rôle of Propaganda in a Democracy." *Annals of the American Academy of Political and Social Science* 179 (1935), pp. 219-226.
This article is driven by the realities of the 1930s; its purpose is to put propaganda in perspective relative to the needs of democracy, and the realities of fascism and communism. Democracy is defined summarily as government of toleration as compared to such intolerant forms of government as exist in fascist and communist states. The author then defines propaganda as spreading ideology by appealing to emotions as well as reason, and then applies its uses to democracy in comparison to authoritarianism. He argues that in a two-party system, propaganda helps sustain democracy, whereas in a one-party system it becomes a means of coercion and control, which is the opposite of democracy.

Childs, Harwood Lawrence, ed. *Propaganda and Dictatorship: A Collection of Papers*. Princeton, N.J.: Princeton University Press, 1936.
No one puts the point of this collection of six papers presented at the American Political Science Association in Chicago in 1934 better than does DeWitt Clinton Poole, who wrote in the foreword that the dictatorships of Europe, "now in power," hold their power through manipulating public opinion through propaganda dissemination. To this the editor adds that "the world is both propaganda-conscious and dictator-conscious," and therefore it is essential to examine how the one promotes the other and how dictatorship differs from democracy in

relation to manipulating public opinion. The papers include Fritz Marx on Germany, Arnold Zurcher on Italy, Bertram Maxwell on the Soviet Union, Oscar Jászi on the Balkans, Harold Lasswell on research on propaganda and dictatorship, and George Catlin on propaganda and democratic government. These were among the leading scholars of the day in the field of political dictatorship and propaganda, whose insights into both the subject matter of the papers and the concerns of the historical period in which they appeared set the standards over many years for research and writing on political propaganda.

Conquest, Robert. *The Politics of Ideas in the U.S.S.R.* New York: Praeger, 1967.
This volume offers an explanation for how the Soviet Union regulated the expression of ideas through censorship and manipulation of information, which is to say through propaganda. The author discusses a wide range of areas where Soviet propaganda is applied, from politics proper to the humanities and sciences. He begins with a commentary on "the theory" behind Soviet politics (Marxist determinism) and then explains how this theory has been regulated through thought mobilization, systematic restriction of public expression, state organization of the press, literature and broadcasting, and specific techniques of thought control as introduced after World War II. The bibliography lists mainly Russian-language publications.

Ebenstein, William. *Fascist Italy*. New York: American Book Company, 1939.
This book provides an analysis of the origins, development, and structure of fascist Italy on the eve of World War II. While the author surveys all aspects of the fascist system, chapter 4 is devoted exclusively to how propaganda was used to create it, and continued to be used to maintain it. The underlying theme of the book as a whole is the danger which a system predicated on an extremist, dictatorial ideology poses to democracy, and to the existing democracies. The author's interpretation of fascist Italy indicates his conviction that this ideology was sustained by propaganda which, as it did in Nazi Germany, glorified the leader, war, and conquest. Limited bibliography.

Ebermayer, Erich, and Hans-Otto Meissner. *Evil Genius: The Story of Joseph Goebbels*. Translated by Louis Hagen. London: Allan Wingate, 1953.
First published in German in 1952, this biography of Third Reich propaganda minister Joseph Goebbels has been "freely adapted" by the translator. It reads like a biographical novel. All the same, it presents details of the life of Germany's master propagandist, making the point that

Goebbels indeed was an evil genius. He is treated as a thorough cynic who believed little of the propaganda he created. Later studies of Goebbels made more of the psychological element in his life, such as his need to overcome a physical deformity, which led him to become both a woman-izer and an elitist. The treatment of Goebbels in this book is almost romantic in nature. Illustrations but no bibliography. See Ernest K. Bramstead, *Goebbels and National Socialist Propaganda* (entry above).

Ekstein, Modris. *The Limits of Reason: The German Democratic Press and the Collapse of Weimar Democracy*. London: Oxford University Press, 1975.
The response of the liberal press in Weimar Germany to the rise of National Socialism is the subject of this book. The author looks at three Jewish-owned newspaper firms, each of which distributed several papers, and examines their editorial policy and how it was formulated. He concludes that the real failure of these and other papers that constituted the liberal press in Germany was that they did *not* do an adequate job of disseminating anti-Nazi propaganda. Appendixes note the political affiliation of major Weimar newspapers and their circula-tion figures. Select bibliography.

Flavell, M. Kay. "Kitsch and Propaganda: The Blending of Myth and History in Hedwig Courths-Mahler's *Lissa geht ins Glück* (1936)." *German Studies Review* 8, 1 (February 1985), pp. 65-87.
Hedwig Courths-Mahler wrote romance novels in the 1930s. Kay Flavell here challenges the convention that these novels were simple folk myth, and thus outside the parameters of the nationalist volkish traditions of the National Socialist political movement. Rather, she argues that they were squarely within that tradition, and that *Lissa geht ins Glück* is a case in point. While refusing to follow Joseph Goebbels' suggestion that she make her villains Jews and her heroes SA men, she nevertheless contributed to the Nazi mythos of the Aryan hero who is strong, patriotic, and loyal, while the Aryan heroine is also strong but, more important, is obedient to male authority. Therefore, the author con-cludes, Courths-Mahler's stories contributed, whether intended or not, to the political-cultural propaganda of the National Socialist movement.

Fraser, Lindley. *Germany Between Two Wars: A Study of Propaganda and War-Guilt*. New York: Oxford University Press, 1945.
This book was written in German by an English expert on broadcast propaganda in order to show the Germans how they had been misled by propaganda. It was then translated into English for the benefit of British and American officers and others who would have contact with

the Germans after World War II. The book covers the period between the world wars with special reference to propaganda that was designed to deny defeat in World War I, bring the National Socialists to power, and justify the war that began in 1939. Some of the topics covered are the "stab-in-the-back" theory, the "dictated peace," German rearmament, propaganda favoring war, and the origins of World War II. Much of the contents of this volume appeared first in British news broadcasts made by the author as counters to German propaganda. They became, in their own right, propaganda justifying the allied cause in World War II. This book links primary and secondary source material on British wartime propaganda. Select bibliography.

Gadberry, Glen W., ed. *Theatre in the Third Reich: Essays on Theatre in Nazi Germany*. Westport, Conn.: Greenwood Press, 1995.
This collection of essays cover a wide variety of subjects concerned with German theater in the Nazi period. The underlying theme of each essay which provides unity for the entire collection is the attempt by the Nazi regime to purge German theater of everything which did not further the racial and other objectives of Nazi ideology. At least one contributor, Rufus J. Cadigan, treats this theme with a touch of humor by referring to his subject, Eberhard Wolfgang Möller, as a "politically correct playwright of the Third Reich." Select bibliography.

Graham, Cooper C. *Leni Riefenstahl and Olympia*. Metuchen, N.J.: Scarecrow Press, 1986.
A detailed and archive-based study concerned with every aspect of how cinematographer Leni Riefenstahl made her documentary film of the 1936 Olympic Games in Berlin. The author is chiefly concerned with describing the process of organizing, planning, making, and distributing the film rather than with the politics that surrounded it, though each of these activities had political connections at some level. He indicates at the outset that the style of the film reflected aspects of Nazi ideology and certainly was an affirmation of Nazi worship of physical culture, with all of its racial overtones. While the propaganda elements of the film cannot be and are not overlooked, the main point is that Riefenstahl, regardless of what her politics may have been (she maintained that she was apolitical, an artist only), was the greatest woman filmmaker of the twentieth century. An appendix includes, among other documents relevant to the subject, Riefenstahl's contract with the German propaganda ministry. Extensive bibliography of primary and secondary sources, and a single illustration, a photograph of Riefenstahl.

Hardy, Alexander G. *Hitler's Secret Weapon: The "Managed" Press and Propaganda Machine of Nazi Germany*. New York: Vantage Press, 1967.

The author was a United States prosecutor at the Nuremberg war crimes trials, and this volume is based largely on the "lessons" learned from that experience. Subjects examined include the nature of managed news, the Nazi press and propaganda machine, the Nazi "propaganda lords" ranging from Joseph Goebbels through broadcaster Hans Fritzsche, Nazi propaganda posters, German public opinion as influenced by propaganda to support both foreign conquest and the mass murder of Germany's domestic "enemies," and finally, a detailed analysis of propaganda and the Holocaust. The text and extensive appendixes include many widely varied documents related to Nazi propaganda. Despite the sense of personal outrage at the Nazi experience which the author clearly felt, the text is remarkably free of unsubstantiated judgments. No bibliography.

Hartsough, Denise. "Soviet Film Distribution and Exhibition in Germany, 1921-1933." *Historical Journal of Film, Radio and Television* 5, 2 (1985), pp. 131-148.

Between 1921 and 1933, the Communist International (Comintern) used Soviet film to propagandize communist doctrines and support for Soviet economic aid in Weimar, Germany. This was not altogether successful, owing to German censorship and taxes on imported film. This article examines the objectives of Comintern film policy as it passed through several stages in which efforts were made to improve Soviet film export to Germany and thereby achieve better propaganda results. The author also notes the more important films that actually were circulated, with commentary on their content. The article is based upon a mix of primary and secondary sources. While there is much of value here, the author has not developed a historical context for her analysis as fully as would have been desirable.

Hollander, Gayle Durham. *Soviet Political Indoctrination: Developments in Mass Media and Propaganda Since Stalin*. New York: Praeger, 1972.

This volume concerns internal Soviet propaganda techniques, which the author describes as the means by which political socialization takes place. Indeed, she describes political socialization as being a virtual preoccupation of the Soviet Communist party, which makes little distinction between political communication and political persuasion. The author examines the mass media and agitprop apparatus with an eye toward explaining the role of mass communications and agitprop in the process of adult political indoctrination. Topics include the nature of the Soviet system, newspapers and magazines, books, radio and television broadcasting, film, Soviet audiences, and the structure of organizations devoted to domestic propaganda. Appendixes include details of Soviet mass communications channels. Extensive bibliography.

Horak, Jan-Christopher. "Zionist Film Propaganda in Nazi Germany." *Historical Journal of Film, Radio and Television* 4, 1 (1984), pp. 49-58. Odd as that might seem at first glance, Zionist film propaganda was disseminated in Nazi Germany with the cooperation of Nazi authorities. The fact seems less odd when it becomes clear that such film propaganda encouraged Jews to emigrate to Palestine. This article examines the overall Zionist film campaign, including how the films were distributed and the difficulties associated with distribution. It also describes and analyzes specific films, many of which were made by German Jews who had already gone to Palestine. After World War II began, Zionist propaganda ceased to circulate in Germany. Outside Germany it was limited largely to propaganda about Jewish contributions to the war effort; even then, the basic message remained that Jews should plan to emigrate to Palestine once the war was over.

Inkeles, Alex. *Public Opinion in Soviet Russia: A Study in Mass Persuasion.* Cambridge, Mass.: Harvard University Press, 1950. The purpose of this volume, the author begins, is to explain the functioning of the mass communications media in the Soviet Union, with the particular object of evaluating its implications. That is, in his words, "since exposure to a steady flow of propaganda and agitation is a major facet of the daily life of every Soviet citizen, no assessment of his life situation can be complete if it does not take account of that fact." The principal topics covered follow accordingly: part 1 concerns propaganda exclusively; part 2 explores "oral agitation," or agitprop, which is a form of propaganda featuring the party leader "agitating" a mass audience with reference to some particular party program; parts 3, 4, and 5 respectively cover the Soviet press, broadcasting, and film. In reading this volume, some background in Soviet history will be helpful. Extensive bibliography.

Kenez, Peter. *The Birth of the Propaganda State: Soviet Methods of Mass Mobilization, 1917-1929.* Cambridge, England: Cambridge University Press, 1985. There is little about the inner workings of the Communist party or the Soviet government in this excellent study of propaganda in the early

Soviet Union. Rather, the book concentrates on the organization of Soviet propaganda in the 1920s and on the contents of books, films, and newspapers that were read and viewed by Soviet citizens and the mass meetings in which citizens participated during that period. This book is about the role of propaganda in mobilizing the Soviet people. The Soviet leaders were not cynical originally, the author argues, but they were manipulative, a factor born out of both ideology and necessity. In his words: "They came to their task of ruling an almost ungovernable country . . . with no clear ideas about propaganda." They quickly learned. Part 1 sets the stage, including a chapter on the "political use of books, films, and posters," and part 2 describes how these communications media were turned into propaganda channels by the Soviet state. Extensive bibliography.

Kershaw, Ian. *The "Hitler Myth" : Image and Reality in the Third Reich.* Oxford, England: Clarendon Press, 1987.
In the author's own words, "this book . . . is not, in fact, primarily concerned with Hitler himself, but with the propaganda image-building process, and above all with the reception of this image by the German people. . . ." What follows is a thorough and revealing study of how propaganda "made" Adolf Hitler and promoted his popularity far beyond that enjoyed by the National Socialist party. Subjects include the Hitler image in the Weimar era, the propaganda profile of Hitler, the "Fuhrer without sin," the Hitler image in relation to Radicals, the Church, the Jews, and the concept of war and peace, and what happens to the Hitler image in the context of defeat and disaster in World War II. Select bibliography.

_____. "Ideology, Propaganda, and the Rise of the Nazi Party," in Peter D. Stachura, ed., *The Nazi Machtergreifung*. London: George Allen and Unwin, 1983.
This essay examines the role of ideology-driven propaganda in the National Socialist rise to power in Germany, which was, in the author's words, a phenomenon "less obvious than it initially may seem." The problem is, what exactly was Nazi ideology? How did the propaganda used to disseminate it function and with what actual effect? These are the author's basic questions, and while these sixteen pages hardly provide a study in depth, they do provide an overview of the problem in its historical context, and draw the conclusion that ideological propaganda had its greatest impact only after it was put across as "national goals rather than party politics."

Kiffer, Monika. *Mussolinis Afrika-Feldzug 1935/36 im Spiegel von Literatur und Propaganda der Zeit*. Bonn: Romanistischer Verlag, 1988. Italy invaded Ethiopia in 1935, and despite international protests including appeals to the League of Nations, persisted in the assault until that East African country had been conquered and made part of Mussolini's Italian empire. This campaign did not have the enthusiastic backing of the Italian people, however. The author of this volume argues that this being the case, the reports and enthusiastic endorsements of the campaign, written by intellectuals and journalists, were simply examples of fascist propaganda favoring Mediterranean and East African expansion as part of the development of Mussolini's imperial master plan. The first chapter describes the contribution to nationalist literary propaganda after World War I by poet Gabriele D'Annunzio. Subsequent chapters detail the contents of similar work in the context of the Abyssinian campaign by such writers as Biagio Pace, F. T. Marinetti, and Paolo Cesarini. Select bibliography of both Italian- and German-language sources.

Kingston, Paul J. *Anti-Semitism in France During the 1930s: Organizations, Personalities, and Propaganda*. Hull, England: University of Hull Press, 1983.
This book is a study of anti-Semitism and its impact upon an otherwise civilized nation in an age of crisis. Jews suffered in France the same as elsewhere, during the decade when authoritarian political ideologies were on the rise. This book analyzes such anti-Semitic newspapers as *La France Juive*, *La Libre Parole*, and *Le Petit Journal*, and looks at anti-Semitic leaders like Eduoard Drumont and organizations such as *La Crois de Feu* and its leader, Colonel de la Rocque. The second half of the book is devoted exclusively to the nature of anti-Semitic propaganda in France in this period. Extensive bibliography.

Kracauer, Siegfried. *From Caligari to Hitler: A Psychological History of the German Film*. Princeton, N.J.: Princeton University Press, 1974. First published in 1947.
While this volume deals with all aspects of German film from what the author terms the "archaic period" (1895-1918) to the end of World War II, the bulk of its analysis concerns the period between the world wars. Parts IV and V examine films that were either anti-Nazi propaganda or pro-Nazi propaganda. In each case, as the book's subtitle indicates, the author's concern is to illuminate the role of psychological manipulation in the films. In the process, he provides technical as well as content analysis of the films discussed. His interpretive conclusion

is that German film both reflected and encouraged those tendencies within German society that led inexorably to the rule of Hitler. An appendix provides a structural analysis of each film discussed. Illustrations and an extensive bibliography. See David Welch, *Propaganda and the German Cinema* (entry below).

MacKenzie, A. J. *Propaganda Boom*. London: John Gifford, 1938.
The author finds the "propaganda boom" of the 1930s, which he describes in this volume, somewhat alarming because of the uses made of it by both communists and fascists. On the other hand, he sees a value in propaganda for promoting democracy. The book includes the author's views on what propaganda is, how it works, and why it has become so pervasive in the post-World War I era. Specific topics include Nazi, Italian fascist, and Soviet communist propagandists, the role of film and broadcasting in propaganda dissemination, censorship, and the role of propaganda in education. Written as a contemporary think piece, the volume does not include a bibliography.

Mancini, Elain. *Struggles of the Italian Film Industry During Fascism, 1930-1935*. Ann Arbor, Mich.: UMI Research Press, 1985.
The author contends that Italian cinema in these critical years was far from being an ideological instrument in the service of the Mussolini regime. Rather, the filmmakers "relied on public opinion to determine the cinematic themes and stories." Indeed, she argues, filmmakers often "bit the hand of Fascism" with their subject matter. Be that as it may, chapter 5 of this volume details the activities of LUCE, the state-controlled company which produced newsreels, documentaries, and educational films, all of which contained some pro-fascist propaganda themes. The basic premise of this book is not altogether convincing as argued. Several appendixes include analysis of particular films and lists of feature films with descriptions. Select bibliography.

Marx, Fritz Morstein. "Propaganda and Dictatorship." *Annals of the American Academy of Political and Social Science* 179 (May 1935), pp. 211-226.
The author briefly explains dictatorship, and then discusses how dictators employ propaganda to maintain their ideological identity. He argues that such employment requires "governmental primacy if not monopoly over all instrumentalities of opinion dissemination, particularly the press." Much of this article draws for examples on the writings of Joseph Goebbels with reference to Nazi propaganda, and much of its purpose is to dispute with other political scholars in the

United States the nature and function of propaganda in relation to dictatorship.

Meyer, Michael. "The Nazi Musicologist as Myth Maker in the Third Reich." *Journal of Contemporary History* 10, 4 (October 1975), pp. 649-665. This article analyzes the roll of musicology in Nazi propaganda. The author explains how noted German composers, performers, educators, critics, and musicologists made statements, issued manifestoes, and wrote articles and books justifying Nazi totalitarian ideology and practice. In short, they became propagandists for a new musicology that helped legitimize Nazi power. This power, the author concludes, rested upon the Nazi leadership's profound understanding of human nature, and an equal understanding of how to manipulate it through cultural as well as political propaganda.

Reuth, Ralf Georg. *Goebbels*. Translated by Krishna Winston. New York: Harcourt Brace, 1993. This is the first biography of the Nazi propaganda minister to have full access to all available materials on his life, including the complete Goebbels diaries. Reuth makes full use of these materials and offers a complete portrait of his subject. The book chronicles Goebbels' life and includes many quotes and anecdotes. The result is an eminently readable biography, which provides an in-depth context within which to place Goebbels' skills as a Nazi propagandist. Accessible to every intelligent reader interested in Goebbels' place in the history of propaganda. Extensive bibliography.

Shlapentokh, Dmitry, and Vladimir Shlapentokh. *Soviet Cinematography, 1918-1991: Ideological Conflict and Social Reality*. New York: Aldine de Gruyter, 1993. This volume provides a thorough examination of the evolution of Soviet film since the end of World War I. Its object, in the authors' words, is to "examine the influence of official ideology, i.e. the ideology supported by the centralized state, on the presentation of social reality by Soviet cinema." In other words, the book is about the role of propaganda in the history of Soviet film. Part 1 concerns the theory behind the interaction of social reality and state ideology. In part 2, the postrevolution decade is explored in terms of a "cordial acceptance of official ideology," with the caution that a few films were produced which were anti-Bolshevik. Part 3 covers the Stalin era, when there was "total submission to official ideology." Part 4 is about the film-makers' challenge to official ideology during the "first thaw" (1954-

1968), and part 5 describes the rejection of official ideology by Soviet cinematographers. A concluding chapter reviews films that took a nostalgic look at the period immediately following the "Fall of the Empire," which films are said to be a reflection of disillusionment with post-Soviet Russia. Illustrations, a select bibliography, a list of film directors and another of Soviet films with titles in English.

Taylor, Richard. "A Medium for the Masses: Agitation in the Soviet Civil War." *Soviet Studies* 22, 4 (April 1971), pp. 562-574.
The new Bolshevik government of Russia held power only marginally and even its survival was questionable immediately following the 1917 Revolution. Its aims were to mobilize the masses behind it and at the same time train them in a new way of thinking about society and the world. Cinema was one of the first mass mediums to be taken over by the Soviet state for the dissemination of propaganda in pursuit of these aims. This article analyzes that process, notes the many difficulties associated with it, and draws appropriate conclusions about the effectiveness of cinema propaganda in the particular context of the Russian Civil War that began in 1919.

_____. "Soviet Cinema: The Path to Stalin." *History Today* 40 (July 1990), pp. 43-48.
This short article explains how silent film was a vital propaganda tool for the Bolsheviks following the 1917 revolution and subsequent civil war. Film proved a useful way to win over a "heterogeneous and largely hostile and illiterate population." During the 1920s, Russian avant-garde films set revolutionary ideals within the context of conventional melodrama, as a way to appeal to Soviet audiences. In 1930, however, the film industry was reorganized and films, now "talkies," were made in which revolutionary or civil war themes paralleled the Stalin personality cult. The musical comedy was also employed in the 1930s as a propaganda channel.

Thompson, Doug. *State Control in Fascist Italy: Culture and Conformity, 1925-43.* Manchester, England: Manchester University Press, 1991.
The general context here is the nature of the political right transcending time and place; the specific context is fascism of the Italian sort, defined as "an extreme form of conservatism," which the author argues is latent within each Western society. The study is of how in fascist Italy this extreme conservatism with its class-based social, economic, and political privilege was promoted and developed, and how it played out. One chapter is devoted entirely to the role played in the process

by "culture as propaganda," and while Italian fascist propaganda is not
the main theme of this study, the author makes clear that propaganda
nevertheless was a factor in each step of transforming Italy into a fascist
state. Select bibliography.

Welch, David. *Propaganda and the German Cinema, 1933-1945*. Oxford,
   England: Clarendon Press, 1983.
   One of the first complete studies of German film propaganda in the
   Nazi period, and arguably the best. The author begins with a historical
   background on the German film industry and the reorganization of that
   industry under Joseph Goebbels. There is also a description of Goebbels as propagandist. The bulk of the volume analyzes the major
   propaganda films produced over the years, from *SA-Mann Brand*
   (1933) through *Kolberg* (1945). The films are grouped for analysis
   according to which aspect of Nazi ideology they stressed: comradeship
   and heroism, the Nazi party, blood and soil, the leadership principle,
   images of war and of the enemy, and anti-Semitism. Illustrations,
   filmography, and select bibliography. See Siegfried Kracauer, *From
   Caligari to Hitler* (entry above).

Channels and Techniques

Berezin, Mabel. "The Organization of Political Ideology: Culture, State,
   and Theater in Fascist Italy." *American Sociological Review* 56 (October 1991), pp. 639-651.
   This article is a conceptual study of the interaction between state and
   cultural institutions using fascist Italy as a model. The author concludes
   that while the fascist regime presumed to use theater as an ideological
   vehicle, that is, as a channel for disseminating fascist propaganda, that
   presumption fell well short of the mark, even though state paternalism
   over theater was established. In short, compared to the exploitation of
   theater and other cultural forms for propaganda purposes in Soviet
   Russia and Nazi Germany, theater in Italy did not become a significant
   propaganda channel for fascist ideology. The article features a select
   bibliography. See also Taylor Cole, "The Italian Ministry of Popular
   Culture" (entry below).

Carter, Huntley. *The New Theater and Cinema of Soviet Russia*. London:
   Chapman and Dodd, 1924.
   Written by an English journalist stationed in Soviet Russia, this lengthy
   volume provides a detailed and thorough description and analysis of

the nature and purpose of Soviet theater and cinema from the 1917 revolution to 1924. He makes clear that these media have been organized for propaganda purposes, specifically for creating a new and revolutionary industrial social mindset, and concludes that this is a phenomenon needing to be studied. Topics include the state organization of Soviet theater, variations within the theater such as the "proletcult theater," Jewish theater, Stanislavsky theater, and such new Soviet film organizations as Goskino and Proletkino. There are references as well to new writers on the scene, Maxim Gorky being, in the author's judgment, one of the most important. Illustrations, appendixes containing official pronouncements on theater, but no bibliography.

Chakotin, Serge. *The Rape of the Masses: The Psychology of Totalitarian Political Propaganda.* New York: Alliance Book Corporation, 1940.
A period piece inspired by the rise of authoritarian politics in the 1930s, this study of propaganda used in conjunction with terror is based upon psychological analysis of human response to certain kinds of stimuli. The book draws upon examples ranging from ancient Greece to the twentieth century. The main theme is the application of psychological manipulation as a feature of twentieth century totalitarianism, which the author explores with reference principally to Nazi Germany and fascist Italy, but by implication to Soviet Russia as well. Topics covered include the science of psychology, "collective" psychology, the use of symbolism in propaganda, why Hitler succeeded, and a few examples of when propaganda is a "good thing"—such as when it is used to counter fascism. The volume is written for the informed reader, although social scientific jargon is kept to a minimum. The select bibliography is of limited value to historians.

Clews, John C. *Communist Propaganda Techniques.* New York: Praeger, 1964.
The author's opening chapter defines propaganda with reference to some of the leading authorities on the subject such as Leonard W. Doob, and to how propaganda has played a role in selling ideas at least since Roman emperor Nero trained a corps of 5,000 young men to "incite crowds at the circus, when fervor had to be stimulated for the execution of the Christians." Beyond that, the volume concentrates on the history of communist propaganda practices, beginning with the Bolsheviks. The campaign to persuade the world that the United States used biological warfare in Korea between 1950 and 1951 is used as a classic case study of techniques. Of particular interest in this volume are the appendixes, which provide lists of communist propaganda

journals and organizations in various countries, international communist fronts between 1945 and 1962, and an analysis of communist hate propaganda and propaganda art. No bibliography.

Cole, Taylor. "The Italian Ministry of Popular Culture." *Public Opinion Quarterly* 2, 3 (July 1938), pp. 425-434.
Written by a contemporary observer, this article describes the Italian culture ministry as an outgrowth of the fascists' desire to regulate the presentation of the Italian image. The ministry's main objective, therefore, is to concentrate control over cultural channels in State hands, thus ensuring their infusion with fascist propaganda material. The author describes the ministry's organization and the kinds of activities it controls, such as tourism and radio broadcasting.

Deutschmann, Linda. *Triumph of the Will: The Image of the Third Reich.* Wakefield, N.H.: Longwood Academic, 1991.
In this volume, the author provides a complete and thorough examination of *Triumph of the Will*, the Leni Riefenstahl propaganda masterpiece. The author notes that this film has often been described as "a great and brilliant achievement in the history of film propaganda; a 'magnificently controlled work of art'; and as a lethal psychological weapon aimed at destroying the will to resist." She puts the film in historical and political context, describes the context of the film and preparations that went into making it, analyzes its contents, and devotes one chapter to the nature of Nazi propaganda and another to Riefenstahl herself. Curiously, while portions of film dialogue are reproduced, there are no illustrations. An appendix provides biographies of the Nazi *prominenti* who appear in the film. Extensive bibliography. See *Triumph of the Will* (entry below under "Propaganda Material").

Freeman, Ellis. *Conquering the Man in the Street: A Psychological Analysis of Propaganda in War, Fascism, and Politics.* New York: Vanguard Press, 1940.
A long and detailed study of the psychology of propaganda in the context of the 1930s. Hitler's use of mystical ritual shares space with the romanticizing of Western heros in Hollywood films, in order to make the point that propaganda works by playing upon psychological responses to a wide variety of stimuli. The volume is in part a warning against such manipulation in political and wartime contexts, and is clearly a response to circumstances facing the United States on the eve of its entry into World War II.

Gallo, Max. "1925-1945: Propaganda and Ideology," in *The Poster in History*. Translated by Alfred and Bruni Mayor. Secaucus, N.J.: Wellfleet Press, 1989.
This chapter covers the rise of totalitarian regimes in Europe, political warfare before 1939, and World War II. The illustrations are explained, and are selected so as to be fully representative of every subject about which propaganda posters were made during that period.

Garber, William. "Propaganda Analysis: To What Ends?" *American Journal of Sociology* 48 (1942-1943), pp. 240-245.
The object of this short article was to criticize how Harold Lasswell and the Institute for Propaganda Analysis were going about their work in 1941. That work was to analyze what was being disseminated as propaganda and to devise ways to defend against it. The author argues that in order to do a proper job in the study of propaganda, new and better techniques must be devised. The point is made that the characteristics of the "field," meaning context, in which propaganda is deployed must be considered in determining the meaning of the specific techniques used. It is necessary, he concludes, to go beyond the study of the "rhetorical and psychological tricks" that propaganda employs; not to do so leaves the impression that the only way to defeat propaganda is to emulate it.

Geldern, James von. *Bolshevik Festivals, 1917-1920*. Berkeley: University of California Press, 1993.
This volume describes the use of festivals in the early years of Bolshevik Russia as a medium for spreading enthusiasm for the new regime; in other words, festival as agitprop. Reference is made to artists such as Marc Chagall covering buildings in Vitebsk with murals and Nathan Altman redesigning Palace Square in Petrograd, all with an eye toward celebrating the victory of the revolution. Popular culture, including the circus, was exploited for propaganda festival purposes. The author makes the argument that the tradition of this "propaganda by festival" had its origins in the czarist period. However, the Bolsheviks made far more extensive use of the concept than the czarist regimes ever did. Illustrations and extensive bibliography.

Grandin, Thomas. *The Political Use of the Radio*. New York: Arno Press and *The New York Times*, 1971. First published in Geneva, 1939.
Published originally on the eve of World War II, this volume presents a view of radio as a problematic medium of communication that contains the potential for much misuse as a propaganda channel. The

theme is set in the context of radio broadcasting in the later 1930s. Broadcasting is examined statistically and qualitatively from countries as diverse as Latvia and Great Britain. The volume is driven by the reality of fascist and Nazi propaganda that filled the airwaves in the 1930s. Appendixes contain specific information for 1939 on power ratios for long and medium wavelengths, numbers of receiving sets in countries around the globe, and broadcast schedules. One discovers that in Slovakia, for example, one could tune in to English language newscasts every Wednesday at 10:30 P.M., local time.

Hitler: February 10, 1933. Prod. International Historic Films, 31 min., 1985. Chicago: International Historic Films.
One week after Hitler was appointed Chancellor of Germany, he gave a speech at the Berlin Sports Palace in which he exhorted the German people to vote for Nazi candidates in the upcoming parliamentary elections. This is a copy of the original film of that speech, made by Universum-Film-Aktiengesellschaft in 1933, and distributed across Germany. All of Hitler's considerable oratorical skills and ability to manipulate his audience are on display in this film.

Janowitz, Morris. "The Technique of Propaganda for Reaction: Gerald L. K. Smith's Radio Speeches." *Public Opinion Quarterly* 8, 1 (Spring 1944), pp. 84-93.
Gerald L. K. Smith was an American fascist who delivered propaganda speeches by radio to a Midwestern audience during the 1940s. The context for these speeches was, in the author's words, "'Christian' paternalistic expression of 'fundamentalist' reaction." This article analyzes Smith's technique as a radio propagandist, and includes tables depicting the frequency with which he used certain themes, such as "his enemies are persecuting him." Such themes served to draw Smith's listeners into his world of paranoia and hate. A comparison is drawn between Smith's manipulative skills and those of Senator Huey P. Long of Louisiana; both men are described as being on the authoritarian fringe.

Joseph Goebbels. Prod. Coronet/MTI Film and Video, 26 min., 1966. New York: Sterling Educational Films.
This film examines the life and personality of Third Reich propaganda minister, Joseph Goebbels, and evaluates his techniques for creating propaganda. It also argues that the German people were willing participants in war as a result of this propaganda, which the evidence suggests is not an altogether accurate judgment. The film is too short

to provide more than an overview on any level, but does at least introduce viewers to the chief Nazi propagandist.

Knudson, Jerry W. "The Ultimate Weapon: Propaganda and the Spanish Civil War." *Journalism History* 15, 4 (Winter 1988), pp. 102-111.
The Spanish Civil War, 1936-1939, was a struggle between democracy and fascism, or so it was thought. This article details how propaganda was used in that struggle, concentrating on the channels and techniques by which the Nationalists on the one hand and the Republicans on the other targeted both enemies and supporters. The analysis is illustrated with reproductions of Spanish press items and leaflets. Documentation is limited to newspapers from the period, and there is no reference to archival material. This piece was written for journalists by a journalist, rather than for historians.

Kris, Ernst, and Hans Speier, eds. *German Radio Propaganda: Report on Home Broadcasts During the War*. New York: Oxford University Press, 1944.
In 1941, the Research Project on Totalitarian Communication at the Graduate Faculty of the New School for Social Research in New York set out, under the direction of the authors of this volume, to "develop methods for the study of enemy propaganda and to train American social scientists for prospective government work in this field. . . . [T]he study of German home broadcasting seemed to offer the best opportunities for training and research." This volume was the outcome. Divided into three parts labeled "The State," "The Actors," and "Situations," the study details the nature of Nazi home propaganda, the structure of the Nazi radio system which disseminated it, the people who ran propaganda and others who provided the images which the propaganda extolled (the Führer, and German soldiers, for example), the enemy who were used as scapegoats in the propaganda, and specific situations (the war in Yugoslavia, for instance) which were explained to the German people in propaganda language. No bibliography, but appendixes detail the subject matter and the dates of German broadcasts of war news.

Landy, Marcia. *Fascism in Film: The Italian Commercial Cinema, 1931-1943*. Princeton, N.J.: Princeton University Press, 1986.
The author argues that commercial Italian film during the fascist period was much more than mere propaganda. However, this analysis of the relationship between the film industry and the fascist government is a study of how filmmaking and the fascist state interacted, how the state censored film according to the needs of state propaganda, and how the

contents of many commercial films contained themes that were ideologically fascist in nature. Her argument that there is more here than propaganda is well developed all the same, as she shows how many of these films also show unresolved conflict between fascist ideology and "more traditional ideological structures." There were about 700 commercial films produced in Italy during the period in question. Illustrations and extensive bibliography. See Elain Mancini, *Struggles of the Italian Film Industry During Fascism* (entry above under "History and Function").

Lasswell, Harold D. *Propaganda and Dictatorship*. Princeton, N.J.: Princeton University Press, 1936.
In this study of the interaction of propaganda and power in authoritarian states such as Nazi Germany and the Soviet Union, the author takes into account force, violence, and coercion as part of overall propaganda techniques. The focus is on how authoritarians use propaganda to gain power. It is no coincidence that Lasswell, a leading authority on propaganda in the United States, completed this volume just three years after Adolf Hitler came to power in Germany.

Lasswell, Harold D., and Dorothy Blumenstock. *World Revolutionary Propaganda: A Chicago Study*. New York: Alfred A. Knopf, 1939.
The authors analyze the propaganda efforts of the Communist Revolutionary Movement of Chicago, as it was called, in an attempt to assess its appeal and the extent to which it might be effective. This was one of the earliest efforts by propaganda theorists to apply systematic measurement to the volume and impact of revolutionary political propaganda. Lasswell and his associates in propaganda study are always worth reading, and this volume is no exception. No bibliography.

Lavine, Harold. *Fifth Column in America*. New York: Doubleday, Doran, 1940.
Prepared with the assistance of the Institute for Propaganda Analysis, this volume deals with the question whether or not there were already Fifth Columnists operating in the United States on behalf of fascist or communist movements when war began in Europe in 1939. The author argues that professional Fifth Columnists—from the Soviet Union or Nazi Germany, for example—are not a problem in the United States. Rather, the "real Fifth-Column menace" to the United States are the hypocrites, patriots, and "frustrates" exercising their right of free speech to disseminate their own propaganda in an effort to change the United States' form of government. The first chapter, "This Is the Problem," describes the various anti-Semitic, pro-fascist or pro-

communist agitators that operate in the United States, and how they seek to undo democracy in the United States through their lies, half-truths, and sensationalist literature. Subsequent chapters deal with specific individuals who fit this category: Major General Van Horn Moseley, who "hates Jews, dogs and gonorrhea," Father Charles E. Coughlin, editor of *Social Justice*, and Fritz Kuhn, leader of the *Amerikadeutscher Volksbund*, which operated out of upstate New York, among others. No bibliography.

Lenin, N. (Vladimir Ilich). *Agitation und Propaganda*. Vienna: Verlag für Literatur und Politik, 1929.
This is a translation into German of a set of writings on how to use propaganda to agitate the masses toward revolution attributed to the leader of the Bolshevik Revolution in Russia in 1917, Vladimir Ilich Lenin. The collection explains how "agitprop," as the concept came to be known, was used in Russian radical politics before 1905, during the uprising which occurred in 1905, and in the period after, leading to success in 1917. While these essays explain the process of agitprop as a propaganda technique, they are also propaganda in their own right. From the beginning, Lenin was an advocate of the use of propaganda in achieving revolution, and here is the evidence.

The Master Race. Prod. Granada Television, 20 min., 1985. Princeton, N.J.: Films for the Humanities.
This twenty-minute British production briefly explores how the 1936 Olympics, *Mein Kampf*, the Nuremberg Laws, and Joseph Goebbels' concept of the Big Lie were incorporated into the anti-Semitic propaganda that shaped the German mind in the 1930s. Its brevity renders the treatment somewhat superficial.

Minister of Hate. Prod. Columbia Broadcasting System, 25 min., 1959. Carlsbad, Calif.: CRM Films.
The life and work of German propaganda minister Joseph Goebbels in twenty-five minutes. Interviews with German filmmaker Fritz Lang and British historian Hugh Trevor-Roper help tell the story of how Goebbels used print, broadcast, and film propaganda to build up Hitler and the Nazi state. However, like *The Master Race* (entry above), it is too brief to provide more than an overview.

Remington, Thomas. "The Mass Media and Public Communications in the USSR." *Journal of Politics* 43, 3 (August 1981), pp. 803-817.
This article describes and analyzes the cause-and-effect relationship between de-Stalinization and the recognition, by the Soviet state, of a

public opinion separate from that expressed on behalf of the public by the State. This is a theoretical article which examines the type of evidence from which models can be constructed to explain the formation of Soviet public opinion in the Western sense of that phrase. The model that works, the author contends, is based upon both social and political factors—that is, avenues of communication of opinion within subgroups in Soviet society, such as families, villages, and ethnic minorities. He concludes that in the post-Stalinist Soviet Union, state-controlled media address themselves to the public with this fact clearly in mind, which is a dramatic departure from the practices of the Stalinist period itself.

Rentschler, Eric. "Ministry of Illusion: German Film, 1933-1945." *Film Comment* 30 (November/December 1994), pp. 34-42.

During the period of the Third Reich, 1,100 narrative feature films were produced, which included "hideous propaganda, formal bombast, and unbearable kitsch." The author describes the kinds of messages these films sent: anti-Semitism, German patriotism, xenophobia, the insignificance of women other than to serve men, and a general idea that everybody was out to get Germany. The work carried on under propaganda minister Joseph Goebbels by major film figures such as Veit Harlan, G. W. Pabst, Emil Jannings, and Werner Krause is noted, as is the fact that eighty-six percent of the 1,100 feature films produced in the Third Reich had no propaganda or ideological purpose at all, but rather were "light and frothy entertainments set in urbane surroundings and cozy circles, places where one never sees a Swastika or hears a 'Sieg Heil'." See David Welch, *Propaganda and the German Cinema* (entry above under "History and Function").

Riegel, O. W. "Propaganda and the Press." *Annals of the American Academy of Political and Social Science* 179 (1935), pp. 201-210.

This article argues that a rising lack of sympathy with the press in the United States is brought on by awareness among the public of "that awesome monster, propaganda." The point is to comment on the use being made of the press as a channel of propaganda through purchased advertising—the bulk of which ends up in the wastebasket, the author claims—and through the "daily barrage of items of so-called 'news'" that are laid on the press by publicity men and propagandists. Specific comment is offered about "subsidized news," "social obligations of the press," and comparisons between commercial and political propaganda. There is even a discussion of "freedom of propaganda," meaning the right of all propagandists to peddle their wares. This article was

inspired by concern over the nature of propaganda in the rising totalitarian states in Europe and the potential of this fact for the freedom of
the press in the United States.

Roth, Paul. *Cuius Regio-Eius Informatio: Moskaus Modell für die Welt-
informationsordnung.* Vienna: Styria, 1984.
This volume examines how the Soviet Union operates its *Neue Weltin-
formationsordnung* (New World Information Order, or more accurately,
external propaganda organization). Beginning with the "selling" of the
Bolshevik Revolution abroad, the author examines the techniques,
channels, contents, and targets of Soviet propaganda in the context of a
history of that propaganda dissemination over more than seven decades.
The volume contains extensive descriptions of some of this material,
in the form of annotations of the contents. Select bibliography.

Rudnitsky, Konstantin. *Russian and Soviet Theatre, 1905-1932.* Translated by Roxane Permar. New York: Harry N. Abrams, 1988.
The author describes the evolution of Russian theater from the late
czarist period, in which its experimentation had a primarily artistic
purpose, through the first decade and a half of the Soviet period, when
the theater's equally experimental outlook had a primarily agitprop
purpose. The volume is a historical treatment of this evolutionary
process, but within that context, the author is focused on the structure
and intent of theatrical writing, staging, and performance. For example,
when describing the theater of the first years of revolution, he makes
reference to the fact that "the slogans of 'Theatrical October' declared
war on the apolitical character of the old stage art. . . .The 'leftists'
wanted the stage to become a platform for Revolutionary ideas right
there and then and to celebrate the victory of the Proletariate." Extensive illustrations and limited bibliography.

Saerchinger, César. "Radio as a Political Weapon." *Foreign Affairs* 16
(January 1938), pp. 244-259.
Set in the context of rising tension in Europe, this article argues for
greater understanding of the uses to which radio may be put for
propaganda purposes: who should control broadcasting, how it should
be deployed both at home and abroad, and how its use by the wrong
people (fascist dictators, for example) can be countered. The author
ends by warning that the absence of radio censorship and government
control in broadcasting in the United States, though desirable in
peacetime, will have to end in the event of war if the full propaganda
potential of broadcasting is to be realized.

Schnitzer, Luda, Jean Schnitzer, and Marcel Martin, eds. *Cinema in Revolution: The Heroic Era of the Soviet Film*. London: Secker and Warburg, 1973.

There are twelve essays in this volume, all by Soviet experts on cinema, who are recalling the "astonishing and wonderful days," as Sergei Yuykevitch phrased it, of revolutionary filmmaking in the Soviet Union. The filmmakers' task then was "to build a new, a revolutionary, a socialist art" for a new, ideal, socialist society. Therefore, the films they made were works of art as well as of propaganda. They included such classics as *Strike* and *Battleship Potemkin*. This short volume is illustrated with stills and photographs of filmmakers, and includes a glossary of some prominent artists and others who contributed to this period of filmmaking. No bibliography.

Short, K. R. M., and Richard Taylor. "Soviet Cinema and the International Menace, 1928-1939." *Historical Journal of Film, Radio and Television* 6, 2 (1986), pp. 131-159.

This excellent article by two leading British film scholars details how Soviet cinema during the eleven years preceding World War II reflected a rising sense that the outside world, in particular Nazi Germany, threatened Soviet security. The authors discuss various films which demonstrate how Soviet film expressed this viewpoint, including *The Outskirts*, *The Revolt of the Fishermen*, *The Deserter*, and the best-known of these films, the historically based *Alexander Nevsky* (entry below under "Propaganda Material"), in which the medieval prince of Muscovy leads the Russians to victory over the invading Teutonic Knights. Not surprisingly, this film was withdrawn following the signing of the Nazi-Soviet Nonaggression Pact in August 1939. A list of major Soviet films from the period is appended.

Smith, Woodruff. "The Colonial Novel as Political Propaganda: Hans Grimm's *Volk Ohne Raum*." *German Studies Review* 6, 2 (May 1983), pp. 215-235.

With an eye on novels about life in the colonies generally, the author concentrates on a German example published in 1926, which within a decade sold more than 300,000 copies. He concludes that such novels had enormous popularity because they used the colonial metaphor to address the question of the colonial nation's place in the world. *Volk Ohne Raum* urged Germans to see themselves as a force in the world at a time when they were still recovering psychologically from the Great War. The novel was embraced by the Nazi party and became, whether Grimm intended it or not, a propaganda piece for German expansion.

The Speeches of Adolf Hitler. Prod. MPI, 45 min., 1989. Oak Forest, Ill.: MPI Home Video.
This documentary contains excerpts from some of Hitler's speeches delivered over a ten-year period, beginning in 1927, and including the famous "Thousand Year Reich" speech. The emphasis is on the "demonic" phrases he used to stir up his audiences against various enemies.

Taylor, Richard. "Boris Shumyatsky and the Soviet Cinema in the 1930s: Ideology as Mass Entertainment." *Historical Journal of Film, Radio and Television* 6, 1 (1986), pp. 43-64.
Soviet filmmakers certainly made propaganda features in the prewar years. What has been overlooked, the author notes, is that they fully understood the importance of making the propaganda entertaining. Hence filmmakers such as Sergei Eisenstein and Boris Shumyatsky, and actors like Ilyinsky and Cherkasov, were associated with a Soviet film quality that had nothing to do with the ideological content of their product. In this well-researched and well-crafted article, the work of Shumyatsky is examined in detail in the context of a wide range of Soviet films from this period. See K. R. M. Short and Richard Taylor, "Soviet Cinema and the International Menace, 1928-1939" (entry above).

_____. *Film Propaganda: Soviet Russia and Nazi Germany.* London: Croom Helm, 1979.
Written by a specialist in Soviet cinema, this volume is a comparison of two similar, yet different, authoritarian regimes with reference to how they used film as propaganda. The author opens with the mildly questionable assertion that the importance of both political propaganda and film as propaganda has been "undervalued," but that is a minor point. This volume is a major contribution to the history of film propaganda in Soviet Russia and Nazi Germany, which draws upon comparisons of specific films to make its point. The volume includes illustrations, an appendix of films cited complete with cast of characters and production credits, and an extensive bibliography of primary and secondary sources in Russian, German, and English. This volume should be part of any informed propaganda library.

_____. *The Politics of the Soviet Cinema, 1917-1929.* Cambridge, England: Cambridge University Press, 1979.
While this volume goes beyond the idea of Soviet cinema as a propaganda channel, explaining that element is nevertheless an important part of the author's purpose. Indeed, chapter 2 is titled "The Bolsheviks, Propaganda, and the Cinema," and subsequent chapters detail

how the Communist party in the Soviet Union employed film propaganda against "reactionary elements in society" that were making a last stand against the party. The bibliography is extensive but includes mostly Russian-language sources. See Richard Taylor, *Film Propaganda* (entry above).

Thornton, Sinclair. "The Nazi Party Rally at Nuremberg." *Public Opinion Quarterly* 2, 4 (October 1938), pp. 570-583.
The author was present for the 1938 Nuremberg party rally. This article is a description and analysis of what happened, emphasizing that the purpose of the rally was "lavish and skillful propaganda." He breaks the rally down into "constituent parts." These are: the Congress, the special assemblies, the mass demonstrations and parades, and the amusements and exhibitions. Each of these is considered in detail, and appropriate conclusions are drawn regarding their propaganda function. Of course, the greatest propaganda moment at the rally was the arrival of the Führer.

Tiger at the Gate. Prod. Granada Television, 20 min., 1985. Princeton, N.J.: Films for the Humanities.
This film offers an explanation for Hitler's rise to power and for his wide support among the German people, all in twenty minutes. Central to both is the role of propaganda in appealing to middle-class resentments, working-class antagonism toward other social classes, anti-Semitism, and a sense of grievance against those who "betrayed" Germany in 1918. Unfortunately, twenty minutes is not long enough to avoid overgeneralization.

The Twisted Cross. Prod. National Broadcasting Company, narr. Alexander Scourby, 55 min., 1958. Del Mar, Calif.: CRM/McGraw-Hill.
A documentary based in part on Alan Bullock's seminal book *Hitler: A Study in Tyranny*, this film portrays Hitler as succeeding in Germany mainly through the effectiveness of the propaganda disseminated by Joseph Goebbels' propaganda ministry. The film is, in its own way, a work of propaganda as much as was the propaganda it is explaining. For example, authentic German film footage is occasionally supplemented with film of scenes created in the studio to make certain points. In one instance, a shadowy figure contemplating the retreat of German forces late in World War II is presented as being Hitler, but clearly is not.

Wanderscheck, Hermann. *Weltkrieg und Propaganda*. Berlin: E. S. Mittler und Sohn, 1936.
While this book represents a German study of British World War I propaganda, its purpose is made perfectly clear in the foreword. The

author notes that by understanding the techniques and organization of British propaganda, the German propaganda ministry under Joseph Goebbels will be able to improve its own efforts and be more effective in instilling the ideals of the Third Reich in the German people. The author examines the basis of English war propaganda and its various techniques, including the use of censorship. The point is made clear that the techniques are all negative, an effort at demeaning German culture, leadership, and purpose. Lord Northcliffe, the head of British war propaganda efforts through much of the war, comes in for a careful analysis also. There are a few illustrations, and an extensive bibliography of printed English propaganda materials, as well as of retrospective materials on the propaganda war.

Weinberg, David. "Approaches to the Study of Film in the Third Reich: A Critical Appraisal." *Journal of Contemporary History* 19 (1984), pp. 105-126.
Written by a distinguished historian of Germany, this article argues for more research into how the Third Reich used film for propaganda purposes. The author points out that while the research that has been done is useful, there is not enough of it. The importance of such research is made clear by the well-known fact that both Hitler and Goebbels were obsessed with movies, a fact demonstrated in Gerd Albrecht's *Nationalsozialistische Filmpolitik*, which the author surveys here. The author also offers some critical observations on the nature of Nazi organization for filmmaking, and its commitment to making propaganda films, particularly those advancing anti-Semitic themes.

Wilson, Charles H. "Hitler, Goebbels, and the Ministry of Propaganda." *Political Quarterly* 10, 3 (1938), pp. 83-99.
This article aims to "disparage . . . the utterances of Hitler and Goebbels on the theory of propaganda" and to "exhibit" their technical achievements in propaganda with regard to the Ministry of Propaganda. The author contends that Hitler's and Goebbels' views on propaganda, which came out of the early Nazi movement, are no longer relevant in an era of "monopoly propaganda"—that is, propaganda controlled by the State which also censors everything that differs from the official line. He also contends that anything useful Hitler and Goebbels had done in the propaganda arena since they took power lay entirely in the way the ministry developed broadcasting, film, theater, music, art, and literature as propaganda tools. The article examines and characterizes the structure and activities of the propaganda ministry in considerable detail.

Young, John Wesley. *Totalitarian Language: Orwell's Newspeak and Its Nazi and Communist Antecedents.* Charlottesville: University Press of Virginia, 1991.

In this volume, the author uses George Orwell's *Nineteen Eighty-Four* as a metaphor through which to evaluate the nature of totalitarian language, which is to say, the language of totalitarian propaganda. He cites, for example, a Stalinist Five-Year Plan slogan "2 + 2 = 5," which is mathematically impossible but which expresses "the desire of the Soviet Communist party . . . to accelerate its drive to meet industrial and agricultural goals." The author includes equally bizarre examples from the Nazi period as well. The topics covered are "fanatical" language, ideology and language, and rhetorical "treachery," among others. Appendixes contain lists of specific Russian and German words that were used by the totalitarian systems as part of their particular "newspeak." Select bibliography of writings by George Orwell in addition to bibliography of sources on Nazi and Soviet history.

Young, Robert G. "'Not This Way Please!' Regulating the Press in Nazi Germany." *Journalism Quarterly* 64 (Winter 1987), pp. 787-792.

A brief but well-crafted article on how Joseph Goebbels molded the German press into a "pliable instrument for disseminating the new regime's propaganda." The author examines the concept of the "organic national community" which proscribed the idea of a free press as understood in democratic nations, and upon which Goebbels based his concept of a press that spoke with a single voice. He then explains the *Zeitschriften-Dienst* (periodical service) which Goebbels established as a collection of weekly directives sent from his minister to chief editors of German periodicals. Its purpose was quite simply to tell them what it was desirable to print. The ZD also contained a censorship section, in which materials that ought not to be printed were included under the subheading *"Bitte Nicht So!"* ("Not This Way Please!"). Over time, the author concludes, this method of control reduced the number of journals in Germany and impaired the quality of those that remained.

Zeman, Z. A. B. *Nazi Propaganda.* London: Oxford University Press, 1964.

The thesis of this book is that propaganda created the Third Reich and sustained it. Propaganda was Hitler's first priority, the author avers, and notes that it was his ability at propaganda that "raised him from the ranks after the war, and it gained him entry into the political group that he was to make his own party." The author dissects Nazi propaganda from beginning to end, taking on a particular aspect of the problem in each chapter. He looks at foreign as well as domestic Nazi propaganda; the consistent themes within both such as anti-Semitism, anti-communism, and the appeal to German blood; the specific propaganda campaigns against Britain; and war propaganda. Illustrations include examples of poster propaganda, and there is an extensive bibliography.

Propaganda Material

Aelita. Dir. Yakov Protazanov, Mezhrabpom, 70 min., 1924. New York: Kino International.
This is the first Soviet science fiction film, in which two Russian soldiers land on Mars, a planet ruled by the autocratic Queen Aelita. They organize a Bolshevik-style revolution, out of which comes a system that looks remarkably like the New Economic Policy introduced by the Soviet government in 1921. The film makes clear that this policy will transform Mars and by implication the Soviet Union as well, all for the good. The film is based upon a story by Alexei Tolstoy, author also of a historical novel about the life of Czar Peter the Great, whose contribution to modernizing Russia rings remarkably like the contribution to Soviet Russia made by Lenin as described by party propagandists.

All My Good Countrymen. Dir. Voitech Jazny, Filmove Studio Barrandov, 126 min., 1968. Chicago: Facets Video.
One of the "Prague Spring" films that repudiated the Stalinist style of the Czechoslovakian government. It describes life in a Moldavian village punctuated by the death of a postman, a young Communist party member, and a farmer who refuses to give up his land to the collective, among others. The film was banned in Czechoslovakia when the Prague Spring ended, and the director fled to Germany.

Animal Farm. Prod. John Halas, narr. Gordon Heath, DCA, 75 min., 1955. Chicago: Facets Video.
An animated adaptation of George Orwell's allegorical novel of the same title, the story is of a barnyard rebellion led by Napoleon, a pig who perverts the revolution and takes on the evil characteristics of the overthrown regime. It is all about the Bolshevik revolution, of course, and Stalin's remaking of it for his own totalitarian purposes. The operative line which sets the leaders apart from their followers has passed into legend: "All animals are equal, but some are more equal than others."

Arsenal. Dir. Alexander Dovzhenko, Vseukrainskii-Fotografichiskii-i-Kinoustroistvo (VUFKU), 99 min., 1929. Chicago: International Historic Films.

This film, made by a Ukrainian director, tells the story of the Bolsheviks' struggle to overcome opposing forces and to impose collectivization in the Ukraine. It is filled with "agitprop" and features a tractor in a leading role. A classic example of early Soviet "docudrama" in which the propaganda purpose and technique are perfectly obvious to all but the most naive viewer. It also is a lead-in to the "Socialist Realism" that dominated Soviet film in the 1930s, and which has been described facetiously as "boy meets tractor, boy falls in love with tractor, and they live happily ever after on the Collective."

Baltic Deputy. Dir. Alexander Zarkhi and Joseph Heifits, Lenfilm/Amkino, 107 min., 1937. Chicago: International Historic Films.

A romanticized version of how the Russian scientist and former Oxford University don Klement Timiriazev (who is given a different name in the film) joined the Bolsheviks in 1918 and became a hero of the revolution. His Bolshevik idealism is maintained despite ostracism by his Oxford colleagues. This is a reasonably well-made film in which the propaganda elements do not altogether overwhelm the elements of good cinema.

Battleship Potemkin. Dir. Sergei Eisenstein, Goskino, 75 min., 1925. Chicago: Facets Video.

A classic of Soviet cinema and of Sergei Eisenstein's work as both an innovative and talented filmmaker and a film propagandist for the Soviet Union. It tells the story of an incident involving the crew of a czarist battleship, the *Potemkin*, during the revolution of 1905. The setting is the port of Odessa on the Black Sea, and the cinematography shows some of Eisenstein's best work. It is a propaganda film all the same, in which Cossacks brutalize innocent women and children, a priest aboard the *Potemkin* is portrayed both in image and action as the personification of evil, and common seamen are abused by their czarist officers.

Bismarck. Dir. Wolfgang Liebeneiner, Tobis Rota, 118 min., 1940. Chicago: International Historic Films.

A film biography of the famous nineteenth century German chancellor who, as minister-president of Prussia, orchestrated the unification of Germany in 1871. Made as a propaganda film by Tobis Rota, the only major German film company besides Universum-Film-Aktiengesellschaft before World War II, the point was to emphasize absolute obedience to leadership as the key to the success of the nation. Hitler was meant to be understood as Bismarck's heir. See David Welch, *Propaganda and the German Cinema* (entry above under "History and Function").

Blanco White, Amber. *The New Propaganda*. London: Victor Gollancz, 1939.
The Left Book Club was started in England by Victor Gollancz in the 1930s as a vehicle for publishing books which called for radical social and political reform. This is volume 35 in the Left Book Club series. It addresses the issue of how propaganda serves fascist dictatorships (there is no mention of propaganda in Stalin's dictatorship) and asks whether propaganda, the tool of fascism, might serve the left in a democracy if used with care. The answer to the last is no, largely because propaganda is designed to create robots, whereas the goal of the left is to create the New Man. This person is to be "a self-respecting citizen, possessed of a social and political conscience . . . capable of forming and defending [his] own social judgements." The author proudly proclaims herself a socialist and a Labour party candidate in parliamentary elections. This book is a good example of leftist British propaganda in the 1930s, much of which addressed socialism's battle against fascism.

Carl Peters. Dir. Herbert Selpin, Universum-Film-Aktiengesellschaft, 110 min., 1941. University Park: Pennsylvania State University.
The nineteenth-century German colonialist Carl Peters is the subject of this feature film. In this story, Peters is falsely accused of mistreating Africans by an African bishop who works for the British secret service. He must face the anger of his superiors; however, the bishop is exposed as a British agent, and Peters is exonerated and emerges a hero in the process. This film contains many ideological elements of National Socialism, including the hero principle, xenophobia, anti-Semitism, and even elements of the leadership principle. However, the Carl Peters in the film bears little resemblance to the real Carl Peters, whose brutal treatment of Africans is well documented.

Chapayev. Dir. Sergei Vasiliev and Georgi Vasiliev, Lenfilm, 99 min., 1934. Sandy Hook, Conn.: Videoyesteryear.
Socialist Realism is the style of this early Soviet sound docudrama. It tells the story of a famous Red Army commander, Chapayev, who fought against Czech and Kolchak forces during the Civil War of 1919. He was impulsive, heroic, and an icon of the revolution. The film was

made for the fifteenth-anniversary celebration of Soviet cinema, and was well received both in Russia and abroad. With *Chapayev*, Soviet film propaganda made a great leap forward in sound-era quality.

Confessions of a Nazi Spy. Prod. Robert Lord, dir. Anatole Litvak, Warner Brothers, 110 min., 1939. Los Angeles: UCLA Film and Television Archive; Madison: Wisconsin Center for Film and Theater Research; Washington, D.C.: Library of Congress.
One of the first uncompromising anti-Nazi feature-length propaganda films to come out of Hollywood prior to World War II. In rural Scotland, a woman's strange behavior arouses suspicion. A Scotland Yard investigation reveals she is part of a Nazi spy ring. Intercepted information reveals the existence of a similar spy ring in the United States. British and American government agents cooperate to root out this Nazi underground. Eventually the mastermind is uncovered and proves to be the leader of a Nazi *Bund* group who is recruiting young Americans into Hitler Youth organizations. Nazi brutality is a constant theme, and German Nazi leaders are openly vilified.

The Cranes Are Flying. Dir. Mikhael Kalatozov, Mosfilm, 97 min., 1957. Chicago: International Historic Films.
A post-Stalinist film by Mikhael Kaltozovin in which the emphasis is still on patriotism for the Soviet Union. However, here it is expressed by real people rather than by the two-dimensional extensions of the State that were the characters in many Stalin-era films. The setting is World War II. Soldiers departing for the front are of widely varied backgrounds: an intellectual bids farewell to his wife and colleagues; a father parts from his family. The hero is Boris, who volunteers for the front specifically to defend his fiancée, Veronica, who symbolizes the motherland. Boris is killed without his relationship to Veronica ever being consummated. The point seems to be that while it is good to die for the motherland, it can also be tragic. This is understated propaganda which departs from the pure emotionalism of the prior decade and attempts to appeal to the viewers' intelligence.

Le Dernier Milliardaire. Dir. René Clair, Pathé/Natan, 90 min., 1934. London: Cannon Video.
A fictitious country, Casinaria, supports its economy through gambling (which sounds slightly like Monte Carlo) and finds itself on the verge of bankruptcy. The queen lures a financier to her country to marry her daughter, though the girl loves the national band leader. The financier ends up appointed dictator, but a blow on the head leads to some mad

behavior, such as ordering all of the citizenry to run for hours around the public square as a fitness activity, and confession that he is not the wealthy man he pretended to be. This is a satire of dictatorship which probably would have gone unnoticed as propaganda had not both fascist Italy and Nazi Germany banned the film, the Soviet Union praised it, and French fascists rioted against it.

Diary for My Children. Prod. Eva Martin, dir. Marta Meszaros, Mafilm/ Hungarofilm, 106 min., 1984. Unable to locate copy.
This film tells the story of political purges that took place in Hungary between 1953 and 1956 in the interests of maintaining the strict Stalinism of the Hungarian regime. A Hungarian family reside in the Soviet Union. The father is arrested without explanation and disappears into the Soviet gulag system, leaving behind his wife and teenage daughter. When the mother dies, the daughter returns to Hungary, where she lives with a former revolutionary who is now a politically committed newspaper editor. His strong views alienate the girl, who retreats in the afternoons into movie houses with the editor's friend, a factory worker who ends up in prison for his beliefs. She pays him regular visits because he reminds her of her father. There is an autobiographical element in the film, as the director had similar experiences. The overall product is a profound indictment of Stalinism in retrospect and a call for reform of the system that continued to exist in Hungary even after Stalin died.

Earth. Dir. Alexander Dovzhenko, Vseukrainskii-Fotografichiskii-i-Kinoustroistvo (VUFKU), 90 min., 1930. Chicago: International Historic Films.
This film features the triumph of Ukrainian collectivization over opposition from the Kulaks (landowners) in the 1920s. They are the heavies in this film, while the peasants are the heroes. When the dust settles, the collective farm emerges as a rural paradise. Some of the original scenes depicting relatives of a slain peasant mourning him naked and peasants urinating on a tractor were cut on order of the puritanical Soviet censors. See in conjunction with Dovzhenko's *Arsenal* (entry above), which also extols the triumph of collectivization.

Enthusiasm. Dir. Dziga Vertov, Ukrainfilm, 96 min., 1931. Chicago: Facets Video.
A documentary which extols the efforts of workers in the Donets Coal Basin in the eastern Ukraine to meet the goals of the Five Year Plan. Its symphony of noise and futuristic visual poetry is a celebration of

both Soviet workers and Soviet cinema art. Charlie Chaplin much admired this film.

The Eternal Jew. Dir. Fritz Hippler, 62 min., 1940. Chicago: International Historic Films.
A documentary filmed in part by Nazi cameramen in the Jewish ghetto of Lodz in occupied Poland, with the cooperation of the Jewish community, who either had no choice in the matter or else were unaware of the purpose for making the film. This footage is combined with clips from international newsreels and excerpts from various cultural films, all designed to portray Jews as swindlers and parasites. The film combines traditions of European anti-Semitism with Nazi ideology and attempts to justify the policy of "cleansing" Europe of its Jewish population. In German with English subtitles.

The Extraordinary Adventures of Mr. West in the Land of the Bolsheviks. Dir. Lev Kuleshov, Goskino, 78 min., 1924. Chicago: Facets Video.
This Soviet film satirizes stereotypes of "mad" Russian Bolsheviks held by Americans at a time when anti-Bolshevik fever was high in the United States. The story, told with gags and some slapstick, is of a YMCA president, Mr. West (portrayed as Hollywood comic actor Harold Lloyd's double), who tours the Soviet Union with his faithful cowboy aide, Jed. While there, he falls among evil companions who seek to rob him and pretend while doing so that they are the very evil, leering Bolsheviks of his imagination. Actually, the crooks are former aristocrats of whom little else can be expected, and who are uniformly ugly as well. In the end, Mr. West sees the "real" Bolsheviks, who are decent, hardworking, noble people—and generally quite handsome.

The Fall of the Romanov Dynasty. Dir. Esther Shub, 90 min., 1927. Chicago: Facets Video.
A documentary of the collapse of czarist Russia, drawing upon some remarkable historic footage. The editing is radical, however, in order to show the triumph of communism over the czars. It is historical drama with an unapologetic propagandistic purpose.

Foreign Correspondent. Dir. Alfred Hitchcock, United Artists, 120 min., 1940. Stamford, Conn.: Lightning Video.
Hitchcock began making films warning against the rising power and wickedness of the authoritarian states in Europe as early as 1934, when Hitler canceled Germany's participation in the disarmament conferences. In this film, an American journalist is covering a pacifist conference in London. He becomes romantically involved with the

daughter of a diplomat who is involved with the pacifists and holds the secret of peace. When the diplomat disappears, the correspondent goes to work and finds that a Nazi spy ring has engineered the disappearance. There is also an assassination, and in the end, the correspondent manages not only to rescue the diplomat but also to alert his editor in the United States that the country must wake up to the horrible reality of fascist terrorism.

Fridericus. Dir. Johannes Meyer, 101 min., 1936. Chicago: International Historic Films.
The exploits of eighteenth century Prussian king Frederick the Great are the subjects of this film. The theme is that Prussia is surrounded by enemies, all of whom are out to conquer Frederick's state. The only hope is in the genius of his leadership. The juxtaposition with Hitler is obvious. This particular copy of the film is in German without subtitles.

The General Line—Old and the New. Dir. Sergei Eisenstein, Sovkino, 70 min., 1929. Minneapolis: Festival Films.
This film by Sergei Eisenstein reflects the official view of collectivization. Peasants are plagued by poverty which is only encouraged by individualism, and two brothers, so greedy that they literally cut their ancestral house in two rather than cooperate to preserve their family, are the symbol of this Marxist view of capitalism. As a result of the brothers' action, the peasants see the evils of individualism, and the peasant women start a cooperative to produce milk. The proceeds pay for a machine that produces butter, productivity increases, and the advantages of collectivization are made clear. Ilia Kopalin made films with identical themes at this time: *For the Harvest* (1929), *Rejuvenated Labor* (1930), and *Countryside* (1930).

German Propaganda Shorts. Prod. Universum-Film-Aktiengesellschaft (UFA), 50 min., 1938. Indianapolis, Ind.: German Language Video Center.
This fifty-minute reel includes three German propaganda short films, made ca. 1938. *Tag der Freiheit* (Day of Freedom) is a Leni Riefenstahl film from 1935 which glorifies the German army and all of its equipment by showing it off in parades and drills with Hitler and Goering looking on. The film was ordered by Hitler to make up for the fact that there was very little of the army present in Riefenstahl's classic, *Triumph of the Will*. The other shorts are *Munich, 1938 Arts Festival* and *The Eternal Jew*, which propagandize, respectively, national pride and racial antagonism. In German without subtitles.

Germany Awake! (Deutschland Erwäche). Prod. and dir. Erwin Leiser, 89 min., 1968. Chicago: International Historic Films.

Erwin Leiser was a refugee from the Third Reich who made a postwar career of the study of German cinema from that period. This film is his creation. Leiser analyzes Nazi propaganda feature films made between 1933 and 1945, through his commentary on excerpts from twenty-two different examples. *Jud Süss*, *Ohm Krüger*, and *Kolberg*, three of the most ambitious creations of the Goebbels-directed film industry, are among the samples.

The Great Dictator. Prod. and dir. Charlie Chaplin, United Artists, 128 min., 1940. Chicago: Facets Video.

This film was a personal matter for Chaplin. It is a satire on fascism in which Chaplin plays the role both of a Jewish barber and his look-alike, Adenoid Hynkel (Hitler), the dictator of the imaginary totalitarian state of Tomania (Nazi Germany). At a critical point in the story, the two are mistaken for one another, which provides the barber, pretending to be the dictator, an opportunity to make a plea for humanity and tolerance and against racism and dictatorship. There is some creative use of Wagner's *Lohengrin* theme music, the usual Chaplinesque deployment of slapstick, and a marvelous performance by Jack Oakie as Benzino Napaloni (Mussolini), dictator of Bacteria (fascist Italy). This was not the first antifascist propaganda feature, but it was one of the best.

Happiness. Dir. Alexander Medvedkin, Moskino Kombinat, 90 min., 1934. Chicago: Facets Video.

A poor peasant and his wife are dispossessed by the evil czarist regime for failing to pay the heavy taxes demanded by it. He is sent off to World War I, but when he returns the revolution has happened, and he and his wife are able to find happiness by joining a collective farm. This is Socialist Realism in its orthodox praise of collectivization, but presented with humor and a surrealism reminiscent of the early days of Soviet cinema. That was an unusual quality in films of the Stalinist period.

Hitler, Adolf. *Mein Kampf.* Translated by Ralph Manheim. Boston: Houghton Mifflin, 1971. Originally published in 1925 in German.

This is the book through which Adolf Hitler and the Nazi party promoted Nazi ideology before and after they came to power in Germany. It was written while the author was in Landsberg Prison, to which he had been sentenced for his part in the attempted overthrow of the

Bavarian state government in 1923. Part 1 describes Hitler's early life
and his encounter with war, propaganda, and the idea of nation and
race. Part 2 contains his views on everything from the philosophy of
the Nazi movement to the organization of the SA. The point is clearly
made that propaganda is the means through which Germany will come
to accept Hitler and the Nazi philosophy. After Hitler became chancellor in January 1933, this book was promoted virtually as a new German
bible. It sold millions—but many have argued that this was mainly
because it was required reading in schools and elsewhere. In fact, the
book did not sell widely until after Hitler came to power.

Hitlerjunge Quex. Dir. Hans Steinhoff, Universum-Film-Aktiengesellschaft (UFA), 102 min., 1933. Chicago: Facets Video.
A Nazi feature film based upon an incident from the early days of the
Nazi youth movement; this was one of the better propaganda features
produced in the early days of the Third Reich. Quex is the name given
to real-life Herbert Norkus, a member of the Hitler Youth who was
killed by communists while on an errand for the party. He became a
martyr and hero of the Hitler Youth, in a manner similar to Horst
Wessell for the SA. The subtitle translates: "A Film about German
Youth and Its Spirit of Sacrifice." This edition is in German with
English descriptions of content rather than subtitles as such. See Jay
Baird, "From Berlin to Neubabelsberg," and David Welch, *Propa-
ganda and the German Cinema* (entries above under "History and
Function").

Hitler's Children. Prod. Edward A. Golden, dir. Edward Dmytryk, RKO
Radio Pictures, 83 min., 1943. Chicago: Facets Video.
Based upon Gregor Ziemer's book *Education for Death*, this emotion-
ally charged film depicts the preparations of the Hitler Youth for war
and totalitarian rule. Done in a docudrama style, the film begins with
the lads swearing obedience to Hitler and from there focuses upon one
boy, who grows with the movement until he becomes an SS man, and
a girl who resists Nazism. Both were born in the United States into
German families, and with those families found their way back to
Germany. She is a student in an American school and must be forced
to participate in Nazi youth activities. He, on the other hand, joins the
Hitler Youth gladly. Eventually, he becomes the cause of her death,
speaks out against the Nazis, and is killed in consequence. Singlemind-
edly anti-Nazi from start to finish and, in the context of the times,
effective propaganda. Tim Holt, famous as a star of Hollywood West-
erns, was an odd choice for the youth.

Huxley, Aldous. *Brave New World*. New York: Bantam Books, 1953. First published in 1932.
In this novel, Aldous Huxley lends his imagination to describing a utopia that is actually a totalitarian world in which all semblance of human individuality and free choice has long since been eradicated. The opening paragraph, for example, refers to the "Central London Hatchery and Conditioning Center," which is where human life is now produced in a test tube. Over the door is the "World State's motto, Community, Identity, Stability." That this novel took Soviet Russia (already in the early 1930s turning into a Stalinist nightmare) as its inspiration may be inferred from the overly technocratic and mechanistic world the novel creates, and as well from the name of its heroine, "Lenina." When the novel was republished in 1946 virtually without change, it seemed equally relevant as a cry of protest against the ideology of a futuristic totalitarian utopia.

Ich Klage An. Dir. Wolfgang Liebeneiner, Universum-Film-Aktiengesellschaft (UFA), 105 min., 1941. Chicago: International Historic Films.
This film tells the story of a doctor's wife who suffers from multiple sclerosis and becomes increasingly depressed. Finally, she persuades her husband to kill her. This film was propaganda in support of the Nazi policy of killing the mentally and physically handicapped.

The Iron Crown. Dir. Alexander Blasetti, approx. 120 min., 1941. Chicago: Facets Video.
An Italian film with a pro-fascist message. It is a quasi-historical fantasy that attempts to do for Italy what *Die Nibelungenlied* did for Germany, which is to say it mythologizes the nation in line with those national characteristics Italian fascism was supposed to represent.

Jud Süss. Dir. Veit Harlan, Universum-Film-Aktiengesellschaft (UFA), 100 min., 1940. Chicago: International Historic Films.
Based upon an incident in eighteenth century Wurtemburg involving the duchy's Jewish finance minister, Joseph Oppenheimer, this feature film, made by Universum-Film-Aktiengesellschaft, the German state film company set up by propaganda minister Joseph Goebbels, is a classic of anti-Semitic film propaganda made in Nazi Germany. Every traditional Jewish stereotype was both included and stressed. Veit Harlan co-authored and directed the film, and some of Germany's leading actors appeared in it. Among these were Ferdinand Marian, Kristina Söderbaum, and Werner Krauss. A French-language version, *Juif Süss*, was a central feature of an anti-Semitic exhibition in occupied Paris in 1941.

Kühle Wampe. Dir. Slatan Dudow, writ. Bertold Brecht, Praesens-Film, 90 min., 1932. Los Angeles: UCLA Film and Television Archive; New York: Museum of Modern art.
Germany is in the grips of economic depression, and the Bönike family is dispossessed. They move to Kühle Wampe, a tent city on the outskirts of Berlin. The son commits suicide, and the daughter marries a chauffeur who becomes a leftist political activist. Both Dudow, the director, and Brecht, the writer, were communists. Their film is intended to be passionate pro-communist propaganda. Consequently, it was censored by the German government for "endangering the safety of the State." This was ironic in light of what lay just around the corner for Germany when the film was released.

Lenin in 1918. Dir. Mikhail Romm, Mosfilm, 133 min., 1939. Unable to locate copy.
A docudrama which portrays Lenin's heroic struggles, aided by writer Maxim Gorky, to bring order out of chaos in revolutionary Russia. It is hagiographic to a fault, hero worship being one of the main propaganda themes. The other is that Stalin was Lenin's heir from the start, which constitutes a significant rearrangement of historical fact. This is a sequel to Romm's *Lenin in October* (1937), which is an equally propagandistic appraisal of Lenin's orchestration of the October Revolution in 1917.

Mädchen in Uniform. Dir. Leontine Sagan, Deutsche Film-Gemeinschaft, 110 min., 1931. Chicago: Facets Video.
As an all-female enterprise, this film was written, directed, and acted by women. The story is set at a boarding school, where the principal character attempts suicide in the context of an aggressively austere and oppressive environment. The uniforms, methods of discipline, and the attitude of the headmistress presage the political authoritarianism then creeping into German political life. The undertones of lesbianism in this powerful film are secondary to its propaganda message, which is a call for resisting authoritarian and repressive politics.

Der Marsch Zum Führer. Prod. Universum-Film-Aktiengesellschaft (UFA), 50 min., 1940. Chicago: International Historic Films.
Each summer, thousands of Hitler Youth marched across Germany to Nuremberg to participate in the annual Nazi party congress. This film shows them marching across mountains, through forests, fields, and towns. It is a pilgrimage climaxed by colorful ceremonies and rituals. At the rally, they are addressed by Hitler Youth leader Baldur von Shirach, deputy party leader Rudolf Hess, and Hitler himself. Much

splendid pageantry went into this film, the point of which is to show how skillfully the regime is preparing Germany's youth, physically and psychologically, for the future, including for war.

My Universities. Dir. Mark Donskoi, Soyezdctfilm, 104 min., 1940. Chicago: Facets Video.
Part of Donskoi's Gorky Trilogy, consisting of three docudramas extolling the life of Soviet writer Maxim Gorky. In this film, Gorky goes from job to job witnessing the exploitation of the workers. At the end he envisions the coming of a better future. Filled with patriotism and Soviet ideology, the film is a masterpiece of Socialist Realism. The others in the trilogy are *The Childhood of Maxim Gorky* and *My Apprenticeship.* All are based on Gorky's autobiography.

Nazi Agent. Prod. Irving Asher, dir. Jules Dassin, Metro-Goldwyn-Mayer, 82 min., 1942. Atlanta: Turner Movie Classics.
Twin brothers, one a German expatriate to the United States and the other the German consul in New York, represent opposite poles on the issue of Nazism. The consul is a hard-core Nazi who uses his office to spy on the United States; his twin is an anti-Nazi bookseller who deplores what his brother has become. A clash between them results in the death of the Nazi brother. His twin takes his place and in this "disguise" tries to undo some of the harm the "evil brother" has done. Konrad Veidt, a German expatriate actor, plays the twins.

The New Gulliver. Dir. Alexander Ptoushko, Mosfilm, 85 min., 1935. New York: Museum of Modern Art.
The story in this film is told by puppets. It is that Jonathan Swift's *Gulliver's Travels,* when read to a group of Young Pioneers (the Soviet version of the Boy and Girl Scouts), gives the Pioneers ideas about how the story would be in their own day. They imagine Gulliver's situation being filmed, the giant being fed with devices designed by modern engineering, and, of course, the giant, when freed helping to win the class war for the oppressed masses. The message is characteristic of most Stalin-era Soviet films, but delivered in an unusual way.

The Nibelungen Saga—Kriemhild's Revenge. Dir. Fritz Lang, Decla Bioskop/Universum-Film-Aktiengesellschaft (UFA), 118 min., 1924. Chicago: International Historic Films.
The second of two Fritz Lang films based on the famous *Song of the Nibelungen,* which also provided inspiration for Richard Wagner's famous operatic Ring Cycle. Here, Kriemhild takes revenge on the Burgundians for killing her husband, Siegfried, who is the subject of

the first film. See *Siegfried* (entry below). In both films, Teutonic mythology, gods, heroes, villains, and a clear connection with *das Volk*, the particular brand of populism dear to Nazi hearts, are prominent. This is one of Fritz Lang's earliest films, and it was not intended as propaganda. Nevertheless, it had a great impact upon later Nazi propaganda disseminated through film and other channels.

The Nibelungen Saga—Siegfried. Dir. Fritz Lang, Decla Bioskop/Universum-Film-Aktiengesellschaft (UFA), 131 min., 1924. Chicago: Facets Video.
The first of Fritz Lang's two film adaptations of the Nibelungen saga. See *Kriemhild's Revenge* (entry above). In this film, Siegfried marries Kriemhild and journeys from Iceland to Burgundy with Brunhild, who is to marry Siegfried's brother-in-law, Gunther. She is not pleased, and arranges for the evil Hagen to kill Siegfried. Siegfried is the classic Teutonic type, who rides through the film on a white horse, worships power and war, and is graced with golden hair, all perfectly consistent with the Nazi ideology which was taking shape even as the film was made.

Ninotchka. Prod. and dir. Ernst Lubitsch, Metro-Goldwyn-Mayer, 110 min., 1939. Chicago: Facets Video.
Based on a play by Melchior Langyel, this film satirizes communism, and is not all that kind to capitalism. Ninotchka is a stern representative of the Soviet Union in Paris, who slowly but surely warms to French champagne and a French playboy. Three Soviet commissars come to Paris to sort her out, but they too fall prey to the city's seductive charm.

Olympia: The Film of the 1936 Olympic Games, parts 1 and 2. Dir. Leni Riefenstahl, Tobis Rota, 215 min., 1936. New York: Phoenix/y BFA Films and Video.
This is the English-language version of Leni Riefenstahl's four-hour-long record of the 1936 Berlin Olympics. While the exploits of such non-Aryan olympians as Jessie Owens were faithfully recorded, the film nevertheless preached the ideals of the Nazi mythos. Each of the two parts depicts the ideal of Aryan beauty, the first in male, and the second in female athletes. During the early stages of the German invasion of Russia, the film was exported for anti-Soviet propaganda purposes, the point being that the Soviet Union had not participated in the Berlin games.

Orwell, George. *Nineteen Eighty-Four.* New York: Harcourt Brace, 1949.
Orwell was a novelist with a cause, or sometimes several causes. Any bibliography on propaganda must include Orwell, who in his later years

propagandized against propaganda. *Nineteen Eighty-Four* is arguably his most famous work, a novel which imagines a future totalitarian world created and maintained by propaganda (herein defined as "brain-washing") and within which war has become a way of life. Inspired by Orwell's disillusionment with communism, intellectuals, and spe-cifically totalitarian dictatorship of the Soviet type, this novel is a warning against the use and abuse of propaganda. *Nineteen Eighty-Four* long ago became a classic of literature on propaganda as a tool of anti-democratic politics, and was made into feature films twice. The second effort, released in 1984 with John Hurt as Winston Smith, is, in the opinion of this author, far superior to the 1954 original.

Our March. 21 min., 1968. Chicago: International Historic Films.
Made to commemorate the fiftieth anniversary of the Bolshevik Revolu-tion, this film glorifies communism and its impact upon the world. The film presents the most famous events of the period of the revolution in dramatic scenes of blood and glory: ringing speeches by Lenin, the massacre of peasant marchers in city streets, the final storming of govern-ment buildings (all in 1917), achievements in collectivization in the 1920s and 1930s, and finally, the great Soviet victories in World War II.

Paracelsus. Dir. G. W. Pabst, Bavaria-Filmkunst, 104 min., 1943. Chi-cago: Facets Video.
This was one of three films Pabst made at the invitation of the Third Reich. The story is of Paracelsus, the town physician in medieval Basel, who confronts reactionary academics, medical superstitions, and greedy merchants as he does battle against a plague that is infesting the city. The film has all of the elements characteristic of Nazi propa-ganda films: anti-intellectualism, including a line in which the doctor says "resolute imagination can accomplish all things" (which is more or less the same as Hitler's frequent line that he distrusted the mind and relied rather on the heart), and a rebel hero cleaning the old ways out of Germany and replacing foreign influence with things German. After World War II, Pabst sought to atone for these Nazi films by making *Jackboot Mutiny* (entry in chapter 7 under "Propaganda Material") in 1955, about the attempt to assassinate Hitler.

Rosenberg, William G. *Bolshevik Visions: First Phase of the Cultural Revolution in Soviet Russia*. Ann Arbor, Mich.: Ardis, 1984.
This volume includes writings by Bolshevik leaders in the early 1920s in which they instruct (propagandize) the populace on thinking and behaving in the new Russia. The authors include V. I. Lenin, N. Krup-

skaya, N. Bukharin, Leon Trotsky, Alexandra Kollontai, and many others. The editor has grouped the collection under eight categories. Examples of headings include: "The New Man and New Woman: Sex Roles, Marriage and the Family," "Religion, Language, and Other 'Awkward Habits' of Everyday Life," "Proletarian Legality," and "Vodka, the Church, and the Cinema: Workers' Films and the Uses of Visual Art." Within these categories are such essays as Kollontai on "The Fight against Prostitution," Trotsky on "The Struggle for Cultured Speech," and a Central Committee report on "Anti-Religious Agitation and Propaganda among Women Workers and Peasants." All of the materials were written between 1919 and 1924. Illustrations and limited bibliography.

Sabotage. Prod. Michael Balcon, Ivor Montagu, dir. Alfred Hitchcock, Gaumont, 76 min., 1936. Chicago: Facets Video.
In the later 1930s, Alfred Hitchcock carried on a subtle but unmistakable one-man film propaganda campaign against Britain's policy of appeasing totalitarian dictators. British film censors would not permit overt political criticism of foreign leaders, but Hitchcock managed it all the same in this and several other films between 1934 and 1940. In *Sabotage* a terrorist with a distinctly Germanic-sounding name is on a bombing spree in London, using a trusting young boy to deliver the bombs without his knowing the contents. This was clearly a metaphor for the British government's blindness to the dangers posed by Hitler and other European dictators. The villains in the film are sinister and have foreign accents, the boy is naive, and the people who suffer from the acts of terrorism are innocent victims. Interestingly, censors in some countries banned the film because they thought it advocated terrorism. This was not the objection to it in Britain, however.

Shchors. Dir. Alexander Dovzhenko, Kiev Film Studio, 140 min., 1939. Cambridge, Mass.: Harvard University Widener Library.
A feature film in which pro-Bolshevik Ukrainians liberate Kiev from the Germans in 1918. Later, the hero of the event, Nikolai Shchors, founds a school for Red Army officers. This heroic epic was made at the specific request of Stalin. The director responded with a film which extolled Shchors' achievements in the manner of a "cult of personality" statement, which was precisely what Stalin wanted. The idealized character of Shchors is rarely off the screen, and the story is overwhelmingly didactic.

Storm over Asia. Dir. Vsevolod Pudovkin, Mezhrabpom, 93 min., 1928. Chicago: Facets Video.
A nomadic fur trapper in 1918 claims to be the heir of Genghis Khan. British interventionist forces in Mongolia set him up as a puppet

monarch. However, he realizes his national identity and rouses the Asian hordes against their British oppressors. A good example of early Soviet anti-Western propaganda cinema. The film was banned in Britain for some years, probably because it made the British out to be tyrannous villains.

Strike. Dir. Sergei Eisenstein, Goskino, 82 min., 1924. Chicago: International Historic Films.

It is 1912, and after the suicide of a worker who had been fired, cavalrymen are sent by the State to slaughter workers and their families who have gone on strike. This was one of Eisenstein's early film efforts, and while he employs the kind of cinemagraphic techniques that made him one of the great early Soviet filmmakers, the substance is, as always, propaganda that celebrates the victory of the workers in the October Revolution of 1917.

Ten Days That Shook the World. Dir. Sergei Eisenstein, Sovkino, 164 min., 1928. Chicago: Facets Video.

Also known as *October*, this is the story of the ten days that brought down the Provisional Government in 1917 and put Lenin and the Bolsheviks in power. Needless to say, they are the heroes of the film. Other propaganda elements include expunging the scenes featuring Trotsky, who, by the time the film was released, had been officially rejected by the Politburo. This was the best of several films commissioned by the Soviet government in celebration of the tenth anniversary of the Revolution.

Three Songs of Lenin. Dir. Dziga Vertov, Mezharbpomfilm, approx. 100 min., 1934. New York: Kino International.

Made for the tenth anniversary of Lenin's death, this film extols his virtues, identifies him with the masses whom he liberated, and shows these ordinary people pouring out their love for Lenin in the form of three songs from the Soviet East which are identified as songs of the Revolution. Lenin is identified at the outset as "the leader of the oppressed of the whole world." The content of the film is largely a survey of the great achievements accomplished by the Soviet revolution, in particular the collectives, in which proud peasants are depicted as being happy that they are living as part of what is identified as "their Collective," and grateful that Lenin gave it to them.

Triumph of the Will. Dir. Leni Riefenstahl, Universum-Film-Aktiengesellschaft (UFA), 110 min., 1934. Rye, N.Y.: Images; Logan: Utah State University, Merrill Library.

This is the edited, two-hour-long English-language version of Leni Riefenstahl's documentary film of the 1934 Nuremberg Nazi party rally, *Triumph des Willens*. The original version is much longer. The point is nevertheless clear. Every element of Nazi mythology is present, from the Führer's airplane descending from the sky, a messianic metaphor, to the image of healthy German youth representing a superior blond race. This is a propaganda classic, and one of the most effective such films ever made. See Linda Deutschmann, *Triumph of the Will* (entry above under "Channels and Techniques").

Turksib. Dir. Victor Turin, Vostok Kino, 60 min., 1929. New York: Museum of Modern Art.
This is a documentary which describes the building of the Turkestan-Siberian Railway. The climax is the completion of the railway, and it comes with the workers straining cheerfully as well as successfully to meet the objectives of the first Five Year Plan. An exuberant Soviet morale booster that was actually finished ahead of the railway. British documentary filmmaker John Grierson is said to have been much influenced by the technical aspects of this production.

Underground. Dir. Vincent Sherman, Warner Brothers, 98 min., 1941. Hanover, N.H.: Dartmouth College.
If the United States was neutral prior to December 1941 in terms of the war that began in Europe in September 1939, Jack Warner, head of Warner Brothers studio, was not—at least not where Nazi Germany was concerned. This film is a story about resistance to the Nazi regime within Germany, and whether or not there was much resistance is beside the point. A German underground organization broadcasts anti-Nazi propaganda within Germany over clandestine radio. They are found out, and their leaders are executed, but the rest of the movement remain defiant. The broadcasts continue.

Watch on the Rhine. Prod. Hal B. Wallis, dir. Herman Shumlin, Warner Brothers, 114 min., 1943. Chicago: Facets Video.
Lillian Hellman wrote the play upon which this film is based. Set in the prewar United States, it tells the story of Kurt and Sara, refugees from Nazi Germany, who arrive with their children to visit Sara's mother in Washington, D.C. There they encounter a Rumanian count who is chummy with the Germans at the embassy and comes to suspect that Kurt is actually leader of an anti-Nazi resistance movement in Europe. He offers to spy for the Germans, and at the same time tries to blackmail Kurt. Kurt responds by killing him in order to protect his family and himself. This is among the earliest American films to present fascism as a real philosophical danger to the United States, rather than just a military one.

We Are from Kronstadt. Dir. Efim Dzigan, approx. 90 min., 1936. New York: Museum of Modern Art.
This film glorifies the Bolshevik Revolution. Red sailors from the Kronstadt naval base near Petrograd heroically face death rather than yield to the White Army during the Civil War. However, they must be shown the way, as they are prone to anarchy. Commissar Martynov manages to influence them, through his own courage, to hold fast against the Whites. Martynov is killed in the battle, and after his funeral, each surviving member of the naval regiment joins the Communist party. That Soviet propaganda had become enormously successful at home is indicated by this anecdote: the real story of Krondstadt was that these same sailors rebelled against the Bolsheviks in 1921 and were stopped only by a counterattack ordered from the Kremlin.

We the Living. Dir. Goffredo Alessandrini, Scalera/Duncan Scott, 174 min., 1942. Chicago: Facets Video.
An Italian production based upon Ayn Rand's novel about her youth spent in Russia in the early years of the Soviet Union, this film features heroic renunciations and suicides in the name of lost ideals. Kira and Leo are anti-Red lovers. When he is arrested, she becomes the mistress of two men, an idealistic party member and a secret police officer, in order to earn money to pay for Leo's treatment for tuberculosis. However, Leo becomes as corrupt as his oppressors, while the party member becomes disillusioned with the party and shoots himself when he learns that Kira does not love him. Finally, still firmly anti-Red, Kira leaves both Leo and the Soviet Union. Anti-communist propaganda is a constant theme throughout the film, but despite that fact, it was banned in Mussolini's Italy when it first appeared.

Ziel im den Wolken. Prod. Universum-Film-Aktiengesellschaft (UFA), 101 min., 1937. Chicago: International Historic Films.
This tells the story of a young cavalry officer trying to convince his military superiors of the future role aircraft will play in army reconnaissance. He encounters ridicule and hostility but is supported and encouraged by the woman who loves him. Her devotion subjects her to skepticism from her parents, but she persists. The hero finally abandons the military and pursues aviation as a civilian. In the process, he forsakes the old order and strikes out in new progressive directions, fighting resistance the whole way. He is the Nazi revolution personified. This copy is in German without subtitles.

Zvenigora. Dir. Alexander Dovzhenko, Vseukrainskii-Fotografichiskii-i-
Kinoustroistvo (VUFKU), 73 min., 1928. Chicago: Facets Video.

An early Soviet propaganda film made by a Ukrainian director in
which an old man and his two grandsons, one a revolutionary and the
other a reactionary, go in search of buried treasure. While they travel,
grandfather dreams of the long history of the Ukraine; the reactionary
grandson demonstrates the corruption of the old order by advertising
his own suicide at a theater in order to get money. The characters are
metaphors for the past, present, and future. In this film, ancient culture
is brought together with the flowering of the Soviet New Order—a sort
of film propaganda symbol of the Marxian dialectic in which thesis
meets antithesis, and they merge into synthesis.

Chapter 5

PROPAGANDA AND WORLD WAR II, 1939-1945

Propaganda came into its own as a weapon of war during World War II. It was spread at home and abroad by every belligerent state, each of which abetted its propaganda by maintaining a strict censorship watch over the press, post, and other forms of communication. Between the wars, the science of public relations and advertising had taken great strides forward. These advances were attached to World War II propaganda from the first day, in terms of organization, style, and technique. Moreover, propaganda channels were now more numerous and sophisticated than those used in World War I. Press, pamphlet, poster, leaflet, film (including documentary, feature, and cartoon), broadcasting, "whisper campaigns," and the new "science" of disinformation—that is, true information presented in such a way as to create a false conclusion—all of these played a role in the propaganda war. Government propaganda agencies were much larger than in World War I and were brought into existence upon the outbreak of war rather than developing over time; or, as in the case of Italy and Germany, they already existed and were simply expanded to include war propaganda.

Entries in this chapter cover the history, function, channels, techniques, and materials of World War II propaganda in all of their variety. This includes an extensive listing of propaganda films, for film became one of the most popular propaganda channels during this particular war, and perhaps the most effective.

History and Function

Allport, Gordon W., and Leo Postman. *The Psychology of Rumor.* New York: Henry Holt, 1947.

This book, published two years after World War II ended, analyzes "rumor mongering," a phenomenon which became a problem "of grave national concern in the tense years of 1942 and 1943." The authors describe rumor as an ordinary part of social conversation. They chose to undertake this study because "in wartime, rumors sap morale and menace national safety by spreading needless alarm and by raising extravagant hopes." Therefore, they concluded it is important to understand the psychology and sociology of rumor mongering, presumably in the event of future national crises. This study includes such topics as how and why rumors circulate, examples of rumors that circulated in World War II, and different experiments that shed light on rumor. The discussion of such topics is especially interesting in light of the fact that one of Britain's many propaganda techniques in neutral countries during World War II was the "Whispering Campaign," which was specifically a process of rumor mongering. Limited bibliography and an appendix containing "Standards for Agencies Working on the Prevention and Control of Wartime Rumor," which was put out during the war by the Massachusetts Committee on Public Safety.

Baird, Jay W. *The Mythical World of Nazi War Propaganda, 1939-1945*. Minneapolis: University of Minnesota Press, 1974.
This book provides an analysis of Nazi propaganda within the context of a chronological historical survey of World War II in Europe, from the German invasion of Poland through the last days in the Berlin bunker. It is one of the earliest scholarly historical treatments of Nazi war propaganda based upon archival research. The author characterizes Nazi propaganda as "focused on the irrational through myth and symbol." Jews were "The Enemy," the British were a plutocracy deserving to be brought down, the Bolsheviks were Jews, to die for the Fatherland was to experience joy, and so forth. By 1945 time was running out for the Nazi leadership, and the author sees them taking leave of reality altogether and entering the mythical world created by their propaganda. A few illustrations and a select bibliography.

Baker, M. Joyce. *Images of Women in Film: The War Years, 1941-1945*. Ann Arbor, Mich.: UMI Research Press, 1980.
This book is indirectly about propaganda. The author's aim is to write an analysis of how women were portrayed in Hollywood feature films during World War II. In the process, she draws the inevitable conclusion that in most instances, the portrayal sent persuasive messages about the role women were playing, or ought to be playing, in wartime. The author's topics include heroines on the home front, heroines in military life, women as resisters, women supportive of men at war, mothers, and the impact of wartime film imagery upon the actual lives of women. Illustrations and a select bibliography that includes film lists.

Balfour, Michael. *Propaganda in War, 1939-1945: Organizations, Policies and Publics in Britain and Germany*. London: Routledge and Kegan Paul, 1979.
The author served in both the British Ministry of Information and the Political Warfare Executive during World War II. The latter office was devoted to propaganda aimed at enemy and enemy-occupied countries.

This volume provides explanation of propaganda on both the British
and German sides, with definitions and analysis of how the various
propaganda agencies did their work. This was the first study of World
War II propaganda that provided a comparative analysis of British and
German efforts. It is based on archival research. Select bibliography.

Bell, P. M. H. *John Bull and the Bear: British Public Opinion, Foreign Policy
and the Soviet Union, 1941-1945*. London: Edward Arnold, 1990.
This volume provides a model for how to analyze wartime policy,
censorship, and propaganda as an integrated study. The subject is the
work of the British government in attempting to persuade British public
opinion to be pro-Soviet for purposes of winning the war against Hitler.
Two "case studies," the Katyn Graves episode and the Warsaw Uprising, are presented to show how opinion and policy interacted at critical
moments during the war, and how propaganda was used to try to move
that opinion in directions desired by foreign policy makers. Limited
illustrations, select bibliography of primary and secondary sources, and
an appendix which demonstrates the main theme of the book in reference to a subject not related to the Soviet Union, the Anglo-American
"deal" struck in 1942 with French Admiral Darlan in North Africa.

Bishop, Robert L., and LaMar S. Mackay. "Mysterious Silence, Lyrical
Scream: Government Information in World War II." *Journalism Monographs* 19 (May 1971), pp. 1-39.
This pamphlet is a straightforward history of the principal problems
the United States government faced in setting up its information
agencies for World War II. It has the additional purpose of suggesting
"some conclusions which may be relevant now"—that is, of use to the
present government (1971) in terms of disseminating information. The
title derives from a *New Yorker* column which described news disseminated during World War II as having "undulated in the mysterious
region somewhere between the mysterious silence of the censor and
the lyrical scream of the propagandist." The pamphlet is in two parts,
the first dealing with the news release organization and the second with
the Office of War Information, which was the wartime propaganda arm
of the United States government.

Black, Gregory D. "Keys of the Kingdom: Entertainment and Propaganda." *South Atlantic Quarterly* 75, 4 (Autumn 1976), pp. 434-446.
The co-author of *Hollywood Goes to War* (entry below under Koppes)
prepared for that book in this article, by discussing World War II feature
entertainment films made for propaganda purposes. He surveys their

propaganda function, describes the role played in Hollywood by the Office of War Information, and analyzes *Keys of the Kingdom* (entry below under "Propaganda Material") as an example. The author explains how in this instance, the OWI "managed to change a film from a Hollywood version of early twentieth-century missionary life in China to an OWI epic that reflected the wartime relationship between Washington and Chungking." He notes that OWI influence turned some 500 Hollywood features into propaganda, which was roughly 200 more specifically propagandistic films than Joseph Goebbels inspired throughout the existence of the Third Reich.

Boelcke, Willi A., ed. *The Secret Conferences of Dr. Goebbels: The Nazi Propaganda War, 1939-43.* Translated by Ewald Osers. New York: E. P. Dutton, 1970.
Joseph Goebbels was Nazi Germany's chief propagandist. Almost every morning from the beginning of the war, he met with his closest collaborators at the propaganda ministry and issued his directions for propaganda activities. By 1941 there were about fifty participants in these conferences. This volume contains the minutes of some of those meetings. In these documents and in the editor's introduction, Goebbels' philosophy of propaganda is made clear, and it is made clear also that his philosophy was far more cynical than that which applied to British propagandists at the same time. "Propaganda has nothing at all to do with truth," the reichsminister once noted, and then pointed out that the main task of the propagandist is to master the art of "lying credibly."

Briggs, Asa. *The History of Broadcasting in the United Kingdom.* Vol. 3, *The War of Words.* London: Oxford University Press, 1970.
"Words do not win wars," the author begins, but goes on to note that World War II is sometimes known as a war of words because so many were broadcast in order both to inform and to persuade millions of people at home and abroad. This long volume (more than 700 pages) is a history of the British Broadcasting Corporation (BBC) in wartime. It explains in exacting detail what the BBC did and did not do, the role it played as a propaganda channel for Britain and against Britain's enemies, who worked for it, and what, if anything, broadcasting accomplished in the process. If there is anything not covered in this volume, it could not have been important, at least not in the author's judgment. Illustrations, a limited bibliography, and several appendixes indicating BBC wartime broadcasting schedules at home and externally, and major personnel.

Capra, Frank. *The Name Above the Title: An Autobiography*. New York: Macmillan, 1971.
Frank Capra made many films, including the propaganda documentary series *Why We Fight* (entry below under "Propaganda Material") in 1943. In this somewhat novelistic autobiography, Capra tells the story of his association with Hollywood. One section is devoted entirely to his labors during World War II on behalf of the Office of War Information, and in connection with such filmmakers as Sidney Bernstein of the British Ministry of Information. Though Capra's autobiography is valuable to the study of wartime film, it should be remembered that autobiographies are not noted for their objectivity. The author's observations about personalities and events connected with making propaganda films should be taken with a grain of salt. Illustrated with photographs, no bibliography. See Clayton Koppes and Gregory Black, *Hollywood Goes to War* (entry below).

Clarke, Peter B. *West Africans at War: 1914-18; 1939-45: Colonial Propaganda and Its Cultural Aftermath*. London: Ethnographica, 1986.
This short volume begins with a discussion of the role of West Africans in the two world wars, and then moves to its primary point, British propaganda and its role in West Africa. The author's principal theme is that British anti-German propaganda before and during World War II played a pivotal role in bringing the West Africans within reach of their postwar independence—which was quite the opposite of what the propaganists intended.

Coers, Donald V. *John Steinbeck as Propagandist: "The Moon Is Down" Goes to War*. Tuscaloosa: University of Alabama Press, 1991.
Was Steinbeck's 1942 novel *The Moon Is Down* propaganda? Critics thought so at the time, and, as the author of this well-crafted study indicates, they did not like it. Apparently, it was Steinbeck's intention to write a propaganda novel, on the premise that a novel would be a more effective propaganda channel than the "customary propagandistic hype." This volume describes the novel, criticism of it, argument over it, and the fact that it was clandestinely published in such enemy-occupied countries as Norway, Denmark, Holland, and France. The author concludes with praise for Steinbeck, noting that while *The Moon Is Down* was not among his great works, it nevertheless "was a beacon of hope in a seemingly endless night." This volume sheds needed light on a World War II propaganda channel, literature, that receives less attention that the more conventional channels of film, broadcasting, and the press.

Colby, Benjamin. *'Twas a Famous Victory: Deception and Propaganda in the War with Germany*. New Rochelle, N.Y.: Arlington House Publishers, 1974.
A revisionist history, this book describes the deception, propaganda, and falsehood used to promote trust in the Soviet Union and hatred of Germany, during a war which "brought unconditional military victory and disastrous political defeat." By that last the author seems to mean that allied propaganda did not seek to undermine Hitler so much as it sought to condemn the German people, with the result that they fought to the bitter end. And that, he concludes, guaranteed that communism would take control of half of Europe. Source material is indicated in endnotes. The author's arguments might be more compelling if this material was archival rather than limited to memoirs and newspaper items. There is a strong flavor of 20-20 hindsight in this book.

Cole, J. A. *Lord Haw-Haw—and William Joyce*. London: Faber and Faber, 1964.
William Joyce, the "renegade" Irish-American who made propaganda broadcasts on behalf of Germany during World War II, came to be known as Lord Haw-Haw because of the excessively "English" accent he employed for the broadcasts. This biography seeks to explain Joyce's fascination with fascism and Hitler's Germany, and, as the author explains it, to look beyond the hatred expressed by postwar writers about Joyce in order to present the real character of the man. William Joyce was, he concludes, neither a joke nor a crackpot, but rather "intelligent, well-educated, dedicated, hardworking, fluent and sharp-tongued. . . ." The book traces his history from the Joyce family origins in Ireland through his execution after the war as a traitor. Illustrations but no bibliography, though the author claims to have had access to much primary material about the subject. See Francis Selwyn, *Hitler's Englishman* (entry below).

Cole, Robert. *Britain and the War of Words in Neutral Europe, 1939-1945: The Art of the Possible*. London: Macmillan, 1990.
This volume examines British propaganda efforts directed at European neutrals in World War II. The neutrals were an important target of the propaganda "war of words." The volume covers British propaganda work in Belgium, Denmark, Finland, Greece, Holland, Norway, and Yugoslavia before these countries were overrun by German armies, and Portugal, Spain, Sweden, Switzerland which were never invaded and remained neutral throughout the war. It describes the organization and channels for propaganda dissemination, the content of the propa-

ganda material, and assesses the extent to which the propaganda efforts
were successful. The volume also describes the harrowing experiences
of the press attachés who ran propaganda dissemination in neutral
countries for the Ministry of Information, when they had to flee
invading German armies. The author does not include neutral Ireland
or the Soviet Union and Italy during their neutral period, as each of
these involved what the British considered to be special circumstances
and were dealt with differently than the others. Extensive bibliography
of primary and secondary sources. See Michael Balfour, *Propaganda
and War* (entry above).

_____. "The Other 'Phoney War': Britain and the 'War of Words'
in Neutral Europe, September-December, 1939." *Journal of Contemporary History* 22 (1987), pp. 455-479.
This article describes the first four months of British propaganda
efforts in neutral Europe, with particular emphasis upon confusion and
shortcomings in the the Foreign Publicity Division of the Ministry of
Information, the organization that had responsibility for this effort. The
author draws the conclusion that even as the shooting war remained on
hold from September 1939 until the spring of 1940, so too did the
propaganda war, at least until the end of 1939. The article describes
what was not happening and why. See Robert Cole, *Britain and the
War of Words* (entry above).

Cornick, Martyn. "The BBC and the Propaganda War Against Occupied
France: The Work of Émile Delavaney and the European Intelligence
Department." *French History* 8, 3 (1994), pp. 316-354.
This article is an "oral history" of the subject, based upon an interview
with Émile and Madame Delavenay, who made French-language
broadcasts into occupied France for Britain during World War II. An
in-depth introduction explains the various propaganda agencies that
operated in Britain and against Britain in France and Germany, and
makes an assessment, based upon postwar interviews, of how much
the French public relied upon British radio for news of the war. The
introduction provides context for the interview.

Costello, David R. "*Searchlight Books* and the Quest for a 'People's War,'
1941-42." *Journal of Contemporary History* 24, 2 (April 1989), pp.
257-276.
This article describes the hopes of prominent British leftists to turn
World War II into an opportunity to transform Britain socially. The
means to this end was to be a series of books called *Searchlight Books*,

put out by Secker and Warburg publishers, and written by the likes of George Orwell and Tosco Fyvel. These books were a form of social propaganda which called for, among other things, a postwar classless society. In the end, only ten such books were published. The author describes them as an "impressive effort," despite their having had only limited impact.

Coultass, Clive. "British Feature Films and the Second World War." *Journal of Contemporary History* 19, 1 (January 1984), pp. 7-22.
Feature films played an important role in World War II in both reassuring and propagandizing British cinema audiences. This article describes both aspects of British wartime features and argues for expanding historical study of the subject. The author describes feature films as diverse in content and purpose as Lawrence Olivier's *Henry V*, Carol Reed's *Night Train to Munich*, and the docudrama *Target for Tonight* (entries below under "Propaganda Material"). The latter is explained as being among the earliest British feature films to be promoted as straight propaganda. See Clive Coultass, *Images for Battle*, and Anthony Aldgate and Jeffrey Richards, *Britain Can Take It* (entries below under "Channels and Techniques").

Cruickshank, Charles. *The Fourth Arm: Psychological Warfare, 1938-1945*. Oxford, England: Oxford University Press, 1981.
This is a history of Britain's Political Warfare Executive (PWE) in World War II, which was in charge of propaganda to enemy and enemy-occupied countries. The book opens with a description of how the Sudeten crisis of September 1938 encouraged the government to move forward in its preparation for the kind of wartime propaganda activity that the PWE would undertake, which was sometimes referred to as "sykewar." The author explains how the PWE was organized, how it carried out its operations, the content of materials disseminated, and how its audiences responded. Illustrated, select bibliography, and an appendix describing archival sources.

Cull, Nicholas John. *Selling War: The British Propaganda Campaign Against American "Neutrality" in World War II*. New York: Oxford University Press, 1995.
The history of the British propaganda aimed at the isolationist United States in the first year and a half of World War II is based upon thorough archival research. The record reveals, the author argues, that this propaganda made a major contribution to preparing the United States for the war which followed the Japanese attack on Pearl Harbor.

However, when the war was over, the British government "seems to have tried to destroy the evidence of its war propaganda in the United States. It hoped to avoid the embarrassment that followed exposure of its similar campaign to draw America into World War I." Nevertheless, the evidence remained, and when the archives were opened, that evidence indicated clearly that the British propaganda campaign in the United States "stands as one of the most diverse, extensive, and yet subtle propaganda campaigns ever directed by one sovereign state at another." Topics covered include the development of a propaganda policy for the United States before 1939, propaganda activities during the "phoney war" (1939-1940), projecting the Battle of Britain, projecting British courage during the Blitz, asking for American aid, and orchestrating propaganda in the last months before Pearl Harbor. Illustrations and extensive bibliography.

Duus, Masayo. *Tokyo Rose: Orphan of the Pacific*. Translated by Peter Duus. Tokyo: Kodansha International, 1979.
"Tokyo Rose" was the name American soldiers and others in the Pacific theater in World War II gave to the voices of all English-speaking female Japanese propaganda broadcasters. However, one particular woman, Iva Toguri, a *nisei* (born in the United States of Japanese parents) left stranded in Japan by the war, fell heir to the mantle of Tokyo Rose. This book tells her story. She apparently continued to believe in the United States, even though that country abandoned her and sentenced her to prison after the war. Written by a *nisei* journalist, the book is reasonably objective but is not a work of scholarship. It does shed light on Tokyo Rose propaganda, however, and perhaps even more on the kind of propaganda that myth and racial prejudice can generate quite on its own.

Evans, Gary. *John Grierson and the National Film Board: The Politics of Wartime Propaganda*. Toronto: University of Toronto Press, 1984.
John Grierson, creator of the Documentary Film Movement in Britain in the years between the world wars, became the "propaganda maestro" of Canada during World War II. This book is a history of that experience. The author claims that Grierson turned Canadian war propaganda into a crusade with "near-religious overtones," the point being that Grierson's propaganda aimed at building "a brave new world based on the changes he could see coming as a result of the new age and techniques of mass communications." That it did not work out quite the way he anticipated was not owing to shortcomings of Grierson himself, but rather to the government involved, which concluded that

"once the crisis had passed, there was no need to preach about a better world to come." The author examines the National Film Board, documentary propaganda, "political cockfights," and practical politics against idealism, among other topics. Numerous illustrations but only minimal bibliography, save for what is contained in endnotes.

Gerdes, Peter R. "'*Ciné-Journal Suisse*' and Neutrality, 1940-1945." *Historical Journal of Film, Radio and Television* 5, 1 (1985), pp. 19-35.
This article details how Switzerland maintained a delicate but necessary neutral balance between the belligerent powers in World War II. That balance became increasingly difficult when *Ciné-Journal Suisse* (C-JS) was started early in the war period, which took it upon itself to become a tool of "spiritual defense" of the nation, and provide war information, sustain traditional Swiss democracy and national values, all without "sounding too cock-sure and propagandistic," or offending any of the belligerents. The author takes up a wide variety of subjects within the context of neutrality and the C-JS, including discussion of the intricacies involved in official neutrality. See Robert Cole, *Britain and the War of Words in Neutral Europe* (entry above).

Hargrave, John. *Words Win Wars: Propaganda, the Mightiest Weapon of All*. London: Wells Gardner, Darton, 1940.
This volume is a study of propaganda function, and it makes such a strong case for the use of propaganda in war that it virtually becomes propaganda itself. The setting is Britain in 1940, the year following the beginning of World War II. "All wars begin—and end—with words," is how the author opens. His argument in favor of word use to further Britain's cause—which is to say the Cause of Right—never wavers from that moment onward. Part of the argument is that the Ministry of Information, Britain's propaganda organization, does not do a proper job, or else is prevented from doing it by interference of the official censor's office. The author is perplexed regardless of where the fault lies. Drawing upon history, literature, and the Bible for example and inspiration, he pleads for the expansion of a truth-based propaganda that will overcome the enemy. This volume is primary material for the historian of British propaganda in World War II. No bibliography.

Honey, Maureen. *Creating Rosie the Riveter: Class, Gender, and Propaganda During World War II*. Amherst: University of Massachusetts Press, 1984.
The purpose of this book is to assess why war work for women did not in the end "legitimize women's entry into nontraditional occupations,"

and to examine the contradiction between propaganda that praised the capacity of women to perform public work and other propaganda that relegated them to the kitchen once war was over, using the argument that "that is where their 'natural' limitations and strengths place them." The author explains the cultural context out of which wartime working women came, as part of her evaluation of the propaganda techniques that first drew them into factories, and then persuaded them to leave that work and go home. Illustrations, bibliography, and appendixes listing propaganda publications aimed at women. See *The Life and Times of Rosie the Riveter* (entry below under "Channels and Techniques").

Jarvie, I. C. "Fanning the Flames: Anti-American Reaction to *Operation Burma* (1945)." *Historical Journal of Film, Radio and Television* 1, 2 (1981), pp. 117-137.
Noting first that Anglo-American relations during World War II were "far from harmonious," and giving some incidental reasons why, the author analyzes the impact on that less than harmonious relationship by *Operation Burma*, a Hollywood feature adventure film with the usual war propaganda themes, which was released in 1945. The basic British criticism of the film was that it misled its audiences regarding the role played by both the United States and Britain in the war, encouraging in the process a grossly chauvinistic view of the United States. This article explains the film in terms of what it contained that was offensive to so many Britons, and reactions to the film that included criticism of its contents by American servicemen. Several appendixes contain documents relevant to the article.

Kirwin, Gerald. "Allied Bombing and Nazi Domestic Propaganda." *European History Quarterly* 15 (July 1985), pp. 341-362.
Allied bombing intensified as World War II progressed, creating an ever expanding problem for Nazi propagandists. Their task was to maintain civilian belief in ultimate victory, which was not easy with allied bombs raining down nightly on their homes—or so it was always assumed. This article opens with a description of the ongoing debate over whether or not Nazi propaganda offset the demoralizing effects of bombing, and points out that the debate too often has overlooked such important questions as what is actually meant by "propaganda success." The bulk of the article describes the nature of the propaganda used in response to allied bombing and the nature of the difficulties it attempted to address, concluding that, given the overall difficulties Germany faced in the winter and spring of 1944-1945, "a real and lasting 'propaganda success' was hardly feasible. . . ."

Koppes, Clayton R., and Gregory D. Black. *Hollywood Goes to War: How Politics, Profits and Propaganda Shaped World War II Movies.* New York: Free Press, 1987.

Probably the most complete extant study of the wartime film industry in the United States, this volume presents in detail the history of how the Hollywood film industry and many of its leading producers and directors—Frank Capra and William Wyler, among others—were recruited by the Office of War Information to make propaganda documentaries and features. The authors also describe how and why Hollywood filmmakers turned out many of the latter without being asked. Propaganda feature films are described as being usually simplistic, often racist, rarely ever realistic or accurate—a classless England in *Mrs. Miniver* and a benign Stalin in *Mission to Moscow*, for example—but uniformly popular with audiences ready to believe everything good about the United States and its allies at war, and everything evil about their enemies. Illustrations and a bibliographic essay.

_____. "What to Show the World: The Office of War Information and Hollywood, 1942-1945." *Journal of American History* 64, 1 (June 1977), pp. 87-105.

This article provides an overview of the role of the Office of War Information (OWI) in influencing the ideological content of Hollywood feature films during World War II. Along the way the authors raise such questions as whether or not the administration's propaganda strategy may have undermined some of its avowed war aims, and why historians to this point in time had largely ignored such a vital part of war history as analysis of the United States government's relationship to propaganda filmmaking. They demonstrate clearly that OWI and Hollywood worked well together, as the anti-Nazi sentiments of the government were fully shared by the likes of Frank Capra and Jack Warner.

Lavine, Harold, and James Wechsler. *War Propaganda and the United States.* New York: Garland Publishing, 1972.

Originally published in 1940 by Yale University Press for the Institute for Propaganda Analysis, this volume provides an analysis of war propaganda in the context of the first year of World War II. The authors define propaganda as opinion formation through stimulation, and indicate how important this stimulation can be in wartime. The opening chapter is called: "They Do Not Lie in Vain," in which the authors describe the role propaganda plays on the home front and abroad. Each subsequent chapter examines a different aspect of war propaganda. Illustrations but no bibliography.

McLaine, Ian. *Ministry of Morale: Home Front Morale and the Ministry of Information in World War II*. London: George Allen and Unwin, 1979.

This volume describes and analyzes the domestic work of Britain's Ministry of Information during World War II, including both criticism and approval of its efforts. The author begins by describing the structure of the ministry, and proceeds from there to explain how the ministry strove to carry out its primary domestic function, sustaining morale in a Britain faced with a Europe conquered by Germany, and years of German air raids on British cities. Censorship of war news in the press through the issuance of "D-Notices" (Defence Notices) is explained thoroughly, as are the wide variety of poster and other campaigns launched to remind the civilian population that "Careless Talk Costs Lives," to encourage Britons to not be wasteful, and above all, that they should believe in ultimate victory. Illustrations and a select bibliography.

Meo, L. D. *Japan's Radio War on Australia, 1941-1945*. Melbourne: Melbourne University Press, 1968.

A study of Japanese propaganda broadcasts to Australia during World War II, this volume provides a history of the process and an assessment of the various reasons why it was bad propaganda and therefore unsuccessful. The author admits that the book is driven by the fact that despite being a member of the British Commonwealth, Australia since 1960 had become more economically engaged with Japan than with Great Britain, and argues that the content of Japanese war propaganda would suggest that even in the 1940s, the Japanese saw this development coming. Other historians may question this hypothesis, in light of Japan's advocacy in the 1930s of a Japanese-controlled Asian co-prosperity sphere, but it is worth considering all the same. After all, Japanese broadcast propaganda aimed at Australia needed specific objectives that would offer the Australians a viable reason to prefer Japan to Britain and the United States. Limited bibliography.

Pronay, Nicholas, and Jeremy Croft. "British Film Censorship and Propaganda Policy During the Second World War," in James Curran and Vincent Porter, eds., *British Cinema History*. Totowa, N.J.: Barnes and Noble Books, 1983.

This essay describes how the British Board of Film Censors (BBFC) continued to operate during World War II, and how the Ministry of Information (MOI) cooperated with it in the censorship of film. Part of the reasoning was that propaganda films ought not to appear to be

propaganda films; if so, their effectiveness might be reduced. Therefore, the MOI, the BBFC, the War Office, the Air Ministry, and the
Admiralty cooperated in seeking to influence commercial film producers in order that through their treatment of wartime subjects on
film, they would put the war interests of Britain in the most positive
light. Subtle censorship with a propaganda objective, but censorship
all the same.

Riley, Norman. *999 and All That.* London: Victor Gollancz, 1940.
There were 999 employees in the Ministry of Information (MOI) when
it came officially into existence on September 4, 1939, the day after
Britain declared war on Germany. The number 999 was also what a
person dialed to get Scotland Yard. Meanwhile, *1066 and All That* was
the title of a popular send-up of British history that had appeared a few
years earlier. All of the above enabled the author to provide a title for
his book full of metaphor and symbolism. The book is a send-up of the
MOI. After a year in operations, the ministry was anything but an
effective instrument of propaganda dissemination, and because of this
fact was being criticized, reviled, and rapidly turned into the butt of
jokes. The author, a journalist, takes on the ministry and suggests ways
it could improve its operations, such as distributing actually useful
information to the British public. His chapters have such titles as "The
News Machine," "The Westminster Follies," "Blue Pencils, Red
Tape," and "Never Too Late." He acknowledges the importance of
what the MOI was trying to do; the problem was that it was not doing
it well, or even adequately. He concludes with a general overview of
how important it might be to continue an information *qua* propaganda
office after the war, but warns: "Whatever its name, it must never be
called a Ministry of Information. It would sound too much like a weak
old music-hall gag revived." No bibliography.

Robertson, James C. "British Film Censorship Goes to War." *Historical
Journal of Film, Radio and Television* 2, 1 (1982), pp. 49-64.
Feature film censorship in Britain was well established prior to World
War II and was fully as much political as moral. This article describes
the application of censorship by the British Board of Film Censors to
feature films, before and during the war, which had political content
that ran counter to what was deemed beneficial to British foreign policy
(prewar) or to the British war effort. The article also is a survey of
existing literature on the subject by such historians as Nicholas Pronay
and Philip M. Taylor. See James C. Robertson, *The British Board of
Film Censors* (entry in chapter 1 under "General Studies").

Rossignol, Dominique. *Histoire de la propagande en France de 1940 à 1944: L'Utopie Pétain.* Paris: Presses Universitaires de France, 1991. After France fell to Germany in June 1941, the Vichy regime was established in unoccupied France, under Marshall Pétain, hero of World War I. It was to be a neutral state benevolent toward Germany. This volume is a history of the propaganda produced in France by both Vichy and German propagandists. Topics covered include the structure of the Vichy propaganda machine, German propaganda and how it made use of French political movements, the objectives of Vichy propaganda such as anti-communism, anti-Semitism, and anti-Allies, and above all, propaganda aimed at creating the "myth" of Pétain as the *saveur de France.* The volume includes reproductions of a wide range of propaganda posters, and select bibliography.

Rupp, Leila J. *Mobilizing Women for War: German and American Propaganda, 1939-1945.* Princeton, N.J.: Princeton University Press, 1978. An illustrated history of propaganda campaigns aimed at women in Germany and the United States in World War II, this volume argues that in the first place, women were encouraged to play a role in industry and elsewhere, but that in the second place, they were not encouraged to forget that they were women and thus took second place to men. In short, the war necessitated a degree of liberation which was not intended to last past the war. Topics include the Nazi image of mothers, the American housewife image, propaganda policies aimed at mobilizing women for war work and for supporting men as warriors in both the United States and Germany, and the specific image of Rosie the Riveter that was adapted by propaganda campaigns in the United States. Extensive bibliography of primary and secondary sources, and an appendix explaining mobilization numbers for both Germany and the United States. See Maureen Honey, *Creating Rosie the Riveter: Class, Gender, and Propaganda During World War II* (entry above), and *The Life and Times of Rosie the Riveter* (entry below under "Channels and Techniques").

Selwyn, Francis. *Hitler's Englishman: The Crime of Lord Haw-Haw.* London: Routlege and Kegan Paul, 1987. This book tells how the Irish American William Joyce, described here as "Hitler's secret weapon of the airwaves," came to sell his services to Hitler's Germany as a propaganda broadcaster during World War II, for which he was hanged after the war. He was known as "Lord Haw-Haw" because of the nasal tones and exaggerated English accent he employed. The author asks whether Joyce really was a traitor, or was he "sent to the scaffold as a necessary sacrifice?" He answers by saying that Joyce was, in fact, a "street-corner fanatic of the Fascist movement," who got what he deserved. Select bibliography. See J. A. Cole, *Lord Haw-Haw* (entry above).

Soley, Lawrence C. *Radio Warfare: OSS and CIA Subversive Propaganda.* New York: Praeger, 1989.
A study of how post-World War II radio propaganda got its start; the volume mainly concerns the wartime efforts of the United States Office of Strategic Services (OSS), which was the predecessor to the Central Intelligence Agency. The author begins with an assessment of what radio propaganda is and how it works, and then he describes the relative successes and failures of such radio propaganda put out by the British Broadcasting Corporation and Radio Paris Mondial in the years before and during World War II. This is followed by an assessment of early subversive radio stations operated by the United States, a study of OSS "psychwar" stations in Europe and Asia. The author concludes with a discussion of Soviet psychwar broadcasting and the onset of the Cold War. Select bibliography.

Steele, Richard W. "Preparing the Public for War: Efforts to Establish a National Propaganda Agency, 1940-41." *American Historical Review* 75, 6 (October 1970), pp. 1640-1653.
The American public seemed not to share President Franklin D. Roosevelt's anxieties over what the European situation after 1939 portended for the United States. This article describes the results of his conviction that public opinion in the United States must be brought into line with his own. The solution was to launch a domestic propaganda campaign to alert the public to the danger—or at least to try. The author describes various proposals which were advanced for creating a propaganda organization and assesses the president's response to them. He makes clear that Roosevelt did not want to be seen as emulating Joseph Goebbels, though at least one advisor saw no objection to the United States developing an organization like the German propaganda ministry. It was not until the Office of War Information was conceived that a propaganda machine emerged with clear goals and methods.

Strebel, Elizabeth Grottle. "French Cinema, 1940-1944, and Its Socio-Psychological Significance: A Preliminary Probe." *Historical Journal of Film, Radio and Television* 1, 1 (1981), pp. 33-45.
When is a propaganda film not a propaganda film? This article takes on writers in the 1950s who argued that leading French filmmakers

(other than those in Vichy) during the years of German occupation made films that more often than not presented pro-Nazi materials. The author contends that much of this is misdirected, and that many films later regarded as propaganda actually were "a way of working out the relationship of France to the occupying power and . . . a way of coming to grips with the 1940 defeat and the ensuing modification of political structure as well as life style." An interesting hypothesis, but perhaps questionable in light of the evidence presented here.

Thomson, George P. *Blue Pencil Admiral.* London: Sampson Low, Marston, 1947.
    Admiral George P. Thomson was the chief press censor in Britain during World War II. This is his story. The volume is written in memoir form and at times reads almost like a novel. This is not a criticism, for *Blue Pencil Admiral* is one of the most readable books extant on World War II, and the subject matter is of vital importance to the study of war propaganda. The author worked for the Ministry of Information and was responsible for keeping an occasionally contentious press from revealing sensitive information regarding Britain's war effort. The volume makes clear the importance of suppressing such information in order to keep the enemy in the dark and at the same time to enhance the effects of propaganda disseminated at home and abroad. The chapter title "Keeping Hitler in the Dark" has more than one meaning. Above all, the author makes clear that censoring the press was never easy and was a concept never agreed upon by all, but at the same time that it was an essential aspect of mass war. No bibliography.

Winkler, Allan M. *The Politics of Propaganda: The Office of War Information, 1942-1945.* New Haven, Conn.: Yale University Press, 1978.
    Among the earliest works of historical scholarship on the United States propaganda agency in World War II, this volume does for the Office of War Information (OWI) what Ian McLaine's *Ministry of Morale* (see entry above) does for the British Ministry of Information. The author presents a straightforward narrative history of the organization and operations of the OWI. Starting with the origins of the organization, he progresses through discussion of how it operated at home, internal conflicts regarding its operations abroad and the nature of its campaigns. He concludes with a brief "epilogue" which suggests that as a result of OWI efforts, the United States would never again be able to avoid propaganda as an instrument of policy, and that in its postwar foreign relations—again a result of the positive spin OWI propaganda placed on information concerning the United States—it would tend to project "an unfortunate

sense of American superiority." The author researched this volume thoroughly in government archives and interviewed many of those who worked for OWI including actor John Houseman. Extensive bibliography.

Channels and Techniques

Aldgate, Anthony, and Jeffrey Richards. *Britain Can Take It: The British Cinema in the Second World War*. Oxford, England: Basil Blackwell, 1986.

Film played an important role in Britain's war effort, both as a source of escape from the ordeal of war on the home front and as a propaganda channel for sustaining morale. Average weekly attendance at British cinemas was 30 million by 1945. This book is introduced by a general survey of the role film played in wartime Britain, including the activities of the Ministry of Information Films Division and various British filmmakers and distributors. For the rest, it is a detailed examination of specific films, most of which had a propaganda purpose: *49th Parallel*, *Pimpernel Smith*, *Let George Do It*, *In Which We Serve*, and *Western Approaches*, among others. Much attention is paid to how and by whom the films were written and made, and to the individuals who acted in them. Leslie Howard, for example, is described as having been among Britain's best propagandists as a film actor, and the Germans detested him for his effectiveness in this regard. Illustrations and filmography. See Clive Coultass, *Images for Battle* (entry below).

Begley, George. *Keep Mum! Advertising Goes to War*. London: Lemon Tree Press, 1975.

This short volume describes how advertising played a role in Britain during World War II as a propaganda channel and as a way of keeping the civilian population informed as to what was in short supply. An example of the latter was a recipe for "cheese chops." The advertisement was headed: "To make one cheese ration do for four." It then detailed the cheese chop, in which beans, cheese, onions, and spices were mixed together and shaped to resemble a pork chop, and then grilled. An entertaining as well as informative volume. Illustrations but no bibliography.

Childs, Harwood L., ed. *Public Opinion Quarterly* 7, 1 (Spring 1943). Special issue, "Office of War Information."

The entire issue is devoted to describing the role of the World War II Office of War Information (OWI), beginning with an introductory article by OWI director Elmer Davis. Topics include OWI organization, OWI overseas and at home, OWI and Hollywood, OWI intelligence gathering, enemy response to OWI work, and Voice of America broadcasting. Save for the Davis article, the contributors were "outsiders" with regard to OWI work, but all were experts on propaganda, public opinion, or publicity.

Childs, Harwood L., and John B. Whitton, eds. *Propaganda by Short Wave*. Princeton, N.J.: Princeton University Press, 1942.
Clearly inspired by the entry of the United States into World War II, this collection of eight essays examines the role played by international radio broadcasting in propaganda dissemination, beginning with a brief history of the medium in that context. Specific topics covered include radio in international politics, Nazi shortwave propaganda theory and strategy, British, Italian, and French broadcast propaganda and who in the United States listens to it, atrocity propaganda broadcasts, and techniques of persuasion. Each article provides background for its subject, followed by analysis and explanation of various elements that comprise it. No bibliography.

Coultass, Clive. *Images for Battle: British Film and the Second World War, 1939-1945*. Newark: University of Delaware Press, 1989.
The British film industry shot millions of feet of film during World War II, documentary and feature, mostly in 35 mm black and white. Some of these films were strictly informational; many others were made for propaganda purposes. This illustrated book opens with a description of the industry prior to the war, and then goes through the war from beginning to end, describing the contents of a wide variety of features and documentaries. The author was, at the time of writing, a film archivist at the Imperial War Museum in London. He makes clear the variety of biases that appear in these films, perhaps unthinkingly, such as in Alexander Korda's *The Lion Has Wings* (entry below under "Propaganda Material"), which gives the impression that the Britons most ready to fight are upper-middle class. *Convoy* sends a similar message, though certainly without intending it. The author notes that by 1942, films, documentaries, and features, were beginning to include a broad social range of British "heroes," civilian and military. Select bibliography and title index of the more than 650 films referred to in the text.

Delmer, Sefton. *Black Boomerang*. New York: Viking Press, 1962.
The author was born in Berlin in 1904, the son of an Australian father who lectured on English literature at Berlin University. Hence, he grew

up speaking English as naturally as he spoke Berliner German. Therefore, as an officer of the British Political Warfare Executive during
World War II, he was able to create and carry out with considerable
effect a program of "black" radio propaganda, a form of disinformation
directed against the German government. One technique was to take
on the persona of a retired German officer and loyal follower of Hitler
who broadcast warnings that people at various levels of government
were betraying Hitler and the army. The character created was known
as "Der Chef." This volume is Sefton Delmer's story, written by himself.

Der Fuehrer Schenkt der Juden eine Stadt. Prod. Institut für Film und
Bild, 22 min., 1971. Berlin: Institut für Film und Bild.
In the later years of World War II, the German government made a
propaganda film for domestic consumption, about the Theresienstadt
concentration camp. The audience saw inmates living comfortable,
happy, and productive lives in pleasant surroundings. This film incorporates that film, and adds interviews with those who were forced to
participate in its making. These include Karl Ancerl, who, in 1944, was
conductor of the Jewish inmate orchestra.

Dickinson, Margaret, and Sarah Street. *Cinema and State: The Film
Industry and Government, 1927-84.* London: BFI Publishing, 1985.
The authors have written a history of government involvement in the
British film industry, rather than a history of film as government
propaganda. However, chapters 6 through 8 deal with issues relevant
to the history of British film propaganda. In these chapters, the authors
describe how filmmaking was adapted to war propaganda needs by the
Ministry of Information, how the British and United States governments
interacted on the issue of American films in the British wartime market
and vice versa, and how the wartime experience with film propaganda
influenced political thinking about the role film might play in postwar
cultural and social education. A few illustrations and a very limited
bibliography, as source material is largely indicated in endnotes.

Doherty, Martin. "Black Propaganda by Radio: The German Concordia
Broadcasts to Britain, 1940-1941." *Historical Journal of Film, Radio
and Television* 14, 2 (1994), pp. 167-197.
This article analyzes the propaganda broadcasts made for Germany by
William Joyce, the infamous "Lord Haw-Haw." It examines the output
of "Buro Concordia," described here as the "black propaganda" department within the external department of Reichsrundfunk Gesell-
schaft. "Black propaganda" is a term coined during World War II to

describe a kind of disinformation used against enemy civilian morale. The analysis includes reports of surveys taken to see how many
people actually heard the broadcasts, the results of which indicate that
they were not listened to by a very large proportion of the populace.
Appendixes include government reports on the Buro Concordia broadcasts, sample transcripts, and a sampling of listener surveys. See Sefton
Delmer, *Black Boomerang* (entry above).

Douglas, Roy. *The World War, 1939-1945: The Cartoonists' Vision.* London: Routledge, 1990.
The cartoon has long been an effective propaganda channel. This book
describes how cartoons served in World War II as propaganda, and have
served since the war as an avenue through which historians can assess
how the cartoonists actually viewed the war. The author places each
cartoon reproduced in the book in the context of the events that inspired
it, and then explains its contents in terms of the messages it projected.
Almost without exception, the cartoons reproduced contain very specific propaganda material. They are drawn from Soviet, American, and
British sources, among others. The author also discusses censorship.
No bibliography.

Dyer, Sherman H. *Radio in Wartime.* New York: Greenberg, 1942.
Written by the director of radio productions at the University of
Chicago, this book addresses the question of how radio may function
in wartime as both a source of information and a propaganda channel.
Topics include broadcast censorship, planning in order to maximize
the effects of broadcast information, definitions of propaganda, morale, wartime news broadcasting, radio talk programming, radio drama,
and programming specifically created and sponsored by government
agencies. The volume is illustrated with graphs and charts indicating
costs and revenues associated with radio. The author's ultimate purpose is to define how wartime radio could serve as a source of
information and, in the process, to explain its value for propaganda
dissemination. An appendix reproduces the United States wartime
broadcast censorship code, and each chapter ends with a commentary
from some expert on the subject of that chapter, such as Harold D.
Lasswell on propaganda at the conclusion of chapter 3. For all practical
purposes, this volume is a primary source on radio propaganda. No
bibliography.

Edwards, John Carver. *Berlin Calling: American Broadcasters in Service
to the Third Reich.* New York: Praeger, 1991.

Both a history and an analysis of propaganda technique, in this case, broadcasting by United States citizens for Nazi Germany. They were "United States expatriates and naturalized German-Americans all," who spent much of their lives prior to World War II living in Europe or traveling back and forth regularly between the United States and Europe. These broadcasters took their place along side "Lord Haw-Haw" and "Tokyo Rose" (one of them, Mildred Gillars, was known as "Axis Sally," a European theater of operations version of "Tokyo Rose"), as wartime turncoats. The author's purpose is to examine their lives in an effort to discover their motives for doing what they did. In the process, he also evaluates what they broadcast in terms of its propaganda content. The volume includes photographs of the broadcasters and a select bibliography.

Eye of the Eagle: December 7. Prod. Encyclopaedia Britannica, 54 min., 1987. Chicago: Britannica Films.
Richard Schickel hosts this controversial documentary about propaganda and poetic license. The subject is John Ford's 34-minute film *December 7* (entry below under "Propaganda Material"), released in 1943, which purported to be news film of the Japanese attack on Pearl Harbor. Actually, much of the film was of a staged re-creation of the event, which neither the credits nor the narrator mentioned. There is footage here also from the original 83-minute version of the Ford film, which the War Department suppressed for years because it was considered too controversial to be shown.

Farago, Ladislas, ed. *German Psychological Warfare: Survey and Bibliography.* New York: Committee for National Morale, 1941.
The Committee for National Morale was established in 1940 "in the conviction that morale represents a decisive force in human affairs. . . ." This volume addresses that issue by presenting the public with an analysis of German psychological warfare techniques and purposes. "The present war is, in large measure, ideological," goes the preface; consequently, in the interest of maintaining "national morale," the committee presented this analysis as a "first line of defense" against such propaganda. The contents include an assessment of how Germany rationalized its defeat in World War I, developed techniques for psychological manipulation in preparation for the next war, and then deployed these techniques with reference to the German people and others when that war began. Annotated bibliography of exclusively German-language sources on propaganda and psychological warfare.

Friedmann, Otto. *Broadcasting for Democracy*. London: George Allen and Unwin, 1941.

This pamphlet was written by an Oxford University don, who also engaged in war work during World War II. It is designed to make the case for broadcasting democratic propaganda by radio. As such, it is a primary source on British wartime propaganda. The pamphlet is in two parts, the first explaining the nature and methods of Nazi propaganda, those elements within British society which that propaganda could exploit, and what democratic propaganda could and could not use to counter the Nazi material. Part 2 examines what is needed to make allied propaganda broadcasts successful. The author concludes by noting that some of his ideas already were being employed by British propaganda broadcasts but notes that many faults and shortcomings were still to be overcome. The pamphlet is dedicated to Jan Masaryk, the foreign minister of Czechoslovakia who was then in exile in Britain.

The Life and Times of Rosie the Riveter. Prod. and dir. Connie Field, Clarity/National Endowment for the Humanities, 60 min., 1980. Los Angeles: Direct Cinema Limited.

A documentary featuring five women who recall their experiences as war workers during World War II, this film has, as its main theme, how women moved forward in their struggle for equality within American society as a result of "going to war." A secondary theme is the way in which propaganda was used to encourage them into the work place, and then to encourage them to leave when the war was over. It was their duty, they were told, to leave in order to make room for male workers who were returning home at war's end.

Life Goes to the Movies: The War Years. Prod. Twentieth Century-Fox Film Corporation, Time-Life Films, 34 min., 1976. New York: Time-Life Video.

The second in a series of documentaries on Hollywood film history, this segment uses clips from feature films to show how Hollywood turned to war themes after 1941. The Western hero (John Wayne, for example) becomes the war hero, and the female stars (Ginger Rogers, for example) become heroines on the home front. The clips also show how Hollywood depicted Germans and Japanese as immoral and depraved, while presenting Americans, British, Russians, and the French resistance as heroic characters. Such propaganda was hardly subtle, but it apparently was effective.

Nieuwenhof, Frans. "Japanese Film Propaganda in World War II: Indonesia and Australia." *Historical Journal of Film, Radio and Television* 4, 2 (1984), pp. 161-177.

The Japanese government well understood the value of propaganda, and of film propaganda in particular. This article examines Japan's use of film in advancing the "Greater East Asia Co-Prosperity Sphere," which combined Asian nationalism with anti-European, anti-white racist propaganda, and in preparing for the invasion of Australia, which featured Australian prisoners in POW camps. The author provides excerpts from documents pertaining to the making of some of the films in question, as well as examples of their dialogue, in order to demonstrate how they attempted to persuade their audience. This is an important topic which deserves clear exposition as well as good documentation. Unfortunately, it does not receive such exposition here.

Powers of Persuasion. CD-ROM, Apple Macintosh, 1995. Santa Barbara, Calif.: Intellimation.

This disk contains a collection of posters, radio and film excerpts, speeches, and communications drawn from World War II propaganda materials. It has been created as a guide for students in understanding what official propaganda is and how it functions in wartime. It also makes clear in general terms how bias, stereotype, and information manipulation are all part of persuasion technique, and therefore of propaganda.

Prisoners of Propaganda. Prod. Film Australia, 60 min., 1987. Denton: University of North Texas.

This Australian documentary film analyzes the Japanese World War II propaganda film *Calling Australia*. It includes clips from the film and describes how the Australians used the film later for anti-Japanese propaganda purposes, under the title *Nippon Presents*.

Raack, R. C. "Nazi Film Propaganda and the Horrors of War." *Historical Journal of Film, Radio and Television* 6, 2 (1986), pp. 189-195.

This short article points to the value of German film, despite the limitations of "cinematic verisimilitude," in learning more about the history of the Third Reich during World War II. A major question raised is, Why did the Germans not use atrocity films as a mass propaganda technique? After all, such films likely would have had a powerful effect on the emotions of German film audiences. In fact, the author contends, such films were made, as in the example of *Im Wald von Katyn*, which told the story of the massacre of 4,500 Polish officers captured by the Soviet Union in 1939. However, such films were rarely shown in

German cinemas, though why is not made clear. This article is of value mainly in that it argues for more research on its subject.

Renov, Michael. *Hollywood's Wartime Women: Representation and Ideology.* Ann Arbor, Mich.: UMI Research Press, 1988.
This volume examines how women were presented in World War II Hollywood films. The author covers the general history of the times, including patterns of life and work among American women, the wartime film industry, social ideologies then extant, propaganda as theory and practice, and finally, the films themselves, which are analyzed in order to explain what messages about women were sent to audiences. Renov also assesses how those messages were received. Most of the films covered—*Tender Comrade, The Mortal Storm, Mission to Moscow, Hitler's Children*, among many others—were made initially for propaganda purposes, and part of that propaganda, whether intended or not, applied to how women should behave and be perceived: women as inscrutable, women as evil, women as good, women as martyrs, women as helpers, and so forth. Illustrations, bibliography, and appendixes with film lists and studio distribution figures.

Right in Der Fuhrer's Face. Prod. Public Broadcasting Service, 28 min., 1989. Alexandria, Va.: PBS Video.
This documentary shows how Hollywood, Tin Pan Alley, and Madison Avenue were brought into the war to make propaganda for the home front. Hitler and his Axis partners are made into comic figures by advertising experts, while Hollywood makes them into villains and Tin Pan Alley produces songs that encourage resistance to them. Much of this material was very heavy-handed and often naive, yet some of the techniques depicted in this film have remained in use since, particularly the appeal to fear as a way of selling certain products and ideas.

Roeder, George H., Jr. *The Censored War: American Visual Experience During World War Two.* New Haven, Conn.: Yale University Press, 1993.
Images and the messages they project are basic to propaganda. This volume describes how censorship of reality was used in World War II to alter certain images, thus sending an altered image to the viewer. For example, faces of wounded soldiers in news photographs were often altered in order to make them unrecognizable to family or friends who might see the photograph. A similar practice was undertaken by the British. Realistic photographs of war dead were also suppressed, because of the sometimes shocking manner in which they died. Both Britain and

the United States considered this necessary in the context of a war which grew daily more destructive. There are four chapters, each including what is termed a "visual essay," on such subjects as "playing the death card," "moving pictures," "war as monologue," and "war legacies." The variety of censored photographs and film was enormous, the author points out, including "carefully selected images" of blacks and whites working together for victory, and others which suggested that life was cheap among Asians. Illustrations and select bibliography.

Shindler, Colin. *Hollywood Goes to War: Films and American Society, 1939-1952*. London: Routledge and Kegan Paul, 1979.
The author drew upon oral evidence from Frank Capra, Henry Fonda, and others, as well as the archives of various Hollywood film studios in creating this volume. The point is both the content and the making of films during World War II and the Korean War. In the latter case, the author has demonstrated an admirable sense of humor by including reference to *Red Planet Mars* (entry in chapter 6 under "Propaganda Material"), a film which connects Korea to the Cold War and which "suggests quite vividly that the world could be clearly divided into wrong-thinking atheistic perverted communists and right-thinking heterosexual Christian democrats." The text is illustrated with stills from every film referenced. Limited bibliography.

Short, K. R. M., ed. *Film and Radio Propaganda in World War II*. London: Croom Helm, 1983.
The fifteen articles in this anthology cover a wide spectrum of media propaganda in World War II. The preface includes a brief description of the argument made by each contributor and an overview of what constituted film and broadcast propaganda in wartime. Specific topics include racial, political, and social aspects of film and broadcast propaganda from France, the Soviet Union, Germany, the United States, and Japan. Each article includes endnotes, and several have appendixes.

_____. "Hewing Straight to the Line: Editorial Control in American News Broadcasting, 1941-42." *Historical Journal of Film, Radio and Television* 1, 2 (1981), pp. 167-176.
The theme here is censorship. This article is a collection of documents which pertain to how certain American news broadcasting services organized control over what went out as news over radio. The author's introduction describes the general situation, indicates the problems involved in organizing controls, and gives a brief overview of the development of news broadcast controls before and during World War II.

The documents are six letters exchanged between Herbert Moore of Transradio Press Service in New York and various broadcast editors.

_____. "'The White Cliffs of Dover': Promoting the Anglo-American Alliance in World War II." *Historical Journal of Film, Radio and Television* 2, 1 (1982), pp. 3-25.
Forty percent of Americans in 1939 believed that the United States had been lured into World War I by "propaganda and selfish interests," presumably associated with Britain. This created a problem for British propagandists seeking to circumvent United States neutrality prior to December 1941, and to sustain Anglo-American relations once the United States was in the war. A 1940 poem "The White Cliffs," which concerned an American woman married to an Englishman, seemed to suggest a way. The feature film *The White Cliffs of Dover* (entry below under "Propaganda Material"), released in 1944 by MGM, was based on the poem and aimed specifically, as the author notes in his title, at "promoting the Anglo-American alliance." This article analyzes reasons why there were difficulties between America and Britain over whether the United States would enter the war, describes a number of films, American and British, which addressed those difficulties, and concludes with an assessment of *White Cliffs of Dover*.

Shulman, Holly Cowan. *The Voice of America: Propaganda and Democracy, 1941-1945*. Madison: University of Wisconsin Press, 1990.
This is a history of Voice of America (VOI) propaganda broadcasting during World War II. It describes how VOI was founded and the occasional internal organizational problems that accompanied its efforts. The bulk of the book analyzes VOI propaganda campaigns in relation to encouraging resistance movements, describing audiences, and examining the relationship between propaganda and wartime foreign policy. The volume is dedicated to the memory of the author's father, who spent World War II working for the Overseas Branch of the Office of War Information. In the later years of the war, he was director of broadcasting operations for Europe, Africa, and the Middle East. She writes of him: "His belief in the power of ideas and the importance of propaganda pervaded our house, like the background sound of music." Extensive bibliography.

Simone, Sam P. *Hitchcock as Activist: Politics and the War Films*. Ann Arbor, Mich.: UMI Research Press, 1985.
Alfred Hitchcock was among the most innovative filmmakers of the early years of the "talkies." This volume examines those of his films

made during World War II in order to understand Hitchcock's own politics: that is, the films reveal his commitment to democracy and opposition to Nazism, and his conviction that film was a useful and necessary propaganda channel in connection with the defense of democracy against Nazism. Of course, as the author points out, never did Hitchcock lose sight of the importance of making his films entertaining even while they were purveying propaganda themes. Among the films discussed are *Foreign Correspondent* (1940), *Saboteur* (1942), and *Lifeboat* (1944). Select bibliography.

Taylor, Edmond. *The Strategy of Terror: Europe's Inner Front.* Boston: Houghton Mifflin, 1940.
Written by an American journalist before the United States entered World War II, this volume offers an explanation for what the author describes as "the battle-front of the mind," by which he means the propaganda war. His concern in writing this "history" of the propaganda war—it begins with the interwar years—is to explain "the impact on human beings of ideas used as weapons." While the book is far from objective, it contains extensive selections from European newspapers and other contemporary sources that provide the reader with a useful guide to who was saying what in the battle to control minds at the moment when the war in Europe was beginning to gather steam.

Taylor, Philip M., ed. *Britain and the Cinema in the Second World War.* New York: St. Martin's Press, 1988.
A collection of nine articles introduced by the editor, which cover such topics as the British society which went to see wartime films, the British film industry, feature films, documentaries, the war as portrayed on film, propaganda films, and women on film. The editor is one of the preeminent historians of propaganda writing in the twentieth century. His introduction comments on the importance of understanding film in the context of World War II. The essays go beyond discussion of propaganda as such but provide an overall context in which the role of propaganda film, feature or documentary, can be more clearly understood. The articles derive from a war film conference held in London in 1985.

_____. "Techniques of Persuasion: Basic Ground Rules of British Propaganda During the Second World War." *Historical Journal of Film, Radio and Television* 1, 1 (1981), pp. 57-65.
This entry is a document titled "Memorandum by the International Broadcasting and Propaganda Enquiry," dated June 21, 1939. It was part of the planning process for the Ministry of Information that would

come into existence upon the outbreak of World War II. This document indicates that propaganda planning in Britain for wartime was more advanced when war broke out than was previously thought. See Mariel Grant, *Propaganda and the Role of the State in Inter-War Britain*, Robert Cole, "The Conflict Within," and Philip M. Taylor, "If War Should Come" (entries in chapter 3 under "History and Function").

The War Years, No. 2. Prod. Time-Life Films, 35 min., 1977. New York: Time-Life Video.
Featuring Henry Fonda, Shirley MacLaine, and Liza Minnelli, this documentary examines Hollywood's contribution to both morale through entertainment and the war effort through propaganda during World War II.

World War II: The Propaganda Battle. Prod. Public Broadcasting Service, 55 min., 1984. Alexandria, Va.: PBS Video.
Bill Moyers interviews Fritz Hippler and Frank Capra, filmmakers respectively for the Nazi party and the United States Office of War Information, to highlight this assessment of the revolutionary advances that the technologies of mass media brought to propaganda dissemination in World War II.

Propaganda Material

Above Suspicion. Prod. Victor Saville, dir. Richard Thorpe, Metro-Goldwyn-Mayer, 90 min., 1943. Chicago: Facets Video.
A spy thriller in which the hero and heroine (Americans working for British intelligence) travel from Oxford, England, to Paris and across Germany in pursuit of a missing agent who has vital information concerning a Nazi secret weapon. Basil Rathbone plays a particularly ominous Nazi who once had been the American's friend at Oxford University. Once a Nazi always a Nazi, the message is, even if it was before he was a Nazi. As usual, the "good guys" win while the "bad guys" are shown to be not only bad but incompetent as well.

Across the Pacific. Prod. Jerry Wald and Jack Saper, dir. John Huston, Warner Brothers, 97 min., 1942. Chicago: Facets Video.
An early Hollywood war film in which Humphrey Bogart appears at first to be a disgraced ex-army man who has been court-martialled for selling military secrets. The action takes place aboard a Japanese ship which Bogart has boarded to cross the Pacific via the Panama canal. Bogart is soon revealed to be an undercover agent of the United States

planted on board the ship to deal with a Japanese espionage operation. The American hero is brave, honorable, and smart; the Japanese enemy are evil, sadistic, and not to be trusted.

Action in the North Atlantic. Prod. Jerry Wald, dir. Lloyd Bacon, Warner Brothers, 126 min., 1943. Chicago: Facets Video.
This film tells the story of the merchant marines who kept the supply lines open between the United States and Mermansk in Soviet Russia. The propaganda message is the heroism of American seamen and their dedication to winning the war, with the additional message that the Soviet Union is a worthy ally against the Nazis. There is plenty of action, including the merchant mariners sinking a U-boat by ramming it. They also shoot down several German bombers. In the end, they deliver their cargo and make preparations to go back home for more.

Air Force. Dir. Howard Hawks, 124 min., 1943. Chicago: Facets Video.
A typical war propaganda film in which the courage and skill of a B-17 crew is chronicled from Pearl Harbor to the Battle of the Coral Sea. The theme is the heroism of American airmen who are fighting for democracy and against tyranny.

Army-Navy Screen Magazine Highlights. Prod. U.S. War Department, 53 min., 1945. Washington, D.C.: National Audio-Visual Center.
This film is a compendium of features produced for the *Army-Navy Screen Magazine* during 1943-1945 for showing to United States servicemen. It includes film of the likes of Bob Hope and Dinah Shore performing in USO shows, the story of Corporal Jolley, a first-person account of courage under fire, a segment called Jubilee which is aimed at African-American soldiers, and cartoon character Snafu learning that a "slip of the lip can sink a ship."

Assignment in Brittany. Prod. J. Walter Ruben, dir. Jack Conway, Metro-Goldwyn-Mayer, 90 min., 1943. Atlanta: Turner Classic Movies.
A member of the Free French forces in England is co-opted by British intelligence to masquerade as a look-alike French collaborator in Brittany. The object is to find the location of a German submarine base. Evil Nazis, heroic resistance fighters, and sleazy collaborators parade across the screen, and in the end British commandos land in a surprise raid, opening the doors on the submarine pens so that British torpedo boats can—and do—destroy the U-boats. The message is clear: in the words of the British commander, "We beat them!" If this film was meant to suggest to viewers that the commando raid which actually took place in 1942 on Dieppe was a success, then it truly is propaganda.

That raid was a total disaster in which much of the largely Canadian force that undertook it was either killed or taken prisoner.

Autobiography of a Jeep. Prod. United States Office of War Information, 10 min., 1943. Washington, D.C.: National Audio-Visual Center.
Made for cinema distribution during World War II, this documentary celebrates, through the metaphor of the Jeep, the achievement of the United States in developing the auto industry. In wartime, the Jeep symbolized the new United States presence in the world, which was the point. Upbeat and aimed at encouraging pride among Americans.

Back to Bataan. Prod. Theron Warth, dir. Edward Dmytryk, RKO Radio Pictures, 97 min., 1945. Chicago: Facets Video.
John Wayne leads Filipino guerrillas against the Japanese in this film. The main theme is heroic resistance to the oppressor, with the racial undertones characteristic of wartime Hollywood anti-Japanese propaganda. There is also a warning to be on guard against subversion in the form of a woman who is suspected of being a Tokyo Rose style broadcaster.

Barsis, Max. *They're All Yours, Uncle Sam!* New York: Stephen Daye, 1943.
A collection of cartoons by Max Barsis, which bears the subtitle "The Story of the Twins, Maribelle and Claribelle, Two Babes in Arms Who Became Women at Arms." The cartoons tell the story of women entering the military in World War II and make two basic points: one, that women have "pretty well emerged into the light," which means that men are learning about them in ways they had never done; and two, that the contribution women are making to the war effort is positive, important, and to be encouraged. A woman, the introduction says, "can be relied upon with complete faith to offer herself, freely and gladly, for whatever sacrifice is needed." This collection fits perfectly with the propaganda campaigns carried on in the United States to encourage women into war work in factories, shipyards, and, of course, the military. Typical of this propaganda, Barsis' cartoons are frequently patronizing, as in one which shows a line of women in naval uniforms marching, while two onlookers remark: "Whad'ya know, the Rockettes."

Bataan. Prod. Irving Starr, dir. Tay Garnett, Metro-Goldwyn-Mayer, 115 min., 1943. Chicago: Facets Video.
A documentary-style film that tells the story of soldiers fighting on Bataan as the Japanese advance, knowing they face certain death but

are prepared to die while delaying the Japanese so that others may escape. One by one the soldiers are killed, until only a handful remain to face the horrors of the Bataan Death March. The emotional impact of the film is enormous, and the audience is left in no doubt who are the heroes and who the villains, or that someday, the Americans will return. See *Back to Bataan* (entry above).

The Battle of Kharkov-1942. 27 min., 1984. Chicago: International Historic Films.

Re-created from the original German wartime newsreels, this film depicts German forces preparing for and carrying out a massive attack on the Russian city of Kharkov. There is footage of Hitler arriving to survey the battle sight afterward, and of masses of Russian prisoners being marched off to POW camps. This documentary demonstrates how the German propaganda ministry used war footage to promote the idea at home of the invincibility of the German army. In German with English subtitles.

Behelfskriegsbrücken über die Donau. Prod. Universum-Film-Aktiengesellschaft (UFA), 44 min., 1942. Los Angeles: Classic Film Exchange.

This German-language film documents a Nazi pioneer (engineer) battalion building a bridge across the Danube which will be used by the German army. Propaganda elements include praise of the abilities of the pioneers, the cooperation of the Rumanian workers, speed of construction, quality of the finished product, and at the end, the invincible Wehrmacht invading Bulgaria.

Betrayal from the East. Prod. and dir. William Berke, RKO Radio Pictures, 82 min., 1944. Chicago: Facets Video.

The evil and vicious Japanese war machine sets out to take over the Panama Canal but is foiled by a heroic American agent. This film employs that aspect of war propaganda which aims at dehumanizing the enemy. *Across the Pacific* (entry above), made two years earlier, tells almost the same story.

Black Dragons. Dir. William Nigh, Republic Pictures, 61 min., 1942. Chicago: Facets Video.

One of the first Hollywood anti-Japanese propaganda films to appear after Pearl Harbor. This potboiler features Bela Lugosi as a Nazi plastic surgeon who transforms six Japanese spies so that they can masquerade as American industrialists. The title derives from an actual "Black Dragon" Japanese society, and features, along with Lugosi, Clayton Moore without his Lone Ranger mask.

Blood on the Sun. Dir. Frank Lloyd, Republic Pictures, 98 min., 1945. Chicago: Facets Video.
Based upon the Tanaka document scandal of 1927, this film has James Cagney playing an American newspaper editor in Tokyo who discovers from two reporters that the Japanese have a plan to conquer the world. The reporters are murdered, and Japanese agents accuse the editor. In the end he prevails, demonstrating along the way that the Japanese are not to be trusted and that it is the duty of the United States to save the world from them.

Bombardier. Prod. Robert Fellows, dir. Richard Wallace, RKO Radio Pictures, 99 min., 1943. Chicago: Facets Video.
This film tells the story of how American bombardiers (known in the Royal Air Force as "bomb aimers") in World War II were trained, the dangers they faced, and their vital importance to the success of bombing operations. A United States Army Air Corps general introduces the film, which means that it was sponsored at least implicitly by the War Department. Replete with patriotism, "gung-ho," and a certain childlike innocence on the part of the trainees when they finish their course and head off for war. Film audiences in the United States seem to have viewed their warriors as innocents; at any rate, such is the image of them in most wartime Hollywood films.

Bugs and Daffy: The Wartime Cartoons. Narr. Leonard Maltin, 80 min., 1989. Chicago: Facets Video.
This video contains twelve cartoons from World War II, many of which feature Bugs Bunny or Daffy Duck. These are among the best of the war cartoons with propaganda themes: Daffy making a fool of German soldiers; Bugs making a fool of Goering and Hitler; a collection of Gremlins making a fool of Hitler; and so on. *Hare Meets Herr* and *Gremlins from the Kremlin* are two of the selections.

Casablanca. Prod. Hal B. Wallis, dir. Michael Curtiz, Warner Brothers, 102 min., 1942. Chicago: Facets Video.
Possibly the most famous Hollywood film from World War II, this romantic Humphrey Bogart adventure feature contains every propaganda device known to Hollywood filmmakers: evil Nazis, desperate refugees, a heroic resistance leader, a scene in which patriotic bar patrons overwhelm a group of German soldiers by singing *La Marseillaise*, and the hero, Rick, finally persuaded that he cannot refuse to join the fight against Nazi tyranny. This last theme is linked to the film having been made shortly after the United States became involved in

the war following two years of neutrality. Rick is a cynical United States expatriate who owns a bar in Casablanca, many of whose patrons are refugees and exiles desperately seeking passage to safety. After a number of negative experiences with the Nazis and their Vichy collaborators, and the appearance of a woman who once was his lover in Paris and is now married to the resistance leader, Rick takes sides. In the end, he and an equally cynical French police official are persuaded to join the resistance.

Convoy. Prod. Michael Balcon, dir. Pen Tennyson, Ealing Studios, 90 min., 1940. Chicago: Facets Video.
Among the earliest war propaganda feature films produced in Britain, this is the story of the British navy protecting the convoys of transport ships that are Britain's lifeline from North America from German submarines. The film depicts evil Nazis prepared to slaughter innocent women and children because that is what the Führer told them to do; heroic British navy men saving innocent women and children while selflessly giving their lives; and British destroyers refusing to give up even when confronted by a more powerful German pocket battleship. Understated by contrast to this genre in American World War II propaganda films, but it shares many of the same qualities.

Cremieux-Brilhac, Jean-Louis, ed. *Les Voix de la liberté: Ici Londres, 1940-1944*. Paris: La Documentation Français, 1975.
These five volumes contain transcripts of radio broadcasts from London into occupied France during World War II. Volume 1 includes an introduction by the editor which provides a historical overview of the German occupation and of the psychological warfare the broadcasts represented. Much of the appeal, the editor suggests, was that they were "les Français parlent aux Français" (the French talking to the French). The volumes were prepared in cooperation with the British Broadcasting Corporation, whose facilities were used for the broadcasts. The contents reveal that broadcasts covered every conceivable topic, from warnings that Radio-Paris broadcasts were German propaganda to special messages of hope from Winston Churchill, Franklin D. Roosevelt, and General de Gaulle. The set also includes samples of anti-German and anti-Vichy propaganda leaflets dropped in France by the Royal Air Force. Limited bibliography.

The Cross of Lorraine. Prod. Edwin Knopf, dir. Jay Garnet, Metro-Goldwyn-Mayer, 100 min., 1944. Atlanta: Turner Classic Movies; Washington, D.C.: Library of Congress.

This feature film pays tribute to the heroes of the French resistance in World War II. It shows them fighting the occupying Germans through sabotage, rescuing downed allied airmen, and helping pave the way for the allied landing at Normandy in June 1944. The Free French, whose symbol is the Cross of Lorraine, also receive praise as courageous allies of Britain and the United States.

Darracott, Joseph, and Belinda Loftus. *Second World War Posters.* London: Imperial War Museum, 1972.
In 1972, the Imperial War Museum in London held an exhibit of mostly British World War II propaganda posters. This volume is a retrospective on that exhibition, presenting as examples of poster art put to the use of propaganda. It contains work by Fougasse (Cyril Kenneth Bird), among others. In their way, such artists as Fougasse virtually illustrated World War II in Britain through posters like those reproduced in this volume. Limited bibliography.

Days of Glory. Prod. Casey Robinson, dir. Jacques Tourneur, RKO Radio Pictures, 88 min., 1944. Chicago: Facets Video.
A tribute to heroic Russian partisans fighting against Germany. Gregory Peck, in his first film role, is the Partisan leader who organizes his band to join in a big push against the German army. The heroism knows no limits, whether of age or gender. In one scene, a teenage boy is to be hanged by the Germans. He is promised that he will be spared if he or anyone in the assembled crowd will name the members of the Partisan groups. Not only does the crowd remain silent, the boy cries out "Death to the Germans!," at which point the hangman proceeds with the execution. There is occasional background narration, through which a documentary flavor is introduced. This was not an unusual technique in World War II propaganda features. It lent a degree of verisimilitude to the presentation.

December 7th. Prod. United States Navy, 29 min., 1943. Washington, D.C.: National Audio-Visual Center.
A half-hour-long Navy Department film showing footage of the Japanese attack on Pearl Harbor. There were few motion picture cameras in place at Pearl Harbor at the time of the attack; therefore, much of the footage had to be "created" in order to get the point across. This was perfectly consistent with propaganda techniques from the war period. The film is considered a classic of wartime documentaries. See *Eye of the Eagle: December 7* (entry above under "Channels and Techniques").

Desert Victory. Prod. British Army and Royal Air Force, 61 min., 1943. Chicago: International Historic Films.

Made by RAF and Army film units, this hour-long documentary is a history of the allied victory (emphasizing the British Eighth Army) in North Africa. It includes the usual propaganda themes: heroic British soldiers and fliers, an invincible British army, determination to succeed, commanders outsmarting the enemy, and the privations of war in the desert. This film marked the first great triumph in the war which could be celebrated by audiences at home in Britain.

Desperate Journey. Prod. Hal B. Wallis, dir. Raoul Walsh, Warner Brothers, 119 min., 1942. Chicago: Facets Video.

After being shot down on a bombing raid over Germany and captured, five allied airmen escape. They make their way across Germany, doing the enemy grave harm as they go. Finally, they steal a captured British bomber—which conveniently has a bomb aboard—and fly away to England in a hail of German bullets. As they pass over the French coast, the character played by Ronald Reagan manages to drop the bomb on a German submarine base. Classic Hollywood war hero propaganda which presents the Germans as both malevolent and incompetent. *Desperate Journey* is proof that propaganda feature films need not also be subtle. It ends with Errol Flynn delivering the immortal line, "Now for a crack at those Japs!"

Edge of Darkness. Prod. Henry Blanke, dir. Lewis Milestone, Warner Brothers, 120 min., 1943. Chicago: Facets Video.

Hollywood World War II propaganda featuring the Norwegian resistance. A German patrol boat sails into a Norwegian port and discovers that the entire German occupation force and the local population have been killed, apparently in a bloody battle that ended with the Norwegian flag flying over the occupiers' garrison. The film proceeds from that point as a flashback to show how the battle happened: the audience learns that the local underground organized to fight the Nazis because its members are prepared to die rather than submit further.

Fight for the Sky. Prod. United States Office of War Information, 20 min., 1945. Stillwater, Okla.: Oklahoma State University.

This Office of War Information film recounts the record of American air crews flying out of Britain from a particular base in East Anglia to bomb Germany during World War II. The theme is the heroic contribution of these flyers, which has a determining effect on the outcome of the war, and that all Americans can and should be proud of them.

The Fighting Sullivans. Prod. Sam Jaffe, dir. Lloyd Bacon, Twentieth
   Century-Fox, 111 min., 1944. Los Angeles: UCLA Film and Television
   Archive; Philadelphia: Movies Unlimited; Washington, D.C.: Library
   of Congress.
   The fact-based story of five brothers who were killed during the battle
   of Guadalcanal while serving together on the cruiser *Juneau.* The film
   begins with their boyhood in a small Iowa town, where their father
   works for the railroad. They are brought up properly with discipline
   and respect and love for country, and when the war begins, they
   volunteer for the Navy and insist on serving together on the same ship.
   News of their death is received at home with grief but also with pride.
   The family is comforted by knowing that the sacrifice was in the cause
   of right, and by the fact that the brothers were together to the very end.

Film Communique: 1-11. Prod. United States Office of War Information,
   20-25 min., 1943. Columbia: University of Missouri.
   A series of eleven documentaries for home consumption put out by the
   Office of War Information covering aspects of the United States war
   effort. They range from 20 to 25 minutes in length. Subjects include
   Japanese bombing raids, naval battles, the war in North Africa, and
   even a glimpse of Private Snafu, an animated cartoon G.I., who appears
   in a segment called "The Home Front."

49th Parallel. Prod. and dir. Michael Powell, Ortus Films, 122 min., 1941.
   New York: VidAmerica.
   A tribute to Canada and Canadians in the early days of World War II,
   this British film provides propaganda that vibrates with loyalty to the
   Empire and Commonwealth equally from Canadians of English,
   French, and native origins. The story is that Canadian bombers have
   sunk a German U-boat in the Gulf of St. Lawrence, leaving six Nazis
   stranded. They set out to find their way back to Germany, leaving
   mayhem behind them. One compelling scene is when their philosophy
   is rejected by a religious community of German immigrants. They are
   finally hunted down and either killed or captured. The outstanding cast
   includes Laurence Olivier as a French-Canadian fur trapper.

The German Invasion of Poland: 1939. Prod. International Historic Films,
   60 min., 1985. Chicago: International Historic Films.
   This German newsreel of the invasion of Poland both shows the power
   of the Wehrmacht and illustrates Hitler's claim that German residents
   in the Polish Corridor were being persecuted. This was the first look
   the world had of Germany's army in action, and the message is clear:

German troops are devoted to the Führer, and the German army is irresistible. German dialogue with English subtitles.

German Propaganda Swing: Charlie and His Orchestra, 1940-1941. London: Harlequin, 1987.
A recording of German propaganda songs that were broadcast in English from Germany into Britain and the United States, and into prisoner of war camps where English-speaking soldiers were incarcerated. The musicians played mainly American popular swing songs from the 1930s as written, and then replayed them with propaganda lyrics. For example: "Let's Go Slumming" becomes "Let's Go Bombing," the point being that the British enjoy bombing the French, a message probably intended to sow discord between the British and the French Free Forces. It is unlikely that it had much impact. Among other songs are "Stormy Weather," "Goody Goody," "You Can't Stop Me from Dreaming," and "St. Louis Blues."

German Wartime Newsreels: 1941-1945. Prod. International Historic Films, 85 min., 1980. Chicago: International Historic Films.
This collection includes selected weekly newsreels with the original commentary. They are rife with anti-Semitic, anti-Anglo-American, and anti-Soviet propaganda, and much footage is devoted to encouraging the German people to support their heroic soldiers and their Führer. The themes are the progress of the war from the German point of view and the importance of resistance as the war nears its end. The collection includes film of the invasion of Russia, the battles of Kursk and the Rhineland, and the defense of the German homeland in March 1945. A guide provides the English translation of the German narration.

Germany Calling. 44 min., 1944. Sandy Hook, Conn.: Videoyesteryear.
A typically British approach to anti-Nazi propaganda in that the film pokes fun at the Nazis. "Schickelgruber Doing the Lambeth Walk, assisted by the Gestapo Hepcats" is the subtitle. Using newsreel footage, the filmmakers managed to give the appearance of the German leader and his followers doing song and dance in full military and party regalia, and in the process appearing ridiculous.

Gregory, G. H. *Posters of World War II.* New York: Gramercy Books, 1993.
A brief introduction offers an explanation for the general inspiration behind wartime posters in the United States, noting that they touched on every possible subject and arguing that they were unique in their equation of patriotism with democracy, rather than merely espousing jingoism and nationalistic fervor. Norman Rockwell figures promi-

nently among the creators of posters, notably the famous "Four Freedoms" series inspired by Franklin D. Roosevelt's 1941 state-of-the-union address. Poster subjects include military recruitment, bonds sales, dedication and sacrifice for victory, and the strength of American workers. That these posters represent war propaganda there is no doubt; that they represent positive rather than negative propaganda is equally clear. No bibliography.

Der Grosse König. Dir. Veit Harlan, Universum-Film-Aktiengesellschaft (UFA), 116 min., 1942. Chicago: International Historic Films.
German propaganda minister Joseph Goebbels took a direct hand in making this film about Frederick the Great, the eighteenth-century Prussian monarch who was famous as a military leader. This version of his life clearly makes him out to be a man of destiny, who has much in common with Adolf Hitler. However, by the time the film was released, final victory no longer seemed certain, and the tone of *Der Grosse König* emphasizes heroic resistance, stoicism, and absolute faith in Nazi leadership, rather than the arrogant enthusiasm that characterized earlier Nazi propaganda films.

Guadalcanal Diary. Prod. Bryan Foy, dir. Lewis Seiler, Twentieth Century-Fox, 93 min., 1943. Chicago: Facets Video.
Based upon Richard Tregaskis nonfiction book about the Battle of Guadalcanal, this film is a docudrama of American heroism in the first major conflict in the Pacific involving United States Marines. It is powerful propaganda; the enemy is treacherous, the Marines are drawn from all walks of life and are uniformly heroic, and, like *Gung Ho!* (entry below), the film takes them from training camp to victory.

Gung Ho! Prod. Walter Wanger, dir. Ray Enright, Universal, 88 min., 1943. Chicago: International Historic Films.
Based upon the actual exploits of a Marine unit known as Carlson's Raiders, this film tells with considerable hyperbole the story of these Marine volunteers from training camp to combat. It is filled with action, patriotism, and glory. When asked why they want to "kill Japs," each recruit has a reason, such as "my brother was killed at Pearl Harbor" or "I don't like Japs."

Hangmen Also Die! Prod. and dir. Fritz Lang, United Artists, 131 min., 1943. Chicago: Facets Video.
Reinhard Heydrich was the Deputy Reich Protector of Czechoslovakia until his assassination. This film depicts that assassination by Czech partisans after Heydrich has treated the Czechs in the most brutal

manner. His assassination, however, leads to the atrocity of the destruction of Lidice, with all of its male inhabitants being executed, and the
rest sent to concentration camps. Despite this consequence, the film
suggests that the assassination of Heydrich was worth it, his death
standing as a symbol of hope. The film is anti-Nazi propaganda from
start to finish by a German director, and while it is reasonably good as
propaganda, it is somewhat below Fritz Lang's usual film standard. It
is overlong, the characters are two-dimensional, and it is filled with
impassioned patriotic speeches.

Hollywood Goes to War. Prod. Office of War Information, 41 min., 1945.
Chicago: Facets Video.
This video contains a collection of short subjects featuring Hollywood
entertainers who contribute to the war effort by, among other things,
helping to sell war bonds and sustain the morale of overseas troops.
The subjects featured here include *The All Star Bond Rally* with Bob
Hope, Frank Sinatra, et al., and *Hollywood Canteen Overseas Special*
featuring Dinah Shore, Red Skelton, Martha Raye, et al. See *Army-
Navy Screen Magazine Highlights* (entry above).

I Was a Fireman. Prod. Ian Dalrymple, dir. Humphrey Jennings, Crown
Film Unit for the Home Office, Ministry of Home Security, and the
National Fire Service, 72 min., 1943, on *Wartime Homefront*. New
York: Kino International.
This production by Ian Dalrymple of the Crown Film Unit is an early
example—one of many from Dalrymple's effort with the British Documentary Film Movement in Britain—of the "docudrama." In this case,
actual members of the National Fire Service in London perform roles
showing fire fighters coming to work, relaxing until the air raids begin,
then being despatched to face danger and, in one case, even to die in
the line of duty. Women and men are shown as equally important in the
service. The heroism and dedication to duty of quite ordinary English
people is the theme of this artistically and substantively well-made film.

The Immortal Battalion (The Way Ahead). Prod. John Sutro and Norman
Walker, dir. Carol Reed, Two Cities, 89 min., 1944. Chicago: Facets
Video.
Virtually a British army training film, this feature starring David Niven
(a lieutenant colonel in the British army at the time and who suggested
the film) tells the story of a group of ordinary conscripts who are trained
into an effective fighting force that helps defeat Rommel in North
Africa. The film is typical patriotic propaganda featuring a citizen

army. Adventure and spy novelist Eric Ambler wrote the script with help from Peter Ustinov.

In Which We Serve. Prod. and dir. Noël Coward, Two Cities, 115 min. 1942. Isleworth, Middlesex, England: Rank Home Video.
Noël Coward wrote, composed, produced, and directed this docudrama based upon the experiences of Queen Elizabeth II's uncle, Lord Louis Mountbatten, who was a naval officer serving in the Mediterranean in the early years of World War II. The film tells the story of the British destroyer *Torrin* and its crew, who participate in the Dunkirk evacuation, fight naval battles off Crete in the Mediterranean, are torpedoed, and are finally sunk by dive bombers. An early British war propaganda film, this effort, like *The Lion Has Wings* (entry below), exhibits a patronizing class consciousness.

Japanese Relocation. Prod. United States Office of War Information, 11 min., 1943. Chicago: International Historic Films.
This documentary film provides a whitewash of the United States government's relocation of Japanese Americans from their west coast homes to various "relocation camps" in such places as Delta, Utah. It employs xenophobia, patriotism, and racism to persuade its audiences that the relocation is justified.

Joan of Paris. Prod. David Hempstead, dir. Robert Stevenson, RKO Radio Pictures, 91 min., 1942. Chicago: Facets Video.
Several allied airmen, shot down during a bombing raid over Germany, make their way to Paris with the Gestapo in hot pursuit. They encounter Joan, a barmaid, whose name clearly connects her role in heroic French resistance to foreign occupation to that of Saint Joan of Arc centuries earlier. In this case, Joan helps the airmen escape and in the process is herself caught by the Gestapo. Like her fifteenth-century namesake, she sacrifices her life for France and for victory over the foreign aggressors. It is ironic that her sacrifice is on behalf of downed English pilots, while Saint Joan's sacrifice was in resistance to an occupying English army.

Judd, Denis. *Posters of World War Two*. New York: St. Martin's Press, 1973.
This collection of World War II posters is drawn principally but not exclusively from neutral, western allied, and occupied nations sources. There are a few German and Japanese examples, but they are far outnumbered by the others. The point is to demonstrate the style of propaganda poster art associated with particular themes. These are indicated in chapter headings such as "Recruitment," "Patriotism," "Women in Wartime," "Production," "National Security," "War Fi-

nance," "Anti-Semitism and Anti-Bolshevism," and so on. An excellent introductory essay outlines war origins, describes the general course of the conflict including its expansion into the Pacific, addresses life on the home front, and ends with an analysis of the role posters played.

Justice. Prod. United States Office of War Information, 3 min., 1944. Columbia: University of Missouri.
This newsreel shows Japanese troops ravaging Shanghai and Nanking, with a voice-over commenting on "Japanese justice." The purpose was war bond appeal, a message sent through images of violence and racial stereotypes.

Keys of the Kingdom. Prod. Joseph L. Mankiewicz, dir. John M. Stahl, Twentieth Century-Fox, 137 min., 1944. Chicago: Facets Video.
Based upon a novel by A. J. Cronin, this film tells the story of a missionary priest at work spreading the gospel and hope for a better life, in early twentieth century China. The themes are the benevolence of the West toward the Chinese, whose best interests (in this case spiritual) Westerners have at heart. The Office of War Information encouraged the making of this film, with the idea that it would be a plus for relations between the United States and the Nationalist Chinese government.

Kolberg. Dir. Veit Harlan, Universum-Film-Aktiengesellschaft (UFA), 118 min., 1945. Chicago: International Historic Films.
Incredibly, at a moment when Germany was being hard pressed on both fronts, Joseph Goebbels ordered thousands of German soldiers away from the front to play soldiers in this film about German defiance of Napoleon at the Battle of Kolberg in the early nineteenth century. The film is laced with anti-Christian symbolism and Nazi ideology, and mirrors Hitler's own struggle to survive. The besieged citizens of Kolberg are a metaphor for the besieged citizens of Germany near the end of World War II, and this film about the heroism of the Kolbergers seeks to instill the same fanatical will to resist in their latter-day German counterparts.

Kutuzov. Dir. Vladimir Petrov, Mosfilm, 94 min., 1944. New York: Macmillan Films.
Based upon the life of the czarist general who organized the defeat of Napoleon in Russia in 1812, this film glorifies Russians in defense of the motherland. Kutuzov is not only the equal of Napoleon as strategist, he is better than the French emperor. The message is clear. Soviet generals and armies are superior to those of Nazi Germany. Since by 1944 Soviet armies had defeated the Germans at Stalingrad and Kirsk,

and were driving them steadily westward all along the Soviet-German front, the film was a success from a propaganda standpoint. However, it is not one of the great triumphs of Soviet cinema from the viewpoint of artistic quality. In Russian with English subtitles.

The Last Chance. Dir. Leopold Lindtberg, 103 min., 1945. Ames: Iowa State University.
A docudrama which portrays how three allied officers in World War II help a group of refugees escape from Italy through the Alps into Switzerland. The performers are not professional actors, but are actual victims of the war who are reliving their experiences. The theme is the heroism of both the officers and the victims, who are prepared to face death rather than live under the tyranny of the fascist regime.

The Life and Death of Colonel Blimp. Prod. and dir. Michael Powell and Emeric Pressberger, Archers, 115 min., 1943. New York: VidAmerica. Made with the support of the Ministry of Information, this British production tells the story of a well-meaning but outdated British gentleman soldier who finds himself heading up a Home Guard division in World War II. In the process, he learns that gentlemanly traits are of little value in a nasty war against a nasty enemy, and having learned this, he cheers the new generation of soldiers who will win the war for Britain. Winston Churchill objected to this film because the central figure, Clive Wynn-Candy, was of Churchill's generation, and the prime minister did not like the idea that his view of the British man at war being a man of honor might be outdated. The film was enormously popular all the same. It covered the years of Wynn-Candy's life from the turn of the century to the early years of World War II. As that moment nears, he takes on the appearance and out-of-date world view of the Colonel Blimp character made famous by cartoonist David Low during the 1920s and 1930s. Regrettably, the American version was cut drastically, restored only in 1986 to its original length of 163 minutes.

The Lion Has Wings. Prod. Alexander Korda, dir. Michael Powell, Brian Desmond, Adrian Brunel, London Films/United Artists, 76 min., 1939. Chicago: Facets Video.
A docudrama which features men and women associated with the Royal Air Force (RAF) and their commitment to Britain's victory in World War II. Scenes involving professional actors are interspersed with newsreel and other documentary footage in order to tell the story of the RAF going to war against Germany. The film is typical of early British war propaganda. The RAF officers and their wives and girl-

friends all have upper-class accents, while the rest speak variations of Cockney. Ian Dalrymple of the Documentary Film Movement wrote the script and was associate producer.

Listen to Britain. Prod. Ian Dalrymple, dir. Humphrey Jennings and Stewart McAllister, Crown Film Unit, 19 min., 1942, on *Wartime Moments*. New York: Kino International.
This Crown Film Unit production has no narrative; rather, for the length of its nineteen minutes, the viewer listens to the sounds of Britain: London radio, BBC World Service, people singing around pianos, children playing and clapping, factories at work, pianist Myra Hess performing with a Royal Air Force orchestra, and the like. The film ends with members of a concert audience singing "Rule Britannia." Early and late scenes include fields of grain waving while music is played in the background. The theme is that Britain is worth fighting for, and that the British are a resilient people who will never give in to aggression.

London Can Take It. Dir. Harry Watt, Humphrey Jennings, Government Post Office for the Ministry of Information, 24 min., 1940, on *Wartime Homefront*. New York: Kino International.
A production meant largely for overseas audiences, as indicated by the fact that it is narrated by American *Collier's Magazine* correspondent Quentin Reynolds. This documentary describes how Londoners not only survive the "blitz" of German bombers but are made stronger and more determined as a result of it. An interesting but unintended message sent by the film is this: if the British maintained a stiff upper lip during mass bombing raids, it was reasonable to suppose that the Germans would also, a fact military historians such as Basil Liddell-Hart and Robin Higham established beyond reasonable dispute during the 1960s.

Man Hunt. Prod. Kenneth MacGowan, dir. Fritz Lang, Twentieth Century-Fox, 105 min., 1941. Bloomington: Indiana University.
Based on the novel *Rogue Male*, this film is the story of a big game hunter in the Bavarian Alps who discovers that he has a chance to assassinate Hitler. He is caught and tortured but survives and escapes back to England, where he is pursued by a sadistic Gestapo agent. That chase ends with an unusually imaginative showdown in an underground tunnel. In the final scene, the hunter is parachuting back into Germany for another try at Hitler. The message is clear. The Nazis are sufficiently evil that it is quite justifiable to kill their leader, even though he is also the head of a state with which the United States is at peace.

The Memphis Belle: A Story of a Flying Fortress. Prod. William Wyler,
Paramount Studios, for the Office of War Information, 43 min., 1944.
Chicago: International Historic Films.
   William Wyler, best known as the director of such films as *Mrs.
Miniver* (entry below), a wartime propaganda feature film, and *Ben
Hur*, a Hollywood epic of the postwar years, was a major in the United
States Army Air Force in 1943. His orders were to make a documentary
about the role of the B-17 Flying Fortress in the European war. This is
the film. It follows a specific airplane, *The Memphis Belle*, on its
twenty-fifth and final mission, a raid that begins in England and is
directed at Wilhelmshaven, Germany. The entire film is footage shot
by 8th Air Force photographers and combat crew members. The film
is domestic morale propaganda; it makes clear the danger the crew is
in from the moment the aircraft crosses the coastline into Germany,
extols the courage of its individual members and, in the process, notes
how they represent a cross section of the United States (the inference
being that we are all in this together), describes the superior qualities
of the B-17, and stresses the vital role that aircraft plays in the European
theater. At the end, as *The Memphis Belle*'s crew is being sent home,
they are visited by King George VI and Queen Elizabeth—which
reminds those at home of the importance in this war of cooperation
between the United States and the United Kingdom.

Midnight. Prod. United States Office of War Information, 10 min., 1944.
Columbia: University of Missouri.
   A docudrama of sorts, this Office of War Information film follows the
United States Navy around the globe. Training, fleet preparation,
combat, and the sailor at work are all part of depicting naval action as
the heroic defense of democracy against Japanese and German aggressors. At ten minutes, the coverage is superficial, but that is an advantage
from a propaganda viewpoint on this kind of subject.

Mrs. Miniver. Prod. Sidney Franklin, dir. William Wyler, Metro-Goldwyn-
Mayer, 134 min., 1942. Chicago: Facets Video.
   This is the story, told by a Hollywood filmmaker, of the British people
at war, their courage in the face of German bombing raids, and how
they are prepared to fight to the end for their nation and their human
dignity. There is a remarkable scene, in which thousands of civilian
boats head across the channel to rescue British soldiers from the
beaches at Dunkirk following the fall of France in June 1940. The
British are brave, the Germans evil, and in the final scene through the
gaping hole in the bombed church where the funeral of an innocent

young woman who was killed in an air raid is taking place, one can see a flight of British aircraft heading toward Germany, while the vicar extols the ideals for which Britons fight and for which they are willing to die. Winston Churchill remarked that this film was as valuable as six divisions toward winning the war.

My Japan. Prod. United States Office of War Information, 14 min., 1943. Pocatello: Idaho State University.
In this Office of War Information (OWI) film made from captured Japanese footage, a Japanese narrator's blunt and direct commentary is used to sell the OWI propaganda message. As he talks about Japanese plans for conquest in Asia, the point is made to audiences in the United States that there is no room for complacency or overoptimism regarding the war in the Pacific. The film is short, but the message is clear.

Negro Colleges in Wartime. Prod. United States Office of War Information, 10 min., 1943. Columbia: University of Missouri.
This Office of War Information documentary describes how black colleges in the United States, along with the rest of the country, have joined the war effort. Their scientists work to produce vital war materials, their male students study chemistry, meteorology, and animal husbandry, and their female students prepare for medicine and technical work. The message is that Americans are in this fight together, regardless of race.

The Negro Soldier. Dir. Frank Capra, United States Office of War Information, 40 min., 1944. Chicago: International Historic Films.
Langston Hughes hailed this documentary on African American soldiers fighting in United States forces in World War II. However, if it was intended to end racism in the United States military, the evidence suggests that it failed. If it was intended to promote the idea that American blacks could be as patriotic as white Americans, then it likely enjoyed some success.

New Philippines News. Prod. United States Treasury, War Finance Division, 2 min., 1945. Pullman: Washington State University.
A war bond drive trailer, this brief film uses captured Japanese propaganda film called *New Philippines News* and compares it with footage from American films, to show how Japanese propagandists lie about providing rice for POWs in camps in the Philippines. The American film shows graves and signs of starvation in the camps, and the trailer ends with the appeal, "Let's speed the war, America. Let's speed it with bonds."

Night Train to Munich. Prod. Edward Black, dir. Carol Reed, Gaumont, 95 min., 1940. Chicago: Facets Video.

This film was showing in London during some of Britain's worst months of World War II. A spy thriller set in the months between the German occupation of Prague and the invasion of Poland, the film tells the story of a Czech technical expert who, with his daughter, is lured under false pretenses to Berlin, where they are held against their will. A British spy infiltrates the German Navy ministry and tries to get them back. Aimed at encouraging the hard-pressed British by showing the ability of British intelligence to outwit the Nazis, this film does not emphasize the two-dimensional confrontation between good and evil that characterizes later war propaganda films.

The North Star. Dir. Lewis Milestone, 106 min., 1943. Ames: Iowa State University.

Commissioned by President Franklin D. Roosevelt, this feature film, also known as *Armored Attack*, was a tribute to the Russian allies of the United States in World War II. A Russian collective, "The North Star," tries to fend off the Nazi invasion of their community. They are beaten, but come back as partisans and overcome their oppressors. This film is a perfect example of Hollywood's pro-Russian propaganda, but one which should not be mistaken for pro-Soviet propaganda. See *Days of Glory* (entry above).

Objective, Burma! Prod. Jerry Wald, dir. Raoul Walsh, Warner Brothers, 142 min., 1945. Chicago: Facets Video.

This is the story of fifty American paratroops who drop behind enemy lines to destroy a Japanese radar station. The commandos succeed, but while waiting for their rescue planes, they are attacked by the Japanese and forced to fight their way through the Burmese jungle on foot. The usual Hollywood propaganda jargon is subdued in this film, perhaps because it comes so late in the war. In its place is the message that the United States is now in charge of Asia as well as of Europe. At least that is how British audiences took the film, and critics trashed it because it gives the impression that the war in Burma was an affair of the United States, whereas Britain, which had been fighting there since the war began, hardly received a mention.

Ohm Krüger. Dir. Hans Steinhoff, Tobis Rota, 135 min., 1941. Chicago: International Historic Films.

A German propaganda film in which the heroic Boers led by Paul Kruger, president of the Transvaal, fight against the oppressive British

Empire in South Africa in 1899-1902. The propaganda images are classic: Kruger is heroic, Queen Victoria is a whiskey-swigging drunk, the British are brutal, and the Boers are valiant. This was one of the most lavish propaganda films made at Joseph Goebbels' inspiration prior to *Kolberg* in 1945.

One of Our Aircraft Is Missing. Prod and dir. Michael Powell and Emeric Pressburger, Archers/British National, 90 min., 1942. Los Angeles: NTA Home Entertainment.
Classic early British war propaganda in which the points are subtle, but there is no question who is in the right and who in the wrong. Based upon actual events, this film tells the story of six British airmen downed in occupied Holland. The Dutch underground (including "wizard" Dutch girls) help them escape. There are several scenes in which collaborators are put in their place and the occupiers are shown to be harsh and brutish.

Passage to Marseille. Prod. Hal B. Wallis, dir. Michael Curtiz, Warner Brothers, 110 min., 1944. Chicago: Facets Video.
A group of French prisoners have escaped the dreaded Devil's Island prison and are picked up by a passing French freighter. They claim they are from a torpedoed submarine. The captain of the freighter is a Free French loyalist, but he must hide his loyalties from a French army major on board who is sympathetic to Vichy. The identity of the escaped prisoners finally is revealed. It turns out that they are all loyal to the Free French, and they seize the ship from the Vichy officer and his men and sail off to join in the war. Patriotism, courage, and Hollywood's obvious preference for the Free French over Vichy are the messages here, along with the wickedness of anyone with fascist views.

Pimpernel Smith. Prod. and dir. Leslie Howard, British National, 110 min., 1942. Chicago: Facets Video.
Clearly a takeoff from *The Scarlet Pimpernel*, a nineteenth-century novel about an English aristocrat who drives French revolutionaries crazy during the Reign of Terror (the mid-1790s) by rescuing French aristocrats from the Guillotine right under their noses. The film version of this novel in 1936 featured Leslie Howard, who plays the main character in *Pimpernel Smith*. The story is that an Oxford don secretly operates a rescue ring for persecuted victims of Nazi tyranny. He is confronted—unsuccessfully—by a corpulent Gestapo officer who is determined to find the "elusive Pimpernel." There is much stiff-upper-lip heroism here, the symbolic presence of a student from the United

States, and a clear indication that no Gestapo man is the equal of a dedicated English patriot. Leslie Howard died in 1943 when his airplane was shot down by German aircraft. British propagandists claimed at the time that the Germans targeted him specifically because he was so good at anti-Nazi film propaganda.

Polish Campaign. Prod. Universum-Film-Aktiengesellschaft (UFA), 33 min., 1939. Chicago: International Historic Films.
The Germans made this half-hour documentary in English about the fall of Poland in September 1939. It was the first of many such films for export, the point being to counter anti-German propaganda and to justify the German view of the war. The Poles are made culpable for creating the situation that made war inevitable. German military prowess is emphasized in the ensuing invasion.

Priestley, J. B. *Britain Speaks*. New York: Harper and Brothers, 1940.
Joseph Priestley was a prominent figure in English literary circles who, like others of his ilk, volunteered for service in Britain's propaganda ministry in World War II. This volume is a collection of his radio broadcasts to the United States during the first year of World War II, in which he explains to the neutral United States what Britain expects to achieve in the war. That these broadcasts were propaganda is clear from such titles as "Civilization Can Defend Itself as Fiercely as Barbarism Can Attack," "Nazi Propaganda for Export," "Comic Fairy Tales from Berlin," and "Three Typical Factories That Are Replying to Hitler." These and other broadcasts are typical of British propaganda in the early days of the war in that they (1) accentuate positive aspects of Britain at war, such as dedication, courage, and a "stiff upper lip," and (2) make light of anti-British propaganda from Germany.

The Purple Heart. Prod. Darryl F. Zanuck, dir. Lewis Milestone, Twentieth Century-Fox, 99 min., 1944. Beverly Hills, Calif.: Fox Home Entertainment.
In this film, two United States bomber crews, who have been captured after the 1942 Doolittle raid on Tokyo, are brought to trial in Japan as war criminals. The are also tortured by a sadistic Japanese officer who wants to know the location of their bases and to have them confess to bombing hospitals and schools. They admit to nothing and in the final scene are led off to their execution. The film is full of patriotic speechifying, and the Japanese are presented as the stereotypically devious, sneering, buck-toothed sadists who are mortal enemies of the United States—by this time standard.

The Ramparts We Watch. Dir. Louis de Rochemont, March of Time, 100
min., 1940. Chicago: Macmillan Films.
This was March of Time's first full-length film. The subject was an
explanation and justification for the United States going to war in 1917;
the object was to push the United States toward involvement in World
War II. The setting is a small New England town where complacency
was rife in 1914, but which eventually was turned by events to total
commitment. Documentary footage is interwoven with dramatic
scenes played by real people.

Rhodes, Anthony. *Propaganda, the Art of Persuasion: World War II.*
London: Angus and Robertson, 1976.
This volume examines World War II propaganda mainly with an eye
toward propaganda posters, but with some references to, and stills from,
propaganda feature films. Samples come from all of the major belligerents
in World War II and represent a wide variety of topics. The illustrations
are accompanied by an explanatory text. The main text is divided between
"The Propagation of the Reich," "Mussolini's New Rome," "Britain
Improvises," "United States: Isolation and Intervention," "Rule and Resistance in the New Order," "The Soviet Union: Propaganda for Peace,"
and "The Rise and Fall of Japan." Victor Margolin wrote a foreword and
Daniel Lerner an afterword for the volume. Select bibliography.

Sahara. Prod. Harry Joe Brown, dir. Zoltan Korda, Columbia, 97 min.,
1943. Chicago: Facets Video.
Directed by one of the famous Korda family who made their film
reputation in prewar Britain, this film features Humphrey Bogart as an
American tank commander in North Africa who, with his tank and
crew, is separated from his unit after the fall of Tobruk. There is a
devious captured Nazi, a repentant Italian, and a siege of the tank by a
large German force searching for the well that the tankers have already
located and are defending. The tankers hold off the German force until
thirst forces them to lay down their arms. There is the usual propagandistic speech-making, but the enemy, save for the devious Nazi captive,
are shown as more human than is usually the case in Hollywood
propaganda films from the mid-war years.

Sieg im Westen. Prod. International Historic Films, 120 min., 1985.
Chicago: International Historic Films.
Originally released in Germany in 1941 following the victory of the
German army in Western Europe, this collection of combat films was
designed to glorify German arms and project among the French and

others the image of their own defeat at the hands of the Germans. There is the triumphant Germany army parading on the Champs Élysées, scenes of despairing, vanquished enemies in prisoner of war camps, and the moment of triumph when the French sign the surrender in the same railway car at Campiègne where the Germans signed the armistice in 1918. Behind it all is appropriately bombastic music composed by Herbert Windt, who also wrote the score for Leni Riefenstahl's propaganda masterpiece *Triumph of the Will*.

Slosson, Preston. *Why We Are at War*. Boston: Houghton Mifflin, 1943.
This pamphlet was written for dissemination in public schools as part of a policy to educate youth on the nature of war and the issues involved in World War II. As the publishers indicate in a foreword, "it is the purpose of this book to show what we are fighting for, why we *must* win this war, and what we must not do when the fighting is over if we are to build for permanent peace and a democratic civilization." The author was a historian at the University of Michigan at the time of writing. He appeals to his readers with such analogies as going to war against tyranny is like organizing a police force to catch burglars. Illustrations but no bibliography.

So Proudly We Hail. Prod. and dir. Mark Sandrich, Paramount, 126 min., 1943. Salt Lake City, Utah: Sight and Sound.
In this film, women are the heroes, specifically three army nurses who survive Bataan and Corregidor, and witness with courage and resolve some of the war's most brutal moments. Naturally, they find love and romance along the way, and the film ends with them joining, on a ship to Australia, the survivors of this first confrontation between the United States and invading Japanese soldiers. There is the usual propaganda material in terms of patriotic language and American heroism, and also an element of revenge taking. The boyfriend of one of the nurses was killed at Pearl Harbor, and she is ready to take it out on a wounded Japanese prisoner, until she is talked out of it by one of the other nurses. An actual army nurse, Lt. Eunice Hatchitt, served as technical advisor for the film.

The Soviet Paradise. Prod. Universum-Film-Aktiengesellschaft (UFA), 15 min., 1941. University Park: Pennsylvania State University.
This film was produced and distributed in Germany to justify the invasion of Russia in 1941. It depicts life in Russia after twenty years of Soviet rule as bleak. The "Soviet Paradise" is depicted as being populated with youth gangs, cowed laborers, wretched peasants, and starving children. In German with English subtitles.

Spitfire. Prod. and dir. Leslie Howard, Misbourne/British Aviation, 90 min., 1943. Chicago: Facets Video.

A film biography of R. J. Mitchell, who designed the British Spitfire. At is was one of the most effective fighter aircraft of World War II, it may be argued that the Spitfire was more responsible than any other single factor in winning the Battle of Britain—at least this film implies that conclusion. Therein lies the propaganda message of this film, which is strongly put and compelling; in sum, another Leslie Howard propaganda triumph.

Target for Tonight. Prod. Ian Dalrymple, dir. Harry Watt, Crown Film Unit for the Ministry of Information, 49 min., 1941, on *Wartime Moments*. New York: Kino International.

A Crown Film Unit production which takes a British bomber crew from briefing and flight preparation, through takeoff, to bomb run over the target, and return home. Along the way, they experience the usual dangers: a crew member is wounded by flak and they return to land in a hazardous fog. This is another Ian Dalrymple "docudrama," in which real Royal Air Force officers and enlisted men play roles in this hypothetical raid. At least some of the shots are studio shots with the camera filming the inside of the bomber through windows. A well-made film which is a classic of British propaganda documentaries.

Tender Comrade. Prod. David Hempstead, dir. Edward Dmytrick, RKO Radio Pictures, 102 min., 1943. Chicago: Facets Video.

The theme is women contributing to the war effort in the United States. The propaganda lies in their courage and resourcefulness. Four women working in an aircraft plant in California team up to share a house and offer moral support to each other, while their husbands are off fighting the war. Ironically—because of the word "comrade" in the title, the implication that the shared house was a sort of commune, and the script's being written by Dalton Trumbo, who had definite Marxist leanings—this film came to be regarded as as subtle pro-communist propaganda. Trumbo was among those who were blacklisted during the McCarthy era, in part because of this film.

This Above All. Prod. Darryl F. Zanuck, dir. Anatole Litvak, 110 min., Twentieth Century-Fox, 1942. Hanover, N.H.: Dartmouth College.

The United States was in the war as Britain's ally when this Hollywood film was made. An upper-class Englishwoman volunteers for the Womens' Auxiliary Army Field Service as an enlisted person rather than as an officer. She falls in love with a working-class man who was wounded at Dunkirk and is bitter about the British aristocracy. He believes that aristocrats rule Britain in their own interest, and it is not worth his life to save theirs. In due course, he deserts and his upper-class lover must persuade him that England is worth fighting for, despite class conflicts. The film seems to send a double message: fight for Britain, but fight against the English class system as well.

This Land Is Mine. Prod. and dir. Jean Renoir, RKO Radio Pictures, 103 min., 1943. Chicago: Facets Video.
Though it is not specified, the setting clearly is director Renoir's France, part of which is occupied by Germans while the rest is ruled by the collaborationist Vichy government. This film is the story of a frightened schoolteacher who tries to go about his business and not get involved. He comes to the attention of a fellow teacher who is sympathetic to the resistance, of which her brother is a bomb-throwing member. She begins to nurture a latent sense of patriotism in her timid colleague. In the end, he takes a stand and pays for it with his life. It has been said that the absence of the usual propaganda clichés in this film, the fact that it sees no black or white, good or evil, but only gray, made it anti-propaganda. In light of the evolution of the cowardly, low-profile teacher into a patriot willing to stand up to the enemies of his country and die for that principle, this is a difficult argument to sustain.

To Be or Not to Be. Prod. and dir. Ernst Lubitsch, United Artists, 99 min., 1942. Chicago: Facets Video.
This film has been described accurately as a masterpiece of satire and "a brilliant example of how comedy can be as effective in raising social and political awareness as a serious propaganda film, while still providing hilarious entertainment." The setting is Poland when the Nazis invade. The story revolves around an actor whose only ambition is to play Hamlet but who ends up pretending to be a Nazi officer in order to uncover a Nazi spy. The real message in this film is Polish heroism in what for the moment is a lost cause. It features Polish pilots who must leave Poland and fly their aircraft to Britain in order to join the fight against the Nazis from there. The film was controversial because some critics thought that director Ernst Lubitsch, a German, was making fun of the Poles.

Voice of Truth. Prod. United States Office of War Information, 3 min., 1943. Pocatello: Idaho State University.
A war bond drive short film which employs the voice of Tokyo Rose, the Japanese propaganda broadcaster, and makes its point by showing

film clips of how United States soldiers in the Pacific Theater responded to her broadcasts: they laughed at her. This was very reassuring to the folks at home. See also Masayo Duus, *Tokyo Rose: Orphan of the Pacific* (entry above under "History and Function").

Wake Island. Prod. Joseph Sistrom, dir. John Farrow, Paramount, 78 min., 1942. Chicago: Facets Video.
The defense of Wake Island in the early days of World War II in the Pacific was doomed from the start. This patriotic potboiler demonstrated that even in defeat there was victory and provided much-needed inspiration to a nation now several months at war, but still waiting to see a victory. The Marines on Wake Island are calm in the face of their impossible situation. They fight courageously and never give up until they are overwhelmed by the hordes of Japanese soldiers. This was an early Hollywood contribution to flag-waving war propaganda. Hollywood never looked back, as evidenced by the films with nearly identical propaganda characteristics which flooded the market through the war years that followed.

We Dive at Dawn. Prod. Edward Black, dir. Anthony Asquith, Gainsborough, 96 min., 1943. Chicago: Facets Video.
The saga of a British submarine crew who proceed from shore leave to sea duty in pursuit of the German battleship *Brandenburg*. There is a harrowing trip through a mine field, followed by circumstances which make it impossible for the crew to know if they succeeded in disabling the *Brandenburg*. Then the submarine runs out of fuel and has to sneak into an occupied Danish port, where there is a Danish tanker. With the help of the Danish resistance and their own courage, the British crew hold off the Nazis and refuel, then make it back to England. The theme is that, through the heroism of British submariners and the Danish resistance, the Germans can be beaten.

West, W. J., ed. *George Orwell, the War Commentaries*. Harmondsworth, Middlesex, England: Penguin Books, 1987.
This volume reproduces the scripts for some of the propaganda broadcasts directed to India that George Orwell wrote and delivered for the British Broadcasting Corporation during World War II. The editor's introduction provides a context for the broadcasts, including the rules of censorship which established what Orwell could and could not say. He argues that this collection gives "a unique picture of an actual propaganda war, broadcast over public address systems in offices and canteens, and from radio sets in homes and villages, throughout an

entire sub-continent." There is an appendix of selected Axis propaganda broadcasts which it was Orwell's job to counter, and several maps of the world at war. No bibliography.

White Cliffs of Dover. Prod. Sidney Franklin, dir. Clarence Brown, Metro-Goldwyn-Mayer, 126 min., 1944. Chicago: Facets Video.
Inspired by Alice Duer Miller's poem "The White Cliffs," this MGM feature film tells the story of an American woman who marries an Englishman just prior to World War I. He is killed in the war, but not before they have a son. The son grows up in time to fight in World War II, where he also is killed. In the final scene, his mother, a Red Cross volunteer, looks out the window of the bedroom where her son has just died of his wounds and sees a battalion of soldiers from the United States marching by, the first to arrive in Britain. The message is clear: there is a natural affinity between Britons and Americans, which means that it is worthwhile for the United States to fight for Britain. The film was an effort to strengthen the Anglo-American connection in wartime, and perhaps after the war as well.

Why We Fight. Prod. Frank Capra, 7 films, 55-83 min. each, 1942-1944. Chicago: International Historic Films.
Frank Capra was a major in the United States Army Signal Corps when he began this series of war propaganda documentaries at the direction of Army Chief of Staff General George C. Marshall. The purpose was to explain to American soldiers why the United States was engaged in World War II. The films were shown also in cinemas across the country. Individual titles include: *Prelude to War* (1942) which shows events leading up to war, with Nazis and Japanese suitably stereotyped; *The Nazis Strike* (1943), which describes Nazi aggression up to and including the invasion of Poland, and denigrates appeasement; *Divide and Conquer* (1943), which follows the early successes of Nazi armies in Europe; *The Battle of Britain* (1943), which extols the courage of the British people faced with the barbarous Nazi attack from the air; *The Battle of Russia* (1944), which depicts the Nazis being defeated at Stalingrad and the heroism of the Red Army; *The Battle of China* (1944), which focuses on the Chinese people in their fight against the Japanese aggressor; and *War Comes to America* (1945), which shows the American people being wrenched out of isolationism and into the fight to save the world from tyranny and for democracy.

Wing and a Prayer. Dir. Henry Hathaway, Twentieth Century-Fox, 97 min., 1944. Chicago: Facets Video.

It is the Battle of Midway, the first decisive battle of the Pacific which the United States won. This is the story of the carrier air pilots. It extols their courage, resourcefulness, willingness to sacrifice all, and the anguish suffered by their officers, who must remain on deck and send them into harm's way. No patriotic American of the time would not have been moved by the heroism and drama portrayed in this film.

Winged Victory. Prod. Darryl F. Zanuck, dir. George Cukor, Twentieth Century-Fox, 130 min., 1944. Washington, D.C.: Library of Congress. Based on the broadway play by Moss Hart, this film celebrates the Army Air Force (AAF) training program. Many of the cast were actual members of the AAF. The hero and his friends and comrades are followed through the course of their training until they receive their wings and go off to war to become heroes.

Wings and the Woman. Prod. and dir. Herbert Wilcox, RKO Radio Pictures, approx. 110 min., 1941. St. Cloud, Minn.: St. Cloud State University.
This film tells the story of Amy Johnson, one of the first women to break into British aviation as a pilot. At the outbreak of World War II, she entered the Auxiliary Transport Corps and ferried aircraft from base to base for the Royal Air Force. On one such mission early in the war, she crashed and was killed. Though made in the United States, the film featured a British producer/director and a British cast. The message is that in this war, women are heroes the same as men, and will play roles in the war formerly reserved for men.

Yass, Marion. *This Is Your War: Home Front Propaganda in the Second World War*. London: Her Majesty's Stationery Office, 1983.
A collection of examples of British government propaganda distributed on the home front in World War II, and a guide to propaganda documentation contained in the Public Records Office in Kew, Surrey, England. The examples are accompanied by a narrative which explains their use and comments on their quality as propaganda. At the time of assembling the collection, the author was on the staff of the Public Records Office.

Chapter 6

PROPAGANDA AND THE COLD WAR, 1945-1989

Even before World War II ended in 1945, indications were clear that leadership in the postwar world would be in the hands of the United States and the Soviet Union. For at least a decade and a half after 1945, much of the rest of the world appeared to have become mere pawns in the Cold War these superpowers waged for dominance of what international relations theorists now termed a "bi-polar world." "Cold War" meant a nonshooting war conducted mainly through secret intelligence operations with an occasional military confrontation in such regions as Korea, Malaysia, and Vietnam, and above all through propaganda. For all practical purposes, the Cold War was primarily a propaganda war in which intelligence agencies played an important and usually covert role. The perception of world politics held by millions of people on both sides of the "iron curtain" (Winston Churchill's term) that divided East from West was created by propagandists who had access to materials gathered—and sometimes invented—by intelligence operatives. These propagandists used journalism, literature, film, the visual arts, radio and television broadcasting, cartoons, posters, and public oratory. Their techniques were those established through the experience of a half century of war and peace, and especially that gained in World War II; moreover, these techniques were even more effective in the Cold War era, owing to steady advances in communications technologies. Entries in this chapter reflect those advances. They also reflect a more intense distrust of propaganda than existed even in the 1930s, but which was accompanied by a paradoxical sense of resignation to propaganda's now being a regular feature of political and social action.

History and Function

Adler, Leo K., and Thomas G. Paterson. "Red Fascism: The Merger of Nazi Germany and Soviet Russia in the American Image of Totalitarianism, 1930s-1960s." *American Historical Review* 75, 4 (April 1970), pp. 1046-1064.
   The authors describe how, since the advent of Stalinism and Hitlerism, it was the tendency of Americans to "deliberately articulate distorted similarities between Nazi and communist ideologies." They contend that this analogy shaped American perceptions of the Cold War world.

Further, they argue that this development was a direct result of the sense given to the word "totalitarianism" by anti-Nazi propaganda of the 1930s; the word was applied with equal certainty by anti-Soviet propagandists to the Soviet system. The anti-Nazi propagandists encouraged the anti-Soviet propagandists until the idea of "red fascism" was a firmly entrenched and well-articulated part of Cold War propaganda.

Alexandre, Laurien. *The Voice of America: From Détente to the Reagan Doctrine*. Norwood, N.J.: Ablex, 1988.

This volume analyzes the nature and impact of Voice of America (VOA) broadcasting as a propaganda weapon employed in the service of United States foreign policy. The time period considered is from the latter stages of the Cold War through the Reagan presidency. The author explains that before that period, the purpose of VOA had been to "fight for the hearts, minds, and pocketbooks of the world's peoples against what was perceived to be a despotic, expansionistic, atheistic, and anti-American enemy." The book picks up the story in the 1970s and analyzes VOA propaganda work, including its technique and style, in the context of such developments as détente, cutbacks in VOI funding, the Watergate debacle, the horrors of Kampuchea (Cambodia), and President Reagan's "Evil Empire" crusade against the Soviet Union. Extensive bibliography, and appendixes which list VOA directors and broadcast schedules.

Allen, George V. "Are the Soviets Winning the Propaganda War?" *Annals of the American Academy of Political and Social Science* 336 (July 1961), pp. 1-11.

The author argues that the Soviet Union, at the time of writing, is more adept than the West at waging a propaganda war. He contends that Soviet propagandists get their message across with more flair and more conviction than do their Western counterparts. However, this is a short-term advantage, because the Soviet propagandists face problems that the contents of their material do not resolve: the issues of "nationality and rising expectations" in those countries where Soviet propaganda is most active. The West has the advantage here, the author concludes, because the liberal democracy and free- enterprise economics of the United States can address these issues far more effectively than can Soviet internationalism and socialist control.

Allen, V. L. *The Russians Are Coming: The Politics of Anti-Sovietism*. Shipley, England: Moor Press, 1987.

This book analyzes the roots and nature of anti-Soviet prejudice and the propaganda which perpetuates it. The author argues that the Soviet

Union is seen by Western capitalist societies as a continuous threat to capitalism. By definition, "anti-Sovietism is an attempt to distort and exaggerate that threat by the constant drip of hostile propaganda, denigrating Soviet principles and practices of government, Soviet mannerism and ideology, indeed all facets of Soviet life and re-constituting them as alien, hostile, frightening, and threatening to everything good for which Western democracies are alleged to stand." The volume is not entirely objective, a fact demonstrated by the startling assertion that the Soviet system simply represents a general social trend of the twentieth century. Even so, the author makes a credible case for many of his other assertions in the context of stereotyping the Soviet enemy, legitimizing capitalism, dissent in the West, and Soviet democracy. Bibliography is included in endnotes.

Barrett, Edward W. *Truth Is Our Weapon*. New York: Funk and Wagnalls, 1953.
A Cold War period piece by an American propagandist, the purpose here is made clear when the author dedicates the volume to his wife and to those "other propagandists dedicated to the frustrating toil of trying to convert men to the cause of freedom." The introduction is a call to propaganda arms. It opens with a reference to needing to win minds in order to win the Cold War, and moves on to insist that the only effective propaganda in this cause is the truth. The book links the propaganda before and during World War II to postwar propaganda, using examples of the former to point out how the latter must be conducted. Subjects covered include learning to overcome confusion and to recognize propaganda needs, the negative impact of McCarthyism, the nature of the enemy—be it Hitler before the war or the Soviet Union after—and the role of various individuals and government bodies in charting the future course of propaganda. More than a little subjective. The classic political, social, and ideological assumptions characteristic of the Cold War are evident on every page.

Bogart, Leo. *Premises for Propaganda: The United States Information Agency's Operating Assumptions in the Cold War*. New York: Free Press, 1976.
This book is based upon a 1954 report on the United States Information Agency (USIA) commissioned by that agency in order to improve its Cold War propaganda efforts. The report was never acted upon and remained locked up under a "confidential" classification. When this volume was written, the report had long been declassified, and the author presents it here, with commentary, in order to show a picture of

how a United States propaganda agency worked during the most intense period of the Cold War, the early 1950s. There also are comparisons with later reports on the USIA with reference to its work in Vietnam in the 1960s. Topics upon which the 1954 report and consequently this volume focus include propaganda objectives in the Cold War, truth and credibility, media, propaganda personnel, and what it was like to be "in the field" doing propaganda work. Limited bibliography of books about the USIA.

Ceplair, Larry, and Steven Englund. *The Inquisition in Hollywood: Politics in the Film Community, 1930-1960*. Garden City, N.Y.: Anchor Press/Doubleday, 1980.
This volume is a history of the political context in which Hollywood films were made, during a particularly tempestuous period in the affairs of both the United States and the world. It has been argued that the Cold War began with the victory of Bolshevism in Russia in the early 1920s. This may be the premise upon which the volume is based, since much of the political ferment the authors describe involved conflict between communist writers and filmmakers, left-wing production crew unions, and "reactionary producers" between 1930 and 1960. Topics include the Screen Writers Guild, pro-Spanish Republic attitudes in Hollywood during the Spanish Civil War, Hollywood communists' influence on American films and politics, the activities of the House Committee on Un-American Activities before, during, and after World War II, the Hollywood blacklist, and the almost perpetual tension between left and right over how and for what purposes the film industry should function. It is an ugly story. Illustrations and an extensive bibliography.

Choukas, Michael. *Propaganda Comes of Age*. Washington, D.C.: Public Affairs Press, 1965.
The author is no fan of propaganda, which he describes as "one of the great shibboleths of our times," seductive and comforting in times of moral, political, and social uncertainty, but not a substitute for rational thought. The author is a veteran of the United States Office of Strategic Services in World War II, which ran propaganda as well as other wartime operations. Therefore, he is well qualified on his subject, which is the nature and uses of propaganda in the Cold War era. The volume analyzes propaganda in a historic setting and closes with a discussion of its role in democratic societies. The underlying theme is that propaganda is here to stay. This is a Cold War period piece, and a good one. No bibliography.

Dunham, Donald. *Kremlin Target: U.S.A. Conquest by Propaganda*. New York: Ives Washburn, 1961.
Donald Dunham worked in Bucharest, Rumania, until the Rumanian government forced him to leave in 1949. This book warns the United States against Soviet propaganda. It was the fault of Soviet propaganda, the author claims, that while in Rumania he was "forced to switch from cultural-information representative of the United States to propagandist, from a person trying to cultivate cordial relations for my country to competitor in a new arena of international conflict." This volume defines Soviet propaganda as a "critical challenge," the target of which is the United States. It also explains what is the "critical challenge" that United States propaganda faces in this propaganda war. The author's Rumanian experience provides the context for his analysis and perhaps explains why the line is so thin here between what is propaganda analysis and what is propaganda. No bibliography.

Evans, F. Bowen, ed. *Worldwide Communist Propaganda Activities*. New York: Macmillan, 1955.
This volume is dedicated to "the devoted group of Americans who serve their country in the world-wide battle against Communist propaganda," though it is not clear exactly who these people are. The book is described as a "report" or "general account of Communist propaganda activities during 1954 in all parts of the world." It opens with a description of the objectives, theory, and organization of international communist propaganda, the aims of which are "to divide the nations of the Free World and, particularly, to isolate the United States." Following this chapter, others concentrate on the volume of and expenditures on communist propaganda, themes in communist propaganda, communist use of international media, and major communist fronts (the World Peace Council and the World Federation of Trade Unions are among those specified). Several chapters detail communist propaganda activities in various parts of the world outside North America. As in other writings of this genre, it is difficult to determine where the analysis ends and anti-communist propaganda begins. No bibliography.

Gordon, George N., Irving Falk, and William Hodapp. *The Idea Invaders*. New York: Hastings House, 1963.
This volume was inspired by Cold War propaganda and is dedicated to the defense of free thought from propagandists, "the idea invaders" of the title, without regard for whether they reside on the East or West side of the Iron Curtain. The author aims at "exposing" propaganda and propaganda language contained within the media and other

sources. With that in mind, he writes in a quasi-journalistic style, and draws heavily upon both opinion-page writers and scholars, including in the latter case the eminent linguistics scholar of the 1940s and 1960s S. I. Hayakawa. Select bibliography.

Grothe, Peter. *To Win the Minds of Men: The Story of the Communist Propaganda War in East Germany*. Palo Alto, Calif.: Pacific Books, 1958.
This book examines how communist propaganda was disseminated in East Germany in order to "change the very consciousness of the 17,900,000 persons living in the Soviet Zone." The author surveys media, education, the justice system, culture, and agitation (agitprop) in order to make the East German propaganda process clear in all of its particulars. His own perspective is clear enough: part 1 is titled "The Big Lie," and there is the implication throughout that East German propaganda had much in common—stylistically, at any rate—with Nazi propaganda from before World War II. A section on counterpropaganda refers to churches and other anti-communist groups in the East. The book ends with a warning that if the West is not careful, communism will overwhelm it and subject it to the same kind of propaganda that distorts the minds of people in East Germany. Limited bibliography.

Hogan, J. Michael. "The Rhetoric of Historiography: New Left Revisionism in the Vietnam era," in J. Robert Cox, Malcolm O. Sillars, and Gregg B. Walker, eds., *Argument and Social Practice: Proceedings of the Fourth SCA/AFA Conference on Argumentation*. Annandale, Va.: Speech Communication Association, 1985.
Political debate is often fueled by so-called lessons from history, the author begins, and proceeds to suggest that historians often write history "with an eye toward influencing political decision-making." The remainder of the essay analyzes "competing frameworks" for explanation of United States foreign policy in the historiography of the Vietnam era—not writings about Vietnam, but historical writing influenced by the reality of that conflict. The overall conclusion drawn is that much of this historiography was politically motivated, i.e., either critical of the United States government or favorable to its policy as a logical extension of the Cold War—which is to say, historiography with a propaganda purpose. No bibliography.

Inkeles, Alex. *Social Change in Soviet Russia*. Cambridge, Mass.: Harvard University Press, 1968.
This volume represents the evolution of the author's views on Soviet culture and society by reproducing essays he had written over a number

of years. Of interest to Cold War propaganda are chapters 16 through 18, organized under the general heading "International Propaganda and Counterpropaganda." Chapter 16 evaluates ideological and political premises on which the initial Cold War Soviet propaganda offensive was mounted, while the others treat the propaganda war in the context of radio wars between Soviet broadcasting and Voice of America (VOA). The author suggests here that VOA may not have been so effective as its advocates claimed. Extensive bibliography.

Joyce, Walter. *The Propaganda Gap*. New York: Harper and Row, 1963.
   "Propaganda is a major weapon in the ideological conflict" of the Cold War, the author begins. It is his contention that "we [the United States] as a nation must rid ourselves of the strange queasiness we feel about propaganda if our conduct in the ideological conflict is to be anything but haphazard." From this premise, he advances a detailed argument in favor of the United States conducting an extensive campaign of disseminating democratic propaganda in opposition to communism, and outlines specific strategies for the purpose. The author was a journalist and a World War II B-25 pilot, who flew psychological warfare leaflet-drop missions over Italy. Limited bibliography.

Leab, Janiel J. "How Red Was My Valley: Hollywood, the Cold War film, and *I Married a Communist*." *Journal of Contemporary History* 19, 1 (January 1984), pp. 59-88.
   The author describes how the Hollywood film "took its lead from the politics of the day," and came on board virtually from the first salvo fired by the United States government in the Cold War. He notes that to some degree, Hollywood's enthusiasm for making anti-communist film was inspired by fear of the House Committee on Un-American Activities, which led the anti-communist witch hunts of the 1950s. This article lists a number of Hollywood films which blatantly propagandized against communism but reserves the bulk of its pages for an in-depth analysis of the filming of *I Married a Communist* (RKO 1950, released finally as *The Woman on Pier 13*), which was one of the prime examples of the Cold War propaganda feature film genre.

Liebovich, Louis. *The Press and the Origins of the Cold War, 1944-1947*. New York: Praeger, 1988.
   This volume examines four major American journals from the 1930s through the 1940s with an eye toward explaining how they interpreted the deteriorating relations between the United States and the Soviet Union that resulted in the Cold War. The journals are *Time*, the *New*

York Herald Tribune, the *Chicago Tribune*, and the *San Francisco Chronicle*. They were selected on the basis of philosophical and regional representation. The author's object is to "answer questions about foreign affairs reporting, about decision making within news organizations, about Franklin D. Roosevelt's and Harry S. Truman's influence over journalists during the specific period." The result is an interesting and revealing study of political influence on the press and press influence on public opinion in the early stages of the Cold War. Select bibliography.

Lilly, Carol S. "Problems of Persuasion: Communist Agitation and Propaganda in Post-War Yugoslavia." *Slavic Review* 53 (Summer 1994), pp. 395-413.
Initial efforts by the new post-World War II communist government of Yugoslavia to recruit young people to work at rebuilding the infrastructure of the war-torn country met with resistance. Coercive policies followed, which gave a hollow ring to the ideal of such labor's being voluntary. The idea behind the labor was that it was necessary to create a "new people" who would embrace the concept, in order to build a new socialist society. Therefore, the Communist Party of Yugoslavia (CPY) initiated a program of agitprop (agitation and propaganda) in order to achieve that end. This article explains the process, the successes and failures, and the hard reality that agitprop did not produce the desired results. After 1948, the CPY resorted to "administrative measures," a euphemism for coercion.

Lowry, Montecue J. *Glasnost' : Deception, Desperation, Dialectics*. New York: Peter Lang, 1991.
Written by a former Central Intelligence Agency analyst, this volume purports to warn the West not to be taken in by *glasnost*, the policy of openness introduced into the Soviet Union in the 1980s by Mikhail Gorbachev. "Many people today," the author writes, "even in the United States, view the Soviet Union and other communists as merely another struggling people who are misunderstood, misrepresented, and mistreated because of prejudices lingering from a misunderstood past." Not necessarily so, he argues, and looks at the history of the Soviet Union, especially at its employment of disinformation and other forms of propaganda, as evidence. In short, the United States should not take the rhetoric of *glasnost* at face value, for within that rhetoric the old ideology still exists. The final sentence leaves no doubt: "The Soviet Union and the insidious communism which it propagates continue to pose a threat to the West, ideologically, politically, and militarily." Select bibliography.

MacDonald, J. Fred. "The Cold War as Entertainment in Fifties Television." *Journal of Popular Film and Television* 7, 1 (1978), pp. 3-31.
From Sergeant Bilko to Bishop Sheen, American television reflected Cold War rivalries throughout the 1950s. As it had become by then the most popular postwar entertainment medium in the United States, television was the perfect channel for both informing and propagandizing audiences in the United States regarding the vital issues of Cold War conflicts. The author describes *I Led Three Lives*, for example, as a series (it was also made into a film) based upon the true story of an FBI agent who infiltrated the Communist Party of the United States. Children's programming also carried the message. Two characters on the animated series *Rocky and Bullwinkle* were the inept but sinister Soviet spies Boris and Natasha. Illustrated with stills from some of the programs analyzed.

Marett, Sir Robert. *Through the Back Door: An Inside View of Britain's Overseas Information Services*. Oxford, England: Pergamon Press, 1968.
These are the memoirs of Sir Robert Marett, who progressed from a war propagandist in the Ministry of Information (MOI), 1939-1945, to a full-time Cold War British diplomat, working mostly in the Foreign Office's publicity department. This is an insider's view of how the Central Office of Information (COI), postwar heir to the MOI, worked to put across Britain's point of view during the Cold War years. The author discusses in some depth such things as the Drogheda Report in 1954, which defined in clear detail both Britain's overseas propaganda and the COI's role as its principal postwar disseminater. No bibliography.

McCarthy: Death of a Witch Hunter. Dir. Emile de Antonio, 45 min., 1971. Chicago: International Historic Films.
Senator Joseph P. McCarthy became the symbol of anti-communist witch hunting during the early 1950s in the United States. In time it came to be understood that his motives were as much political as ideological. Even so, through his instigation of Senate subcommittee hearings into alleged communist infiltration of the United States government, "Joe" McCarthy conducted what amounted to an anti-communist propaganda war. This documentary looks at the man and his motives through such film footage as the famous "Army/McCarthy" hearings televised in the spring of 1954.

Michie, Allan A. *Voices Through the Iron Curtain: The Radio Free Europe Story*. New York: Dodd, Mead, 1963.
The author was Deputy European Director for Radio Free Europe (RFE) in the 1950s, and elected to write this book after he left his post,

convinced that the RFE story, which he describes as a "unique adventure in psychological warfare," is one that "deserved to be told and that it should be told against the ongoing developments of the cold war." This volume is a history of RFE operations in a Cold War context. It includes such chapters as "The Cold War Begins," "Sky Waves over the Iron Curtain," and "Music as Propaganda." There is no doubt where the author's sympathies lie. In one instance, he refers to "puncturing Communist lies," and in another he assures readers that "the Hungarian freedom fighters did not die in vain," a reference to the anti-Soviet uprising in Budapest in 1956. Illustrated with photographs of various barriers which at the time of writing divided Eastern and Western Europe, as well as RFE broadcast facilities, including its headquarters building in Munich. Select bibliography.

Morale for a Free World: America and Not America Only. Twenty-Second Year Book. Washington, D.C.: American Association of School Administrators, 1944.

This rather idealistic volume was created by the AASA's Commission on Education for Morale. Published a year before World War II ended, it looks ahead to the postwar period and lays out what public education in the United States must do to ensure a population both capable and determined to build a better life for humanity. What physical heroism achieved in the war, the commission notes, "must be matched by the moral heroism of informed and devoted citizens." The volume deals with such issues as problems of motivating citizens, the nature of morale in both groups and individuals, children as citizens, schools as morale builders, and many related topics. This is a guidebook for educators as propagandists who must sustain postwar morale and propagate democracy and other good causes. Select bibliography, a collection of official reports of the American Association of School Administrators, and a list of association members.

Nagorski, Zygmunt, Jr. "Soviet International Propaganda: Its Role, Effectiveness, and Future." *Annals of the American Academy of Political and Social Science* 398 (1971), pp. 130-139.

The author argues that as "a closed society has little to offer an open one," Soviet propaganda to the West is shot down even before it is delivered. There is altogether too much looking at the West through Marxist glasses, he claims, which produces poor propaganda results in the West. Even in the Third World, where the message is intervention in the internal affairs of the target country, the Soviet message loses its effect. The author, an anti-communist Polish exile from Kracow, sees little improvement in this situation for the future unless a complete change occurs in the Soviet system. However, he avers that the Soviet Union must achieve a deeper understanding of the West before that will happen.

Parry-Giles, Shawn J. "Propaganda, Effect, and the Cold War: Gauging the Status of America's 'War of Words.'" *Political Communication* 11, 2 (April-June 1994), pp. 203-213.

The author examines the relationship between propaganda, the effects of propaganda, and the Cold War in the context of congressional debates regarding the first Cold War propaganda programs launched by the United States. This is a case study which argues that for Congress, the "war of words" metaphor heightened the need for empirical evidence regarding how the United States was faring in the propaganda war. In particular, congressional critics required objective evidence that Voice of America, the particular program in question, had actually achieved what it was purported to have achieved. The result of such enquiry was development of a communications research paradigm that rejected anecdotal evidence. The paradigm became institutionalized, the author concludes, owing to the longevity of the Cold War.

Pirsein, Robert William. *The Voice of America: A History of the International Broadcasting Activities of the United States Government, 1940-1962.* New York: Arno Press, 1979.

This volume is a Northwestern University Ph.D. thesis from 1970. It is, as the title says, a history of Voice of America (VOA) as a propaganda broadcasting system. It covers every aspect of VOA operations during World War II and the most intense period of the Cold War, including descriptions of internal and external arguments over the effectiveness of these operations. Fifteen appendixes include such items as executive orders relating to oversees broadcasting and the setup of United States propaganda organizations, various VOA scripts, and relations between the United States military and propaganda broadcasters. Select bibliography.

Post War Hopes, Cold War Fears. Prod. Public Broadcasting Service, 55 min., 1984. Alexandria, Va.: PBS Video.

Part of Bill Moyers' *Walk Through the 20th Century* series. Moyers explores the issues of conformity and the Cold War fears that dominated the United States during the period after World War II, looking at how Americans, economically well off and optimistic, evolved into being fearful and distrustful of anyone who was "different." This film documents the hysteria of censorship and blacklisting that accompanied the McCarthy era, when artists, university professors, filmmakers, and other intellectuals were blacklisted, ostracized, and suppressed. Moyers makes the point that anti-communist propaganda was "mass merchandized" in this period. See *McCarthy: Death of a Witch Hunter* (entry above).

Skinner, James M. "Cliché and Convention in Hollywood's Cold War Anti-Communist Films." *North Dakota Quarterly* 46, 3 (Summer 1978), pp. 35-40.
Brief but illuminating, this article surveys Hollywood Cold War propaganda feature films in the context of the "communist under every bed" paranoia that had Hollywood as well as the rest of the country in its grip during the 1950s. In particular, the author identifies the characteristic clichés, most of which were developed in pre-World War II *film noir* and were applied after the war to a different kind of villain. Films discussed include *I Was a Communist for the FBI*, *The Red Danube*, *The Enemy Within*, and *Crime of the Century*. The author argues that as Hollywood had been the great wartime disseminater of anti-Nazi propaganda, it felt obligated after the war to take on the new enemy, communism.

Sorensen, Thomas C. *The Word War: The Story of American Propaganda*. New York: Harper and Row, 1968.
This history of American propaganda begins with World War I and continues through to the time of writing. The aim throughout is to demonstrate how the United States learned to use propaganda in the context of foreign policy after 1945. The underlying theme is American propaganda and the Cold War, with particular emphasis on the post-1945 role of the United States Information Agency. A foreword by then Senator Robert F. Kennedy underscores that emphasis. Written in a style more journalistic than historical, the volume nevertheless sheds valuable light on the United States' side in Cold War propaganda. The select bibliography of secondary material is supplemented by chapter endnotes which include references to primary sources.

Taylor, Philip M. "Power, Propaganda and Public Opinion: The British Information Services and the Cold War, 1945-57," in Ennio Di Nolfo, ed., *Power in Europe?* Vol.2, *Great Britain, France, Germany and Italy and the Origins of the EEC, 1952-1957*. New York: Walter de Gruyter, 1992.
"The Cold War provided Britain with a formidable propaganda challenge," the author begins. He goes on to explain how and why that was the case. Part of the issue was whether what Britain disseminated

actually was propaganda, as everyone else thought, or merely "self-advertisement," which was what the British preferred to call it. There was a further question as to whether the British should be doing even that. The author argues that it was a mistake when the postwar British government decided to cut back on funding for the Central Office of Information (which, amusingly enough, was established on April Fool's Day). In the event, British postwar information services in that crucial first decade of the Cold War failed to achieve much, and that was because they operated without adequate consideration for the practical problems of creating as well as disseminating propaganda. That failure was owing to shortage of funds, but also to not building on the lessons learned in World War II.

Wagnleitner, Reinhold. *Coca-Colonization and the Cold War: The Cultural Mission of the United States in Austria After the Second World War*. Translated by Diana M. Wolf. Chapel Hill: University of North Carolina Press, 1994.
   The author is an Austrian whose childhood occurred during that period when the United States Army occupied the region of Austria where he lived. In his words, "We children religiously waited for the best action of the year: the annual U.S. Army maneuvers and our rations of chewing gum." His purpose in this volume is to examine the concept of cultural imperialism, or cultural hegemony, and its impact on postwar Austria. He looks at the role of Radio Free Europe and the Coca-Cola Corporation in bringing this "cultural imperialism" to pass, and assesses the extent to which American propaganda, whether subtle or direct, tried to sell its audiences on the idea that everything American was "equal if not superior to European 'high culture'." He argues that such propaganda was not successful. This volume is in part autobiographical and covers such topics relative to Austria as United States cultural foreign policy, radio politics, United States information centers and their publications, the propagation of English, the influence of Hollywood, and, lastly, "the children of Schmal(t)z and Coca-Cola." Illustrations and extensive bibliography.

Whitton, John Boardman, ed. *Propaganda and the Cold War*. Washington, D.C.: Public Affairs Press, 1963.
   This collection of thirteen essays came out of a Princeton University symposium on the Cold War. They are by scholars and other experts on subjects relevant to Cold War propaganda, among them being Allen Dulles, Central Intelligence Agency director from 1953 to 1961, George Gallup, director of the American Institute of Public Opinion, and Robert

Holt, a political scientist at the University of Minnesota who had written on aspects of psychological manipulation and foreign policy. The editor's introduction makes the point that "'political communication'—a refined term for propaganda—is a major factor in the Cold War," and the contributors take it from there. The authors address such topics as Soviet political warfare, Radio Free Europe, Radio Liberty, and how political communication can be improved. Select bibliography.

Channels and Techniques

Are We Winning, Mommy? America and the Cold War. Prod. and dir. Barbara Margolis, Cinema Guild, 87 min., 1987. Seattle: University of Washington.
Have the media in the United States orchestrated Cold War anti-communism over the years? Such is the question raised in this film. It is answered in the affirmative. The film was written by L. S. Block and John Crowley, and narrated by Anne Jackson. It comprises television news film clips and presents the case that the media controlled and encouraged the development of anti-communist feelings in the United States before and after World War II.

Artyomov, Vladimir, and Vladimir Semyonov. "The BBC: History, Apparatus, Methods of Radio Propaganda." *Historical Journal of Film, Radio and Television* 4, 1 (1984), pp. 73-89.
The author of this article is not listed. The names above are the authors of the book of which the article is an analysis. The title here is the English translation of the title of the book, originally written in Russian and published in the Soviet Union. The anonymous author of the article indicates that the book was "the first monograph on the BBC ever to be published in Russia," and has as its main purpose to show up the BBC as a "biased, unreliable source of information." The main point of the article is that the book was Soviet propaganda masquerading as counterpropaganda.

The Atomic Cafe. Prod. and dir. Kevin Rafferty, Jayne Loader, Pierce Rafferty, Thorn/EMI, 92 min., 1982. Buffalo, N.Y.: Buffalo State College.
This film is a chilling though sometimes amusing compilation of newsreels and United States government propaganda films from the 1940s and 1950s which promoted atomic weapons. Anti-communist paranoia is featured as well. Materials include musical numbers, military training films, and a piece called "Duck and Cover," in which a

cartoon turtle shows schoolchildren how to hide under their desks in the event of a nuclear attack.

Benn, David Wedgewood. "Soviet Propaganda: The Theory and the Practice." *World Today* 41, 4 (April 1985), pp. 112-115.
Brief but instructive, this essay argues that even Soviet propaganda has rarely been as effective as Soviet governments would like to believe. With that premise in mind, the author describes how Soviet propaganda was originally organized, its reliance upon ideology rather than social science (an interest in the psychology of propaganda was "ruthlessly suppressed" under Stalin), and the widening gap between what Soviet propagandists expect to accomplish and what actually is accomplished. The author concludes that an inclination for independent thinking among Soviet citizens is a reality, but warns that this does not necessarily mean that they oppose the Soviet regime.

Bittman, Ladislav. *The KGB and Soviet Disinformation: An Insider's View*. Washington, D.C.: Pergamon-Brassey's, 1985.
This retrospective from a Czech defector, who had worked in Czech intelligence and security, provides an "insider's view," as the title says, of how the disinformation aspect of Soviet propaganda operated. He is also author of *The Deception Game* (1972), which was a description of his own contributions to disinformation. The purpose of the present volume is to "describe disinformation methods and techniques used by the Soviet bloc, and to assess the impact of those operations against the United States in the last decade." The author focuses specifically on "how Communist nations misuse democratic communication systems." While hardly an objective treatment, this explanation of the disinformation aspect of Cold War propaganda battles is made by an insider, and that makes it primary material in the study of Cold War propaganda techniques. The book concludes with a warning that in its own interests, the United States must learn from KGB techniques. This is ironic, since the volume was published just when *perestroika* and *glasnost* were beginning the process of bringing down the Soviet Union. Select bibliography.

_____, ed. *The New Image-Makers: Soviet Propaganda and Disinformation Today*. Washington, D.C.: Pergamon-Brassey's, 1988.
There are eleven essays in this volume, including the editor's introduction. Writing in the 1980s, the contributors clearly did not believe that the Cold War was over, at least not so far as its propaganda element was concerned. They wrote on such topics as Soviet propaganda and disinformation under Gorbachev, disinformation versus public inter-

est, Radio Moscow's North American propaganda service, Soviet propaganda literature distributed in the United States under the label of social science, the KGB and mass media, and Soviet manipulation of "religious circles." Bibliography in endnotes.

Boyd, Douglas A. "Broadcasting Between the Two Germanies." *Journalism Quarterly* 60 (Summer 1983), pp. 232-239.
The author notes that as East and West Germany speak the same language, both sides of the dividing line listen to broadcasts from the other side. He describes broadcasting organization in both East and West Germany, and some of the broadcast content—noting that West German broadcasting plays down the idea that its material might contain propaganda. East German broadcasting, on the other hand, makes no such pretense. Rivalry between East and West is discussed as being a major part of broadcasting between these two Germanies.

Bright Days of Tomorrow (1945-1956). Prod. DNA "Poland" Ltd. with WNET/New York and Norddeutsche Rundfunk/Hamburg, narr. Roger Mudd, 60 min., 1988. Laramie: University of Wyoming.
This film is part 6 of *The Struggle for Poland* series. It draws upon archival newsreels, photographs, interviews, and readings to document how the Polish Workers party (communist) used propaganda, election fraud, and terror to gain power after World War II. It is significant that this film was produced during the period when the Solidarity Movement, led by Lech Walesa, was in the process of overthrowing the Polish Communist party.

Cantril, Hadley. *Soviet Leaders and Mastery Over Man.* New Brunswick, N.J.: Rutgers University Press, 1960.
Propaganda is one of several themes in this volume. The general purpose is to explain the relationship between Soviet ideology and the shaping of Soviet citizens to fit within it. In this volume, that shaping is generally termed mind manipulation, which occurs as the result of propaganda dissemination. The author's concern is that Soviet manipulation of Soviet citizens is aimed at imposing a view of humanity that contradicts the Western view of humanity, and that if the West assumes that its view of humanity is entirely right and that of the Soviet Union is entirely wrong, the West may be, with regard to the future of democracy, "very shortsighted indeed." Bibliography in endnotes.

Catlin, George. "Propaganda and the Cold War." *Yale Review* 43, 1 (September 1953), pp. 103-116.
The author speculates on whether the arguments between journalists and politicians over the deployment of Cold War propaganda should favor

the journalists (anti-propaganda) or the politicians (pro-propaganda). He agrees that bad propaganda does no good. Good propaganda, on the other hand, might be useful, and in any case, as it seems that the Soviet Union is not cutting back on its propaganda, "do we dare *not* to have a propaganda program?" The second half of the article suggests criteria that need to be taken into account in constructing a good national propaganda program for the Cold War.

Class Warriors. Prod. Vestron Video, 54 min., 1992. Stamford, Conn.: Vestron Video.
Originally produced for television in 1990 with Robert Conquest and Sin Phillips, this documentary claims that communism continues to draw the attention and praise of people around the world because of the rhetoric produced years before by Joseph Stalin. The film charges that Stalin's call for rights and contributions of all workers belies the reality of his brutal, ruthless, and terror-driven regime in the Soviet Union. It is not entirely clear which is the strongest element in the film, the provision of documentary information or the dissemination of anti-communist propaganda.

Communist Accent on Youth. Prod. Pepperdine College, 30 min., 1961. Columbia: University of Missouri.
Young people are presented here as being the primary target of communist agitation and propaganda. The film examines the way in which communist propaganda appeals to youthful idealism, and argues that the purpose of that appeal is to serve communist objectives.

Communist Target: Youth. 31 min., 1962. Washington, D.C.: National Audio-Visual Center.
Various communist movements' persuasion techniques and methods to indoctrinate young people are examined in this documentary. The message here is that communism must be discredited. This makes the film propaganda in its own right, even though its avowed aim is to explain communist propaganda techniques. The message is aimed at a general audience. See *Communist Accent on Youth* (entry above).

Culbert, David. "*Reds:* Propaganda, Docudrama and Hollywood." *Labor History* 24, 1 (Winter 1983), pp. 125-130.
This is a review essay on the film *Reds*, which, broadly speaking, is a film version of John Reed's personal history of the Bolshevik Revolution: *Ten Days That Shook the World*. The reviewer notes that some critics castigated the film as pro-communist propaganda. He argues that it is the opposite, that it is actually anti-communist propa-

ganda in that it attacks communist ideology. The author dissects various scenes in the film to make this and other points about the film's purpose.

Dyer, Murray. *The Weapon on the Wall: Rethinking Psychological Warfare*. Baltimore: Johns Hopkins University Press, 1959.
Written by a veteran of the Office of War Information in World War II, this volume argues that in the Cold War era, propaganda remains a necessary weapon in the arsenal of democracy; however, he would prefer it be renamed "political communication." The author questions "propaganda" or "psychological warfare," terms that he uses interchangeably, as being destructive terminology for political persuasion because both suggest a nation at war. He argues that it would be preferable to accept the *principle* of propaganda as a viable peacetime concept, but to rename it "political communication." No bibliography.

Ebon, Martin. *The Soviet Propaganda Machine*. New York: McGraw-Hill, 1987.
The point here is to warn Western analysts against yielding to the temptation to overstate and overrate changes taking place within the Soviet system in response to *perestroika* and *glasnost*. The author makes this point through an examination of the nature and application of Soviet propaganda. "The struggle for that elusive element, 'world opinion,' is constant and complex," he writes, and argues that while this volume deals only with the Soviet part of it, that part is of paramount importance to the West, even as it is to other parts of the globe. The thirty-two chapters are grouped under four general sections: "Agitprop in Action," "Overt and Covert," "Men and Media," and "Tactics in Transition." Among other topics, specific chapters touch upon *Pravda*, UNESCO, disinformation, the KAL 007 affair, and how Soviet propaganda dealt with the Chernobyl disaster. Appendices include examples of propaganda. Select bibliography.

Emery, Walter B. *National and International Systems of Broadcasting: Their History, Operation, and Control*. East Lansing: Michigan State University Press, 1969.
This enormous volume (more than 700 pages) provides a complete analysis of important broadcasting systems around the world, with particular emphasis on their programming models and how they reflect their national interests. The inspiration for this study lay to some extent in the way international broadcasting was used as a propaganda channel in the Cold War. "Much international radio remains belligerent and

propagandistic," the author notes at the outset, but he goes on to suggest that even so, there are signs of improvement and turning the medium into a positive channel for communication, rather than one mainly devoted to propaganda. Extensive bibliography.

Fable Safe. Prod. Sumner Glimcher, dir. Eric Barnouw, Columbia University Center for Mass Communications, 9 min., 1971. New York: Museum of Modern Art, non-circulating.
This animated film satirizes military rhetoric and the escalation of the Cold War arms race. Birdlike generals, fat atomic bombs, and missiles resembling sharks were created by political cartoonist John Osborn to illustrate the film. The narration claims that the acronyms and propaganda of military strategy are all based on paranoia.

Gordon, Joseph S., ed. *Psychological Operations: The Soviet Challenge.* Boulder, Colo.: Westview Press, 1988.
A collection of eleven essays, this volume evolved out of a panel at the International Studies Association meeting in 1983, which focused on propaganda as used by the Soviet Union and its allies as an instrument of foreign policy. The editor's introduction sets the stage by describing debates in the United States over how, or whether, to use "Psyop" (psychological operations) as a foreign policy instrument in response to Soviet propaganda. It also provides an overview of the other essays. Topics addressed in those essays include Soviet strategic propaganda forces, Soviet Third World propaganda, Soviet-sponsored clandestine radio, military Psyop and United States strategy, and public diplomacy and United States foreign policy. Bibliography is contained in endnotes. See Marian Kirsch Leighton, *Soviet Propaganda as a Foreign Policy Tool* (entry below).

Havighurst, Clark C., ed. *International Control of Propaganda.* Dobbs Ferry, N.Y.: Oceana, 1967.
Inspired by the propaganda battles of the Cold War, this collection of essays examines the issue of whether international propaganda dissemination carries with it inherent dangers, and how such propaganda can be controlled through international law. The question of control has serious implications for international communications at all levels, and while the contributors favor some degree of control, they disagree with one another on how much, and whether, propaganda control interferes with the rights of individual countries. These essays were originally presented as papers at a conference organized by the International Law Society of Duke University. No bibliography.

Houn, Franklyn W. *To Change a Nation: Propaganda and Indoctrination in Communist China*. New York: Free Press of Glencoe, 1959.
The author contends that it is not his intention to attack or apologize for Chinese communist propaganda policy, but simply to describe it. He does so in great detail, making clear that political and social indoctrination is not unique to China. At the same time, he makes it clear that in China, the indoctrination is totalitarian in nature. Written at the height of the Cold War, this book makes references that leave no doubt as to where the author's sympathies lie. In the introduction, for example, he indicates that Chinese communist propaganda is a weapon employed in a "race against time." The communists "must win the hearts of a substantial number of the Chinese before they outstay their welcome." The principal and largely self-explanatory chapter titles include: "Party, State, and Nation," "Schools, Scholars, and Propagandists," "The Printed Word and the Dogma," "One Mind and Many Tongues," and "Stage, Screen, and the Message." Bibliography is in endnotes, and there is an index of Chinese journals and newspapers.

Inkeles, Alex. "The Soviet Attack on the Voice of America." *American Slavic and East European Review* 12, 3 (October 1953), pp. 319-342.
The point of this article is to construct an analytical model for evaluating Soviet broadcast propaganda. The author analyzes the Soviet response to Voice of America (VOI) propaganda broadcasts between 1949 and 1951. The author suggests that by examining the contents of these responses, it is possible to establish patterns of Soviet response, thus gaining further insight into Soviet communist policy and learning more about the nature of international propaganda warfare. Among his conclusions based on analysis of Soviet propaganda materials is that Soviet propaganda appears to concentrate on developing negative counterimages of the United States, rather than on correcting the negative images of the Soviet Union projected by VOA broadcasts.

Janowitz, Morris. "Mass Persuasion and International Relations." *Public Opinion Quarterly* 25, 4 (Winter 1961), pp. 560-570.
This is a review essay in which the author looks at three studies of Soviet and American Cold War psychological operations. His point, in addition to criticism of the books in question, is to comment on the role played by mass persuasion in the age of the nuclear arms race. He also offers commentary on ways in which the United States might improve its foreign-policy image relative to the Soviet Union through more creative and organized deployment of psychological operations—which is to say through propaganda.

Kaplan, Frank L. "The Communist International's Press Control From Moscow." *Journalism Quarterly* 48 (Summer 1971), pp. 315-325.
The author examines Soviet international press propaganda, and concludes that it is highly centralized, well disciplined, and controlling. He describes how foreign communist newspapers such as the Parisian paper *L'Humanité* and in New York *The Daily Worker* were conditioned to respond like Pavlov's dogs to Moscow press direction. The tone of the article is pointedly anti-communist, and the purpose appears to be a warning not to believe that any communist press is ever independent of Moscow.

Kecskemeti, Paul. "The Soviet Approach to International Political Communication." *Public Opinion Quarterly* 20, 1 (Spring 1956), pp. 299-308.
This short article describes the operating principles behind Soviet external mass propaganda, assessing in the process its strengths and weaknesses. The author concludes that with regard to external audiences, the Soviet propagandists seek to instil Marxist ideology only *after* they have brought the people into their sphere of authority and control. He argues that this being the case, it would be the wrong strategy for the West to develop an ideological propaganda as cogent as Marxist propaganda. Instead, the West needs to develop some other strategy for countering Soviet influence. In other words, do not try to fight fire with fire.

Kominsky, Morris. *The Hoaxers: Plain Liars, Fancy Liars, and Damned Liars*. Boston: Branden Press, 1970.
The premise of this book is that the untruths and propaganda lies associated with the Cold War are leading the United States toward fascism and World War III. The author contends that his purpose here is neither to defend nor to attack communism, but rather to expose "the most commonly circulated falsehoods, which are used to create confusion, hysteria, frustration, and apathy." He presents dozens of examples of published falsehoods with analysis of how they are false, organized under such headings as "Poisoning the Minds of the People," "Anti-Semitic Liars," "Racist Liars and Myth-Makers," "Anti-Soviet Liars," "The Red Scare," "Alice in Birchland" (a reference to the John Birch Society), and "The Stalin Fabrication," among others. No bibliography.

Kriesberg, Martin. "Cross-Pressures and Attitudes: A Study of the Influence of Conflicting Propaganda on Opinion Regarding American-Soviet Relations." *Public Opinion Quarterly* 13, 1 (Spring 1949), pp. 5-16.
The author analyzes opinion regarding United States policy toward the Soviet Union as held by trade union members who are exposed to both

communist and Roman Catholic influences. The point is to assess the impact of "cross pressures" on opinion. The study concludes that a majority of the workers were not always aware of the conflicting propaganda (communist and Catholic) to which they were exposed; some who were aware tended to hold confused or conflicting opinions. This article is principally directed toward suggesting research methodologies for studying mass opinion formation.

Kruglak, Theodore E. *The Two Faces of TASS*. Minneapolis: University of Minnesota Press, 1962.
The author examines in depth the nature and work of TASS, the Telegraphic Agency of the Soviet Union, and argues that contrary to popular belief, it is a communication system that can be trusted. This book attempts to counter such charges as that TASS is the "official liar for the Soviet Government" or that TASS is a "recruiting agency for espionage agents." What follows is a history of TASS, an analysis of its relationship with the Soviet government, and the extent to which, trustworthy though it may be as a source of Soviet news, TASS also blurs the line of demarcation between journalism and propaganda— which sounds a little like "damning with faint praise." Bibliography in endnotes.

Leighton, Marian Kirsch. *Soviet Propaganda as a Foreign Policy Tool*. New York: Freedom House, 1991.
There is no doubt where this author stands on the Soviet Union. Her opening line reads: "The manipulation of Western public opinion through propaganda is one of the great success stories of Soviet foreign policy." This short volume provides an analysis of that propaganda, discussing along the way the concept of disinformation and offering the hypothesis that Mikhail Gorbachev is the most polished propagandist of them all. Major topics include Soviet propaganda as a tool of "perceptions management," propaganda in Soviet political culture, the Soviet propaganda "battle order," Soviet propaganda systems and channels, major Soviet propaganda themes, propaganda style and substance under Gorbachev, and countering Soviet propaganda. Bibliography is included in the endnotes.

Lendvai, Paul. *The Bureaucracy of Truth: How Communist Governments Manage the News*. London: Burnett Books, 1981.
Inspired by controversy over international news broadcasting associated with the Universal Declaration of Human Rights that were part of the Helsinki Accords of 1974, this volume addresses the question of

"who decides what is communicated in countries where the print and broadcast media are state-owned and treated as 'the sharpest weapon' of the ruling communist parties in the battle for the minds of the people?" The author was a journalist in Hungary from 1948 to 1956, a self-educated student of communism, and a regular visitor to Soviet bloc countries. Part 1 of the book deals with the structure, function, and control of communist mass media, part 2 examines problems connected with broadcasting to Eastern Europe, and part 3 concerns the significance, consequences, and record of implementation of the Helsinki Accords. "Bibliographical notes" rather than a bibliography.

Lodeesen, Jon. "Radio Liberty (Munich): Foundations for a History." *Historical Journal of Film, Radio and Television* 6, 2 (1986), pp. 197-210. Radio Liberty began as a propaganda adjunct of the Central Intelligence Agency (CIA), but in the 1970s left the CIA to become associated with Radio Free Europe. This article is an introduction to the history of this Cold War propaganda channel. It provides background on the founding and development of Radio Liberty, notes difficulties in maintaining it, discusses the kinds of programs associated with the network, and contains a limited bibliography of largely secondary sources. Written by a former Radio Liberty broadcaster, the piece is seriously lacking in objectivity. At the same time, it does provide illuminating background to an important aspect of Cold War radio propaganda.

Markham, James W. *Voices of the Red Giants: Communications in Russia and China*. Ames: Iowa State University Press, 1967. This volume concerns Russian and Chinese mass communications other than films in the Cold War period. Its purpose is to explain how mass communications systems in "the two largest Communist countries" behave and function and to compare that behavior and function with their Western counterparts. The subject matter is partly historical, partly contemporary, and throughout predicated upon theoretical models. Numerous examples of communications channels are cited, so that the reader has a useful introduction to both the number and variety of communications functions within these countries. Extensive bibliography.

Milenkovitch, Michael M. *The View from Red Square: A Critique of Cartoons from Pravda and Izvestia, 1947-1964*. New York: Hobbs, Dorman, 1966. The purpose of this volume is to "enhance our understanding of Soviet propaganda techniques" in the Cold War by looking at one specific aspect: the political cartoon. This volume contains 120 cartoons taken from the pages of the two leading Soviet newspapers, *Pravda* and *Izvestia*, over a seventeen-year period. A text accompanies the cartoons which explains how they conveyed a particular image of the outside world to Soviet citizens. The author contends that the cartoon is one of the most valuable sources for understanding propaganda imagery, because its combination of visual and written message has an impact that is clear and instantaneous. Part 1 contains observations on the theory, organization, and makeup of Soviet newspapers. In parts 2 and 3, the cartoons themselves are examined as to content, purpose, and the extent to which they mirror the evolution of Soviet foreign policy. Limited bibliography.

Moss, Armand. *Disinformation, Misinformation, and the "Conspiracy" to Kill JFK Exposed.* Hamden, Conn.: Archon Books, 1987.
This volume examines the Warren Commission investigation into the assassination of J. F. Kennedy, with an eye toward explaining how the Soviet Union's disinformation process was the primary means through which reactions to the assassination were shaped in Europe and the United States. The author contends that it worked like this: the Soviet KGB (the mastermind), drawing in a wide variety of "fellow-travellers" in the process—Pierre-Charles Pathé, a pro-communist Frenchman, is named as one example—spread it around that the Warren Commission "did not give the real story" concerning the assassination. This author argues that the commission did give the real story and that "not a line has to be changed in the *Warren Report* with respect to the essential facts." Apparently, Oliver Stone accepted the KGB version, if his film *JFK* (Warner Brothers, 1991) is any indication. Bibliography in endnotes.

No Place to Hide. Prod. and dir. Tom Johnson and Lance Bird, 29 min., 1982. Los Angeles: Direct Cinema.
A retrospective on how Americans were indoctrinated during the Cold War to believe that fallout shelters assured survival in the event of a nuclear attack. Martin Sheen's narration re-creates the nightmares of children growing up in the Cold War era.

Orwant, Jack E. "Effects of Derogatory Attacks in Soviet Arms Control Propaganda." *Journalism Quarterly* 49 (Spring 1972), pp. 107-115.
A highly technical article that draws upon the research of such behavioral psychologists as C. I. Hovland to demonstrate how Soviet-disseminated derogatory propaganda against the United States in connection with arms control negotiations affected the attitude of its recipients, whether they were Soviet citizens or other. The conclusion

is that when Soviet arms control propaganda contained derogatory material relating to American institutions and leaders, it was more effective than when such material was lacking.

Perpetual Revolution. Prod. ABC News, Xerox Films, 11 min., 1973. Urbana: University of Illinois.

A documentary which shows how the people of China are indoctrinated with the "Thoughts of Chairman Mao" in order to ensure that they will carry on, *en masse,* his ideas when he is gone. A feature of the film is the May 7 Schools, which provide manual training for all work cadres and the Red Guard and which comprise high school students and Little Red Guards (a Chinese version of the Soviet Young Pioneers). This documentary is the edited version of another film, *The People of the People's Republic of China.*

Roxburgh, Angus. *Pravda: Inside the Soviet News Machine.* New York: George Braziller, 1987.

"All Soviet newspapers, as well as television and radio, see themselves as arms of the Communist Party," the author writes. "For them, 'propaganda' is not a dirty word." However, in this analysis of *Pravda,* the author argues that not all which appears in that newspaper is propaganda. He maintains that sometimes it is even critical of Soviet life. Part 1 of the book describes the background of *Pravda,* looking at the various roles it has played over the years, its place in the overall news media system, how *Pravda* is planned and produced, and what kinds of news it does and does not contain. This part also examines *Pravda* readership. Part 2 contains selections from *Pravda* on both domestic and foreign affairs. Appendixes include tables showing various types of *Pravda* news coverage, *Pravda* circulation figures, and a list of its editors. Illustrations; bibliography in endnotes.

Short, K. R. M., ed. *Western Broadcasting Over the Iron Curtain.* London: Croom Helm, 1986.

These essays came out of a 1984 conference held at the Freedoms Foundation at Valley Forge, Pennsylvania organized, by *The Historical Journal of Film, Radio and Television,* which is published at Leeds University in England. The subject is Cold War broadcasting, and the presenters include historians, broadcast experts, and broadcasters. The central theme is broadcasting as propaganda, supplemented by assessments of how, and if, it affects its audiences in the ways desired. Soviet censorship of Western journalists is also a consideration in many of the papers, all of which include bibliography in endnotes.

Shultz, Richard H., and Roy Godson. *Dezinformatsia: Active Measures in Soviet Strategy*. Washington, D.C.: Pergamon-Brassey's, 1984.

This volume provides a succinct but illuminating analysis of the techniques of Soviet overt and clandestine propaganda directed at the West, and in particular at the United States. A preface by philosopher Sidney Hook advises that "its perusal is bound to awaken the political sleepwalkers of the Western world." The authors define the Soviet Union's view of its relationship with the non-communist world as being that the Soviet Union is engaged in a constant struggle with non-communists. From that premise they develop their analysis of Soviet propaganda techniques, which are explained as being a key element in that struggle. The book is divided into three major themes: Soviet perspectives and strategy, Soviet overt propaganda themes, and Soviet covert political techniques. It concludes with descriptions of interviews with former Soviet bloc intelligence officers, who confirm the authors' analysis. Bibliography in endnotes and glossary of terms.

Sorrels, Charles A. *Soviet Propaganda Campaign Against NATO*. Washington, D.C.: United States Arms Control and Disarmament Agency, October 1983.

This pamphlet was put out by the United States government. Its purpose was to analyze the propaganda campaign conducted by the Soviet Union against the North Atlantic Treaty Organization (NATO) in 1980. At issue was NATO's decision to "respond" to the buildup of the Soviet SS-20 missile force which, NATO determined, posed a threat to Western Europe. The response was to modernize defensive capabilities and to undertake arms control negotiations with an eye toward eliminating or reducing intermediate-range nuclear forces on both sides. The pamphlet is organized on the premise that Soviet propaganda failed. It argues such points as that there was nothing new in this Soviet propaganda, which followed the time-honored tradition of intimidation. That is, it claimed that NATO's efforts to offset the Soviet buildup constituted a provocative act "which would cause further Soviet actions unfavorable to the West." The pamphlet is illustrated with several charts comparing the numbers of NATO and Warsaw Pact missiles. An appendix contains some documentation of Soviet propaganda. Source references in endnotes.

Wettig, Gerhard. *Broadcasting and Détente: Eastern Policies and Their Implications for East-West Relations*. London: C. Hurst, 1977.

This volume describes the situation in the mid-1970s regarding Western radio broadcasting into Eastern Bloc countries. The purpose is to warn Westerners that the unfolding of détente will not soften the rigor with which communist countries limit the flow of information from the West to the East. The author contends that a change in those policies is likely only when the regimes of such countries cease their "perverse official manipulation of the media and of the news which they transmit." This short volume is well documented from sources on both sides of the Iron Curtain, and there is a useful appendix that provides basic information about radio stations operating out of West Germany, such as Deutsche Welle, Deutschlandfunk, Radio Free Europe, and Radio Liberty. Select bibliography.

White, Ralph K. "Hitler, Roosevelt, and the Nature of War Propaganda." *Journal of Abnormal and Social Psychology* 44, 2 (April 1949), pp. 157-174.
The author applies "value-analysis technique" to the content of Hitler's prewar propaganda speeches and compares the results to a comparable sampling of Franklin D. Roosevelt's speeches. He concludes that the similarities between these speeches were qualities of "successful propaganda in general rather than a distinctive characteristic of 'propaganda for war.'" The object of this study was to distinguish between what is characteristically propaganda leading to war and that which is something other. The outcome of this research has, in the author's view, direct application to analysis of Cold War propaganda disseminated by the Soviet Union and the United States.

_____. "The New Resistance to International Propaganda." *Public Opinion Quarterly* 16, 1 (Spring 1952), pp. 539-551.
This article includes several interconnected points. One is the fact that communications directed at friends and allies abroad face the practical difficulty of being rejected out of hand because they are propaganda. Another is the semantics of communication, including the semantics of the word "propaganda" itself and its connotations in the context of the Cold War. Still another is Soviet propaganda, which the author critiques in the context of semantic usages. He concludes by offering suggestions as to how the difficulty presented by semantics can be minimized with reference to international communications and argues that it is essential to do so if every international communication is not to be discounted as propaganda.

Whitfield, Stephen J. *The Culture of the Cold War*. Baltimore: Johns Hopkins University Press, 1991.
Drawing upon literature, films, art, and the print and broadcast media, this volume examines how Cold War anti-communism in the United

States hammered at the "enemy within, working to subvert the American Way of Life." The result was a cultural assault that "unleashed a fear and loathing that weakened and even subdued traditional commitments to an open society and the Rule of Law." The author looks at the McCarthy era, with its Hollywood witch hunts, the evolution of the concept of "Americanism," and above all, at the impact of Cold War hysteria on film and television. A bibliographical essay both lists and describes a wide variety of books related to the author's subject.

Yu, Frederick T. C. *Mass Persuasion in Communist China*. New York: Frederick A. Praeger, 1964.
The author, a professor of journalism in the United States, claims to neither praise nor condemn, but to describe and analyze mass persuasion in communist China through a study of Chinese communist publications. His thesis is that mass persuasion in communist China "is a startlingly new phenomenon, new both to China and to world Communism." He suggests that the techniques are borrowed from the Soviet Union, and go beyond what Marxist dogma would indicate. Like Franklyn Houn's *To Change a Nation* (entry above), this volume was a product of rising concern in the West regarding what communist China represented for the future of Asia. The author ends on a positive note, writing that it is encouraging to find that after decades of propaganda and isolation, the Soviet Union has not captured the minds of all Soviet citizens, for "the mind of man has a strange way of resisting oppression, and it is not likely that this characteristic will cease to exist altogether." Presumably, that conclusion applied to China as well. Bibliography is in endnotes.

Propaganda Material

Anarchy, U.S.A. Prod. Independent, 78 min., 1966. Sandy Hook, Conn.: Videoyesteryear.
This film attacks the Civil Rights Movement of the 1960s as part of a communist conspiracy orchestrated by the Soviet Union, the objective of which was world conquest. The paranoia which drives this film is very close to the surface.

Atomic Attack. 50 min., 1950. Chicago: International Historic Films.
Walter Matthau stars in this docudrama of what happens to a suburban New York family when New York City suffers a nuclear attack. The film is in part a response to the fact that the Soviet Union had recently

announced its first successful nuclear weapons tests, which meant that
the possibility of nuclear war had to be faced. The objective of the film
is to make perfectly clear just how horrible such a war would be.

The Bedford Incident. Dir. James B. Harris, Columbia, 102 min., 1965.
Burbank, Calif.: RCA Columbia.
The obsessive captain of a United States submarine chaser operating
in the North Atlantic encounters an unidentified submarine. He gives
chase, driving his crew to the point of exhaustion. A journalist questions the captain's motives and procedures, and a conflict develops
between them regarding the lengths to which the captain may go in
forcing the submarine to identify itself. When it will not identify itself,
the captain orders an attack, and three depth charges are fired. Even as
they leave the subchaser, the submarine responds by firing torpedoes.
The film ends with both vessels being obliterated in a nuclear explosion, making clear the dangers inherent in Cold War confrontations
between Soviet and American ships, and the near paranoia that was
possible in the mental makeup of those who had to decide on the proper
course of action in such confrontations.

Big Jim McLain. Prod. Robert Fellows, dir. Edward Ludwig, Warner
Brothers, 90 min., 1952. Chicago: Facets Video.
The film opens in documentary style with a quote from Stephen
Vincent Bénet's poem about Daniel Webster, which begins "Neighbor,
how stands the Union?" From that opening follows a tribute to the
efforts of the House Committee on Un-American Activities (HUAC),
"undaunted by the vicious slander launched against them," to ferret out
subversive elements within the country, John Wayne as Big Jim
McLain is a HUAC investigator who uncovers a group of communist
conspirators and organizes the raid which brings them to justice. One
critic observed that this film offers the lesson that "the fist is mightier
than the brain."

Born American. Dir. Renny Harlin, Cinema Group, 95 min., 1986. Los
Angeles: Continental Video.
Three young Americans vacationing in Finland cross the border into
the Soviet Union as a lark. What follows is a nightmare for them, as
they are caught by Soviet border police, imprisoned, and mistreated.
One dies, one goes insane, and the other finally escapes. The Soviet
people are uniformly evil, save for one girl who befriends the lone
survivor, and even an Orthodox village priest commits a rape/murder
of a village girl. One of the most extreme anti-Soviet films to appear

in American cinema since the 1950s, which is ironic as it premiered on the eve of *glasnost* and *perestroika*. The young Americans are sufficiently arrogant and irreverent that one's sympathies tend to be with the Russians, at least initially. The film was banned in Finland.

Communism. Prod. United States Department of Defense, 29 min., 1950. Washington, D.C.: Library of Congress.
An official government information film which warns that communists operate in every country of the world through the movement's party organization, and, on a more dangerous level, through subversion. From this beginning, the film goes on to explain Communist party activities in the United States through examples of party literature. It also examines various scenes related to the incitement of workers against their employers by communist agitators.

Communism. Prod. United States Department of Defense, 11 min., 1952. Deerfield, Ill.: Coronet/MTI Film and Video.
This short "information" film sends a strong Cold War propaganda message. It asks, among other things, What is communism, how does it threaten our values and way of life, and why has it become such a force in the world? The point is made that a strong defense is the guarantee of peace in the world, as well as a deterrent against communist aggression.

Communism and Coexistence. Prod. Pepperdine College, 30 min., 1963. Columbia: University of Missouri.
This film analyzes developments within Russia between 1917 and 1960. It argues a relationship between internal events and shifts in Soviet foreign policy pursued by communist leaders in the Kremlin, the purpose of which is to consolidate and extend communist rule over large portions of the world. This is anti-communist propaganda in documentary form.

Communist Blueprint for Conquest. Prod. United States Army, 33 min., 1955. Washington, D.C.: National Audio-Visual Center.
The methods and techniques used by the Communist party to seize power in a given country are the subject of this film. After it has seized control of local and central governments, the party moves systematically against other political parties, land owners, businesses, and the middle class, and, by implication, propagandizes individuals into submitting to the absolute authority of the state. Meant to be an information documentary, this film uses classic propaganda techniques to send a strong anti-communist message.

Communist Imperialism. Prod. Pepperdine College, 30 min., 1961. Columbia: University of Missouri.

An anti-communist warning comes through the documentary format of this film. The subject is communist movements at work systematically to subjugate nations and territories. The film begins with an analysis of how the Soviet regime was established in Russia after 1917, and compares that process with the establishment of communist regimes in other countries later on.

Conspirator. Prod. Arthur Hornblower, Jr., dir. Victor Saville, Metro-Goldwyn-Mayer, 85 min., 1949. Atlanta: Turner Home Entertainment.

A British army officer is selling secrets to Russian agents. He does not like doing it, but on the other hand, he is ideologically committed. His wife discovers what he is doing and confronts him. He claims to be an idealist but in fact proves that, beneath it all, he really is a cold, heartless traitor who not only sells secrets to the enemy but traps helpless rabbits in steel snares. This is the real measure of his character. Cold War propaganda is distributed throughout the film in such scenes as a discussion which questions why a man becomes a traitor, another in which it is made clear that "one never questions the party," and another in which the traitor threatens to kill his wife if she does not cover for him. Of course, the war ministry knew about him all along and were using him to send false information to the Soviet Union. Simple justice prevails in the end when the traitor finally does the honorable thing and shoots himself.

Crusade for Freedom: Communist Propaganda vs. Free Europe. Prod. John Daly, Crusade for Freedom, 18 min., ca. 1952. Minneapolis: University of Minnesota.

This film depicts the Radio Free Europe Press fighting back against communist propaganda. It contrasts "evil" communist propaganda with the "truth" of democracy.

Cuba Si! Dir. Chris Marker, Films de la Pléiade, 58 min., 1961. Unable to locate copy.

This documentary tells the story of Cuba from the revolution to the debacle of the Bay of Pigs invasion in 1962. It is a celebration of the Revolution with a strongly Marxist flavor. The tone is anti-United States, pro-Castro, and decidedly propagandistic; sufficiently so that the French government banned the film until 1963.

Dies, Martin. *Martin Dies' Story.* New York: Bookmailer, 1963.

For seven years in the post-1945 period, Representative Martin Dies was chair of the House Committee on Un-American Activities, which, in the view of its critics, carried on an anti-communist witch hunt that blemished, if it did not destroy, the reputations of such prominent Hollywood figures as filmmaker Dalton Trumbo. This volume is Dies' response to the critics, in which he makes a case for the committee's work by arguing that communist infiltrators were present in force in the United States, and working to overthrow democracy. He charges as well that politicians in the United States played into their hands, and in fact abetted them, and that the result was successful disinformation which was costing the United States victory in the Cold War. Dies castigates American liberals as "fellow travelers" of communism and accuses them of everything from helping Castro gain control of Cuba to supporting communism and socialism around the globe. Needless to say, Senator Joseph P. McCarthy emerges in these pages as a knight in shining armor. No bibliography.

Dr. Strangelove: Or, How I Learned to Stop Worrying and Love the Bomb. Prod. and dir. Stanley Kubrick, RCA/Columbia Pictures, 93 min., 1963. Chicago: Facets Video.
This black comedy satirized the paranoia of anti-communism and of those who made national policy at the height of the Cold War. A crazed United States Air Force general is convinced that the communists are plotting to rob Americans of their "precious bodily fluids." He seals off the Strategic Air Command base which he commands, and orders bombers to attack the Soviet Union. However, the Russians have a Doomsday Device which will be triggered automatically if the Soviet Union is attacked, thus bringing about the end of the world. The film ends with numerous atomic blasts going off against the background of a popular love ballad. Characters include a former Nazi scientist, a Royal Air Force liaison officer, an indecisive United States president, and a mentally defective member of the Joint Chiefs of Staff. The film leaves no doubt as to its message.

Don't Be a Sucker. Prod. United States Army, 20 min., 1947. Washington, D.C.: National Audio-Visual Center.
This is an anti-communist propaganda film which uses an examination of German propaganda techniques from before World War II as an example of what to be on the lookout for during the Cold War. The film equates these techniques with those used by postwar rabblerousers in the United States, who are presented as pro-communist. The message is to be on guard against communist propagandists.

Escape from East Berlin. Prod. Walter Wood, dir. Robert Slodmak, Metro-Goldwyn-Mayer, 94 min., 1962. Atlanta: Turner Classic Movies; Washington, D.C.: Library of Congress.

A young East German, who is largely apolitical, finds a cause: circumventing the Berlin Wall, which had been erected between West Berlin and communist-controlled East Berlin. He abandons his self-indulgent habits in order to help his family escape, which they do by tunneling under the wall. The film was inspired by the fact that the wall was there, and by the fact that escaping from East to West had been a part of what might be termed "Cold War romance" since 1945. In this case, the wall complicates matters, and much of the film concerns the technical preparations for the escape. Most of the cast is German, save for the principal character, who is played by an American actor, Don Murray.

Face to Face with Communism. Prod. United States Air Force, 26 min., 1951. Chicago: International Historic Films.
A government docudrama in which a town in the United States is seized by communists. Their tactics of arresting and sentencing citizens are shown, as are the heroic actions of an Air Force sergeant in resisting the takeover.

Fail Safe. Prod. Max E. Youngstein, dir. Sidney Lumet, Columbia, 111 min., 1964. Chicago: Facets Video; Toronto, Ontario: Coliseum Video. This is virtually the same film as *Dr. Strangelove* (entry above), with exactly the same message, except that here the subject is treated with complete seriousness. Following a faulty transmission of orders, a squadron of Strategic Air Command bombers fly off to drop nuclear bombs on Moscow. They cannot be called back, once they have flown past the "fail safe" zone. The president orders fighter planes to try to shoot them down. The attempt fails, and all-out nuclear war seems inevitable. This version of feature film propaganda aimed at showing the danger of nuclear military thinking and anti-communist paranoia was never as popular—and therefore not as effective—as *Dr. Strangelove*.

The Girl in the Kremlin. Prod. Albert Zugsmith, dir. Russell Birdwell, Universal-International, approx. 90 min., 1957. Unable to locate copy. Stalin is still alive! The story is that Stalin had his double executed and then buried in the Kremlin wall. A plastic surgeon altered the real Stalin's appearance and he escaped to Greece to live in pleasant but anonymous retirement. The sister of the nurse who attended his surgery is concerned about what has become of her, and, with the help of an American super sleuth, sets out to solve the mystery. They do, of course, all of which goes to show what a devious lot the Soviets are, and that Stalin was the most devious of them all.

Guilty of Treason. Prods. Jack Wrather and Robert Golden, dir. Felix Feist, Eagle-Lion Films, 86 min., 1950. Chicago: Facets Video.

A docudrama on the Moscow-directed campaign to persecute the Hungarian prelate, Joseph Cardinal Mendszenty, which was an early *cause célèbre* of the Cold War. This film focuses on the nature of communist imperialism in Eastern Europe specifically and everywhere else by implication. The cardinal stands as the symbol of enlightenment and hope, representing a formidable barrier against total communist domination as he gives in to neither torture nor intimidation. While its propaganda message is clear, this feature is of much higher caliber than most of its contemporary Cold War propaganda films.

I Was a Communist for the FBI. Prod. Bryan Foy, dir. Gordon Douglas, Warner Brothers, approx. 90 min., 1951. Washington, D.C.: Library of Congress.

Based on the actual experience of Matt Cvetic, a Pittsburgh steelworker who served as a "plant" in a communist cell for the FBI, this film is a melodrama that exploits the anti-communist paranoia of the early 1950s. It charges communists with furthering their interests by exploiting racial hatred and labor unrest, raises suspicion against public school teachers by introducing one of them as a "diligent party member," and argues throughout that anyone who embraces liberal causes should automatically be suspect. The style is the same as that employed in Hollywood propaganda films from World War II, indicating that by 1945 the techniques had been honed to a fine art: evil villains, handsome infallible heroes, and perfectly clear distinctions between "them" and "us."

Invasion, U.S.A. 90 min., Prod. Alfred Zugsmith and Robert Smith, dir. Alfred E. Green, Columbia, 90 min., 1953. Medford, Oreg.: Sinister Cinema.

The story is the invasion and conquest of the United States by an unnamed foreign power which obviously is the Soviet Union. Scenes include: an atomic bomb dropped on Boulder Dam that releases a torrent of water which catches and drowns a set of parents and their two young children; American cities in ruins; senators being gunned down on Capitol Hill; and near the end, an all-American girl committing suicide rather than be pawed by a brutish and whiskey-swilling enemy soldier. The message is clear: be on guard against the enemy; complacency must be abolished. The film has a trick ending designed to suggest that not all is lost. After all of the horrors of the conquest have been shown, the film suddenly fades to patrons of a bar who discover that they have been hypnotized into imagining all that has happened. The veils now lifted from their eyes, so to speak, they leave the bar *en masse* to donate blood and start building war machines.

The Iron Curtain. Prod. Sol C. Siegel, dir. William A. Wellman, Twentieth Century-Fox, approx. 85 min., 1948. New York: Museum of Modern Art; Washington, D.C.: Library of Congress.
One critic described this film as Hollywood's first shot in the Cold War against Russia. It certainly indicates the continuity between World War II propaganda features and those which Hollywood produced in the Cold War context. This film is the Cold War version of a 1939 Warner Brothers film *Confessions of a Nazi Spy* (entry in chapter 4 under "Propaganda Material"). Significantly, screenwriter Milton Krims worked on both films. Like its predecessor, *The Iron Curtain* is based upon the memoirs of a real person, in this case Igor Gouzenko, a code clerk in the Soviet Embassy in Ottawa, Canada, who defects and tells all regarding Soviet espionage operations in North America. The film has much in common with its wartime predecessors: it incorporates the same arch-villains, who now represent the Kremlin, and advises the audience to hate the enemy, in this case the Reds. The heroes, meanwhile, are stalwart, home-loving, honest, and forthright; the message is that Soviet-sponsored subversion is everywhere.

A King in New York. Dir. Charlie Chaplin, Attica Film Company, Ltd., 105 min., 1957. Chicago: Facets Video.
This film was made in England in 1957 but not released in the United States until 1973. Charlie Chaplin plays a king overthrown by revolution, who comes to the United States in the hope that he can win support for the idealistic reforms he was denied at home: an end to nuclear weapons and adapting nuclear power to create a modern utopia. However, he finds that Americans are overly reliant on technology, ear-splitting music, moronic films, insulting advertising, and political intolerance. Cold War paranoia and the dehumanizing technological world that Chaplin always hated are the objects of this last of several of his personal propaganda efforts on film. One scene takes a clear stab at the House Committee on Un-American Activities hearings made notorious in the early 1950s by Sen. Joseph McCarthy.

A Look at Socialism. Prod. American Heritage Center National Education Program, 15 min., 1955. Minneapolis: University of Minnesota.
An anti-socialist propaganda presentation, this short film begins with an overview of the evolution of socialism, and moves on to the conclusion that the future is inevitably bleak under socialism. What-

ever socialism may promise, the film argues, the reality will be poverty and loss of freedom. The film goes so far as to suggest that Soviet communism and British socialism have common roots, which is a perspective that probably would have drawn loud protests in London.

Man on a String. Prod. Louis de Rochement, dir. Andre de Toth, Columbia, 92 min., 1960. Washington, D.C.: Library of Congress.
This film is based on the confessions of a Russian-born composer and Hollywood producer who, for twelve years, posed as a Russian agent for the FBI. His effort produced a number of trials and convictions of Soviet spies. The film is the story of those twelve years, told as an espionage adventure film but with the propaganda elements less overt than might have been the case a decade earlier. All the same, there is much propaganda involved: the Soviet spy cell operatives are sinister, the undercover agent is level-headed and quietly patriotic, and the implications of what the spying means is made perfectly clear.

Man on a Tightrope. Prod. Robert L. Jacks, dir. Elia Kazan, Twentieth Century-Fox, approx. 90 min., 1953. Los Angeles: UCLA Film and Television Archive, partial print only; Madison: Wisconsin Center for Film and Theater Research; Washington, D.C.: Library of Congress.
This is the story of a circus troupe trying to escape from behind the Iron Curtain. The setting is communist Czechoslovakia (though the filming was done in Bavaria) and the message is pointedly political. The troupe represent ordinary people chafing against the oppressive communist regime, and doing so with sufficient emphasis that a secret police spy is planted among the circus crew to keep an eye on them. He will also practice some intimidation in the process. The "man on a tightrope" of the title is actually the circus clown who is also the circus manager and who is the imperturbable rock to which the troupe members can cling as they seek their escape from Czechoslovakia.

The Manchurian Candidate. Prod. George Axelrod and John Frankenheimer, dir. John Frankenheimer, MC/Essex, 126 min., 1962. Chicago: Facets Video.
Based on a Richard Condon novel, this film tells the story of an American soldier in the Korean War who is captured along with his platoon by Chinese communist soldiers. The Americans are brainwashed by their captors, and one of them is turned into a programmed killer. They do not know that they have been brainwashed until, bit by bit, one of the men puts it all together. Meanwhile, the programmed killer is called upon to assassinate a liberal newspaper columnist, his wife and her

liberal senator father, and a presidential nominee. If he succeeds in the latter assignment, the vice-presidential nominee will take the White House, and he is married to the top communist spy in the United States. This spy is actually the killer's mother, who, unbeknownst to him, is also his controller. A thriller of the first water, this film registers a protest against Cold War extremists of left and right, both of whom are portrayed as being, in the words of one critic, "dangerous fraternal twins." It also suggests that brainwashing, a form of propaganda which was a reality in the Korean War, encompasses the potential for creating a scenario as terrifying as that presented in this film.

Mao's Little Red Video. Prod. United States Central Intelligence Agency, 35 min., 1966. Pullman: Washington State University.

This film is both pro- and anti-Chinese communist propaganda. Made and released in the People's Republic as *The Great Advancement of Mao Zedong's Thinking*, the film contains the radical and histrionic Maoist propaganda that was disseminated to impose the extreme changes of the Cultural Revolution of the 1960s upon the Chinese people. This was a good thing from the Maoist perspective. However, the film was seized by U.S. intelligence in the mid-1960s, who translated the original soundtrack into English and released the film under the new title as proof of the unbending will of Chinese communist fanaticism.

Meeting the Red Challenge. Prod. Norwood Films, 14 min., 1957. Austin: University of Texas.

This film shows how the United States Air Force stemmed the tide of the communist invasion of South Korea in 1950. The communists are depicted as aggressors, while United States armed forces are shown as defenders of freedom and democracy.

My Son John. Prod. and dir. Leo McCarey, Paramount, approx. 95 min., 1952. Washington, D.C.: Library of Congress.

One of the real classics of Cold War propaganda, this film is entirely dedicated to purging the United States of communism. It boils with emotionalism, illogic, and anti-communist paranoia. The story is of a mother who suspects that one of her sons, John, is flirting with communism. She becomes convinced when she learns that he is being investigated by the FBI, though it is not specified that this is because he is suspected of being a communist subversive, and that he has the key to an apartment occupied by a girl who has been arrested and charged with spying. On the basis of such evidence, and the fact that he was less than enthusiastic about his father's superpatriotic pronouncements or about his brothers going off eagerly to participate in the Korean War, John is condemned by his mother, the rest of his family, and virtually everyone else. The film makes heroes of ranting, song-singing patriots, ridicules intellectuals as perverters of the young, and assumes with perfect sincerity that association is evidence of guilt, at least regarding politics.

Nightmare in Red. Prod. National Broadcasting Company, 55 min., 1958. Carlsbad, Calif.: CMI Films VHS.
This was originally a *Project* 20 series program for television. It follows the historical development of Russia beginning with the Revolution of 1905, when violence and insurrection first challenged the czarist regime. From there it proceeds to the Bolshevik Revolution in 1917 and beyond, to end with the rule of Stalin through 1953. As the title indicates, the purpose is to present communist revolution as a violent and bloody exercise, and to suggest that the system it created was little better, if at all, than the one it replaced.

On the Beach. Prod. and dir. Stanley Kramer, Kramer, 133 min., 1959. Chicago: Facets Video.
Based upon a novel by Nevil Shute, this is the story of the apocalypse; that is, the Cold War superpowers have finally pushed the buttons and the world is dying from radiation fallout. Only Australia remains unaffected. The first signs of the radiation sickness begin to appear, and a truly apocalyptic decision is made: suicide pills are dispensed to the population, many of whom are refugees from lands already destroyed, and against the background of nostalgic Australian folk music, people begin killing themselves—a metaphor, no doubt, for the fact that the world has already killed itself through nuclear war.

One, Two, Three. Prod. and dir. Billy Wilder, Mirisch/Pyramid, 115 min., 1961. Chicago: Facets Video.
A comedy and a send-up of both postwar communism and American capitalism. This is the story of the conflict between the self-made American who directs efforts in Berlin to promote the bottling interests of Coca-Cola (a perfect American capitalist metaphor) in postwar Germany. The conflict emerges when the director has to look after the visiting, starry-eyed daughter of a Coca-Cola executive from Atlanta, only to have her fall in love with (and secretly marry) a dedicated East Berlin communist. The American plants a copy of *The Wall Street Journal* on him, which gets him arrested by the Volkspolizei. He then springs the communist from jail and gives him a crash course in American business techniques, thus making him a suitable son-in-law for a Coca-Cola execu-

tive and at the same time achieving a victory for capitalism. Much of the humor derives directly from the Cold War headlines of the time.

Pick Up on South Street. Prod. Jules Schermer, dir. Samuel Fuller, Fox, 80 min., 1953. Chicago: Facets Video.
A melodrama set in the context of the New York City underworld, this film pits United States federal agents against communist spies. A petty crook steals a wallet, but the wallet contains top-secret microfilm that the wallet's owner was unwittingly transporting out of the country for her lover. He, unknown to her, was a communist agent. He, she, and the petty crook pursue each other, and are pursued in turn by federal agents. In due course, she falls for the petty crook and rejects her boyfriend when she learns he is a communist. The spies are foiled in this picture, but the love relationship between the crook and the woman comes to nothing.

The Red Danube. Prod. Carey Wilson, dir. George Sidney, Metro-Goldwyn-Mayer, approx. 85 min., 1949. Atlanta: Turner Classic Movies.
Set in post-World War II Vienna, the administration of which was divided between Soviet and Western allied occupiers, this film presents naive allied officers confronting sinister and cunning Soviet officials within the context of the latter oppressing the Viennese in their section of the city. The story, such as it is, concerns demands by Soviet authorities to force repatriation of displaced persons, including members of a ballet company. One of these commits suicide, which adds a tragic element to allied naiveté. In the end, the allied administration wakes up to reality and puts the Soviet authorities in their place.

The Red Menace. Dir. R. G. Springsteen, Republic Pictures, 87 min., 1949. Chicago: Facets Video.
The subject is the Communist party of the United States. The theme is how the party betrays the idealists and malcontents who join its ranks. The film tells the story of a discontented World War II veteran who is plied with drink, women, and the promise of seeing social justice done, but who is soon led to see that he was duped. Other young communists experience similar disillusionment and become dissidents: a girl from an impoverished background, a black student who thought the party would improve conditions for his race, and a European refugee whose father was a communist. Each seeks to break out of the party, and the villainous party leaders prove unable to stop them in spite of the intimidation and abuse they visit upon the dissidents. The role of the propaganda speech (a ringing declaration of the film's propaganda message) is prominent well beyond what is effective.

Red Nightmare. Prod. William L. Hendricks, dir. George Waggner, Warner
   Brothers, 35 min., 1965. Chicago: Facets Video.
   Produced for the United States Department of Defense, this film depicts
   an American citizen who finds himself in a communist village in an
   unnamed country. The village is a nightmare for the American, and his
   experiences are portrayed as a rude awakening to his civic responsibilities. This example of Cold War docudrama film propaganda is narrated
   by Jack Webb, who was a leading anti-communist in this period.

Red Planet Mars. Prod. Anthony Veiller, dir. Harry Horner, United Artists,
   approx. 85 min., 1952. Salt Lake City, Utah: Sight and Sound.
   Elements of science fiction blend with politics in this film. A German
   Nazi scientist flees Germany, leaving behind plans for a transmitter
   capable of sending signals to and receiving them from the planet Mars.
   American scientists wish to deploy the transmitter in order to probe the
   unknown. However, the Nazi scientist is still alive in a hut high in the
   Andes mountains, where he works for the Russians on a plan to wreck
   the scientists' efforts by feeding them messages from the Martians that,
   among other things, will wreck the world economy. There are other
   messages as well: a call for a revolution in Russia and a call for the
   return of earthlings to religious faith. Are these messages really from
   Mars? Or is the Nazi scientist even more devious as a Russian agent
   than seems possible? The Americans are characteristically heroic and
   the Russians evil from the beginning to the end.

Salt of the Earth. Prod. University of California Extension Media Center,
   94 min., 1954. Berkeley: University of California.
   This film dramatizes the struggle of Mexican-American zinc miners to
   gain living and working equality with Anglo mine workers. It is not a
   propaganda film as such; however, as it first appeared during the
   McCarthy era it was denounced as being pro-communist propaganda
   and was suppressed (censored) until 1965.

Seven Days in May. Prod. Edward Lewis, dir. John Frankenheimer, Seven
   Arts/Joel, 120 min., 1964. Chicago: Facets Video.
   Based upon a novel by Fletcher Knebel (well known for his politically
   conscious fiction during the high days of the Cold War), this is the story
   of an attempt by a right-wing civilian-military clique to stage a *coup
   d'état* in the United States. Their reasoning is that the president is
   selling out to the communists by trying to negotiate a disarmament
   treaty with the Soviet Union. A loyal Marine colonel uncovers the plot
   and foils it with help from various other loyal military and civilian

persons. Those responsible are brought to account. President John F. Kennedy (who did not live to see the film completed) enthusiastically supported the project when it began. The Pentagon, for obvious reasons, was cool toward it. The film well reflects the latent paranoia that characterized the Cold War and pleads for a return to sanity.

Sofia. Prod. John Reinhardt and Robert R. Presnell, dir. John Reinhardt, Film Classics, approx. 90 min., 1948. Hanover, N.H.: Dartmouth College, screenplay only.
    The setting is Sofia, Bulgaria, where an agent of the United States seeks to free a Russian nuclear scientist and his wife from the grasp of the Russians. The film is driven by rising interest in what atomic weapons actually mean for the future—the Soviet Union had not yet exploded a nuclear device when this film was released—and the idea that life behind the Iron Curtain is unremittingly violent. The Russians are portrayed as dark and sinister, while the scientist, his wife, and the agent are just the opposite.

Strategic Air Command. Prod. Samuel J. Briskin, dir. Anthony Mann, Paramount, 114 min., 1955. Los Angeles: Paramount Home Video.
    This film constitutes a docudrama, and does for the Cold War what such films as *Target for Tonight* did for World War II. A professional baseball player in the Air Force Reserve is called to active duty to serve in Strategic Air Command (SAC). Essentially, this film tells the story of SAC, which until the early 1990s, was the air service that patrolled the skies twenty-four hours a day armed with nuclear weapons. The ultimate point is that SAC is such an important part of national defense as to make it worth virtually any personal sacrifice. The SAC commanding officer clearly is meant to resemble Curtis Lemay, who was head of SAC at the time. SAC gave its support to the film, which was immensely popular and, according to one critic, "served to quash the complaints of the taxpayers who were carping about the billions spent on defense."

Three Brave Men. Prod. Herbert B. Swope, Jr., dir. Philip Dunne, Twentieth Century-Fox, 90 min., 1957. Los Angeles: UCLA Film and Television Archive; Washington, D.C.: Library of Congress.
    A Navy Department bureaucrat is accused of being a security risk because of his radical and pro-communist sympathies. He is suspended, then fired. None of the accusations is true, of course. An extensive investigation reveals that much of the evidence against him is the product of hearsay and rumor, circulated by people in his

community with whom he has had differences, and he is reinstated. Based upon a real event, this film is meant to say that communists pose a real threat to the United States and that the government must investigate even the hint of disloyalty among its employees. At the same time, however, the government will go to extraordinary lengths to make sure innocent people are not wrongly treated.

The Woman on Pier 13. Prod. Jack J. Gross, dir. George F. Slavin, RKO Radio Pictures, approx. 85 min., 1950. Los Angeles: UCLA Film and Television Archive; Madison: Wisconsin Center for Film and Television Research; Pullman: Washington State University.
Originally released as *I Married a Communist*, the title was changed because the public seemed not to like it. That it was a mediocre product at best did not help. The film is a straightforward anti-communist potboiler, which paints an ugly picture of communists stirring up labor trouble on the San Francisco waterfront. The party is presented as ruthless and unprincipled, operating according to authoritarian rules and capable of destroying without qualms a young man who decides he no longer wants to be a part of the communist movement. The party also is represented by a group of thugs who in one scene pound on the door of a communist-turned-capitalist who is much involved as a company vice-president in the goings on at the waterfront.

Yankee Go Home: Communist Propaganda. Prod. United States Information Agency, 45 min., no date. Chicago: International Historic Films.
In this documentary film, George V. Allen, first director of the United States Information Agency, explains the purpose of that organization and how he hopes to use it to counter the anti-American propaganda that appears in the popular Soviet media, especially in Soviet films. He examines this propaganda as it exists in several Soviet documentary and feature films, including *Meeting on the Elbe* and *The Partisan*.

Yanks Are Coming! Prod. David L. Wolper, Wolper Productions, 54 min., 1952. Ann Arbor: University of Michigan.
The setting is World War I and United States involvement is explained through authentic film footage. The language is patriotic and nostalgic, and the theme—"saving the world for democracy"—sends a clear Cold War message: that the United States emerged from World War I as the only great power capable of protecting the free world from the communism that had been unleashed through one of the cataclysmic events of that war, the Bolshevik Revolution.

Chapter 7

PROPAGANDA AFTER WORLD WAR II:
More Variations on a Theme

In the years after World War II, propaganda continued to be a staple of politics, social action, foreign policy, war, and revolution, well apart from that which specifically applied to the Cold War. This chapter cites books, articles, films, and other sources concerned with the use of mass communications and public relations for propaganda dissemination after 1945. These sources resemble their counterparts from the pre-1945 period in a number of respects, but most of all in their tendency to criticize the use of propaganda and to charge the media and government with using propaganda techniques to mislead radio, television, and press consumers. On the other hand, many of these entries indicate that propaganda became a normal part of mass communications after the war, and that this may not have been altogether a bad thing.

History and Function

Beloff, Max. "The Projection of Britain Abroad." *International Affairs* 41, 3 (July 1965), pp. 478-489.
At issue in this article is whether Britain should invest public money on cultural and economic propaganda abroad. It is raised because the author sees government policy in this regard falling somewhat short of the mark. Government policy is to "project Britain" in relation to specific areas and to policy requirements within those areas. He contends that to limit cultural and economic propaganda in this way might actually handicap the country's efforts at promoting other commercial and political objectives. "Tourists want to visit museums and antiquities," he points out by way of example, and argues that if this is their sole image of what Britain has to offer, the countries from which they come will not look to Britain as a source of industrial equipment or new ideas in science, education, or social institutions. Britain must "project" on a broad scale if external propaganda is to promote what will serve the country best.

Black, John B. *Organizing the Propaganda Instrument: The British Experience.* The Hague: Martinus Nijhoff, 1975.
This volume concerns post-1945 British propaganda, which the author describes as a "systematic instrument of national and foreign policy."

The author grants that the basis of this propaganda was the organization created for propaganda dissemination in World War II, but contends that the postwar machinery and campaigns were much more systematic, thorough, and competent. His attention is focused on the British Information Service, the external services of the British Broadcasting Corporation, and the British Council. The Central Office of Information, which succeeded the wartime Ministry of Information, was established in 1946 to provide "common production services." The outgrowth of a University of London Ph.D. thesis, this book covers mostly propaganda organization with only perfunctory references to the contents of the propaganda disseminated. There is a short chapter on the "roots" of peacetime propaganda, followed by a chapter each on the various organizations which administered that propaganda. The book concludes with a comparison between United Kingdom and United States overseas propaganda efforts. Select bibliography.

Brownstein, Ronald. *The Power and the Glitter: The Hollywood-Washington Connection*. New York: Pantheon Books, 1990.
Political methods rather than propaganda are the theme of this book. However, the political methods that are described here—the "employment" of Hollywood stars by Washington "pols" to help them get elected, raise election funds, or put across particular programs—are effectively those recognizable as propaganda. This is particularly the case when the author describes the impact of Hollywood glamour on politics in the television age. Television, the author notes, has required politicians "to behave more like actors" in order to sell their policies to the public. As this volume is a history of the Hollywood-Washington connection, several chapters consider the propaganda role of Hollywood feature filmmakers in both World War II and the Cold War. Illustrations and a select bibliography.

Campbell, David. *Politics Without Principle: Sovereignty, Ethics, and the Narratives of the Gulf War*. Boulder, Colo.: Lynne Rienner, 1993.
This short and somewhat philosophical book is about the way the Gulf War was presented to the American people, the ethics of the presentation, and the justifications that lay behind it. The author is concerned to look beyond the surface of the conflict and to demonstrate that the "radically interdependent nature of contemporary world politics renders any attempt to make absolute and emphatic claims about agency, ethics, responsibility, and sovereignty intrinsically problematic." In other words, the rhetoric of moral outrage that surrounded the attack on Iraq and the subsequent news coverage of the event were not

justified by the actuality of the situation. The author's concern is that
United States policy assumed a position of "moral absolutism" and
sold it to the public by employing the various techniques of propaganda. Select bibliography.

Castle, Eugene W. *Billions, Blunders and Baloney: The Fantastic Story
of How Uncle Sam Is Squandering Your Money Overseas*. New York:
Devin-Adair, 1955.
It is difficult to place this volume. On the one hand, the author, a propagandist for the United States in World War II, provides an assessment
of how propaganda functioned—or malfunctioned—in the 1950s as an
element in the formation and implementation of United States foreign
policy; on the other, he makes a case for how the United States has
mismanaged its foreign policy with such vigor as to make his arguments seem propagandistic in their own right. The use of propaganda
is a theme in each of the eighteen chapters, and with few exceptions
the author concludes that propaganda either has been badly done or
cannot serve the ends expected of it. The latter point is central to such
chapters as "We Go Overboard on Psychological Warfare," "Uncle
Sam's Movie Madness," and "Propaganda Can't Win for Americans."
The volume includes photographs purporting to illustrate how the
government wastes money on fancy buildings for embassies, among
other things. No bibliography, however, by which the author might
have more convincingly supported his many negative contentions.

Chomsky, Noam. *Letters from Lexington*. Monroe, Maine: Common
Courage Press, 1993.
A collection of contributions to the anti-propaganda, propaganda journal, *Lies of Our Times*, or *LOOT* (an acronym the metaphoric significance of which is not hard to recognize), that were written by Noam
Chomsky, one of the leading anti-propagandists of the later twentieth
century. At issue is the writing of the "mainstream press" on public
issues. The essays seek to expose all of the ways in which such writing
is propaganda. For one example, the author claims that an A. M.
Rosenthal article in *The New York Times* misleads its readers by
claiming that Israel has always sought to negotiate peace with the
Arabs. This, Chomsky claims, is simply pro-Israel propaganda cooked
up by the Israeli and United States governments. For another, he argues
that the George Bush administration justifed the invasion of Panama
through media propaganda. The disinformation aspect of propaganda
is also addressed. Unfortunately, it is sometimes difficult to determine
whether the disinformation lies in the press material the author criti-

cizes or in the manner of his criticism, which appears to be founded upon the premise that whatever the media say is propaganda.

Crofts, S. W. "The Attlee Government's Economic Information Propaganda." *Journal of Contemporary History* 21, 3 (July 1986), pp. 453-471. The author tries here to fill a gap in writing about post-World War II British prime minister Clement Attlee's economic policies. This first Labour government with a clear majority in the House of Commons was seeking to institute dramatic and far-reaching changes in Britain's economic system. This article provides an overview of the ways in which propaganda was deployed to extend public awareness and appreciation of these new policies. The author notes the extensive public opposition to certain aspects of what the Attlee government was attempting, and that the deployment of propaganda in support of government policy became an absolute necessity. He does not also argue that the propaganda was an overwhelming success. See William Crofts, *Coercion or Persuasion?* (next entry).

Crofts, William. *Coercion or Persuasion? Propaganda in Britain After 1945*. London: Routledge, 1989.
To some extent, this is a history of the Central Office of Information, the successor to the wartime Ministry of Information. The author examines the role this office played in disseminating propaganda about such issues as economics and those industries upon which the postwar economy depended: agriculture, coal mining, and textiles. In this context he considers the nature and impact of propaganda directed at getting women into cotton mills, in which wage rates, working conditions, part-time and nursery facilities, inducements offered by competing occupations, and so forth, were explained. One chapter is devoted to the efforts of "Owd Snack," a fictitious character who appeared in the Lancashire press making his propaganda pitch in a thick North Country dialect: "if tha weshed thisel' proper tha wouldn't need to scrat," for example. Illustrated with poster and newspaper propaganda samples; extensive bibliography.

Curtis, Liz. *Ireland: The Propaganda War. The British Media and the "Battle for Hearts and Minds."* London: Pluto Press, 1984.
"This book tells a story," the author begins, "that is sad, infuriating, and sometimes, in a perverse way, even funny. It is about the propaganda war that has been fought . . . for the hearts and minds of the British people on the question of Ireland." The propaganda to which she refers is British government propaganda which is disseminated in

Green, Fitzhugh. *American Propaganda Abroad*. New York: Hippocrene Books, 1988.
This volume is principally a description of the work of the United States Information Agency (USIA), but it is by no means a conventional treatment of the subject. The author worked for USIA for sixteen years. He describes the agency's efforts in two ways: historical and analytical treatment of how the agency worked, and in several "fictional" vignettes, written in the manner of the short story, on "a typical overseas post" and on "a nation-building post." The result is both entertaining and informative. The author is an enthusiast for the cultural and political benefits overseas propaganda disseminated by the United States brings to the world. So, too, is broadcast journalist John Chancellor, who wrote a foreword to the volume. Bibliography in endnotes.

Jeffords, Susan, and Lauren Rabinovitz, eds. *Seeing Through the Media: The Persian Gulf War*. New Brunswick, N.J.: Rutgers University Press, 1994.
Eighteen contributors including the editors created this collection of perspectives on how the mass media—press and television—forged the "social consensus needed for support of the war and the national identity that defined the shape that consensus would take." The general themes include "seeing through history," "seeing through total television," "seeing through the home front," and "seeing through patriotism." Specific essays deal with the various propaganda techniques—including showing on television children victimized by Iraqi forces and posters which portrayed Muslim women as victims of a repressive society—which formed part of the media presentation of the war. The censorship through which the military helped shape how the media saw and presented the conflict is also an issue. The volume is illustrated with samples of propaganda material. Select bibliography. See David Campbell, *Politics Without Principle* (entry above).

Johnson, Abby Arthur, and Ronald Maberry Johnson. *Propaganda and Aesthetics: The Literary Politics of Afro-American Magazines in the Twentieth Century*. Amherst: University of Massachusetts Press, 1979.
The authors trace the history of African-American literature, as used by black intellectuals to disseminate propaganda advocating freedom from prejudice and discrimination, and for a greater political role for African Americans in the United States, from W. E. B. Du Bois to Richard Wright. Each chapter is written with particular magazines and journals as examples. The authors conclude that "Afro-American magazines" as a whole have been more committed to social and

political expression than the magazines of any other cultural group in the United States, and have self-consciously embraced the concept of art-as-propaganda. Select bibliography.

Lang, Gladys Engel, and Kurt Lang. *The Battle for Public Opinion: The President, the Press, and the Polls During Watergate*. New York: Columbia University Press, 1983.
"What was the effect of the media on the creation, the course, and the resolution of Watergate?" the authors ask. They then examine the impact of the media on opinion formation, using the Watergate experience as context and example. There is much discussion of opinion polling, which draws on opinion responses to specific developments in the Watergate case. The authors also raise the question of whether or not, and to what extent, the various players in the "Watergate game" tried to manipulate opinion through the media. Bibliography in endnotes. Appendixes contain charts and graphs relating to opinion polls.

Laurence, John C. *Race, Propaganda, and South Africa*. London: Victor Gollancz, 1979.
Apartheid in South Africa is this author's enemy, and one which, he argues, is sustained by propaganda. Noting the growing importance of mass communications around the world, he presents an argument that it is mass communications used to transmit race propaganda that has kept the white minority in power. He describes public relations and advertising techniques being employed increasingly for "political, economic and even racial indoctrination, often camouflaged as 'objective information.'" This propaganda prevents the rest of the world from knowing the truth about apartheid. General topics include the "mechanics of misinformation," "propaganda themes," and "the empathy barrier." Within these, the author discusses among other things, race bias, the South African propaganda machine, South Africa and communism, and apartheid in various aspects of South African life. Select bibliography and two illustrations.

Page, Caroline. *U.S. Official Propaganda During the Vietnam War, 1965-1973: The Limits of Persuasion*. Madison, N.J.: Fairleigh Dickinson University Press, 1994.
The author begins with the period when United States involvement in the war in Vietnam began to expand dramatically; she concludes with the withdrawal of United States forces. Her focus is on how the United States sought to persuade its Western allies to back its Vietnam policy during these crucial eight years. She examines propaganda aimed in

particular at Australia, France, Great Britain, New Zealand, and West Germany, and assesses the difference between what was straight information and what was pure propaganda. Part of this assessment concerns information passed by the United States government to allied governments with regard to its amount and veracity, as compared to the kinds and amount of public information regarding the war that was disseminated in these countries. Select bibliography.

Propaganda Message. Prod. National Film Board of Canada, 14 min., 1973. New York: Phoenix Films and Videos.
This Canadian production compares Canadians and Americans in terms of what they believe or disbelieve about themselves, and concludes that there is not so much difference as many in both countries like to think. The film promotes the advantages of federalism and presents federalism with a degree of awe that it works so well, given the many disagreeable constituents within the two federalist systems. Both French and English are spoken in the film.

Sparks, Kenneth R. "Selling Uncle Sam in the Seventies." *Annals of the American Academy of Political and Social Science* 398 (November 1971), pp. 113-123
The author, a former United States Information Agency official, calls for an overhaul of the United States overseas propaganda machine, because as it exists (ca. 1971), it is not focused, not connected closely to national policy, and lacks understanding of the effects of communications media which United States propagandists do not control: the press, radio, and television. In countries where control exists, United States official propaganda has minimal impact, with the result that unofficial channels remain the principal sources of information about the United States. The author argues that a complete reorganization of the machine would enable American propagandists to be more instrumental in the formulation and implementation of foreign policy.

Spitzer, H. M. "Presenting America in American Propaganda." *Public Opinion Quarterly* 11 (1947-1948), pp. 213-221.
The author argues here that opinion regarding the United States held in foreign countries, if left to casual information, might result in the formation of inadequate impressions. Therefore, the United States must continue and expand upon its existing efforts at getting out a truthful picture of the United States to the world. The question is, does that picture need to be presented differently to different nations? The answer is yes, but not altogether differently. Regardless of where it is

directed, American propaganda above all else must stress the importance to the United States of free speech, fellowship, morality, freedom
of opportunity, optimism, and rational curiosity. Only a single paragraph is devoted to how all of this should be presented.

Thompson, Kenneth W., ed. *Rhetoric and Public Diplomacy: The Stanton
Report Revisited.* Lanham, Md.: University Press of America, 1987.
This short volume is a reconsideration of questions raised in the 1975
Stanton Commission report, "International Information, Education
and Cultural Relations: Recommendations for the Future." It contains
a series of discussions involving diplomats and others concerned with
such issues as the use of the United States Information Agency, among
other such services, in the conduct of foreign policy. That such agencies
serve as foreign-policy propaganda channels is a major theme, and the
volume concludes with a specific essay on propaganda and disinformation with respect to Libya during the Reagan administration. A
product of the White Burkett Miller Center of Public Affairs at the
University of Virginia. No bibliography.

Younger, Kenneth. "Public Opinion and British Foreign Policy." *International Affairs* 40, 1 (January 1964), pp. 22-35.
This article speculates about the extent to which there is an activist
public opinion regarding British foreign affairs, and under what circumstances ordinary citizens are most likely to become activists in that
regard. The author's theme is the ability of pressure groups to influence
public opinion in such a way as to cause them, in turn, to influence the
formation of foreign policy by the British government. He cites such
examples as the 1956 Suez Canal crisis and the response to formation
of the European Common Market in 1960, which Britain joined only
a decade later. His objective here is to encourage citizens to take a more
active interest in foreign affairs, lest foreign policy remain exclusively
in the hands of a professional class. Such might not always be good for
British commitment to the democratic process.

Channels and Techniques

Allport, Gordon W. *ABC's of Scapegoating.* New York: Anti-Defamation
League of B'nai B'rith, 1966.
This is the fifth edition of a Freedom Pamphlet on defamation which
first appeared in 1948. It is in two parts. The first part defines scapegoating as shifting blame for something that has happened to someone

who is not actually responsible for it. It tends, the author explains, to involve prejudice, racial or other. This part also describes the personality types of both scapegoats and scapegoaters. The second, and very short part of the pamphlet indicates ways to combat scapegoating. This pamphlet was part of specific campaigns aimed at ending anti-Semitic and other ethnically based discrimination. No bibliography.

Altheide, David L. *Media Power*. Beverly Hills, Calif.: Sage, 1985.
The author is attempting to explain a paradox. There was a time, he writes, when people communicated "in order to do something." However, "today, we must first do something before we communicate." His object is to explain the role of the mass media in "establishing, polishing, and shaping basic communication formats." There are only limited references to propaganda by name; however, every chapter examines aspects of mass communications in connection with social control, how the shape of information is affected by media presentation, and how reception of information is affected by the manner in which the media presents it. The power exercised by the mass media makes it inevitable that it will be used as often as not for propaganda purposes.

Atkin, Charles K., et al. "Quality Versus Quantity in Televised Political Ads." *Public Opinion Quarterly* 37, 2 (Summer 1973), pp. 209-224.
This article is a methodological piece on assessing the effectiveness of televised political propaganda. It draws the surprising conclusion, based upon careful analysis of opinion polls, that voters are generally unaffected by such propaganda, and may even consciously reject it. The point is that "spot ads" may have a temporary effect, but will not necessarily determine how voters respond at the ballot box. There is a detailed explanation of the research methods employed to draw this conclusion. See Edwin Diamond and Stephan Bates, *The Spot* (entry above under "History and Function").

Bagdikian, Benjamin H. "Congress and the Media: Partners in Propaganda." *Columbia Journalism Review* 12 (January/February 1974), pp. 3-10.
The author examines evidence that the media are manipulated by politicians who, in turn, manipulate the public; in short, the media are used for propaganda purposes by people in Congress. The concluding line makes the point clearly: "Most members [of Congress] still do not have to answer pertinent questions for the voters back home, and most continue to propagandize at the constituents' expense with the cooperation of the local news media." A critical piece, but written in an objective style.

Barnouw, Erik. *The Golden Web: A History of Broadcasting in the United States.* Vol. 2, *1933-1953.* New York: Oxford University Press, 1968.
This is the second of a three-volume history of broadcasting in the United States. It opens with the notation that network broadcasting began in 1933 and that this transformed forever the nature of radio's impact upon the American public. The period covered in this volume encompasses the Depression, World War II, and the opening rounds of the Cold War. Topics, therefore, include radio and extremist ideologies, radio and political campaigns, international propaganda broadcasting in wartime, and how Harry Truman used radio in pursuit of his political aims. There is also much discussion of radio advertising, relations between radio and other mass media, and censorship, in particular during the early Cold War period. The volume is illustrated with photographs of famous radio personalities and of devices used in radio to create special sound effects. Extensive bibliography.

_____. *The Image Makers: A History of Broadcasting in the United States.* Vol. 3, *From 1953.* New York: Oxford University Press, 1970.
The final volume in this history of broadcasting in the United States, which concentrates on how radio was joined and then surpassed by television as the principal electronic medium. The topics are as varied as in volume 2, and again the author's purpose is to explain the impact of broadcasting upon the American public on various levels. He writes: "A television-radio system is like a nervous system. It sorts and distributes information, igniting memories. It can speed or slow the pulse of society. The impulses it transmits can stir the juices of emotion, and can trigger action. . . . As in the case of a central nervous system, aberrations can deeply disturb the body politic." This is an appropriate description of a propaganda channel. Photographic illustrations, and an extensive bibliography.

Barron, Jerome A. *Freedom of the Press for Whom? The Right of Access to the Mass Media.* Bloomington: Indiana University Press, 1973.
This volume "chronicles the struggle to open the media." In the 1960s, the author was disturbed by the "failure of our law to provide any right of public access for ideas," that is, by the absence of laws which guarantee the "solitary speaker or the lonely writer" access to the "great engines of public opinion—radio, television, and the press." In consequence, he opened a campaign through the American Civil Liberties Union, among other advocacy groups, to correct this situation. In these pages, in order to state the case for freer access to the media, he describes court decisions, Federal Communications Commission pro-

ceedings, and the efforts of leading figures ranging from Spiro Agnew on the right to Herbert Marcuse on the left. A special subsection acknowledges that propaganda came to play a significant role in the argument. In this subsection, the author speculates on whether it would be a good or a bad thing, if freer access meant more propaganda broadcast across the United States.

Barsamian, David, ed. *Stenographers to Power: Media and Propaganda.* Monroe, Maine: Common Courage Press, 1992.
The object here is clear: the media in the United States pretend to be independent of and adversarial to State power, but in fact they are just the opposite. "The actual purpose which the media serve very effectively is to inculcate and defend the economic, social, and political agenda of privileged groups that dominate domestic society and state." In other words, the media conducts propaganda operations for the fat cats. There are eleven essays in this volume, written by some of the leading critics of propaganda in the United States, including Noam Chomsky, Michael Parenti, and Benjamin Bagdikian. Each essay is presented as an interview with the editor, and the responses uniformly indict the media for being politically and class biased in their coverage of war and politics. Mark Hertsgaard, for example, discusses the "five o'clock follies," by which he means the early evening news. These interviews project that all media coverage is propaganda in the service of thought control by the Establishment. An interesting and sometimes informative collection, which should be read carefully, as the authors and editor clearly have a propaganda agenda of their own. That agenda is easily recognized, however, because their propaganda lacks subtlety.

Beeley, Sir Harold. "The Changing Role of British International Propaganda." *Annals of the American Academy of Political and Social Science* 398 (November 1971), pp. 124-129.
This brief article by a retired British diplomat describes how the British government uses propaganda in the implementation of official foreign policy. It argues that the principal channels of that propaganda, the official information service of the Foreign Office, the British Broadcasting Corporation, and the British Council, have established procedures which are well adapted to the international requirements of a nation that is no longer a global power.

Braestrup, Peter. *Big Story: How the American Press and Television Reported and Interpreted the Crisis of Tet, 1968, in Vietnam and Washington.* Boulder, Colo.: Westview Press, 1977.

At the time this two-volume work was published, the author was a journalist with *The Washington Post*. It was inspired by the author's own experience as a war correspondent in Vietnam, and it is no surprise to discover that the volume is dedicated to journalists who died covering the Vietnam War. However, the author has not written a panegyric to journalists, which would itself be a form of propaganda. Rather, he looks with a critical eye at media coverage of the Tet crisis in 1968, the moment which probably was the turning point in the Vietnam War. He notes that much of the coverage was less than strictly fact-based journalism, and tended to be biased either for or against United States participation in the conflict. Volume 1 "tells the story" of the coverage; volume 2 is a collection of documents and correspondence related to the study. A valuable resource for the study of journalism in wartime as a propaganda channel. No bibliography.

Browne, Donald R. *International Radio Broadcasting: The Limits of the Limitless Medium.* New York: Praeger, 1982.
This book is an examination of how radio has been and continues to be used as a medium for transmitting both information and propaganda. Topics include the process, which is a technical discussion of international broadcasting, how radio served propaganda purposes during and after World War II, and how various national radio systems deployed propaganda internationally before, during, and after World War II. The British Broadcasting Corporation (BBC) is described as the "pace-setter" in this regard. Other examples include Deutsche Welle, Radio Nederland, Radio Japan, Radio Moscow (which, like the BBC, has a separate chapter), Radio Budapest, and many other, lesser, international broadcasting systems. There is also discussion of Vatican Radio and other "voices of faith" and of who listens, and finally, a speculative look at what the future may hold for international broadcasting. Select bibliography and three appendixes containing documents.

Burns, Tom. *The BBC: Public Institution and Private World.* London: Macmillan, 1977.
This is a study set in the historical context of one of the great electronic mass communications systems in the world: the British Broadcasting Corporation (BBC). It is, therefore, a study of the structure, motivation, internal politics, external function, and limitations of a medium that has been used both to disseminate propaganda and to operate against it. Much of the book concerns the BBC in the decades after World War II. The BBC's historic role throughout a significant portion of its existence as a deliverer of both domestic and external cultural and

moral propaganda (the former abroad, the latter at home) is not the principal object of the book. Rather, it is driven by an analysis of BBC operations and constitutes a study that adds much understanding to the corporation's connection to radio propaganda in the twentieth century.

Campaigns and Elections: Classics of Political TV. Prod. Campaigns and Elections, 60 min., 1986. Baton Rouge: Louisiana State University.
This film deals with thirty-five years of modern political advertising. The theme is the impact of television technology on politics. It includes more than seventy-five examples of political commercials selected for their innovation and effectiveness. The purpose is less criticism than information, though the examples should open the viewers' eyes to what political candidates are really saying to voters, as opposed to what they want to be thought to be saying.

Cater, Douglass, and Richard Adler, eds. *Television as a Social Force: New Approaches to TV Criticism*. New York: Praeger, 1975.
This volume is a collection of essays on the impact of television on viewers in the United States. Ninety-seven percent of Americans own a television set, the editor notes, which means that an enormous potential exists for television to be used as a propaganda channel to shape or influence popular thinking and behavior. He adds that it is curious that no one, at least no one qualified to study the facts, seems to have noticed. The contributors seek to make up for that lack, and produce observations on such topics as "Television and Thinking People," "Television Shapes the Soul," "The Viewer's Experience," "Communicating Ideas by Television," and "American Political Legitimacy in an Era of Electronic Journalism," among several others. Bibliography in endnotes.

Chandler, Robert W. *Public Opinion: Changing Attitudes on Contemporary Political and Social Issues*. New York: R. R. Bowker, 1972.
This volume, put out by CBS News, comes at propaganda through the back door. It describes how CBS News polls were conducted (they were conducted for only a few years) and how the results were used as a journalistic tool. The purpose was to link news coverage specifically to events that were prominent in the public mind. The volume discusses the polling results of such matters as the Vietnam War, the Nixon presidency, the environment, and race questions. The book is linked to propaganda in terms of the connection between opinion polls and shaping the content of news reportage, and the subsequent formation of emphases that might, in their turn, shape public opinion regarding certain events and personalities.

_____. *War of Ideas: The U.S. Propaganda Campaign in Vietnam*. Boulder, Colo.: Westview Press, 1981.
The object here is to describe and appraise United States propaganda in the Vietnam War "as an instrument of foreign policy." Many examples of propaganda are included, such as leaflets, posters, handbills, and banners, which indicate the range of propaganda techniques employed. For example, on one poster, a bikini-clad Vietnamese girl invites a Viet Cong soldier to come home to her. The author analyzes the strengths and weaknesses, and successes and failures, of this type of propaganda. He concludes that the experience of World War II was applied in Vietnam only to a limited extent. There is discussion also of the use of television, radio broadcasting, and a wide variety of print channels for propaganda. An objective work, the conclusions drawn are nevertheless critical of the Vietnam propaganda war largely on the basis that it failed to achieve its long-term objective of overcoming Vietnamese nationalism. Select bibliography, appendixes of official directions for pursuing the propaganda war, and illustrations drawn from propaganda materials.

Charnley, Mitchell V. *News by Radio*. New York: Macmillan, 1948.
This study of the impact of radio news was inspired by World War II, in which radio broadcasting played a major role both as a source of information and as a propaganda channel. The point here is to explore the potential and the responsibilities of radio news broadcasting. Topics for analysis include a survey of how radio functioned in World War II, who radio listeners are and what they want to hear since the war, the way radio news differs from press news, how news scripts are written, local as opposed to national radio news reporting, kinds of radio news (agriculture, sports, etc.), and problems of libel and censorship. No bibliography, but four appendixes describe news broadcaster codes, education standards for radio journalism, a radio news stylebook, a "checklist" for radio newsroom self-analysis, and an index of radio stations across the United States.

Cherry, Colin. *World Communication: Threat or Promise? A Socio-technical Approach*. Chichester, England: John Wiley and Sons, 1978.
Rapid advances in technology have altered the nature of communications, particularly international communication. The result, the author argues, is a socio-technical problem. This is an emotional subject, he points out, because much of communication technology is directly related to war, propaganda, profit, and loss. The premise here is that technology is comprehensible only in the context of a social and political environment, and the author has organized this study of world

communications accordingly. There are six parts, arranged into the
nature of human communication, its past and present, its explosion in
the postwar world, its use for politics and pleasure, its economics, and
its impact upon social organization and relationships. The volume
includes graphs, charts, and an extensive bibliography.

Chomsky, Noam. *Towards a New Cold War: Essays on the Current Crisis
and How We Got There*. New York: Pantheon Books, 1982.
A collection of the author's essays that purport to be concerned with
the "evolution of American foreign policy and ideology since the early
1970s," this book actually is an attack on United States foreign policy
and those who make it. It is predicated on the assumption that the media
is subservient to a "state propaganda system," for which they are well
rewarded by the government. In short, only journalists who write
exposés of government skullduggery—which, if the author is to be
believed, is everything governments do in foreign policy—are to be
trusted. Topics include intellectuals and the state, foreign policy and
the intelligentsia, the remaking of history, South Vietnamese aggression, Henry Kissinger, and Israel and the Palestinians, among several
others. There is a strong emphasis throughout on how propaganda
drives all. This is Noam Chomsky at his self-righteous best. Bibliography in endnotes. See Noam Chomsky, *Letters from Lexington* (entry
above under "History and Function").

Cohen, Stanley, and Jock Young, eds. *The Manufacture of News: A
Reader*. Beverly Hills, Calif.: Sage, 1973.
An analysis of the mass media from the perspective of how it manu-
factures and reproduces images with the effect of creating or perpetu-
ating various kinds of bias. The mass media, the volume argues,
"provide the guiding myths which shape our conception of the world
and serve as important instruments of social control." Twenty-six
essays, divided into three sections, make up the text. Part 1 concerns
the process of selecting news; part 2 examines modes and models
which are projected through the news—images of mental illness, for
example; part 3 covers the effects and consequences of news management. The authors are part of what the editors refer to as the "debate
on media," and their work contributes to suggesting new lines for
mainstream media research. Illustrations, but no bibliography.

Combs, James E., and Dan Nimmo. *The New Propaganda: The Dictatorship of Palaver in Contemporary Politics*. White Plains, N.Y.: Longman, 1993.

This volume draws upon historical, conceptual, and analytical perspectives in describing how propaganda is inextricably woven into the fabric of contemporary civilization. The authors argue that it has become an indispensable part of the way we live, and that in our mass media-dominated culture, "propaganda is growing in importance and sophistication and will become a determining force in the way we live, how we think, and what we value." For a start, Santa Claus is described here as a "propaganda icon" that pitches for a commercialized Christmas. Beyond that, the volume covers topics with such titles as "Old Masters and New Propagators," "Palaver in Political Cultures," "Propagated Consumers Consume Propaganda," and "Marketing of Popular Culture." Curiously, despite the occasional flamboyance of chapter titles ("Is There a Sucker Born Every Minute?" for example), the authors are reasonably objective about their subject. Bibliography in endnotes.

Congress and the Media and Congress and the Establishment. Prod. American Political Science Association, 60 min., 1984. Berkeley: University of California.
This documentary is a segment of the *Congress: We the People* series. Part 1 concerns the relationship between the Congress of the United States and the media, in particular how members of Congress try to structure their coverage by local press and television stations, how national media treatment tends to be more objective than local coverage, and how Congress responds to issues concerning funding and regulating the media. Part 2 focuses on the "ethical gulf" that opens when members of Congress are "servicing" themselves at the same time they are representing their constituents.

Conway, Flo, and Jim Siegelman. *Holy Terror: The Fundamentalist War on America's Freedoms in Religion, Politics and Our Private Lives.* Garden City, N.Y.: Doubleday, 1982.
This volume explores religious fundamentalist propaganda through examination of the television, radio, and publications controlled by the likes of Jerry Falwell, Jimmy Swaggart, and Pat Robertson. The title, the authors explain, derives from their conviction that this propaganda is a form of moral terrorism, and that as often as not, its perpetrators are disseminating it as a moneymaking scam. It is made clear that censorship plays a major role in the fundamentalists' propaganda as well. Religious fundamentalism became an increasingly significant factor in conservative politics in the United States after this volume was published. In consequence, the value of this book increased as a study of later-twentieth-century extremist religious propaganda. Select

bibliography of materials relating to terrorism, propaganda, fanaticism, and behavioral psychology.

Cook, Fred J. "Radio Right: Hate Clubs of the Air." *Nation* 198, 22 (May 25, 1964), pp. 523-527.
This essay surveys "hate radio" as it existed in the 1950s and 1960s. It includes a map indicating locations of the hundreds of broadcasting stations across the United States which carried the messages of such organizations as "Twentieth Century Reformation Hour" (Christian Beacon, Inc.), "Life Line" (Texas billionaire Howard Hunt), "Howard Kershner's Commentary on the News" (Christian Freedom Foundation), and several others. The broadcasts are characterized as "hate" propaganda, in which presidents are castigated as disloyal, labor unions are attacked as communist fronts, Catholicism is charged with being an "enemy of freedom," and independents are called Marxist agents. The article is a warning against such broadcasting, and the author stops just short of calling for some form of censorship. That his warning went unheeded is clear from the proliferation of hate radio in the decades following publication of this essay.

Dallek, Robert. *Ronald Reagan: The Politics of Symbolism*. Cambridge, Mass.: Harvard University Press, 1984.
The author is a historian who writes here about a contemporary subject, the Reagan presidency while Reagan is in office—a risky venture for a historian as opposed to a political scientist. Moreover, the author writes this book from a historian's perspective, but also as a critic of Reagan's politics and policies, which he evaluates in the context of the president's use of ideological symbolism. One prominent example of Reagan's use of symbolism for manipulative purposes was the president identifying himself with working-class Americans by putting in an appearance at a neighborhood bar in the presence of television cameras. In reality "Reaganism is a return to old-fashioned Republicanism—large tax cuts for the rich, less government help for the poor, weaker enforcement of civil rights, fewer controls on industry." Reagan politics are effectively described in these pages as the politics of propaganda. No bibliography. See Stephen Ducat, *Taken In*, and *Illusions of News* (entries below).

Dennis, Everette E., George Gerbner, and Yassen N. Zassoursky, eds. *Beyond the Cold War: Soviet and American Media Images*. Newbury Park, Calif.: Sage, 1991.
The Cold War ended officially with the collapse of the old Soviet Union, or so everyone said. This collection of fifteen essays assume

that it did, and their authors examine the critical question of how the traditional images of the Soviet Union and the United States need to be changed for post-Cold War usage. Specifically, they explain that the media constitute both a barometer for the chills and thaws in international relations, and channels for propaganda disseminated in response to chills and thaws. The contributors in this volume come from both the United States and the former Soviet Union. Topics include images of Americans in Russia, images of Russians in the United States, the United States in Soviet newspapers, and content analysis of various newspapers in the United States and Russia. There is a guide to the contributors, but no bibliography.

Ducat, Stephen. *Taken In: American Gullibility and the Reagan Mythos*. Tacoma, Wash.: Life Sciences Press, 1988.
This book evaluates the Reagan presidency in terms of how the former president used techniques of psychological manipulation to win wide support among the people of the United States for policies which the author believes were flawed and even dangerous. Here the "teflon" president is explained and the groundwork is laid for, in the authors words, "a more extensive and definitive future study of American mass-psychology." Questions posed include What factors, historical and developmental, have made Americans psychologically vulnerable to "corporate and governmental propaganda?" and How does such vulnerability "help to sustain relations of domination?" Obviously, this is not the work of a pro-Reagan author, and while the study is well based in psychological theory, there is a political agenda implicit within the text. Illustrations include the *Doonsbury* cartoon strip, and stills from political campaign advertising. The select bibliography is concerned mainly with writings on psychology. See Robert Dallek, *Ronald Reagan* (entry above).

Farrell, John C., and Asa P. Smith, eds. *Image and Reality in World Politics*. New York: Columbia University Press, 1967.
This collection of essays includes contributions by such eminent scholars as Stanley Hoffmann, Reinhold Niebuhr, and Ralph K. White. The link between the essays is their consideration of the various ways in which one nation perceives another, and how such perception helps shape international relations. For example, Niebuhr discusses the "social myths" of the Cold War, while Benjamin I. Schwartz is concerned with the "Maoist image of World Order." These authors do not focus upon propaganda as such, but rather on the imagery which propagandists manipulate for use in international politics. No bibliography.

Frederick, Howard H. *Cuban-American Radio Wars: Ideology in International Telecommunications*. Norwood, N.J.: Ablex, 1986.
The large theme here is the international "war of ideas" which, at the time of writing, included 22,000 hours of international broadcasting from more than eighty countries to more than 250 million listeners around the world. In specific terms, the subject is the application of this war of ideas to the United States and Cuba in the years after the Castro revolution through examination of their respective international newscasts. In the author's words, "in their attempts to woo the opponent's population and to win the hearts and minds of the Americas, both countries emit messages that are rife with competing ideological values about world politics." Extensive bibliography.

Goldie, Grace Wyndham. *Facing the Nation: Television and Politics, 1936-1976*. London: Bodley Head, 1977.
It was decided by the British in 1935 that a national television service would be started in Britain. Little came of it initially owing to the outbreak of World War II, and it was mostly ignored as a political tool until the 1970s. This book provides a history of the evolution of that medium in Britain into a potent channel for political and other kinds of propaganda. It covers the politics of developing the television service as well as the impact of that service on the British nation. Limited bibliography.

Goodfriend, Arthur. "The Dilemma of Cultural Propaganda: 'Let It Be'." *Annals of the American Academy of Political and Social Science* 398 (November 1971), p. 104.
The author, a United States State Department consultant and expert in public relations, claims in this article that contrary to an assumption common among its citizens, the United States does not do better than others in international cultural propaganda. The reason is that when the product being sold is the American ideal and American institutions, official propaganda—meaning government controlled and sponsored—actually runs counter to the real meaning of that ideal and those institutions, simply because propaganda about them is official. The author's point is that such propaganda by the United States government is unethical and immoral, and that the United States should disband such propaganda apparatus as Voice of America and rely instead on the social diversity, variety, and virility of its arts, as well as the "free interplay of unmanaged media" that characterize the United States, to get cultural propaganda messages across.

Gordon, George N., and Irving A. Falk. *The War of Ideas: America's International Identity Crisis*. New York: Hastings House, 1973.
This book, the authors explain, is a new approach to understanding the problems facing the United States in disseminating international propaganda in the post-Cold War era. The emphasis is upon international communications, and they cover a wide range of topics in both contemporary and historical terms. All are presented in a lively and often irreverent manner. The authors admit to bias but claim to have written from the position of "realistic observation and responsible conviction." Themes include the changing nature of international propaganda, the "cracked-mirror image" of the United States abroad, challenges to old myths about methods of international propaganda, the shortcomings of American broadcast propaganda, the crisis of idealism in the United States, and much else of similar nature. Select bibliography.

Graber, Doris A. *Mass Media and American Politics*. Washington, D.C.: CQ Press, 1993.
This comprehensive study is designed as a university-level textbook. It examines the political role of mass media in the United States in terms of press and electronic media, in particular with reference to such new technologies as cable and satellite television transmission. Topics include the mass media as institutions within the American political system, the legal framework of the media, the impact upon policy of newsmaking in all circumstances from wars to floods, the influence of investigative reporting on public policy, new learning about political learning and opinion formation along with new theories about media-induced social and asocial behavior, and the growing media influence on politics and the conduct of foreign policy. Numerous charts and graphs; bibliography in endnotes.

Gustainis, J. Justin. *American Rhetoric and the Vietnam War*. Westport, Conn.: Praeger, 1993.
A specialist in political communications, the author examines the political rhetoric in the United States that came from advocates both for and against the Vietnam War. He notes that wartime rhetoric "is about the creation of consensus." As the Vietnam War dragged on for many years, opinion regarding the war became both acrimonious and divisive. The focus here is on the efforts of the Kennedy, Johnson, and Nixon administrations to build consensus in support of the war, or else to gain a peace that would reflect well upon United States policy and upon the efforts of those who opposed such policies in preference for a unilateral end to the war. Topics include the domino theory, the hero myth (Kennedy

and the Green Berets), the rhetoric of "shared values" (Nixon and the silent majority), the Red Menace (Johnson), the rhetoric of ultra-resistance (Daniel Berrigan), the Students for a Democratic Society, the Weathermen underground, and the use of film and other media to protest the war as in *Apocalypse Now*, or else to support it, as in *The Green Berets* (entries below under "Propaganda Material"). Select bibliography.

Hallin, Daniel C. *The "Uncensored War" : The Media and Vietnam.* New York: Oxford University Press, 1986.
This book looks at how the Vietnam War was covered by the media, and the impact upon the American psyche of the fact that there was virtually no censorship of that coverage. The author wonders whether or not this fact may in itself have determined the outcome, simply because such straightforward reporting became, even if unintentionally, a form of antiwar propaganda. The author also examines the ambivalent relationship between the news media and political authority in the United States during that period. Specific subjects include how *The New York Times* covered the war in the early years, which deals with why that coverage stuck so tightly to official perspectives, the ideology of the war, news management, the special characteristics of war coverage on television, and the growing press disillusionment with the war. Select bibliography.

Hansen, Allen C. *USIA: Public Diplomacy in the Computer Age.* New York: Praeger, 1989.
This volume about the United States Information Agency (USIA) in the age of high tech communications is written by a former USIA information and cultural affairs officer with more than three decades of experience. The book is based upon the premise that political advocacy must take into account that the rapid technological changes in communications systems require "the continuous creation of new public diplomacy techniques." With this in mind, he discusses USIA's mission (providing information and cultural programs related to a democratic society), the relationship between "public diplomacy and propaganda," Voice of America's contribution to the USIA mission, the competition to USIA from abroad, and some analysis of the new communications technologies that require new public diplomacy techniques. Select bibliography.

Herman, Edward S. *Beyond Hypocrisy: Decoding the News in an Age of Propaganda.* Boston: South End Press, 1992.
This is an "exposé" of language manipulation by government and journalism. The author claims that government "doublespeak"—a

term he extrapolated from George Orwell's "newspeak," which figured prominently in his dystopian novel, *1984*—is tied to "political agendas and frames." So too is this "exposé," which uses one kind of political propaganda as a technique for criticizing another one. All the same, the "Doublespeak Dictionary for the 1990s" contained in the last third of the volume is well worth reading. Limited bibliography.

_____. "The Media's Role in U.S. Foreign Policy." *Journal of International Affairs* 47, 1 (Summer 1993), pp. 23-45.
The author notes that the media in the United States—press, radio, and television—like to appear as the "watchdogs" of the country, who root out double-dealing and sleight-of-hand on the part of government. Very nice, he writes, if only it were true. Rather, the "mainstream media" are often "supportive of government policy and vulnerable to 'news management' by the government." The author claims that it was through the media that the Reagan administration sold the people of the United States on such propaganda slogans as the USSR as the "Evil Empire," Muammar Quadhafi as the premier terrorist in the world, and Manuel Noriega as a "villainous drug dealer." He describes media-government cooperation in the Gulf War and concludes that all the available evidence proves that whether wittingly or not, the media allow themselves to be exploited by government for what amount to propaganda purposes.

_____. *The* Real *Terror Network: Terrorism in Fact and Propaganda*. Boston: South End Press, 1982.
This volume is a critique and protest against the use of terrorist propaganda by authoritarian regimes in Third World countries which are linked to the United States. In the author's words, "This work is . . . impelled by a sense of identification and sympathy with the tens of millions of Third World peasants being pushed off the land under a system of 'supply side economics' with machine guns." While the style and language of the volume are themselves propagandistic, the facts are well presented and well supported by cited evidence. This is something of a potboiler, but illuminating for understanding the use of terror as a propaganda weapon. Limited bibliography. This book should be read in conjunction with various contributions by Noam Chomsky and David Barsamian to criticism of the role of propaganda in United States foreign policy, and as well, the author's "exposé" of United States "doublespeak" (entries above).

Hiebert, Ray Eldon. "Global Public Relations in a Post-Communist World: A New Model." *Public Relations Review* 18 (Summer 1992), pp. 117-126.

The author claims that public relations played a part in the collapse of communism by providing an effective means of communicating across national boundaries. He goes on to suggest that in the post-communist era, political ideology may seem less significant than effective communication. That is, the power of communication is less likely to come from the ability of a single authority to control sources of information; information will come instead from the ability of its recipients to assess public attitudes and from the ability of those providing information to communicate it effectively. Public relations theorists in the United States always have argued that two-way communication is preferable to one-way propaganda, and the author concludes that this is a principle which may now become global in an era that has utterly rejected the persuasive effectiveness of centralized control over public communications.

_____. "Public Relations as a Weapon of Modern Warfare." *Public Relations Review* 17 (Summer 1991), pp. 107-116.
Written as a speech by the *Public Relations Review* editor to present in Pretoria, South Africa, this article draws upon a case study of how propaganda (described here as public relations) was used with great success by all sides in the 1991 Gulf War. The conclusion drawn is that the Gulf War demonstrates that governments must deploy propaganda equally with more conventional weapons in order to win a war today, given the vast amount of instantaneous press and television coverage available.

Illusions of News. 55 min., prod. Richard M. Cohen, Public Broadcasting Service, 1986. Alexandria, Va.: PBS Video.
Part of Bill Moyers' *The Public Mind* series, this documentary analyzes how the media in the United States, especially broadcast news, emphasize style over substance. This film concentrates on media manipulation and illustrates how it is accomplished. Michael Deaver, a Reagan adviser, news correspondent Leslie Stahl, and media analyst Benjamin Bagdikian are among those interviewed. Examples from the Reagan presidency of both election campaigns and policy hype are presented in order to make various points.

Index on Censorship: The Magazine for Free Speech. London: Writers and Scholars International, bi-monthly.
This English journal was founded in 1968 by Stephen Spender as a worldwide watch on censorship. Each issue carries an "index" which draws attention to censorship in more than one hundred countries around the globe, but not including the United Kingdom, curiously enough. The journal also publishes propaganda in support of civil

rights and against civil rights abuse. The contributors principally are *literati*, and each issue includes extracts of novels and other writings that have been censored somewhere.

Leff, Leonard J., and Jerold Simmons. "*Wilson:* Hollywood Propaganda for World Peace." *Historical Journal of Film, Radio and Television* 3, 1 (1983), pp. 3-18.
While the Twentieth Century-Fox feature film *Wilson* was released before World War II had ended, its purpose was postwar propaganda. The subject was Woodrow Wilson, who is presented as an idealist for world peace and whose greatest achievement was the League of Nations. A major portion of the film deals with his appearance at the Paris Peace Conference in 1919. The parallels for post-World War II (the founding of the United Nations which was, at the time this film was made, already on the drawing board) are obvious. The authors examine the film in the context of what inspired it, where it fits within a litany of Darryl F. Zanuck films having social or political themes, and reasons why it was not particularly well received in Great Britain. There also is discussion of how the United States war department created censorship difficulties for the filmmakers. See *Wilson* (entry below under "Propaganda Material").

Lerner, Daniel. "Is International Persuasion Sociologically Feasible?" *Annals of the American Academy of Political and Social Science* 398 (1971), pp. 44-49.
A very brief discussion of whether or not the widening economic, social, political, and psychological gap between rich and poor nations makes propaganda "sociologically" feasible. The projection here is that if international propaganda is to remain feasible, global communication must exploit recent technological advances and assist poor nations to "enter into a truly global communication network."

MacArthur, John R. *Second Front: Censorship and Propaganda in the Gulf War*. New York: Hill and Wang, 1992.
This volume describes how the media were manipulated by the governments of both the United States and such Persian Gulf states as Saudi Arabia, in order to have the 1991 Gulf War presented in what was from their individual perspectives the best possible light. For example, "from the moment President Bush committed troops to Saudi Arabia on August 7, the Administration never intended to allow the press to cover a war in the Persian Gulf in any real sense." The author also calls the censorship of news concerning this war "unprecedented" and argues

that the Pentagon used propaganda tactics to manipulate the media into helping start the war in the first place. Bibliography in endnotes.

Mansell, Gerard. *Let Truth Be Told: 50 Years of BBC External Broadcasting*. London: Weidenfeld and Nicolson, 1982.
During World War II, critics of the British Broadcasting Corporation (BBC) complained that its external broadcasts continued to strive for objectivity when what was needed was raw propaganda. The BBC did not listen, and thus maintained the reputation for quality that it had acquired between the world wars. All the same, overseas broadcasting played an important role in British official propaganda operations in World War II, in the Cold War, and as a voice for British cultural propaganda in peacetime. This history of the BBC External Service makes very clear the propaganda role played by one of the most important international communications mediums in the world. Illustrated with photographs and cartoons. Select bibliography.

O'Higgens, Paul. *Censorship in Britain*. London: Nelson, 1972.
The author of this survey of British censorship practices has not presented a scholarly work on the subject. His aim, rather, is to enlighten a popular audience with regard to the subject—in his words, "to make people aware of the different kinds of censorship operating in Britain; and to suggest that censorship poses a number of basic problems for . . . freedom of thought and expression." Topics addressed include legal censorship, extralegal censorship, jobs and censorship, the media, and the "official secrecy" associated with the British government. A concluding chapter, "Why Censorship?," makes clear that the author does not favor censorship and sees it serving no useful function. On the other hand, he does see censorship being used to exercise a form of social control, and thus serving a propaganda function. Select bibliography.

Picturing Derry. Prod. Faction Film Productions, 59 min., 1985. University Park: Pennsylvania State University.
A documentary dealing with photographic propaganda, this film analyzes all that goes into creating a photograph in the city of Derry in Northern Ireland, in the context of ongoing conflict and violence. Themes include propaganda and censorship, as well as the technical and artistic aspects of photography.

Pielke, Robert G. *You Say You Want a Revolution: Rock Music in American Culture*. Chicago: Nelson-Hall, 1986.
Rock music became a channel for antiwar propaganda during the era of the Vietnam War. This volume puts that phenomenon in the context

of post-1945 American culture, with the Woodstock festival figuring as an important galvanizing event in linking rock music to the antiwar movement. Among the many songs analyzed are some of the most famous of the era: "Give Peace a Chance" (John Lennon), "What's Goin' On" (Marvin Gaye), "War Pigs" (Black Sabbath), "Requiem for the Masses" (The Association), and "I-Feel-Like-I'm-Fixin'-to-Die" (Country Joe McDonald). Much consideration also is given to the role these and other rock musicians played in demonstrations, public commentary, and other avenues of antiwar protest. Select bibliography.

Rubin, Bernard. "International Film and Television Propaganda: Campaigns of Assistance." *Annals of the American Academy of Political and Social Science* 398 (November 1971), pp. 81-92.
This article argues the importance of new commnications technology to the emerging Great Power emphasis on informational and cultural propaganda. The author notes a turn away from "hard" propaganda, described as "campaigns of assault," and toward campaigns that stress international assistance. The author looks specifically at international film and television programming in the Western democracies, which sell material change in association with ideology.

Sayegh, Fayez A. *Zionist Propaganda in the United States: An Analysis.* Pleasantville, N.Y.: Fayez A. Sayegh Foundation, 1983.
The author, a Kuwaiti diplomat with a Ph.D. from Georgetown University, was for a number of years a member of the United Nations Committee on the Elimination of Racial Discrimination. In this pamphlet he sets forth a "catalogue" of themes and messages contained in Zionist propaganda disseminated in the United States and an "exposé" of Zionist intentions. The former includes nineteen "durable Zionist themes," among which are the "right of the so-called Jewish nation to Palestine," and the idea that a Jewish nation "has proven itself better able to develop . . . Palestine than the Arabs who owned it." The scope of the pamphlet is made clear in the table of contents: "Setting the Scene," "the Contents of Zionist Propaganda," "The Master Plan of Zionist Propaganda," and "The Privileged Position of the Zionist Propaganda." This pamphlet rests very precariously on the line dividing propaganda technique and channels from propaganda material. Interestingly, four of Dr. Sayegh's speeches at the United Nations are listed in Robert Singerman, *Anti-Semitic Propaganda: An Annotated Bibliography and Research Guide* (entry in Introduction under "Bibliographies and Research Guides").

Schiller, Herbert I., et al. *The Ideology of International Communications.* New York: Institute for Media Analysis, 1992.
Five essays on the United States' role in international communications, which at one time was driven by anti-communist propaganda, but which in the post-Cold War era is driven by what is described here as the determination of the United States to dominate international communications in order to sell "free-market virtues abroad and attack 'statism' where it tries to regulate on behalf of community welfare. . . ." The authors disseminate more than a little "propaganda" of their own when they argue against United States domination of international communications, using such value-laden references as " our minds are being laundered" and "vindictive U.S. power," without providing clear evidence to justify what such phrases imply. See Noam Chomsky, *Towards a New Cold War*, and Edward S. Herman, *The Real Terror Network* (entries above).

The Selling of the Pentagon. Columbia Broadcasting System, 54 min., 1971. New York: Carousel Film and Video.
This documentary film provides examples of promotional public relations activities of the Pentagon. It includes film of businessmen watching war games, officers on lecture tours, sidewalk displays, and indicates films that are available for rental. The propaganda element is twofold: on the one hand, Pentagon propaganda aimed at selling the military is demonstrated; on the other, the filmmakers seek to persuade viewers that the cost of such activity is not warranted in peacetime.

Smear: The Game of Dirty Politics. Prod. Columbia Broadcasting System, 25 min., 1964. Chicago: Macmillan Films.
A smear is defined as an argument that contains untruths or unsubstantiated statements which slander the target and suggests that health as well as careers are sometimes affected by the technique. Print and audio examples trace political smear tactics from the time of George Washington to the presidential race between Richard Nixon and John F. Kennedy. The film warns viewers that they should not believe everything they hear or read.

Tavin, Eli, and Yonah Alexander. *Psychological Warfare and Propaganda: Irgun Documentation.* Wilmington, Del.: Scholarly Resources, 1982.
This volume is an explanation and to some extent justification of propaganda deployed by the Zionist terrorist organization, Irgun, in its quarter-century struggle against British rule in Palestine. It is also a collection of examples of the propaganda. The bulk of the volume

concerns the period of World War II and after, down to the recognition
of Israel by the United Nations in 1948. It constitutes a source book on
"sykewar" and on the role of propaganda in the birth of the Israeli state.
The select bibliography includes memoirs from Irgun leaders of the
period, such as future Israeli prime minister Menachem Begin.

Taylor, Philip M. *War and the Media: Propaganda and Persuasion in the
Gulf War*. Manchester, England: Manchester University Press, 1992.
The 1991 Gulf War seemed to be the most precise execution of warfare
using high-tech weapons and communications in history. It appeared
on television to be "clean" and even humane. However, as the author
indicates in the preface, "most of the information contained in these
pages . . . is gleaned from the media coverage itself—from the press,
television, and radio. This should immediately place one on the alert. . . .
An analysis of Gulf War propaganda is thus in danger of becoming an
extension of that propaganda." The author looks at how the media covered
the Gulf War, and to the extent possible, explains how that coverage was
manipulated. He also examines public response to what was seen on
television and read in the press. This is the first major work on Gulf War
coverage and propaganda to appear, and its purpose is to emphasize how
easily information is manipulated in an age of high-tech communication.
The author's concluding line makes the point nicely: "The conflict belonged to the coalition's armed forces, and to the victors went the spoils
of the information war." Select bibliography and extensive endnotes.

Television's Vietnam: Impact of Visual Images. Prod. Humanitas Films,
150 min., 1982. Stillwater: Oklahoma State University Public Information Office.
This documentary looks at how United States citizens have become
dependent on the mass media. In that context, the film examines the
Vietnam War experience in order to raise questions about the accuracy
and the effects of media reporting on the war. The point is to draw the
viewer into critical thinking about what is actually being presented in
the guise of objective news reportage.

Television's Vietnam: The Battle for Khe Sanh. Prod. Humanitas Films,
60 min., 1983. Stillwater: Oklahoma State University Public Information Office.
A documentary that continues the theme of the above entry by looking
specifically at Marine Corps combat footage of the Khe Sanh battle. It
includes interviews with enlisted and other military personnel, showing how their recollections of the battle conflict radically with the battle

as recorded by still and television cameras. The same conclusion is drawn as above: accuracy was a serious question for television news reporting of the Vietnam War.

Terror! Parts I and II. Prod. Herbert Krosney, 50 min., 1985. New York: Phoenix/BFA Films and Videos.
Part I deals with such terrorist organizations as Black September, the Palestine Liberation Organization, and the Irish Republican Army. Part II considers how governments respond to the activities of such organizations. The underlying theme is that terrorism is an extreme channel of propaganda which delivers an extreme message that can only be countered by governments refusing to compromise with terrorist groups.

34 Years After Hitler. Prod. Columbia Broadcasting System, 19 min., 1979. New York: Carousel Film and Video.
This documentary film describes neo-Nazi activities and the revival of anti-Semitic, Aryan supremacy propaganda in West Germany. It features interviews with Nazi hunter Simon Wiesenthal as well as with neo-Nazi representatives. The film also exposes a German neo-Nazi connection with Lincoln, Nebraska, where a sympathizer supplied the German movement with much of its printed matter.

Whitton, John B. "Hostile International Propaganda and International Law." *Annals of the American Academy of Political and Social Science* 398 (November 1971), pp. 14-35.
The author argues that while hostile propaganda in international relations is commonplace, it is resented and even "violently resisted." He describes how greater attention than in the past is now being focused on propaganda that leads to subversion and outright aggression, and on propaganda that defames sovereign states and their leaders and representatives. This attention has resulted in new international rules and criticism of hostile propaganda, but it has not led to an end of that kind of propaganda. The author calls for more effective enforcement of established norms in dealing with hostile propaganda disseminated in the context of international relations.

Wildy, Tom. "From the MOI to the COI—Publicity and Propaganda in Britain, 1945-1951: The National Health and Insurance Campaigns of 1948." *Historical Journal of Film, Radio and Television* 6, 1 (1986), pp. 3-17.
This article argues that the "large bureaucratic establishment" known as the Ministry of Information, which was set up by the British government to produce and disseminate propaganda during World

War II, was replaced by an only slightly smaller organization called the Central Office of Information. This agency had access to the extensive facilities set up in wartime for producing and distributing official films and adapted those facilities to producing materials aimed at selling the National Health and Insurance schemes to the British public. The author also discusses the role played in this process by another government-connected communication system, the British Broadcasting Corporation. He ends by suggesting that propaganda on behalf of National Health and Insurance marked the acceptance in Britain of domestic propaganda by the British government as both a normal and useful adjunct to implementing national policy.

Wilson, H. H. "Techniques of Pressure: Anti-Nationalization Propaganda in Britain." *Public Opinion Quarterly* 15, 2 (Summer 1951), pp. 225-242.
A Labour government was in power in Britain in 1945 with a clear majority in the House of Commons. As a result, the reordering of British society according to the Labour party's long-standing plan went forward. Labour's program for nationalizing key industries as part of the program met with stiff resistance, however. This article describes the techniques used by British industry in an effort to mobilize opinion against nationalization. For the other side of the coin, see William Crofts, *Coercion or Persuasion?* (entry above under "History and Function").

The World Is a Dangerous Place: Images of the Enemy on Children's Television. Prod. Harvard Medical School Center for Psychological Studies in the Nuclear Age, 13 min., 1989. Phoenix, Ariz.: Maricopa County Community College.
In this documentary film experts on television and child psychology explore the political socialization that television cartoons offer, especially those which portray "enemy" characters. 150 episodes of popular war cartoons were used to show how enemies are negatively stereotyped and how violence is indicated as the only means of resolving conflicts with them. The experts express concern over what such cartoons may teach children about other nations.

Young, Peter R., ed. *Defence and the Media in Time of Limited War.* London: Frank Cass, 1992.
An Australian production, this volume is a collection of papers presented at an international conference in Brisbane following the 1991 Gulf War. At issue was the question of what secrecy demands in a limited war, balanced against the public's right to know. In short, what are the limits of censorship in wartime? Contributors included repre-

sentatives of the military, academia, and the media. They covered such items as theories of media responsibilities in war, specific case studies including Vietnam, Northern Ireland, the Falklands, Granada, the Gulf War, and the specific experience of Australia in various situations. No bibliography.

Propaganda Material

Anatomy of a Lie. Prod. International Association of Machinists, 19 min., 1962. Madison: University of Wisconsin.
   This documentary was made to refute *And Women Must Weep* (entry below), about the 1958 wildcat strike by the International Association of Machinists in Princeton, Indiana. It claims that this National Right to Work film was blatant propaganda which shows union members as dangerous and unlawful. The film includes interviews with union members, clergy, and public officials of Princeton, who argue that the actual events of the strike were much different from those portrayed in *And Women Must Weep*.

And Women Must Weep. Prod. Centron Corp., 27 min., 1962. Madison: University of Wisconsin.
   This film by the National Right to Work Committee dramatizes events surrounding a 118-day wildcat strike called by the International Association of Machinists against the Potter-Brumfield company in Princeton, Indiana, in 1958. It depicts strikers committing violence against nonstrikers, the efforts of a local minister to act as peacemaker, and the impact on the townspeople. The film ends with the minister's wife appealing to people to support right-to-work legislation. See *Anatomy of a Lie* (entry above).

Animal Times: The Magazine That Speaks Up for Animals. PETA, Washington, D.C., bimonthly.
   PETA stands for People for the Ethical Treatment of Animals. Its main publication, *Animal Times*, takes up the cause of protecting animals, tame or wild, from what the magazine terms "injustice": that includes product testing on animals by such manufacturers as Procter and Gamble and Gillette, cruelty to animals in slaughter houses or in mass egg production, malicious treatment of animals by vandals, and any other manner of animal abuse that comes to light. Through its journal, the organization advocates using political pressure—each issue indicates the importance of individuals making their views known to

congressional representatives and other government officials—to achieve improvement in the treatment of animals. It also advocates vegetarianism. "I'm Raising Two Beautiful Vegan Kids," is the title of an article in a 1995 issue. The style of argument embraces all of the techniques that are characteristic of propaganda.

Apocalypse Now. Prod. and dir. Francis Ford Coppola, United Artists, 139 min., 1979. Chicago: Facets Video.
A major anti-Vietnam War film which employs such evocative techniques as a helicopter attack with Wagner's "Ride of the Valkyries" as the background music. Based upon Joseph Conrad's novel *Heart of Darkness*, the story is of a renegade Green Beret colonel who breaks with the United States military and sets himself up as a god among a tribe of Montagnard warriors in the Vietnam highlands. An amoral army captain is sent upriver to assassinate the colonel, as he has become an embarrassment to the United States military. The point is made that United States involvement in the Vietnam War is a form of madness at best, and at worst, pure immorality.

Backing up the Guns. Prod. Illinois Educational Association, 15 min., 1943. Pocatello: Idaho State University.
Already looking ahead to the postwar period, this short dramatic film tells its audience that while guns will win the war, the democracy for which it is being fought can survive the "perils that lie ahead" only if the United States is committed to maintaining a high-quality education for Americans.

The Battle of Algiers. Prod. Antonio Musu and Yacef Saddi, dir. Gillo Pontecorvo, Magna, 120 min., 1966. Chicago: Facets Video.
Sometimes described as a first-class documentary on the struggle of the Algerians for freedom from France, the film is more often described as "a powerful battle cry for Marxist revolutionaries." It was reportedly used as a terrorist training film in the late 1960s. This Italian-Algerian production tells, in psuedo-documentary form, the story of the Algerian struggle for liberation from France which ended in 1962. It is well done in many respects—not all of the French soldiers are brutes, though the French *colons* (colonists) are usually portrayed as both brutal and sadistic. However, the political sympathies of the Italian director are clear. The Algerian Liberation Front is portrayed as a group of innocent martyrs to a cause, and the film overall is a condemnation of imperialism. Appropriately, the opening scene depicts an Algerian rebel being executed on the guillotine.

Born on the Fourth of July. Prod. A. Kitman Ho and Oliver Stone, dir.
Oliver Stone, Fourth of July, 140 min., 1989. Chicago: Facets Video.
Oliver Stone is a perfect example of the propagandist as an individual
with an ax to grind who has access to the mass media. This film tells
the story of a gung-ho young man of "all-American" midwestern
background who goes off to the Vietnam War and is wounded and left
paralyzed from the waist down. He returns home to the United States
to become an antiwar activist. The film is somewhat autobiographical,
for Stone himself followed a similar course, though without the para-
lyzing wound. The point is to challenge "patriotic, God-fearing, macho
all-American" types using the Vietnam War as context. See *Platoon*
(entry below).

Cast a Giant Shadow. Prod. and dir. Melville Shavelson, Mirisch/Llenroc/
Batjac, 144 min., 1966. Washington, D.C.: George Washington University.
Based on the role played in the first Israeli war with the Arabs in 1949
by Colonel David "Mickey" Marcus, who was an American World
War II hero. Marcus was recruited by the fledgling Israeli government
to organize its army into a force that could protect the new state from
its enemies. A variety of Israeli freedom fighters march heroically
across the screen, and a variety of volunteers from the United States—
including Marcus himself—die for Israel. A clear distinction is drawn
between Israeli "good guys" and Arab "bad guys."

Casualties of War. Prod. Art Linson and Fred Caruso, dir. Brian De Palma,
Columbia, 120 min., 1989. Chicago: Facets Video.
This Vietnam War film tells the story of a single bloody patrol, and of
the inhumane treatment of a young Vietnamese girl at the hands of a
sergeant who has gone off the deep end. It is an anti-Vietnam War film
done in the manner of Stanley Kubrick and Oliver Stone, with over-
emphasis on blood and gore at the expense of dealing with the genuine
issues of whether or not the United States should ever have joined in
the conflict.

The China Syndrome. Prod. Michael Douglas, dir. James Bridges, Columbia, 122 min., 1979. Chicago: Facets Video.
Concern over the potential for nuclear disaster at nuclear power
stations rose steadily in the course of the 1970s. That danger inspired
this film. The story is that government, power companies, and others
are seeking to prevent the publication of information that a given
nuclear power station in California poses an immediate danger of
meltdown which, if it happened, would be a colossal disaster. Polemi-

cal but honest in its polemicism, the film makes its point clearly. When seen in the context of the Three Mile Island and Chernobyl nuclear power station disasters that have occurred since this film was made (the Three Mile Island accident occurred only a few weeks after the film's opening), its message acquires much greater potency. As E. H. Carr once observed, nothing makes propaganda more effective than when it is predicated upon the truth.

Connors, Michael F. *Dealing in Hate: The Development of Anti-German Propaganda.* Torrance, Calif.: Institute for Historical Review, 1970.
The Institute for Historical Review is well known for its efforts to rewrite the history of World War II in terms of exonerating Nazi Germany, while making out that the Holocaust was actually part of a Jewish-communist conspiracy. This volume argues that historic "Germanophobia" has created in the public mind a mythic and negative portrait of the Germans as "robot-like, goose-stepping legions of glassy-eyed storm troopers." It concludes that the real villains of World War II were the Allies (the United States, Soviet Union, and Great Britain), whose fault the war was to begin with. The author cites the work of reputable historians of Germany as proof of his arguments, and then cites well-known Jewish writers and statesmen, in the United States in particular, as being those who perpetuate "Germanophobia." The volume is an example of "disinformation"—that form of propaganda which presents factual information in such a way as to induce the reader to draw erroneous conclusions.

Dallas at the Crossroads. Prod. Dallas Citizens Council, 21 min., 1961. Dallas, Tex.: Dallas Public Library.
This film was developed specifically as propaganda by the Dallas Citizens Council for showing to school and community groups in preparation for the desegregation of Dallas schools, which was scheduled for June 1961. It features interviews with white community leaders who argue for peaceful desegregation and for the need to avoid the racial violence that was then occurring elsewhere in the South in the context of school desegregation.

The Damned. Dir. René Clément, Spéva Films, 105 min., 1947. Chicago: Facets Video.
It is the last days of World War II. Nazi officials and their hangers-on, knowing they face war-crimes accountability, take a U-boat from Oslo and head for South America. Along the way they behave in the brutal fashion characteristic of Nazis. A doctor, kidnapped to look after a

woman who was injured when an allied destroyer attacked the U-boat, becomes the hero when he saves the woman and engineers bringing the escaping Nazis to justice. The film combines a thriller motif with the kind of anti-Nazi propaganda that was widely popular in the first years after World War II.

Death Mills. Prod. United States War Department, 26 min., 1946. Baton Rouge: Louisiana State University.
This is the war department film shown to Germans after World War II as part of the de-Nazification program. It provides twenty-six minutes worth of footage of Nazi death camps, and the point is that every German bears responsibility for each victim of the Holocaust. Effective, and long enough to be particularly horrifying.

A Diary for Timothy. Prod. Basil Wright, dir. Humphrey Jennings, Crown Film Unit, 39 min., 1945, on *Wartime Moments*. New York: Kino International.
"Timothy" is a metaphor indicating the post-World War II generation kids born during the war. Timothy's father was a soldier, and his mother did war work of various kinds. The film is both a tribute to the total involvement of the British people in the war of 1939-1945, and a hint at social criticism. It argues that the "people's war" must result in a "people's peace," meaning a more egalitarian social order for the future.

A Dry White Season. Prod. Paula Weinstein, dir. Euzhan Palcy, Metro-Goldwyn-Mayer/United Artists, 97 min., 1989. Chicago: Facets Video.
Apartheid in South Africa is the target of this film polemic, based upon a novel by Andre Brink. An Afrikaner history teacher lives a comfortable middle-class life with wife and family in Johannesburg. However, following the Soweto uprising of 1976 all of his personal and political ties are thrown into question. He can no longer stand aside when his gardener is imprisoned and tortured merely for attempting to recover the body of his son, who was among those schoolchildren massacred during the uprising. The film examines the effect of racism on both whites and blacks in South Africa. This is the first feature film ever directed by a black woman for a major American film studio.

Family Portrait. Dir. Ian Dalrymple, 24 min., 1951. New York: Kino International.
This film is by Ian Dalrymple, who was a major figure in the Crown Film Unit during World War II. It is a public relations effort on behalf of the United Kingdom. The theme is the Festival of Britain, which

argues that the "family" in question is Britain and the peoples of the Empire and Commonwealth. The message is that Britain has got democracy right in all of its diversity; variety is the spice of British life, so to speak. Britain is praised for doing many good things around the globe.

Gallo, Max. "1950-1970: Words and Images," in *The Poster in History*. Translated by Alfred and Bruni Mayor. Secaucus, N.J.: Wellfleet Press, 1989.
This chapter details post-World War II propaganda posters for every occasion from commerce to pro- and antiwar movements. It provides both poster reproductions and explanatory text, illustrating in the process that the poster became an ever more effective propaganda channel as both technical production and manipulative image and language improved.

Gentleman's Agreement. Prod. Darryl F. Zanuck, dir. Elia Kazan, Twentieth Century-Fox, 118 min., 1947. Chicago: Facets Video.
This film is proof that a propaganda film can be well done. The target is anti-Semitism. A non-Jewish magazine writer decides to write a series of articles exposing the extent to which anti-Semitism is endemic to American society. Moreover, he decides that the only way to grasp the subject fully is to experience it firsthand by pretending to be a Jew. This film is a perfect example of propaganda that seeks to turn its audience away from prejudice and toward tolerance—more often than not, propaganda historically has worked the other way around. It is interesting to note that producer Darryl F. Zanuck was one of the few major Hollywood producers of that era who was not Jewish.

Go Tell the Spartans. Prod. Allan F. Bodah and Mitchell Cannold, dir. Ted Post, Spartan, 114 min., 1978. Chicago: Facets Video.
Set in the early days of United States involvement in the Vietnam War, this film tells the story of a detachment of Vietnamese militia commanded by a United States advisor who is a veteran of three wars. The unit is sent to occupy an old French garrison which, the advisor argues, is of no military value, and that to put troops there is to expose them to the Viet Cong. He is overruled on the grounds that because the French abandoned the fortress, they lost to the Viet Minh. Naturally, the old veteran is proved right. The film makes a strong case that the United States should not have been in Vietnam in the first place, and portrays United States Army command as stupid and the South Vietnamese government as thoroughly corrupt.

The Green Berets. Dir. John Wayne and Ray Kellogg, Warner Brothers, 141 min., 1968. Chicago: Facets Video.

John Wayne is at his superpatriotic best in this film, which purports to tell the story of the Green Berets in the Vietnam War, through the *persona* of a Green Beret colonel played by John Wayne himself. He leads a team of United States Green Berets and South Vietnamese regulars on a mission behind the lines. The film features Viet Cong treachery, the heroic death of American soldiers, the superiority of United States war technology, and the ideal of the United States fighting the war on behalf of ordinary South Vietnamese. An orphaned Vietnamese boy befriended by the Green Beret colonel is the metaphor which makes the latter point. The film contains all of the standard characteristics of a World War II propaganda feature: good versus evil, a righteous cause, and a speech that sums up the propaganda message. A United States Army officer once remarked that from the viewpoint of military tactics, "there is the right way and the John Wayne way." This film proves his point.

The Heroes of Desert Storm. Prod. Johanna Persons, dir. Don Ohlmeyer, Capital Cities/ABC Video Productions, 100 min., 1991. Los Angeles: ABC Video Enterprises.

Introduced by President George Bush, this docudrama tells the story of soldiers and flyers from the United States who took part in Operation Desert Storm to liberate Kuwait from Iraq in what has come to be known as the Gulf War. The film concentrates on particular individuals involved in particular military actions, shifting back and forth between them in the field and their families back home. More sophisticated photography and a greater subtlety in making its points is all that separates this film from its World War II predecessors. Patriotism, heroism, and fighting in the just cause are the main themes.

Jackboot Mutiny. Dir. G. W. Pabst, Arca/Ariston, 77 min., 1955. Unable to locate copy.

This film is a dramatic reconstruction of the attempt by a conspiracy of German army officers to assassinate Hitler on July 20, 1944. It is an expiatory anti-Nazi propaganda film by a director who earlier had made three pro-Nazi propaganda films. Hitler is portrayed as the personification of evil, his sycophantic associates as weak and spineless, and the army conspirators as heroes. The argument is made that they would have succeeded had more Germans been as heroic as these officers. In the mid-1950s, those Germans who had grown up during the Third Reich and experienced World War II were seeking a place of comfort within Europe. This film contained a comforting message for them.

Lomas, Charles W., and Michael Taylor, eds. *The Rhetoric of the British Peace Movement.* New York: Random House, 1971.

The Campaign for Nuclear Disarmament was a major force in British antiwar protest in the 1950s and 1960s. This collection of printed speeches from the movement indicates the kinds of arguments, both rational and emotional, that fueled the movement. The introduction describes the nature of protest rhetoric and the historical development of the peace movement, providing a critical framework for the study of the speeches included in the remainder of the volume. Those speeches are taken from various anti-nuclear war rallies organized by the CND. They were made by the likes of Donald Soper, Sir Richard Acland, Aneurin Bevan (a cabinet minister in the first postwar Labour government), J. B. Priestley (who did propaganda broadcasts for the British Broadcasting Corporation during World War II), philosopher Bertrand Russell, and historian A. J. P. Taylor. Debates over nuclear arms at the Labour Party Conference of 1960 are also reproduced. Each example of protest rhetoric is introduced by a brief explanation of context and the identity of the speaker(s). No bibliography.

Man of Iron. Prod. and dir. Andrzej Wajda, Film Polski/Film Unit X, 140 min., 1981. Chicago: Facets Video.

This is a pro-Solidarity propaganda film, made under intense political pressure and only just finished before the Polish government tried to suppress all forms of propaganda which supported Solidarity. The setting is Gdansk and the story is of a Solidarity strike leader who is harassed by the Polish government and by a pro-government journalist. The latter conducts a smear campaign against him, but as the strike continues finds that his own loyalties are being tested to the limit. This is the sequel to *Man of Marble* (entry below).

Man of Marble. Prod. and dir. Andrzej Wajda, PRF/Zespol, 162 min., 1972. Chicago: Facets Video.

Here is the story of a young filmmaker trying to reconstruct an honest picture of Stalinist influence on Poland's history since World War II. This is done by tracing the history of a bricklayer who had been made a "star" for his skills, until his stardom began to interfere with worker politics. Then, through propaganda and disinformation, the government disgraced his name and forced him into obscurity. The worker is a metaphor for Poland under communist rule. Curiously, the film was permitted in Polish cinemas, and when it played to packed houses, the audiences rose to their feet and sang the Polish national anthem. The Solidarity revolt was not far behind. See *Man of Iron* (entry above).

The Master Race. Prod. Robert Golden, dir. Herbert J. Biberman, RKO Radio Pictures, 96 min., 1944. Chicago: Facets Video.

Though made in wartime, this film concerns the peace which is to come. It opens with newsreel footage of the Normandy landings in June 1944, which is followed by a chilling scene that depicts a German colonel sending a group of officers into hiding. Their purpose is to reappear over time and in other guises, in order to once again organize the taking of power by the German "master race." The film projects into the postwar future and follows the efforts of this colonel, who, disguised as a Belgian refugee, strives to re-create in a Belgian border town the climate of totalitarian control through manipulation, intimidation, and disinformation that existed under the Nazis. The film warns its audience that the defeat of Nazism in war must be followed by the eradication of its unrepentant soldiers and its philosophy, during the ensuing peace.

Mission to Moscow. Prod. Robert Buckner, dir. Michael Curtiz, Warner Brothers, 100 min., 1943. Salt Lake City: University of Utah.

The film is introduced by Joseph E. Davies, United States Ambassador to the Soviet Union during the late 1930s, upon whose book by the same name it is based. It is a docudrama made during World War II with a message for postwar audiences. It makes a strong case that the Soviet Union has been much maligned and misunderstood in the West, and that the future security of Europe and the world rests upon cooperation between the United States and the Soviet Union. The distance is considerable between Stalin's prewar Soviet Union, as pictured in this film, and what the evidence indicates was the reality.

Oh! What a Lovely War. Prod. Brian Duffy, Richard Attenborough, and Len Deighton, dir. Richard Attenborough, Accord, 144 min., 1969. Hollywood, Calif.: Paramount Home Video.

One of the best antiwar films ever made, in which the propaganda is disseminated in the form of satire. Based upon a Charles Chilton play, the film traces the main themes of World War I, both on the battlefield and at home, in musical comedy style. For one example, the British aristocracy are shown sacrificing for war only by refusing to drink German champagne; for another, a cricket scoreboard keeps tally of war casualties; and for still another, a unit goes to the front baaing like sheep to the tune of *Onward Christian Soldiers*. The powerful antiwar angle made the film immensely popular with the British left, including historian A. J. P. Taylor, whose *Illustrated History of the First World War* employed satiric techniques also. For example, in that volume a photograph of a bespectacled and timid-appearing German soldier is captioned "A Wicked Hun."

Platoon. Prod. Arnold Kopelson, dir. Oliver Stone, Hemdale, 120 min., 1986. Chicago: Facets Video.
Oliver Stone served in Vietnam and came back convinced that it was the wrong war, in the wrong place, and at the wrong time. This film was inspired by his Vietnam experience and was made in order to promote his antiwar message. While some viewers saw Stone's use of violence in the film as effective antiwar propaganda, others saw it as excessive to the point of being the depiction of violence for its own sake. See *Born on the Fourth of July* (entry above).

Poelchau, Warner, ed. *White Paper Whitewash: Interviews with Philip Agee on the CIA and El Salvador*. New York: Deep Cover Books, 1981.
The name of the publishing house says it all. Former Central Intelligence Agency operative Philip Agee provided the material for these essays, which argue that the Reagan administration engaged in an anti-reform conspiracy with reactionary elements in El Salvador. The essays analyze how the Reagan administration used propaganda, disinformation, and out and out lies "to convince allied governments and the Social Democrats of an international communist plot against freedom in El Salvador." The media are indicted as being part of this conspiracy for refusing to take Agee seriously when he first attempted "to stimulate skepticism" regarding the "captured documents" that formed the basis of the Reagan propaganda. The editor of this collection makes no bones about where he stands. The El Salvador guerrillas "are fighting injustice, illiteracy, exploitation, torture and murder. . . . Their cause is just and the more support they get, from whatever source, the better." Whether justified by the facts or not, there is no question regarding the purpose of this volume. An appendix including United States government documents and El Salvador guerrilla documents are offered as proof of the conspiracy. No bibliography.

Reed, Sally D. *NEA: Propaganda Front of the Radical Left*. No place of publication indicated: Sally D. Reed, 1984.
Apparently privately published by the author, this short book purports to expose the radical "one-world," anti-family-values propaganda of the National Education Association. It purports also to represent the views of an organization referred to as the NCBE, though what these initials are the acronym for is never explained. The book purports to be a counter to NEA "propaganda," the content of which is said to be

undermining patriotism, belief in God, and the hopes of children to have an "education." In the process of these "purports," the author develops a blatant propaganda attack on the NEA, the national government, and all ideas about educational reform. If there is any doubt, here are some of the chapter headings: "Who Has Control of the Children?," "The NEA Spells Disaster for Public Education," "NEA—Socialism's Best Friend," and "The NEA Says Better RED than READ." Dale Evans-Rogers, the former singing cowgirl, wrote the introduction. No bibliography.

Sierra: The Magazine of the Sierra Club. San Francisco, bimonthly.
This bimonthly magazine is a publication of the Sierra Club, one of the oldest environmental lobbying organizations in the United States. The Sierra Club is committed to preserving wilderness and wildlife, and to encouraging enjoyment of these elements without doing them harm at the same time. Much of *Sierra* material is committed to opposing the depredations of overdevelopment, and what its publications sometimes term the shortsightedness of the United States government and American industry where the environment is concerned. While the magazine conveys a great deal of valuable information about the environment, it also employs some classic propaganda techniques in calling for its readers to be activists in preserving it.

State of Siege. Prod. Jacques Perrin, dir. Constantin Costa-Gavras, 119 min., 1973. Chicago: Facets Video.
Set in Uruguay, this political thriller by Costa-Gavras, a filmmaker with an ax to grind, is based on the actual kidnapping and murder of a military "advisor" from the United States, an event that was used as a pretext for shutting down Uruguayan civil liberties. The film condemns clandestine activities by the United States Central Intelligence Agency and other organizations in Central and South America. It is not complimentary to the military regime in Uruguay, either. See *Z* (entry below).

Sword in the Desert. Prod. Robert Buckner, Dir. George Sherman, Universal-International, 95 min., 1949. Washington, D.C.: Library of Congress.
This film preaches the virtues of those Jews, Sabras and European immigrants, who created the new state of Israel. Israel was roughly two years old when the film was released, and less than one year past its first war of survival against surrounding Arab states. The time is immediately after World War II. The cynical captain of a freighter agrees to transport illegal immigrants into Palestine for money. When he has to wait for payment, he becomes unwillingly involved in the

Jews' struggle against both British administration of Palestine and anti-Jewish Arabs. In due course he is converted to the cause and helps in the fight for the new state. The British are treated with some tolerance, but the film is full of anti-Arab propaganda.

Wilson. Prod. Darryl F. Zanuck, dir. Henry King, Twentieth Century-Fox, 154 min., 1944. Chicago: Facets Video.

Though made during World War II, this film is about the peace to follow. It tells the life story of Woodrow Wilson, one of the architects of European peace at the end of World War I. Two themes are central: Wilson as the man who believed in peace and worked hard to establish it throughout his life and career, and Wilson the president who was betrayed at the end of this effort by political opponents, who put personal interest above the national good. This film aimed to convince Americans that this must not be allowed to happen after World War II. See Leonard J. Leff and Jerold Simmons, "*Wilson*" (entry above under "Channels and Techniques").

Z. Dir. Constantin Costa-Gavras, Reggane Films/ONCIC(Algiers), 125 min., 1968. Chicago: Facets Video.

In a nameless Mediterranean country (read Greece) support grows for "Z," the leader of a pacifist opposition party. He is clubbed in the head by a man in a passing truck and killed. An investigating magistrate uncovers a secret organization of thugs supported by police and government, and claims the death is murder. The finger in this film points squarely at the totalitarian regime of the colonels in Greece in the 1960s. It also points at totalitarian regimes generally, sending an unmistakable message that they must be opposed in the name of human rights and freedom.

Abelson, Herbert I., 35
Abrams, Mark, 25
Abrams, Ray H., 88
Adam, Peter, 190
Adler, Leo K., 294
Adler, Richard, 350
Ailes, Roger, 56
Ainsworth, Gardner, 159, 169
Akzin, Benjamin, 134
Albert, Ernst, 160
Albig, William, 20, 25
Aldgate, Anthony, 77, 160, 245, 255
Alexander, Yonah, 364
Alexandre, Laurien, 295
Allen, George V., 295
Allen, V. L., 295
Allport, Floyd H., 25
Allport, Gordon W., 42, 238, 345
Altheide, David L., 39, 71, 346
American Institute for Research, 57
Angell, Norman, 6, 14
Annis, Albert D., 26, 57
Anschütz, Gerhard, 107
Aronson, Elliot, 49, 51-52
Artyomov, Vladimir, 307
Asher, R., 39
Atkin, Charles K., 346
August, Thomas G., 135

Baden-Powell, Robert, 132, 151, 175
Bagdikian, Benjamin H., 71, 346,
   348, 360
Bagley, William C., 135
Baird, Jay W., 191, 227, 239
Baker, M. Joyce, 239
Balfour, Michael, 1, 35, 239, 244
Ball-Rokeach, Sandra J., 39, 77
Bandura, Albert, 40
Barkhausen, Hans, 89
Barnicoat, John, 58
Barnouw, Erik, 58, 347
Barrat, Stephanie, 78

Barrett, Edward W., 296
Barron, Jerome A., 347
Barsamian, David, 348, 359
Barsis, Max, 268
Bartlett, F. C., 14
Bates, Stephan, 340, 346
Becker, Jean-Jacques, 89
Beeley, Sir Harold, 348
Begley, George, 255
Bell, P. M. H., 240
Beloff, Max, 336
Bem, Daryl J., 14
Benn, David Wedgewood, 308
Bent, Silas, 160
Bentley, Eric, 58
Berchtold, William E., 135
Berelson, Bernard, 24, 26, 36, 59
Berezin, Mabel, 204
Bernays, Edward L., 14, 22, 27-28,
   30, 32, 34
Best, James J., 28
Bettinghaus, Irwin P., 72
Bevan, Edwin, 123, 126
Beyle, Herman C., 40
Bigelow, Burton, 160
Bishop, Robert L., 9, 240
Bittman, Ladislav, 308
Black, Edwin R., 72
Black, Gregory D., 240, 242, 249
Black, John B., 336
Blakey, George T., 89
Blanco White, Amber, 221
Blankenhorn, Heber, 112
Bloomfield, Leonard, 73
Boelcke, Willi A., 241
Bogart, Leo, 296
Borchard, Edwin M., 136
Bornecque, Henri, 112
Boyd, Douglas A., 309
Braestrup, Peter, 348
Bramstead, Ernest K., 192, 195
Briggs, Asa, 241

Brock, Timothy C., 46, 50
Brown, Harold Chapman, 161
Brown, J. A. C., 15
Brown, Steven R., 41
Browne, Donald R., 349
Brownlow, Kevin, 104
Brownrigg, Sir Douglas, 113
Brownstein, Ronald, 337
Brucker, Herbert, 59
Bruntz, George H., 90
Buchan, John, 107, 124
Buchsbaum, Jonathan, 136
Buitenhuis, Peter, 90
Burden, Hamilton T., 192
Burns, Tom, 349
Buzzi, Giancarlo, 28
Bytwerk, Randall L., 193

Cadogan, Mary, 114
Calder, Robert Lorin, 161
Caldwell, Jill, 59
Callcott, W. R., 161
Campbell, Craig W., 9
Campbell, David, 337, 342
Campbell, Donald T., 41
Canetti, Elias, 41
Cantril, Hadley, 29, 42, 309
Capra, Frank, 242
Carr, E. H., 162, 371
Carroll, Gordon, 176
Carsten, F. L., 91
Carter, Huntley, 204
Casey, Ralph D., 10-11, 25, 60, 136, 167
Castle, Eugene W., 338
Cater, Douglass, 350
Catlin, George E. G., 193-194, 309
Ceplair, Larry, 297
Chafee, Zechariah, Jr., 73
Chaffee, Steven H., 73
Chaiken, Shelly, 42
Chakotin, Serge, 205
Chambers, Frank P., 91
Chandler, Robert W., 350-351

Chappell, Matthew N., 74
Charnley, Mitchell V., 351
Chase, Stuart, 74
Chenault, Libby, 124
Cherry, Colin, 74, 351
Chester, Edward W., 75
Child, Irvin L., 42
Childers, Erskine, 151
Childers, R. Erskine, 176
Childs, Harwood Lawrence, 30, 162, 193, 255, 256
Chomsky, Noam, 7, 338, 348, 352, 359, 364
Choukas, Michael, 297
Christensen, Terry, 60
Christenson, Reo M., 30
Clark, David C., 163
Clarke, I. F., 31
Clarke, Peter B., 75, 242
Clements, Frank, 137
Cockerill, George, 91
Cockett, Richard, 137
Coers, Donald V., 242
Coggeshall, Reginald, 76
Cohen, Arthur R., 43
Cohen, Stanley, 352
Colby, Benjamin, 243
Cole, J. A., 243, 253
Cole, Robert, 138, 155-156, 159, 243-244, 247, 266
Cole, Taylor, 204, 206
Collins, Ross F., 92
Combs, James E., 15, 352
Combs, Sara T., 15
Connors, Michael F., 371
Conquest, Robert, 194
Constantine, Stephen, 177
Converse, Philip E., 43
Conway, Flo, 353
Cook, Fred J., 354
Cook, Sir Edward, 114
Cooper, Eunice, 48
Corcoran, Paul E., 76
Cornebise, Alfred E., 92, 95, 138

Cornick, Martyn, 244
Costello, David R., 244
Cottrell, Leonard S. Jr., 36, 51
Coultass, Clive, 245, 255-256
Craig, Patricia, 114
Crawford, Anthony R., 125
Creel, George, 114
Cremieux-Brilhac, Jean-Louis, 271
Crew, T., 163
Crewdson, Wilson, 123, 125
Croft, Jeremy, 250
Crofts, William, 339, 367
Crozier, Emmet, 115
Cruickshank, Charles, 245
Culbert, David, 61, 310
Cull, Nicholas John, 61, 245
Curran, James, 76-77
Curtis, Liz, 339

Dahlin, Ebba, 92
Dale, Edgar, 160
Dallek, Robert, 354-355
Dalrymple, Helen, 32
Darracott, Joseph, 126, 272
Daugherty, William E., 61
Davey, Arthur, 138
Davison, W. Phillips, 31, 340
Davitz, Joel R., 77
De Chambure, A., 115
de Grazia, S., 59
Deacon, Richard, 62
DeFleur, Melvin L., 39, 77
Delmer, Sefton, 256, 258
Demartial, Georges, 115
Demm, Eberhard, 116
Dennis, Everette E., 354
DeNoon, Christopher, 178
Deutschmann, Linda, 206, 235
Diamond, Edwin, 340, 346
Dickinson, Margaret, 257
Dies, Martin, 324
Dobyns, Fletcher, 163
Dodge, Raymond, 93
Doherty, Martin, 257

Doob, Leonard W., 16, 20, 24-25, 31,
    36, 42-44, 65, 205
Douglas, Roy, 258
Dovifat, Emil, 16
Drouilly, J. Germain, 112
Ducat, Stephen, 354-355
Dunham, Donald, 298
Duus, Masayo, 246, 291
Dyer, Murray, 311
Dyer, Sherman H., 258

Ebenstein, William, 194
Eberle, Matthias, 139
Ebermayer, Erich, 192, 194
Ebon, Martin, 311
Edwards, John Carver, 258
Ekstein, Modris, 195
Ellul, Jacques, 16-17, 54, 79
Emery, Walter B., 311
Englund, Steven, 297
Ernst, Wilhelm, 93
Evans, F. Bowen, 298
Evans, Gary, 246

Fairbanks, Arthur, 340
Falk, Irving A., 298, 357
Farago, Ladislas, 259
Farrell, John C., 355
Felstead, Sidney Theodore, 93, 109
Ferguson, John, 94
Festinger, Leonard, 44, 56
Fielding, Raymond, 139, 155
Fite, Gilbert C., 182
Flavell, M. Kay, 195
Flynn, John T., 31
Ford, Guy Stanton, 116
Ford, Nick Aaron, 18
Foster, H. Schuyler, Jr., 164
Foulkes, A. P., 59, 62
Fraser, Lindley Macnaughton, 18,
    140, 195
Frederick, Howard H., 356
Fredin, Eric, 75
Freedman, Anne E., 45

Freedman, Jonathan L., 45, 50
Freedman, P. E., 45
Freeman, Ellis, 206
Freeman, Judith, 164, 177
Friedl, Bettina, 179, 189
Friedmann, Otto, 260
Friedrich, Carl J., 18-19
Friedson, Eliot, 78
Fulbright, Senator J. W., 341
Furhammar, Leif, 62
Fyfe, Hamilton, 78

Gadberry, Glen W., 196
Gallo, Max, 116, 119, 207, 373
Garber, William, 207
Garnett, Maxwell, 19
Geldern, James von, 207
George, Alexander L., 45
George, John, 341
Gerdes, Peter R., 247

Gervereau, Laurent, 63
Gilmour, T. L., 94
Ginsberg, Benjamin, 32
Godefroy, Christian H., 78
Godson, Roy, 319
Goldie, Grace Wyndham, 356
Goodfriend, Arthur, 356
Goodrum, Charles, 32
Gordon, George N., 298, 357
Gordon, Joseph S., 312
Gordon, Robbie, 63
Got, Ambroise, 165
Graber, Doris A., 357
Graham, Cooper C., 196
Grahame, Jeanne, 95
Grandin, Thomas, 207
Grant, Mariel, 137, 140, 164, 266
Graves, W. Brooke, 33
Green, Fitzhugh, 342
Greenwald, Anthony G., 46
Gregory, G. H., 275
Grierson, John, 141
Gross, John, 141

Grothe, Peter, 299
Gruening, Ernest, 165
Gurevitch, Michael, 76
Gustainis, J. Justin, 357

Hachey, Thomas E., 95
Hale, Hubert, 9
Hale, Oron James, 141
Hall, Alex, 142
Hallin, Daniel C., 358
Halloran, J. D., 79
Hamlin, Charles Hunter, 165
Hanak, Harry, 95
Hansen, Allen C., 358
Hanson, Elisha, 166
Hapgood, Norman, 127
Harding, T. Swann, 142
Hardy, Alexander G., 197
Hargrave, John, 247
Harrisson, Tom, 33
Hartsough, Denise, 197
Haste, Cate, 96
Havighurst, Clark C., 312
Hawthorne, Jeremy, 19
Hayakawa, S. I., 73-74, 79, 299
Hays, Will H., 142
Henderson, Edgar H., 19
Hennessy, Bernard C., 33
Herman, Edward S., 7, 358-359, 364
Herz, Martin F., 46
Hiebert, Ray Eldon, 33, 359-360
Higham, Charles Frederick, 143
Hiley, Nicholas, 96
Himelstein, Morgan Y., 143
Hitler, Adolf, 226
Hobson, J. A., 111, 143
Hodapp, William, 298
Hogan, J. Michael, 299
Hollander, Gayle Durham, 197
Hollins, T. J., 166
Holt, Robert T., 46
Honey, Maureen, 247, 252
Hooper, C. E., 74
Hoover, A. J., 97

Hopkin, Deian, 77, 97
Horak, Jan-Christopher, 198
Houn, Franklyn W., 313, 321
Hovland, Carl I., 36, 47, 52, 317
Howell, Bill, 99
Howitt, Dennis, 79
Huber, Georg, 97
Hummel, William, 64
Huntress, Keith, 64
Huse, H. R., 64
Huxley, Aldous, 30, 167, 228
Hyman, Alan, 94, 98, 109
Hyman, Herbert H., 34, 47

Ingersoll, William, 116
Inkeles, Alex, 198, 299, 313
Irion, Frederick C., 34
Irwin, Will, 79
Isaksson, Folke, 62
Isenberg, Michael T., 98-99, 102

Jackson, Martin A., 66
Jacobson, David J., 64
Jahoda, Marie, 48
Janowitz, Morris, 26, 61, 208, 313
Jansen, Sue Curry, 65
Jarvie, I. C., 248
Jeffords, Susan, 342
Johnson, Abby Arthur, 342
Johnson, John M., 39
Johnson, Niel M., 144
Johnson, Ronald Maberry, 342
Johnston, Winifred, 99
Jones, Barbara, 99
Jowett, Garth S., 20, 34, 80, 104
Joyce, Walter, 300
Judd, Denis, 278
Juergens, George, 144
Jusserand, Jean Jules, 100

Kamins, Bernard Francis, 21
Kapferer, J. N., 35
Kaplan, Frank L., 314
Karlins, Marvin, 35

Katz, Daniel, 26, 35
Katz, Elihu, 80
Kecskemeti, Paul, 84, 314
Keen, Sam, 64
Kenez, Peter, 198
Kershaw, Ian, 199
Kiffer, Monika, 200
Kingston, Paul J., 200
Kirkpatrick, George R., 181
Kirwin, Gerald, 248
Knightly, Phillip, 80, 87
Knoles, George H., 100
Knowles, Dorothy, 145
Knudson, Jerry W., 209
Kohut, Andrew, 85
Kominsky, Morris, 314
Koppes, Clayton R., 242, 249
Kracauer, Siegfried, 200, 204
Kraus, Sidney, 81
Kriesberg, Martin, 314
Kris, Ernst, 209
Kruglak, Theodore E., 315

Lacey, Kate, 167
Lahav, Pnina, 65
Lakoff, Robin Tolmach, 81
Lambert, Richard S., 21
Landau, Captain Henry, 117
Landy, Marcia, 209
Lane, Robert E., 65
Lang, Gladys Engel, 343
Lang, Kurt, 343
Larson, Cedric, 100-101, 103
Lasswell, Harold D., 10-11, 21, 24,
   30, 36, 48, 82, 90, 117, 194, 207,
   210, 258
Laurence, John C., 343
Lavine, Harold, 210, 249
Lawrence, Raymond D., 12, 167
Leab, Janiel J., 300
Lee, Alfred McClung, 22, 25, 36
Lee, Ivy L., 36
Leeper, R. A., 145
Leff, Leonard J., 361, 379

Leighton, Marian Kirsch, 312, 315
LeMahieu, D. L., 168
Lemert, James B., 82
Lendvai, Paul, 315
Lenin, N., 211
Lerner, Daniel, 82, 361
Lester, Marilyn, 84
Levin, Jack, 168
Lewis, Beth Irwin, 66
Lichtenberg, Bernard, 159, 168
Liebovich, Louis, 300
Lilly, Carol S., 301
Lindzey, Gardner, 49
Linton, James M., 80
Lipsky, Abram, 22
Lodeesen, Jon, 316
Loftus, Belinda, 126, 272
Lomas, Charles W., 375
Low, David, 183
Lowell, Abbott Lawrence, 101
Lowry, Montecue J., 301
Lumley, Frederick E., 20, 22
Lumsdaine, Arthur A., 47
Lutz, Ralph Haswell, 101
Lyons, Timothy J., 98, 101

MacArthur, John R., 361
MacCann, Richard Dyer, 145
Maccoby, Nathan, 44
McCombs, Maxwell E., 83
McCrosky, James C., 83
MacDonald, Callum A., 146
MacDonald, J. Fred, 302
McDowall, Duncan, 36
McEwen, John M., 117
Machiavelli, Niccolò, 45
Mackay, LaMar S., 240
MacKenzie, A. J., 201
MacKenzie, John M., 135, 146, 169
McLaine, Ian, 250
McLaughlan, Andrew Cunningham, 118
MacLean, Eleanor, 65
McWilliams, Robert O., 30

Mancini, Elain, 201, 210
Mansell, Gerard, 362
Marchand, Roland, 146
Marett, Sir Robert, 302
Markham, James W., 316
Marks, Melvin R., 49
Marquis, Alice Goldfarb, 102
Marrin, Albert, 102
Marshall, Herbert, 169
Marshall, Logan, 129
Martin, Kingsley, 147
Martin, L. John, 23, 49
Martin, Marcel, 214
Marx, Fritz Morstein, 194, 201
Meier, Norman C., 26
Meissner, Hans-Otto, 192, 194
Meo, L. D., 250
Merton, Robert K., 50
Messenger, Gary S., 102
Metzl, Irvine, 103
Meyer, Michael, 202
Michie, Allan A., 302
Milenkovitch, Michael M., 316
Millard, Oscar E., 118
Mock, James R., 100, 118
Mock, James Robert, 101, 103
Molotch, Harvey, 84
Montague, Ivor, 169
Morris, A. J. A., 147
Moss, Armand, 317
Mott, Frank Luther, 170
Mould, David H., 103

Nagorski, Zygmunt, Jr., 303
Nelson, Joyce, 147
Nicholson, Ivor, 104
Nielsen, Keith, 104
Nieuwenhof, Frans, 261
Nimmo, Dan, 352
Noble, George Bernard, 105
Noelle-Neumann, Elisabeth, 37

O'Connor, John E., 66
Odegard, Peter H., 37, 148

O'Donnell, Victoria, 20
Ogle, Marbury Bladen, Jr., 37
O'Higgens, Paul, 362
Orwant, Jack E., 317
Orwell, George, 32, 218-219, 231, 245, 291, 359
Osterhouse, R. A., 50
Ostrom, Thomas M., 46
O'Sullivan, Carol, 66

Page, Caroline, 343
Parenti, Michael, 348
Paret, Paul, 66
Paret, Peter, 66
Parry, Robert, 65, 67
Parry-Giles, Shawn J., 304
Passelecq, Fernand, 131
Paterson, Thomas G., 294
Perloff, Richard M., 81
Perris, Arnold, 67
Peterson, H. C., 105, 182
Petrick, Michael J., 73
Petty, Richard E., 50
Phelan, John, 68
Pielke, Robert G., 362
Pirsein, Robert William, 304
Poelchau, Warner, 377
Pohle, Heinz, 170
Ponsonby, Sir Arthur, 109, 118
Pool, Ithiel de Sola, 84
Postman, Leo, 238
Potter, Pitman B., 170
Pratkanis, Anthony R., 7, 51
Price, Vincent, 38
Priestley, J. B., 286, 375
Pronay, Nicholas, 11, 23, 77, 104, 148, 171, 250

Qualter, Terence H., 38

Raack, R. C., 261
Rabinovitz, Lauren, 342
Rappaport, Armin, 106
Rawls, Walton, 119

Read, James Morgan, 106
Reader, W. J., 135, 146, 148
Reardon, Kathleen Kelley, 84
Reed, Sally D., 377
Reeves, Nicholas, 106, 119
Reid, Franklyn, 149
Remarque, Erich Maria, 167, 187
Remington, Thomas, 211
Renov, Michael, 262
Renshaw, Patrick, 149
Rentschler, Eric, 212
Reuth, Ralf Georg, 202
Reynolds, Mary T., 149
Rhodes, Anthony, 287
Rice, Arnold, 150
Richards, Jeffrey, 150, 245, 255
Rickards, Maurice, 68, 131
Riegel, O. W., 125, 150, 172, 212
Riley, John R., 36, 51
Riley, Norman, 251
Roberts, Donald F., 85
Robertson, James C., 23, 150, 251
Robinson, Edward J., 52
Robinson, Edward S., 44
Robinson, Michael J., 85
Roeder, George H., Jr., 262
Roetter, Charles, 119
Rogerson, Sidney, 172
Rokeach, Milton, 52, 54, 341
Rose, Oscar, 10
Rosenberg, William G., 232
Rosenthal, Michael, 151
Rosnow, Ralph L., 52
Rossignol, Dominique, 252
Roth, Paul, 213
Rotha, Paul, 152
Roxburgh, Angus, 318
Rubin, Bernard, 363
Rudnitsky, Konstantin, 213
Rudolph, G. A., 131
Rühlmann, Paul M., 152
Rupp, Leila J., 252
Russell, Bertrand, 152

Saerchinger, César, 213
Sanders, Michael, 107
Sargant, William, 53
Sargent, S. S., 39
Sayegh, Fayez A., 363
Schiller, Herbert I., 364
Schnitzer, Jean, 214
Schnitzer, Luda, 214
Schoenewolf, Gerald, 53
Schramm, Wilber, 85
Schwertfeger, Bernhard, 107
Sears, D. O., 45
Seldes, George, 173
Selwyn, Francis, 243, 252
Semyonov, Vladimir, 307
Shaw, Donald L., 83
Sheatsley, Paul B., 47
Sheffield, Fred D., 47
Shindler, Colin, 263
Shlapentokh, Dmitry, 202
Shlapentokh, Vladimir, 202
Short, K. R. M., 23, 214-215,
    263-264, 318
Shover, Michele J., 108
Shulman, Holly Cowan, 264
Shultz, Richard H., 319
Siegelman, Jim, 353
Silver, Kenneth E., 120
Silverman, Joan L., 153
Simcovitch, Maxim, 153
Simmons, Jerold, 361, 379
Simone, Sam P., 264
Singerman, Robert, 10, 363
Skinner, James M., 305
Slosson, Preston, 288
Smith, A. C. H., 77, 173
Smith, Bruce Lannes, 10-11, 21, 24,
    53
Smith, Chitra M., 11
Smith, M. Brewster, 54
Smith, Ted J., III, 24
Smith, Woodruff, 214
Soley, Lawrence C., 253
Sorensen, Thomas C., 305

Sorrels, Charles A., 319
Southworth, Herbert Rutledge, 153
Sparks, Kenneth R., 344
Speier, Hans, 82, 85, 209
Spitzer, H. M., 344
Spring, D. W., 171
Sproule, J. Michael, 24, 86
Squires, James Duane, 108
Stangor, Charles, 42
Stanley, Peter, 132
Stead, Peter, 154
Steele, Richard W., 154, 253
Steinson, Barbara J., 155
Stenton, Michael, 155
Stevens, John D., 86
Stone, Vernon A, 54
Storey, Graham, 86
Strang, Herbert, 132
Strebel, Elizabeth Grottle, 23, 253
Street, C. J. C., 120
Street, Sarah, 257
Stuart, Sir Campbell, 114, 120
Suleiman, Susan Rubin, 69
Swann, Paul, 152, 155
Swanson, G. E., 54
Swartz, Marvin, 108
Symons, Julian, 94, 109
Szecskö, Tamás, 80

Tanaka, Yasumasa, 55
Tavin, Eli, 364
Taylor, Edmond, 265
Taylor, Michael, 375
Taylor, Philip M., 107, 109, 137, 145,
    148, 155-157, 159, 265-266, 305,
    365
Taylor, Richard, 157, 203, 214-216
Taylor, Wilson L., 49
Thimme, Hans, 109
Thompson, Doug, 203
Thompson, Kenneth W., 345
Thompson, Wayne N., 55
Thomson, George P., 254
Thomson, Oliver, 69

Thornton, Sinclair, 216
Thorpe, Frances, 11
Thum, Gladys, 25
Thum, Marcella, 25
Tschirhart, Mary, 38
Turner, Ralph H., 55

Ursprung, Tobias, 55

van de Velde, Robert W., 46
Vaughn, Stephen, 110
Viereck, George Sylvester, 110

Waddington, Geoffrey, 157
Wagnleitner, Reinhold, 306
Waley, Daniel, 157
Walker, Graham, 158
Wallace, Stuart, 110
Walster, Elaine, 56
Wanderscheck, Hermann, 216
Waples, Douglas, 86
Ward, Larry Wayne, 99, 121, 123-124, 127-128, 130-131
Warner, Arthur H., 121
Warren, Allen, 158
Wasburn, Philo C., 70
Wechsler, James, 249
Weinberg, David, 217
Weiss, Janet A., 38
Welch, David, 122, 201, 204, 212, 221, 227
Wells, Gary L., 50
West, W. J., 291
Wettig, Gerhard, 319

White, Ralph K., 70, 320
Whitfield, Stephen J., 320
Whitton, John Boardman, 162, 256, 306, 366
Wildy, Tom, 366
Willcox, Temple, 158
Willey, Malcolm M., 87
Williams, John, 111
Willis, Irene Cooper, 111
Wilson, Charles H., 217
Wilson, H. H., 367
Wilson, Trevor, 111
Wingate, Pauline, 77
Winkler, Allan M., 110, 254
Wirth, Louis, 87
Wooddy, Carroll H., 71
Woollacott, Janet, 76
Wright, D. G., 112
Wright, Quincy, 174

Yass, Marion, 293
Young, Jock, 352
Young, John Wesley, 218
Young, Kimball, 12
Young, Nigel, 157
Young, Peter R., 367
Young, Robert G., 218
Youngblood, Denise J., 159
Younger, Kenneth, 345
Yu, Frederick T. C., 321

Zajonc, Robert B., 56
Zeman, Z. A. B., 218
Ziffren, Lester, 160

FILM TITLE INDEX

A nous la liberté, 174, 185
Above Suspicion, 266
Across the Pacific, 266, 269
Action in the North Atlantic, 267
The Adventures of Dick Dolan, 122
Aelita, 219
Aerograd, 174
Air Force, 267
Alexander Nevsky, 174, 214
All My Good Countrymen, 219
America's Answer, 122
Anarchy, U.S.A., 321
Anatomy of a Lie, 368
And So They Live, 175
And Women Must Weep, 368
Animal Farm, 219
Apocalypse Now, 358, 369
Architektur des Untergangs, 191
Are We Winning, Mommy? America
    and the Cold War, 307
Army-Navy Screen Magazine
    Highlights, 267, 277
Arsenal, 220, 223
Art with a Message: Protest and
    Propaganda, 57
Assignment in Brittany, 267
Atomic Attack, 321
The Atomic Cafe, 307
Autobiography of a Jeep, 268

Back to Bataan, 268-269
Backing up the Guns, 369
Baltic Deputy, 220
Bataan, 268
The Battle Cry of Peace, 122, 127
The Battle of Algiers, 369
The Battle of Kharkov-1942, 269
Battleship Potemkin, 169-170, 192,
    214, 220
Be Neutral, 123
The Bedford Incident, 322

Behelfskriegsbrücken über die
    Donau, 269
Betrayal from the East, 269
Big Jim McLain, 322
The Birth of Soviet Cinema, 192
Bismarck, 220
Black Dragons, 269
Blood on the Sun, 270
Body and Soul, 175
Bombardier, 270
The Bond, 123
Born American, 322
Born on the Fourth of July, 370, 377
Bright Days of Tomorrow
    (1945-1956), 309
Britain Prepared, 124
Bugs and Daffy: The Wartime
    Cartoons, 270
Building Belief, Part 1, 59

Campaigns and Elections: Classics of
    Political TV, 350
Carl Peters, 221
Casablanca, 270
Cast a Giant Shadow, 370
Casualties of War, 370
Century of Progress, 176
Chapayev, 221
Chicken Little, 15
China Strikes Back, 177
The China Syndrome, 370
Civilization, 125
Class Warriors, 310
Coal Face, 177
Communism, 323
Communism and Coexistence, 323
Communist Accent on Youth, 310
Communist Blueprint for Conquest,
    323
Communist Imperialism, 324
Communist Target: Youth, 310
Confessions of a Nazi Spy, 222, 328

Congress and the Media and Congress and the Establishment, 353
Conspirator, 324
Consuming Hunger, 60
Convoy, 256, 271
The Cranes Are Flying, 222
Le Crime de M. Lange, 177
The Cross of Lorraine, 271
Crusade for Freedom, 324
Cuba Si!, 324

Dallas at the Crossroads, 371
The Damned, 371
Dangerous Hours, 178
Days of Glory, 272
Death Mills, 372
December 7, 259
December 7th, 272
Le Dernier Milliardaire, 222
Desert Victory, 4, 273
Desperate Journey, 273
Diary for My Children, 223
A Diary for Timothy, 372
Dr. Strangelove: Or, How I Learned to Stop Worrying and Love the Bomb, 60, 66, 325
Does It Matter What You Think?, 31
Doin' His Bit, 126
Don't Be a Sucker, 325
Drums, 178
A Dry White Season, 372

Earth, 223
Edge of Darkness, 273
Enthusiasm, 223
Eric Severeid's "Not So Wild a Dream," 178
Escape from East Berlin, 325
The Eternal Jew, 224-225
The Extraordinary Adventures of Mr. West in the Land of the Bolsheviks, 224
Eye of the Eagle: December 7, 259, 272

Fable Safe, 312
Face to Face with Communism, 326
Faces of the Enemy, 44
Fail Safe, 326
The Fall of a Nation, 126
The Fall of the Romanov Dynasty, 224
Family Portrait, 372
FDR and Hitler, 164
Fight for the Sky, 273
The Fighting Sullivans, 274
Film Communique: 1-11, 274
The First Casualty, 116
Foreign Correspondent, 224, 265
49th Parallel, 255, 274
Fridericus, 225
Der Fuehrer Schenkt der Juden eine Stadt, 257

G-Men, 179
The General Line—Old and the New, 225
Gentleman's Agreement, 373
The German Invasion of Poland: 1939, 274
German Wartime Newsreels: 1941-1945, 275
Germany Awake! (Deutschland Erwäche), 226
Germany Calling, 275
The Girl in the Kremlin, 326
Go Tell the Spartans, 373
La Grande Illusion, 179
The Grapes of Wrath, 60, 180
The Great Dictator, 60, 226
The Great Liberty Bond Hold-Up, 127
The Green Berets, 60, 63, 358, 374
Der Grosse König, 276
Guadalcanal Diary, 276
Guilty of Treason, 327
Gung Ho!, 276

Hangmen Also Die!, 276
Happiness, 226

Heart of Humanity, 121, 127
Hearts of the World, 128
The Heroes of Desert Storm, 374
Hitler: February 10, 1933, 208
Hitlerjunge Quex, 63, 191, 227
Hitler's Children, 227, 262
Hollywood Goes to War, 277
Home Front, 1917-1919: War Transforms America, 96
Hunger: The National Hunger March to Washington, 180

I Am a Fugitive from a Chain Gang, 180
I Was a Communist for the FBI, 305, 327
I Was a Fireman, 277
Ich Klage An, 228
Illusions of News, 360
The Image Makers, 34
The Immortal Battalion, 277
In Which We Serve, 255, 278
Industrial Britain, 177, 180
The Informer, 181
Invasion, U.S.A., 327
The Iron Crown, 228
The Iron Curtain, 328

J'accuse, 181
Jackboot Mutiny, 232, 374
Japanese Relocation, 278
Joan of Paris, 278
Joseph Goebbels, 208
Jud Süss, 226, 228
Justice, 279

The Kaiser, the Beast of Berlin, 128
Kameradschaft, 181
Keys of the Kingdom, 241, 279
A King in New York, 328
Kolberg, 204, 226, 279, 285
Kühle Wampe, 229
Kutuzov, 279

The Lady Vanishes, 182
The Last Chance, 280
Lenin in 1918, 229
The Life and Death of Colonel Blimp, 280
The Life and Times of Rosie the Riveter, 248, 252, 260
Life Goes to the Movies: The War Years, 260
The Lion Has Wings, 11, 256, 278, 280
Listen to Britain, 60, 281
The Little American, 128
The Lives of a Bengal Lancer, 182, 188
London Can Take It, 281
A Look at Socialism, 328

McCarthy: Death of a Witch Hunter, 302, 305
Mädchen in Uniform, 229
Man Hunt, 281
Man of Iron, 375
Man of Marble, 375
Man on a String, 329
Man on a Tightrope, 329
The Man Who Was Afraid, 128
The Manchurian Candidate, 329
Mao's Little Red Video, 330
Der Marsch Zum Führer, 229
La Marseillaise, 183
The Master Race, 211, 376
Meet John Doe, 183
Meeting the Red Challenge, 330
The Memphis Belle: A Story of a Flying Fortress, 282
Metropolis, 184
Midnight, 282
Millions Like Us, 184
Minister of Hate, 211
Mission to Moscow, 60, 66, 249, 262, 376
Mr. Smith Goes to Washington, 60, 147, 155, 184

Mrs. Miniver, 4, 249, 282
Modern Times, 185
Morale for a Free World: America
    and Not America Only, 303
A Mormon Maid, 185, 189
Mothers of France, 129
The Moving Picture Boys in the
    Great War, 104
Munich, 1938 Arts Festival, 225
My Four Years in Germany, 130
My Japan, 283
My Son John, 330
My Universities, 230

The National Hunger March, 185
Native Land, 185
Nazi Agent, 230
Negro Colleges in Wartime, 283
The Negro Soldier, 283
The New Gulliver, 230
New Philippines News, 283
The Nibelungen Saga—Kriemhild's
    Revenge, 230
The Nibelungen Saga—Siegfried, 231
Night Mail, 186
Night Train to Munich, 245, 284
Nightmare in Red, 331
Ninotchka, 231
No Place to Hide, 317
The North Star, 284

Objective, Burma!, 284
October, 192
Oh! What a Lovely War, 376
Ohm Krüger, 226, 284
The Old Way and the New, 186
Olympia: The Film of the 1936
    Olympic Games, 231
On the Beach, 331
One of Our Aircraft Is Missing, 4, 285
One, Two, Three, 331
Our American Boys in the European
    War, 130
Our Daily Bread, 186

Our March, 232
Over There: 1914-1918, 105

Paracelsus, 232
Passage to Marseille, 285
People of the Cumberland, 186
Perpetual Revolution, 318
Pett and Pott: A Fairy Story of the
    Suburbs, 186
Pick Up on South Street, 332
Picturing Derry, 362
Pimpernel Smith, 255, 285
Platoon, 66, 377
Polish Campaign, 286
Post War Hopes, Cold War Fears, 304
Prisoners of Propaganda, 261
Professor Mamlock, 187
Propaganda Message, 344
Propaganda Techniques, 68
The Prussian Cur, 131
The Psychology of Mass Persuasion,
    51
The Public Mind: 1—Consuming
    Images, 68
Public Relations: A Founder's
    Perspective, 38
The Purple Heart, 286

The Radio Priest: The American
    Experience, 172
Radio, Racism and Foreign Policy,
    172
The Ramparts We Watch, 287
The Red Danube, 305, 332
The Red Menace, 332
Red Nightmare, 333
Red Planet Mars, 263, 333
Reefer Madness, 187
Return to Life, 188
Right in Der Fuhrer's Face, 262

Sabotage, 233
Sahara, 287
Salt of the Earth, 333

Sanders of the River, 188
The Selling of the Pentagon, 364
Seven Days in May, 333
Shchors, 233
Sieg im Westen, 287
Smear: The Game of Dirty Politics, 364
So Proudly We Hail, 288
Sofia, 334
The Soviet Paradise, 288
The Speeches of Adolf Hitler, 215
Spitfire, 289
State of Siege, 378
Stop Japan, 188
Storm over Asia, 233
Strategic Air Command, 334
Strike, 192, 214, 234
Swat the Spy, 132
Sword in the Desert, 378

Tag der Freiheit, 225
Target for Tonight, 245, 289, 334
Television's Vietnam: The Battle for Khe Sanh, 365
Television's Vietnam: Impact of Visual Images, 365
Ten Days That Shook the World, 234
Tender Comrade, 262, 289
Terror! Parts I and II, 366
Think Twice: The Persuasion Game, 69
34 Years After Hitler, 366
This Above All, 289
This Land Is Mine, 290
Three Brave Men, 334
Three Songs of Lenin, 234
Tiger at the Gate, 216
To Be or Not to Be, 290
Trapped by the Mormons, 188
Triumph of the Will, 1, 60, 206, 225, 234, 288

Truth and the Dragon, 70
Turksib, 235
The Twisted Cross, 216

Underground, 235

La Vie est à nous, 136, 189
Voice of Truth, 290

Wake Island, 291
War Reporters, 87
The War Years, No. 2, 266
Watch on the Rhine, 235
We Are from Kronstadt, 236
We Dive at Dawn, 291
We the Living, 236
Westfront, 1918, 189
What Eighty Million Women Want, 189
The White Cliffs of Dover, 264, 292
Why We Fight, 242, 292
Wilson, 361, 379
Wing and a Prayer, 292
Winged Victory, 293
Wings and the Woman, 293
The Woman on Pier 13, 300, 335
The World Is a Dangerous Place: Images of the Enemy on Children's Television, 367
World War II: The Propaganda Battle, 266

Yankee Doodle Dandy, 130
Yankee Doodle in Berlin, 99, 133
Yankee Go Home: Communist Propaganda, 335
Yanks Are Coming!, 335

Z, 379
Ziel im den Wolken, 236
Zvenigora, 237

Subject Index

Advertising, 7, 13, 15-16, 18-19, 27-28, 32, 36, 51, 61, 64, 66, 69, 71-72, 74, 81, 146-147, 161, 168, 238, 255, 340, 343, 347, 350

Agitprop, 143, 197-198, 207, 211, 220, 301, 311

Anti-Semitism, 10, 144, 150, 172, 192-193, 200, 204, 210-212, 216-217, 219, 221, 224, 228, 252, 275, 279, 314, 346, 366, 373

Art, 1, 3-4, 8, 16, 33, 39, 48, 57-58, 61, 63, 65-66, 68, 90, 94, 96-97, 99, 103-104, 108, 116, 119-121, 124-126, 128-129, 131, 134, 138-139, 141, 146, 148, 152, 155, 158-159, 163, 183, 190-191, 217, 238, 258, 261, 268, 272, 278, 287, 294, 317, 320, 339, 342-343, 351, 355, 373

Axis Sally, 259

Belgium, 111, 118, 128, 132

Black propaganda. *See* Disinformation

Bolshevism. *See* Communism

Bottomley, Horatio, 93, 98, 102, 109

Brainwashing, 1, 40, 53, 232

British Board of Film Censors, the (BBFC), 23, 104, 124, 142, 150, 154, 250-251

British Broadcasting Corporation, the (BBC), 94, 146, 156, 159, 192, 241, 253, 271, 281, 291, 307, 337, 340, 348-349, 362, 367, 375

British Council, 137, 145, 156, 159, 164, 337, 348

Broadcasting, 3-4, 8, 22, 33-34, 42, 44, 47, 50, 56, 59-61, 63, 66, 68, 70-71, 74-77, 79-80, 83, 87, 92, 94, 103, 134, 137, 139, 146, 148, 155, 160, 162-170, 172, 194-195, 198, 201, 208-209, 211, 213, 217,

235, 238, 241, 244, 250, 256, 258-261, 263-265, 286, 291, 294-295, 302, 304, 307, 309-311, 313, 315-316, 318-320, 331, 336-337, 340, 342, 344, 346-351, 353-354, 356-360, 362-363, 365-367, 375

Capra, Frank, 147, 183, 185, 242, 249, 263, 266, 292

Cartoons (animated). *See* Film

Cartoons (print). *See* Art

Censorship, 3, 5, 10, 12-13, 23, 25, 30, 32-33, 38, 59-61, 65, 68, 70, 72-73, 75, 78, 88-89, 91-92, 97, 99, 102-103, 105, 111, 113-114, 116, 121, 125, 135-136, 142, 145, 147, 153, 155, 157, 160, 169, 171, 173, 194, 197, 201, 209, 213, 217, 223, 233, 238, 240, 250-251, 254, 258, 262, 291, 305, 318, 333, 340, 342, 347, 351, 353-354, 358, 360-362, 367

Central Office of Information, the (COI), 302, 306, 337, 339, 367

Children, 15, 66, 132, 227, 302, 378

China, 26, 177, 188, 241, 279, 292, 313, 316, 318, 321, 329-330

Churchill, Winston, 17, 183, 271, 280, 283, 294

Cold War, 7-8, 11, 18, 34, 37, 57, 60-62, 253, 263, 294-300, 302-314, 316-318, 320, 322-328, 330-333, 336-337, 347, 354-355, 357, 362

Committee on Public Information, the (CPI), 27, 88, 96, 100, 103, 110, 114, 116, 121-122, 146

Communications, 3, 5-8, 11, 13, 15-16, 20, 24-28, 30-31, 34, 36-40, 43, 45, 49-50, 55, 57, 59, 61, 63, 68-70, 72-74, 76-85, 88, 117, 136,

138, 143, 151, 162, 168, 172, 197-199, 205, 207, 261, 304, 307, 312, 315, 318, 320, 336, 338, 340, 342, 344, 346-348, 351-353, 357-362, 364-365, 367-368

Communism, 6, 9, 74, 86, 91, 97, 118, 136, 143, 149, 161, 170, 173, 177-178, 185, 189-191, 193, 197-198, 201-203, 205, 207, 210-211, 213, 215-216, 218-220, 224, 227, 229, 231-234, 236, 239, 243, 252, 263, 279, 289, 294, 297-303, 305, 307-310, 313-327, 329-335, 341, 343, 354, 360, 364, 371, 375, 377

Coughlin, Charles E., 47, 140, 172, 211

Counterpropaganda, 16, 50, 70, 161, 299

Creel, George, 88, 93, 103, 110, 114, 121

Creel Committee. *See* Committee on Public Information

Democracy, 1, 3, 6, 14-15, 17, 19, 21-22, 24, 26, 32-33, 36, 38-39, 48, 53-54, 60, 63, 87, 98, 114, 134, 143, 145, 151, 154, 168, 170, 172, 185, 193-194, 201, 209, 211, 221, 232, 260, 263, 265, 267, 275, 282, 295-296, 303, 308-309, 311, 324-325, 330, 335, 345, 363, 369, 373

Disinformation, 1, 7, 62, 64, 71, 92, 172, 238, 257, 301, 308, 315, 317, 325, 338, 345, 371, 376-377

Documentaries. *See* Film

Documentary Film Movement, 141, 155, 171, 180, 187, 246, 277, 281

Drama. *See* Theater

Education, 18-22, 34, 37, 43, 48, 60, 71, 87, 89, 141, 143, 145, 149,

153, 172-173, 201, 288, 303, 351, 378

Eisenstein, Sergei, 169, 174, 192, 215, 220, 225, 234

England. *See* United Kingdom (UK)

Fascism, 2-3, 6-7, 47, 52, 74, 79, 86, 136, 143-144, 146, 149, 152, 154, 157, 172-174, 176, 179, 183-184, 188-190, 193-194, 200-201, 203-206, 208-210, 213, 221, 223, 226, 228, 235, 243, 280, 285, 295, 314

Film, 1, 3-4, 7-9, 11, 15-16, 23, 31, 44, 47, 58, 60-62, 66, 68, 70-71, 80, 84, 87-89, 95-96, 98-99, 101, 103-106, 114, 116, 119, 121-122, 125-126, 134, 136-137, 139, 143, 145-146, 150, 152-156, 159-160, 163-166, 168-169, 171, 175, 177, 180, 184, 186-189, 191-193, 196-204, 206, 209, 211-212, 214-215, 217, 219-221, 224, 226-230, 232-235, 238-240, 242, 245, 248-251, 253, 255-257, 260-267, 269-270, 273-276, 278-280, 282, 285-287, 289, 291, 294, 297, 300, 305, 307-308, 320-324, 326-327, 333-334, 361-364, 366-367, 369, 372, 375-376

Four-Minute Men, 92, 95, 116

France, 4, 10, 18, 58, 63, 69, 89, 91-92, 97, 99-101, 105, 112-113, 115, 120-121, 125, 128-131, 135-136, 138, 152, 165, 169, 177, 179, 181, 183, 188-189, 200, 223, 231, 244, 252-253, 256, 260, 263, 267, 271-272, 275, 278, 282, 285, 287, 290, 317, 324, 344, 369, 373

Germany, 1-5, 10, 23, 29, 60, 62-64, 85-86, 88, 90-91, 93, 97, 99, 101-102, 105, 107-111, 113, 115,

119-129, 131-133, 138-142, 144, 147-150, 152, 154, 157, 160, 162, 164-165, 167, 169-170, 173, 176, 179, 181, 184, 187, 189-192, 194-200, 202, 204-205, 208-212, 214-221, 223-230, 232-233, 235, 238-244, 250, 252, 254, 257, 259-261, 263, 266-267, 269-279, 281-284, 286-288, 290-291, 299, 309, 320, 325-326, 331, 333, 344, 366, 371, 374, 376-377

Gillars, Mildred. *See* Axis Sally

Goebbels, Joseph, 89, 151, 158, 189, 192, 194-195, 197, 201-202, 204, 208, 211-212, 216-218, 226, 228, 241, 253, 276, 279, 285

Great Britain. *See* United Kingdom, the (UK)

Great Depression. *See* New Deal

Grierson, John, 156, 177, 180, 186, 235, 246

Gulf War, the, 2, 8, 33, 43, 337, 359-361, 365, 367, 374

Hitler, Adolf, 18-19, 23, 30, 57, 60, 65, 110, 138, 140, 150, 160, 164, 183, 191, 199, 201, 205-206, 208, 210, 215-218, 221, 224-227, 229, 232-233, 240, 243, 252, 254, 257, 262, 274, 276, 279, 281, 286, 294, 296, 320, 374

House Committee on Un-American Activities (HUAC), 60, 297, 300, 322, 324, 328

Howard, Leslie, 255, 285, 289

Indoctrination. *See* Brainwashing

Information, 2-5, 13, 17, 20, 24, 28-29, 37-39, 47, 59, 66, 68-69, 71, 73, 75, 83, 85-86, 121, 142, 172, 194, 240, 247, 251, 258, 298, 307, 320, 323, 344-346, 349, 358, 360, 365, 370, 378

Institute for Propaganda Analysis, the, 207, 210, 249

Italy, 4, 10, 131, 146, 157, 162, 164, 171, 190, 194, 200-201, 203-206, 209, 223, 226, 228, 236, 238, 244, 256, 287, 369

Japan, 29, 152, 174, 188, 245-246, 250, 259-261, 263, 266, 268-270, 272, 274, 278-279, 282-284, 286-288, 290-292

Journalism. *See* Press, the

Joyce, William (Lord Haw-Haw), 243, 252, 257, 259

Korean War, 8, 43, 205, 263, 294, 329

Ku Klux Klan, the, 131, 143, 149-150, 153, 189

Language, 13, 19, 55, 67, 73-74, 76, 79, 81-82, 84, 152

Leaflets, 3, 31, 35, 46, 65, 88, 108-109, 113, 148, 163, 209, 238, 351

Literature, 3, 7-8, 12-13, 34, 62, 69, 90, 94, 97, 108, 112, 114, 138-139, 141, 146, 161-163, 170, 180-182, 188, 191, 194-195, 217, 232, 236, 238, 242, 247, 294, 320, 342, 345, 369, 372

Long, Huey P., 140, 208

Lord Haw-Haw. *See* Joyce, William

McCarthy, Sen. Joseph P., 18, 70, 289, 296, 302, 305, 325, 328

Mass communications. *See* Communications

Ministry of Information (MOI), 1, 14, 94, 104, 119, 138, 140, 155-156, 159, 164, 239, 242, 244, 247, 250-251, 254-255, 257, 265, 280, 302, 339, 366

Morale, 2, 6, 10, 22, 29, 33, 88-89, 111, 113, 117-118, 125, 238, 258-259, 266, 303

Motion Picture Producers and Distributors of America (MPPDA), 142

Music, 13, 33, 67, 94, 146, 165, 202, 217

Mussolini, Benito, 39, 58, 140, 183, 190, 200-201, 226, 236, 287

National Socialism. *See* Nazism

Nazism, 1, 3-5, 45, 63, 65, 102, 124, 136, 139-140, 148, 151, 160, 167, 170, 174, 182, 184, 187, 189-192, 194-202, 204-206, 208-211, 214-218, 221-224, 226-232, 235-236, 239, 241, 248-249, 252, 254, 256, 259, 265-267, 269-270, 273-277, 279, 281, 284-285, 287, 290-292, 294, 325, 333, 341, 366, 371, 374, 376

New Deal, the, 15, 136, 143, 147, 155, 161, 166, 172, 176, 178, 180, 184-186

Newspapers. *See* Press, the

Newsreels. *See* Film

Office of Strategic Services (OSS), 253, 297

Office of War Information, the (OWI), 125, 146, 240-242, 249, 253-256, 264, 266, 273-274, 279, 282-283, 311

Opinion polls. *See* Public opinion

Pacifism, 57, 86, 91, 119, 125-126, 160, 178, 181, 187, 189

Pamphlets. *See* Literature

Poetry. *See* Literature

Political Warfare Executive (PWE), 239, 245, 257

Posters. *See* Art

Press, the, 1-3, 5-8, 10, 13, 15-17, 24, 26-28, 30-34, 39, 42, 44, 47, 54, 59, 63, 66, 68, 70-73, 75-78, 80, 82-89, 92, 96-97, 102-104, 106, 114-117, 134, 137-139, 141, 144, 147, 149-150, 154-156, 160, 162-166, 168, 170-171, 173-174, 180, 183-184, 194-195, 197-200, 204, 209, 212, 218, 223, 238, 246, 254, 265, 294, 300-301, 309, 314-316, 318, 321-322, 336, 339-340, 342-344, 346-347, 349-352, 355, 357-361, 365, 375

Psychological warfare, 15, 20, 46, 51, 57, 61, 85, 119, 245, 253, 259, 300, 303, 311-312, 338, 365

Psychology, 1, 4, 6-7, 10, 13-15, 24, 26, 33, 35, 37-38, 40-47, 49, 51-53, 55-57, 59, 62, 65, 72, 75, 78, 81, 84-85, 88, 120, 200, 205-207, 214, 238, 307-308, 313, 317, 341, 355, 361, 367

Psyops. *See* Psychological Warfare

Public opinion, 5-7, 10-11, 13-14, 22, 25-38, 41, 44, 48, 51, 54, 66, 68, 73, 76-77, 80, 82-84, 87, 92, 95, 100-101, 106, 115, 117, 135, 139, 141, 147, 149, 151, 157, 160, 165, 170, 172, 174, 193, 197, 201, 212, 240, 249, 256, 301, 306, 315, 341, 343, 345-347, 350, 357

Public oration, 108

Public relations, 7, 10, 13, 15-16, 27-28, 30, 32-34, 38, 68, 142, 166, 169, 177, 180, 186, 238, 336, 341, 343, 356, 360, 364, 372

Racism, 3, 143, 172, 175, 226, 249, 261, 278-279, 314

Radio Free Europe, 302, 306-307, 316, 320, 324

Radio Liberty, 307, 316, 320

Religion, 2, 7, 15, 22, 34, 37, 39, 49, 53, 69, 81, 87-88, 97, 102, 136, 139, 145, 148, 175, 353, 368

Riefenstahl, Leni, 60, 196, 206, 225, 231, 234, 288

Roosevelt, Franklin D., 154, 159, 164, 166, 170, 176, 178, 183, 253, 271, 276, 284, 301, 320

Rumor, 35, 56, 64, 238

Russia. *See* Union of Soviet Socialist Republics (USSR)

Schools. *See* Education

Smith, Gerald L. K., 140, 208

Socialism, 58, 86, 91, 106, 142, 169, 181, 214, 220-221, 226, 230, 325, 328-329, 378

Sociology, 4, 6-7, 13, 35, 38, 44, 72, 78, 84-85, 87, 238, 361

Soviet Union. *See* Union of Soviet Socialist Republics (USSR)

Spanish Civil War, 67, 154, 160, 172, 188, 209, 297

Stalin, Joseph, 5, 159, 174, 190, 212, 218-219, 221-223, 226, 228-230, 233, 294, 308, 310, 314, 326, 331, 375

Stereotypes, 37, 41-42, 261, 286, 296, 367

Suffrage, 179, 189

Sykewar. *See* Psychological Warfare

TASS. *See* Telegrafnoye Agentstvo Suverennykh Stran (TASS)

Telegrafnoye Agentstvo Suverennykh Stran (TASS), 315

Televangelism. *See* Religion

Television. *See* Broadcasting

Terrorism, 150, 158, 173, 182, 205, 233, 309-310, 353-354, 359, 364, 366, 369

Theater, 58-59, 143, 152, 196, 204, 213, 217, 376

Tokyo Rose, 246, 259, 268, 290

"Uncle Sam," 39

Union of Soviet Socialist Republics (USSR), 4-6, 10, 26, 62-63, 81, 104-105, 119, 159, 161, 169, 172-174, 178, 187, 190, 192, 194, 197-199, 202-205, 207, 210-211, 213-216, 218-224, 226, 228-231, 234-237, 240, 243-244, 253, 258, 260-261, 263, 267, 269, 272, 275, 279, 284, 287-288, 294-301, 303, 307-329, 331-335, 354-355, 371, 376

United Kingdom (UK), 1-5, 9-11, 14, 19, 23, 25, 31, 33, 59-61, 63-64, 69, 78, 80, 91-102, 104-114, 116-117, 119-120, 122, 124-125, 128, 131-132, 135-138, 140-143, 145-162, 164, 166, 168-169, 171-173, 175-178, 180-182, 186-188, 195, 204, 208, 211, 214, 216-217, 219, 221-222, 233, 235, 239-245, 247-248, 250-252, 254-258, 260, 262, 264-267, 271-275, 277-278, 280-282, 284-287, 289-293, 302, 305, 318, 324, 328-329, 336-337, 339, 344-345, 348, 356, 360-362, 364, 366-367, 371-372, 375-376, 379

United States Information Agency, the (USIA), 296, 305, 335, 342, 344-345, 358

United States of America (USA), 4-5, 9, 15, 25, 27-33, 38, 42-43, 47, 50, 57, 59-62, 65-68, 71, 73, 75, 85-86, 88, 90-92, 95-96, 98-101, 103-108, 110, 112-119, 121-132, 135-136, 140, 142, 144-150, 152-155, 161-167, 169-170, 172, 176, 178-181, 183-184, 186-188, 195, 197, 202, 205-206, 208-210, 212-213, 222, 224, 227, 230, 235, 240, 245-246, 248-250, 252-254, 256-260, 262-276, 278-279, 281-289, 291-309, 312-314, 317,

319-323, 325-335, 337-338,
341-344, 347-361, 363-365,
369-371, 373-374, 376-378
Universum-Film-Aktiengesellschaft
(UFA), 122, 208, 220, 228

Viereck, George Sylvester, 144
Vietnam war, 8, 43, 60, 63, 66, 80,
132, 294, 299, 341, 349-351,
357-358, 362, 365-366, 368-370,
373-374
Voice of America, 75, 256, 264, 295,
300, 304, 313, 356, 358

Whispering campaigns. *See* Rumor
Wilson, Woodrow, 123, 127, 130,
140, 186, 361, 379
Works Projects Administration
(WPA). *See* New Deal
World War I, 2, 4, 6-7, 9, 12, 14, 16,
18-19, 22, 24, 26-27, 38, 44, 61,
63, 67, 86, 88-121, 123-134,

139-141, 143-144, 146, 148-149,
151-158, 165-166, 173-175,
179-180, 187, 190, 196, 200-202,
214, 216, 226, 238, 246, 252, 259,
264, 292, 305, 335, 376, 379
World War II, 1-2, 4, 7, 9-11, 14,
18-20, 24, 26, 29, 31, 42-47,
50-51, 57, 59, 61-64, 67, 74,
78-79, 81, 89, 103, 106-107, 110,
114, 125-126, 130, 132-133, 137,
139-140, 145-146, 148-150, 156,
158-159, 162, 164, 171, 181-182,
190, 192, 194, 196, 198-200,
206-207, 214, 216, 221-222, 232,
238-266, 268, 270-274, 278-280,
283-284, 286-289, 291-294,
296-297, 299-301, 303-307, 309,
311, 325, 327-328, 332, 334,
336-339, 347, 349, 351, 356,
361-362, 365-366, 370-376,
378-379

About the Author

Robert Cole is a professor of history at Utah State University in Logan, Utah, where he teaches modern British and Western European history. His research area is twentieth century Britain, emphasizing propaganda. He has published several journal articles on British propaganda and other topics, and two monographs: *Britain and the War of Words in Neutral Europe, 1939-1945*, concerning British propaganda efforts in Portugal, Spain, Sweden, and Switzerland; and *A. J. P. Taylor: The Traitor Within the Gates*, a study of Taylor's work over four decades as one of the most prolific and controversial historians in Britain. Another monograph, *Anglo-American Propaganda and Irish Neutrality, 1939-1945*, is in progress. He has given guest lectures at such colleges and universities as Monash University in Australia and the University of Leeds in England, and in 1982-1983 he was a visiting Senior Lecturer at the University of North London.